S0-BSN-395

HOW ADULTS LEARN

HOW
ADULTS
LEARN

J. R. Kidd

Revised, Updated, Completely Rewritten

CAMBRIDGE
The Adult Education Company
888 Seventh Avenue, New York, New York 10106

HOW ADULTS LEARN

Copyright © 1973, 1959 by J. R. Kidd

All rights reserved. No part of this publication may be reprinted, reproduced, transmitted, stored in a retrieval system, or otherwise utilized, in any form or by any means, electronic or mechanical, including photocopying or recording, now existing or hereinafter invented, without the prior written permission of the publisher.

Library of Congress Catalog Card Number: 78-73992

PRINTED IN THE UNITED STATES OF AMERICA

Contents

Introduction to the New Edition   7

1. Learning Throughout Life   13

Learning Means Change . . . Some Myths of Learning . . . Growing Acceptance . . . What Is Learning? . . . Controversy in Learning Theory . . . Some Issues to Be Considered . . . The Plan of This Book

2. The Adult Learner   30

The Adult—In What Ways Different From the Child? . . . Exploring Useful Hypotheses About Adult Learning . . . Changes in Role . . . Growing Old and the Acceptance of Death

3. Physical and Sensory Capacity   53

The Process of Aging . . . Early Studies of Growth . . . Sensory Acuity, Sensation and Sensory Processes . . . Common-Sense Practices for Minimizing Losses Associated With Age

4. Intellectual Capacities   70

The Nervous System and Intellectual Capacity . . . Intelligence and Learning . . . Implications From Results of "Intelligence Tests" . . . A Shift in Opinion . . . Evidence From Follow-Up Studies . . . Cognitive Learning and Thinking . . . Interest and Learning

5. The Affective Domain   93

Feelings and Learning . . . Feelings of Adults . . . Constellations of Feelings . . . Motivation of Adults . . . Motivational Theories and Research . . . Interests . . . Attitudes

5

6. Being and Becoming   124

The Self . . . A Paradox: Self and Humanness . . . Changes in
Role . . . Maturity . . . The Notion of Becoming . . . Transactional
Analysis . . . Identity Crisis and Peak Experience . . . Learning to
Die

7. Theories of Learning   147

Use of Theory . . . Philosophers and Learning . . . New Voices . . .
Other Disciplines . . . Developments in the First Half of This
Century . . . Connections (Trial and Error) . . . Conditioning
(Behaviorism) . . . Gestalt Psychology . . . Field Theory . . . Psy-
choanalysis . . . Cognitive Learning . . . Concepts and Concept
Formation . . . Altered States of Consciousness . . . Some Other
Approaches . . . Is a General Theory of Adult Learning Possible?

8. Some Fields of Practice   193

Large-Scale Training Programs . . . Groups and Group Development . . . Theories and Research About Leadership . . . Communications Practice and Research . . . Learning From Mass Media
. . . Other Fields of Practice

9. Environmental Factors in Learning   234

Emotional Climate . . . The Individual Learner . . . Social Learning . . . Forms and Devices . . . Simulating the Real . . . Motion
Pictures . . . Application

10. The Learning Transaction   268

Needs of the Learner . . . Curriculum . . . The Learning Situation
. . . Evaluation

11. The Teacher in the Learning Transaction   292

Different Roles of the Teacher . . . No Blueprints for Teachers . . .
The Teacher as Learner . . . Other Traits or Skills . . . Responsibility of Teacher

Index   311

Introduction to the New Edition

In his book *The Shape of Things to Come*, H. G. Wells wrote:

> The years from thirty to seventy were formerly a sort of dump for the consequences of the first three decades; now they are the main part of life, the years of work, expression and complete self-discovery, to which these earlier years are the bright, delightful prelude.

Was this statement fact or prophecy? With Wells one could never be sure. Still, one can conclude that the condition he described has come much nearer to being reality during the past fifteen years.

How Adults Learn appeared first in 1959, and the material for it was collected several months earlier. When I interpreted the data available fifteen years ago, my conclusions were considered unduly optimistic by some. In the years since, I have been obliged to reread the text carefully in the light of experience and new research evidence. Many of the views about politics or international affairs I held in 1959 have been modified as the 1960's raced on. But not the main conclusions of this book. I have wished sometimes that I had written with greater lucidity, and I might have chosen other examples and illustrations, but I would not alter the tone or the assessment, except to accentuate the chief message: people of all kinds, in all places, and of all ages have a marvelous capacity to learn and grow and enlarge. As more and more research reports and abstracts come in, what may have seemed rhetoric, an expression of faith, becomes more and more a sober fact, which can be endlessly documented. Here and there contradictory evidence or seeming paradoxes appear, but there is little doubt about the central message.

How Adults Learn was intended for the practitioner in adult education and was written by a practitioner; it was never intended as a textbook. Yet it has been used as a text in universities in two score countries; it has been

7

BRIDWELL LIBRARY
SOUTHERN METHODIST UNIVERSITY
DALLAS, TEXAS 75275

translated into French, Spanish, Arabic, Serbo-Croatian, and Hindi. Does it weather well the storms and stresses of translation into other languages and use in other cultures? I wonder, because I am acutely aware of the fantastic and wonderful differences in perceiving and conceptualizing and thinking that are performed by men and women in varied times and lands and climes. To the extent that the book does speak to people in other cultures, it is because I have learned so much from men and women in these countries.

In the years since *How Adults Learn* was first published much has happened with respect to adult learning. Most of the learned disciplines have contributed to learning theory. There are new fields of practice where more precise observation and evaluation have been carried out: important new concepts have been formulated.

Today it's a cliché to talk about social change; we have all been borne along or dragged along in an avalanche of change, exhilarated or frightened or numbed by what has been happening to us. The feelings of many are best illustrated by the title of the best-selling book, *Future Shock*. It is difficult to be observant about the force and direction of a hurricane when one is in "the eye."

There have been wars, famines, and political revolutions. These cataclysmic events always transform men's lives. But so do other mutations. Despite the development of a growing science of demography, people, at least in North America, have not begun to cope with the changes wrought by a shift in the age composition of the population. Adjustments to provide for the vast numbers of children born in and soon after World War II were agonizingly slow. Now it is a part of conventional wisdom to regard ours as a youthful population and expect that the "problem" of vast numbers of young people will be with us always. Of course, nothing is further from the truth. In many Western nations it is a case of large numbers who are old, large numbers who in the next decade will be approaching middle age, and comparatively fewer young. In Canada, for example, a quarter of the population is fifty-five years and over: it is rapidly becoming a nation of middle-aged and older people. In the United States during the century, the number of people over sixty-five has quadrupled and now makes up almost 10 per cent of the population. While the median age in 1900 was sixteen years, in 1960 it was thirty-one years. Another fact may be of equal or greater consequence: on an average, women in North America cease to bear children after age thirty, with a half-century of productive life ahead of them. Yet most government officials and manufacturers, advertisers and publishers have failed to realize, or act upon, these facts. *The Psychology of Aging* by J. E. Birren and other such books have been purchased, and perhaps read, but those making decisions in society have not begun to act upon the clear implications. Nor have educational officials. Yet all of the people who make up these statistics are already born. If adult educationists fail to count noses and face up to facts, who will?

Institutional changes have been many. An almost new institution—in reality, an entire new field of education—has sprung up and taken root in at least thirty countries—the various forms of the community college. National and international programs to achieve functional literacy are found in most parts of the world, and there have been many efforts to help men and women achieve a minimum standard of education that will enable them to be competent to deal with educational needs within their own culture or circumstance. Despite prodigious efforts (and in the Latin American countries in the 1960's illiteracy was reduced from about 33 per cent to 24 per cent), the world increase in new literates has not kept pace with the increase in new births, so there has been an increase in the total numbers of illiterate people, though not in percentages. However, the "watershed" date at which the gross numbers of illiterates will begin to decline will probably be reached in the 1970's. There have also been many new programs of adult basic education and manpower training, and new kinds of institutions for these purposes have been created. The numbers of men and women engaged in continuing professional education and management education have continued to mount.

In many fields the developments are both promising and alarming. Biologists and geneticists are able to change the genetic balance of cells. The use of drugs and other chemicals has mushroomed: for therapeutic and clinical purposes under the supervision of scientists who know something about the probable consequences; much consumed in dangerous doses by those who don't.

Changes in life-style, in taste, in values have been equally profound, although there are often fads and cycles in these things. One of the most surprising shifts is the re-evaluation of the school and university. Far from being considered the shrine and temple of this century, an institution which, despite shortcomings here and there, was unassailable, there has been a mounting denigration of organized education. When Ivan Illich tells of a schoolboy who was accidentally but painfully kicked by another boy, and who turned on the latter and shouted "School you!" he was telling a joke, but such jokes clothe what is deeply felt, just as clichés do. And yet the invective, whether baseless or well founded, is not directed against learning, but against certain kinds of organized education. The enterprise of learning, as distinct from schooling, has never had such advocacy or so much participation.

Adult education is a field of enormous complexity, and there seem, on the surface, to be more counter-trends than trends, and there is more paradox than consensus. During a recent flurry in the stock market, a customer asked his broker "to wire him the straight dope" about a certain stock. In due course he received a telegram: "Some think it's going up. Some think it's going down. I agree. Whatever you do will be wrong. Act at once."

Experiences in adult education differ markedly, and we don't all use the same languages. How can a practitioner be expected to keep up when, for some kinds of educational research, not only must he know computer and statistical languages but be versed in electronic theory as well? This extremity is illustrated by the plight of the professor of mathematics who was knocked down by an automobile and, later in court, was asked for the license number. "I'm afraid I have forgotten," he replied, "but I remember noticing that if it were multiplied by itself, the cube root of the product would be equal to the sum of the digits reversed."

Of course, it is an impossible task to encompass fully what has happened over more than a decade. In the Preface to *Adult Psychology* published in 1969, author Ledford Bischof says:

> Ten years from now an individual will not be able to write a book like this unaided. Having scoured the literature since 1964, one conclusion is inescapable: the "information explosion" is so vast and rapidly expanding that one person will be totally unable to assimilate or even collate but a portion of it. . . . The bibliography, "Learning and Cognitive Performance in Adults" has 1,591 items. Ninety per cent of the items date since World War II.

The *Overview of Research in Adult Education* was published in 1959. It reported:

> Any examination of research in adult education reveals a rather chaotic situation. A few pertinent areas, such as adult learning, have been explored far more thoroughly than others. Some have received almost no research attention. Where any considerable body of effective research is available, other than in the field of methods, typically it has been conducted, not by adult educators, but by social scientists who had available a considerable body of theory, generalizations and methodologies developed by their disciplines, which could be applied to the problems of adult education.

Adult education continues to benefit from research in several disciplines, but the quantity of investigations carried out by adult educators themselves has increased to the point that, in several countries, but notably in the United States, there are at least annual volumes reviewing the year's product and research abstracts that are now being exchanged by several countries.

Despite efforts to reach agreement on definitions at international seminars and conferences, there are still many difficulties about the precise and accepted meaning of terms. However, efforts by scholars in several countries, many of them engaged in comparative studies in adult education, may bring about the achievement of agreement about most terms and concepts, and the basis for a taxonomy in the present decade.

Despite the press of countless new publications and studies, and many examples of disagreement and dissonance, certain trends seem to be established. Examples:

It now seems accepted that such factors as housing and the economic and social position of the family deeply affect a child's educational performance. This is not less true of adults: it is more true.

The nature of an individual profoundly affects his growth and development, but so does the food he eats and his competence in learning.

As Marshall McLuhan and others have said, the "roles" of many people have become more important to them than "goals," and there is a deep need on the part of many for engagement and involvement.

The differences that distinguish the adult learner from the child are considerable and so are the continuities in learning within the life span of an individual.

The learner of almost any age is capable of large measures of self-management of his learning experience and can be assisted to become increasingly effective as a self-directed learner.

* * *

This is a new edition. It is a revision that has been undertaken at the request of readers in many countries. It is also an invitation to practitioners in adult education to share in the continuing quest for better theory and improved practice in assisting all people, including us, in the improvement of their and our most human quality—learning. Gestalt therapist Fritz Perls said that "learning is the discovery that something is possible." And 300 years ago Sir Thomas Browne wrote: "We carry with us the wonders we seek without us: there is all Africa and her prodigies in us."

1

Learning Throughout Life

This book is about learning. It's not so much about the learning of children as about older youth and adults, although there are continuities in learning that begin at birth or conception and that extend throughout life. The emphasis and focus is on learning throughout the years of adulthood. In the foreword to one of his books, cartoonist Walt Kelly was writing about the kinds of crusades and causes for which many adults strain and struggle in their communities, and he concludes: "Resolve, then, with heads held high and banners waving, we will march out to meet the foe, and not only may he be ours, he may be *us!*" This is a book about us. Can people like us learn well?

To be honest, it should be pointed out that ignorance still abounds concerning the learning of adults. It is not fully understood why it is that some people will put forth effort, will extend themselves and their powers, will try, will take risks, while others are more resistant, more wary, are slow to start and quick to give up. The latter are showered with advice and quickly classified—they are apathetic, or lazy, or not well motivated. It is much easier to apply epithets than it is to understand or help people become effective learners.

However, it is probably true that much more is known than is generally practiced. The increase in knowledge about the learning of adults during the past two decades has been phenomenal. Much of it seems to have happened when the main emphasis was shifted in recent years, from *teaching* to *learning*. This emphasis is rather recent. Think of the millions of books and pamphlets in every language that have as their subject how to teach, how to train, how to instruct, how to propagandize. These books vary in quality and scope but, barring a few distinguished exceptions, by far the majority of them deal with the way one human being imposes his will, or knowledge, or skill, upon another. Consciously or unconsciously, most of them are

13

about how a communication is shaped and directed, almost always from the point of view of the director or the fashioner or giver of that communication.

In all ages, of course, wise men have recognized that learning is the active, not the passive, part of the process: the learner opens up himself, he stretches himself, he reaches out, he incorporates new experience, he relates it to his previous experience, he reorganizes this experience, he expresses or unfolds what is latent within him. The critical part of the process of teaching-learning is how the learner is aided to embark on this active, growing, changing, painful, or exhilarating experience we call learning.

We can put it another way. Most of what has been written about the practice of medicine describes how certain chemicals or herbs, and certain techniques, may be used to heal the body. Yet the most profound fact about the living body is that it is health seeking—that its forces reach out toward health and healing. The art of medicine is not so much doing things to the body but inhibiting destructive influences and enabling the body to achieve healing. It seems to be very much the same with learning. Human beings seem to seek after learning; learning seems to be a condition of a healthy organism. The objective is to provide the climate and atmosphere and freedom and self-discipline in which learning is promoted. It is not so much doing something to the body-mind-emotions but setting up the conditions whereby the person will behave in a learning way.

What a human being needs is a "fair field" for the kind of encounter that is learning. One of the best-known fables of the West is about the hardy pioneer who came face-to-muzzle, on a mountain pass, with a grizzly bear. His hasty prayer to the Almighty was that he needed no special aid—"but please don't help that bear!" Given suitable conditions men and women can be counted on to demonstrate capacity for learning. And, as we shall see in a later chapter, whether an activity is "teacher-centered" or "learner-centered" influences considerably how many facts or skills or attitudes are learned and retained.

To be sure, the dictionary definitions of learning have not always emphasized this active principle. One common definition is "to receive instruction." However, most of the other meanings offered are much more active:

"to ascertain"
"to find out"
"to come to know"
"to come to know how"
"to acquire knowledge or skill"
"to fix in mind"
"to acquire a habit"

The dictionaries go on to note that learning happens as the result of observation, study, experience, or instruction. That is, learning may go on with or without conscious plan or direction. It is thus most easily distinguished from education by the fact that the latter word suggests the conscious planning or organization of experience. Education is planned learning. Some definitions emphasize the lifelong aspect of education: "It is the systematic development and cultivation of the mind and natural powers. It begins in the nursery, continues through school, and also through life."

There is a corresponding close relationship between learning and intelligence. The latter word has often been defined in practice as the "capacity for learning," or "intelligence is the power to learn," particularly learning academic things, utilizing verbal and mathematical symbols. This subject will be dealt with much more thoroughly in Chapter 4.

Learning Means Change

One of the most useful descriptions of a learner was once put forward by the theorist, John Dollard: "The learner is a person who wants something; the learner is a person who notices something; the learner is a person who does something; the learner is a person who gets something." Notice that these are all active verbs. Learning means change. It is not simply a matter of accretion—of adding something. There is always reorganization or restructuring. There may be *un*learning. Indeed, as we shall see, this may be the most difficult part. What there is of pain in learning is not so much coming to terms with what is new, but reorganizing what has been learned.

Learning involves a change in behavior: learning may make us respond differently. Learning may also involve a change in the organism, and over time, in the personality. It is usually assumed that the change will be toward more effective performance, but of course some changes are not for the better. We may learn not only to get along with others, or use new symbols or skills, but we may also learn to worry, to savage others, to become neurotic. Most of the complex behaviors categorized under various labels such as "mental illness" are learned, although there may also be a physiological basis for them.

Usually when we speak of learning we are thinking about changes which we anticipate will occur in the learner. These may be primarily "intellectual" changes—the acquiring of new ideas or some reorganization of presently held ideas. The changes may be in attitude where we hope that people will come to a different appreciation and more positive feelings about a subject, not simply gain more information. Or they may be changes in skill where we expect the learner to become more efficient in performing certain acts—such as operating a machine, maintaining records, submitting reports, counseling others, leading a discussion. Sometimes we hope for changes in many ways—in some combination which we may express as becoming "better citizens," or "more mature."

Much of learning is related to shifts in the tasks or roles that a person performs. The developmental changes of an adult are many. For example:

- becoming independent,
- seeking and maintaining forms of livelihood,
- selecting a mate,
- learning to live with a mate,
- becoming and functioning as a parent,
- interacting with the community and society,
- enlarging responsibilities as a citizen,
- accepting changes in relationships—of parents or children,
- preparing for retirement,
- finding satisfactions in old age,
- preparing for death.

And it is precisely around these developmental roles that the most notable changes have been occurring. For example, one person may, during a lifetime, choose and live with several different mates, or he or she may enter into a "joint family" relationship, or group or commune relationships.

Each of these changes is accompanied by physiological and biochemical and personality changes; some greater, some less.

Recently the president of a great corporation was asked why his company spent large sums of money on the education of its executives and what outcomes had been found. Notice how, in his summary, changes of several kinds are reported:

1. There was tremendous enthusiasm on the part of each year's participants. They tell us they have increased personal identification and self-realization. In other words, this means that the men know where they are going and why, and they also know why they have chosen the path they have.
2. The changes in the men were apparent to those watching them. They have greater intellectual curiosity and self-confidence and are better able to express their ideas.
3. They tell us it has made them better family men, better citizens in their communities, and better individuals.[1]*

This book is about the ways in which adults learn. That is its focus, and most of the examples used will be drawn from the experience of adults. We

* Numbered footnotes are found under "References" at the end of each chapter.

have already pointed out that what we describe as adult learning is not a different kind or order from child learning. Indeed, our main point is that man must be seen as a whole, in his lifelong development. Principles of learning will apply, in ways that we shall suggest, to all stages in life. The reason that we specify adults throughout is obvious. This is the field that has been neglected, not that of childhood.

Not only has there been neglect, but usually, except in novels and plays, adulthood is referred to as one long endless plain or desert. With such a view it doesn't matter much if adults can learn or not. But, seen as Robert J. Havighurst sees it, adult learning becomes crucial, for the community and the race, but not less for the individual human being.

> Adulthood is not all smooth sailing across a well-charted sea with no adventures or mishaps. People do not launch themselves into adulthood with the momentum of their childhood and youth and simply coast along to old age. There are fully as many new problems to solve and new situations to grasp during the adult years as there are during the earlier periods of life. Adulthood has its transition points and its crises. It is a *developmental period* in almost as completely a sense as childhood and adolescence are developmental periods.[2]

Some Myths of Learning

Before proceeding very far it may be well to face squarely one of the most difficult obstacles to effective learning for adults. When we begin to review the data about how adults learn, we are going to note a very curious fact. We shall see that there are two main limits to human growth and development. There is the real, practical limit of one's maximum ability or potential capacity. And there is the *no less real* psychological limit which each man places upon himself. Unfortunately, it would seem that the barriers that most restrict and hobble us, the chains that bind most severely, are those which we fashion for ourselves.

Why is this? Why do we limit ourselves? Why, despite evidence to the contrary, are we so unready, so fearful of trying out and extending our powers?

This is a difficult question to which we shall return from time to time. But a part of the explanation is that much of our tradition is negative and pessimistic about human progress and growth. Myths and fables, religious literature and secular admonitions, learned histories and old wives' tales, are full of references to human inadequacy to learn. Our books, and those parts of our culture which continue to be transmitted orally, abound in myths about learning. Some are as old as the race; some we have created in our own generation. Ancient and superstition-laden or modern and pseudoscientific, these myths and lies affect all of us; for even if we do not bear their imprint, they affect those with whom we work. Part of the task for all of us is the eradication of such falsehoods and half-truths, by replacing them with sound ideas.

Of course there may be some slight aspect of truth to each. Myths or distortions of fact rarely survive unless they contain at least a vestige of truth, enough to make the barb stick. One could compile a sizable array of these myths, but we shall note only some of those which have had the most pernicious influence.

1. *You can't change human nature.* This assertion, delivered with profound confidence from the earliest of times, and often held with the deepest conviction, has been used to show how futile any attempt would be to try to do anything about slavery, or slums, or war, or child labor, or inequality of opportunity for women, or discrimination based on color or creed. Man is what he is: there is something unalterable in his nature and make-up; or so it is claimed. Of course, the truth is that human behavior, in very fundamental ways, is being changed every day, and human nature and human personality can be profoundly reshaped. Consider what was *natural* for our fathers to think and do, and compare this with how we live. Consider what was natural for millions of Asians and Africans well into this century, and what is now natural. Canadian Eskimos continue in a stone-age existence and yet are beginning to take part in the complexities of life in the twentieth century. One of the miracles of humankind is the extraordinary capacity of men and women for change and growth. In the past fifty years our notions about what is specifically human nature have been radically altered, due in part to the evidence about different cultures, supplied by the anthropologists.

2. *You can't teach an old dog new tricks.* Our canine-loving friends have been quick to point out that this is a vile lie, perpetrated and repeated by those who are ignorant about dogs. But of course the charge has been employed for centuries to describe men and women. That it is equally wide of the mark when applied to them will be the main subject of Chapters 3 and 4. Still, it is an observation you will hear again and again. But before you accept any part of the slander, read carefully the evidence about the capacity of adults to learn found in this book and in the suggested readings.

3. *The "hole in the head" theory of learning.* Many people, some of them quite sensible in other respects, talk about learning as if it were some process by which an entrance is somehow forced into the brain and facts are poured in, or pressed in, or stamped in. The process is seen as a simple one. Organize your facts carefully; use repetition and other devices to be

sure that they are properly injected into the mind. One concomitant of this notion is that the heads and minds of children are regarded as being easier to penetrate, as less cluttered than those of adults. The attic isn't yet stuffed with the accumulation of the years and something more may be put in. This is a fantastic theory, much too silly to be dignified by a refutation. It had the appearance of truth only in those eras when there was little social change. But if you will listen and look carefully during any Education Week you are almost certain to hear sermons or speeches, or to read articles in reputable newspapers and magazines in which these conceptions are developed with authority and rhetoric.

4. *The all-head notion of learning.* Many people thing about and talk about learning as if it were completely an affair of the mind. They claim that it is entirely a rational, intellectual process. According to this theory learning is not particularly difficult to understand. You simply select and arrange the content of your subject in a rigorously rational way, and present it to the student. However, unfortunately for this notion, man is actually much more than mind and intellect. Most of us have become increasingly aware that man is a creature of emotions and feelings, and that these have an important part in learning. It has long been recognized that in childhood, emotion is a dominant influence and that one must understand this fact when dealing with the young. But some have assumed that, for the mature, an intellectual approach is all that is needed. Worse still, *intellectual* has often been a euphemism for *dull*.

5. *The "bitter-sweet" notions.* These are two equally fallacious and contradictory views. The first is that learning cannot happen at all unless it is exciting and exhilarating. Unless it is easy and delightful, no learning. Now most of us know from our own experience that much of learning is difficult, wearing, repetitive—the hardest kind of hard work, which we accept only because of the importance of objectives we seek and the satisfactions we shall learn. Yet, we are told by the advocates of the "fun and games" approach that drudgery and effort can be eliminated, that rich, insightful learning can be painless. Of course, some who are attracted by these claims may become quickly disillusioned.

Just as dishonest, and perhaps even more baleful in result, are the views of those who proclaim that there is no learning except when accompanied by harsh unpleasantness. If you will listen to some convocation addresses, or the talk of elderly educational administrators, you will find that it is not uncommon to hear one state, "It doesn't much matter what one studies so long as one detests or hates it sufficiently." It has frequently been claimed that the worth of learning lies in the transformation of the human personality through stern, disagreeable, painful discipline. This perversion of the Puritan ethic is surprisingly widespread. Unfortunately, the effect is to cause most normal human beings to recoil in disgust.

6. *The mental age of the average adult is twelve years.* One of the characteristics of our times is that we pretend to be a little scornful of the fables, superstitions, and myths of previous ages. But that has not prevented us from creating some of our own. A successful myth must always have the appearance of reality and wear some of the coloration of its time of origin. Myths, to be accepted in our era, are all likely to have some appearance of science, to seem to depend upon scientific inquiry for justification. An excellent example of such a myth is, "The mental age of the average adult is twelve years." This is such a perversion, such a misinterpretation of psychological research data, that if its effects were not so serious it could be dismissed as a schoolboy howler, in the same class as "Geometry teaches us to prove what we already know to be true" and "Ambiguity means telling the truth without intending to." This myth, like Minerva, sprang up full armed.

In the American army during World War I there was, for the first time, an opportunity to give thousands of men "intelligence" tests. The tests used were mostly based on academic materials, employed "norms" based on the performance of children, had rigid time limits, and were given to men who, on the average, had had only a few years of schooling. Men tested in this way made average scores which corresponded to the average scores of school children of the years twelve, thirteen, and fourteen. Most of the psychologists understood these results and treated them for what they were. However, some people compared the scores of men and children in school in a way that was completely unwarranted and which led to the foolish assertion that the mental age of service men (and therefore presumably of adults generally) was twelve years. (Sometimes this has been stated as thirteen, sometimes as fourteen.) One might have expected that such a palpable blunder would have been washed away in gales of laughter. Unfortunately it stuck; it has been repeated thousands of times; and, despite the vast amount of evidence to the contrary, it continues to be repeated. If, for example, you ask those responsible for some of the most inane, repetitive film, radio, or television shows, why they choose the content and style that they do, they are quite likely to tell you seriously that their show is aimed at the "average adult who has a twelve-year-old intelligence." This notion has been used with such destructive consequences that we shall return to its discussion in Chapter 4. One aspect of this may need a special footnote—the frequency with which the results of observations of animals or children are applied to adults, as if a man were only a "great big boy." The adult is *not* just a larger child: the cells of his body are different, his experiences are vastly different. Data derived from research with children are only useful if applied with care and if rigorously checked against adult experience as well as with data collected from systematic observation of adults. This is elementary enough, but is is a point that is frequently overlooked.

7. *Unless you have a high IQ, all hope abandon.* This is a strange notion that also has achieved widespread circulation. No sensible person would ever deny the importance of intellectual capacity. We shall all want to cherish every vestige of intellect that can be mustered and seek to encourage its unfolding and development in every child and adult. But there is a great part of human life, human achievement, and human dignity, that is not at all comprehended by even the best intellectual standards. There are other kinds of worthiness to be sought after and nourished. Concentrating all attention on what is measured by rather imperfect instruments (the "intelligence tests") is to omit much of what is richest in life.

Growing Acceptance

But enough of these myths, for, although the continued repetition of error is harmful in its effect, perhaps beyond what we can estimate, there has been at the same time an increasing acceptance of a contrary view, *that adults can learn effectively*. It would be wrong to suggest that such an idea attained recognition only during our own time. The achievements of some older men and women (such as Goethe writing great literature when over eighty), and the success of older people learning new skills or knowledge, have always been recognized. But for the most part these were considered exceptions to the general rule.

Teachers of adults, as far as they were able, strove to correct false claims. "We have known," wrote Robert Peers, "each in his own experience, hundreds of cases of men and women for whom, at the beginning, serious reading was an effort and the putting together of a few sentences in writing a terrifying task, who have overcome these difficulties in their tutorial classes and, by the end of their courses, have acquired new intellectual interests and new powers of expression in speech and writing." [3]

One of the most decisive checks to outworn notions came with the printing of E. L. Thorndike's book, *Adult Learning* [4] in 1928. Upon its publication the book was widely quoted. Thorndike summarized his findings:

In general, nobody under forty-five should restrain himself from trying to learn anything because of a belief or fear that he is too old to be able to learn it. Nor should he use that fear as an excuse for not learning anything which he ought to learn. If he fails in learning it, inability due directly to age will very rarely, if ever, be the reason. Adult education suffers no mystical handicap because of the age of the students.

Notice, the age that he selects is *forty-five*. Forty years later this claim seems modest enough. But it struck against conventional wisdom in the twenties. And it was the first such claim to be supported by evidence from systematic empirical research. In the Introduction to *Adult Learning*, Thorndike wrote:

> There has never been an extensive and systematic enquiry seeking to discover whether and to what extent infancy, childhood and adolescence do have by nature an advantage over the years from twenty to forty in respect to ability to learn. . . . There has been in the main a neglect of the problem or an acceptance of the proverbial conventional opinion that it is especially important to train up the child in the way he should go.

In later chapters we will consider not the age of forty-five as a summit before decline, but perhaps the age of seventy-five, or whatever age signals the termination of a healthy organism. One hears less of *Adult Learning* these days, but in all probability it will always be regarded as a landmark effort in the long uphill struggle to provide education for everyone.

Others, in increasing numbers have joined the inquiry. Many developmental psychologists, faced with the obvious fact that adulthood constitutes the longest period of living, have become interested not only in finding out how older people may decline in performance, but in determining those things that they do better. It has been alleged that the lives of older people were rarely studied because social science, like the movies, has been "youthbound," that most social scientists have been comparatively young. However, to the extent that this was once an important factor, a change has come. Most American adults have a longer life expectancy. Simply on an actuarial basis, it is not difficult to make a case for increased attention to the adult; there are so many more of them. In the United States in 1900 four per cent of the population was sixty-five years and over; this percentage had doubled by 1960, and the numbers had risen from three million to twelve million. The median or middle age in 1900 was sixteen years; in 1960 it was thirty-one years. Life-expectancy tables in 1955 provided the prediction that forty-year-olds could expect approximately thirty-three more years of life.

That is a substantial number of people for a society to support, a very large bloc of voters who can be constructive or destructive in their voting decisions, depending upon their experience and attitudes. According to the United States Department of Labor, the peak earning capacity is found in those years forty-five to sixty-five, two decades after the age that Thorndike used for his terminal point. Even our categories are being modified. What was once considered old age is now considered middle age.

In previous centuries learning was rarely considered a field for psychological or sociological inquiry. Views about learning were much more likely to be associated with philosophy or theology. The conception of how a man learned was intimately tied up with one's general view of man. If one believed, for example, that man was sinful and lost, then it might also be concluded that learning must always be accompanied by pain, hardships, and chastisement.

However, with the systematic development of the social sciences during the nineteenth century, first in Germany and then elsewhere, speculation began to be replaced by direct observation of behavior and by theories deduced from this observation. Experimental psychologists were quite early attracted to the study of learning. Initially they began to watch the behavior of animals, later of children, still later of adults who were living in various kinds of institutions such as sanitariums or reformatories. Only recently has there been much attention given to those of older age, and observations and studies of the "normal" adult in the middle years have only begun to appear. As we shall see, there has always been some application of learning theory to adults, but this has been sporadic.

Since World War II there have been a number of developments which when brought together may provide considerable information about adult learning. This has come about in many ways: through the work of anthropologists, social psychologists, psychiatrists, and counselors; from such fields as linguistics (how a man may learn and begin to think with new symbols), gerontological research, training programs in industry and in various military services; from communication research and theory, to mention only some of the fields. In Chapter 8 an attempt will be made to review a few of these developments and make a rough assessment of their importance.

The term *Mathetics* is coming into use to denote the transition from teaching to learning. It is a term in use by certain researchers in the United States, the U.S.S.R., and some other European countries. Mathetics is "the Science of the pupil's behavior while learning just as pedagogy is the discipline in which attention is focussed on the schoolmaster's behavior while teaching." [5] Included in the scope of Mathetics are any disciplines, chemistry or biology for example, from which relevant information can be obtained about learning.

What Is Learning?

The title of this book is *How Adults Learn*. In one sense there is no answer to this question, just as there is no answer to the question, "What is electricity?" Once a student was asked that question and, very puzzled, he replied, "I did know, but I forgot." The professor smote his brow. "My God! The only man who ever knew what electricity is has forgotten!"

We know how to make electricity, or at least how to induce it, but it still defies definition. Augustine once said, "I understand what time is, but don't ask me." Similarly, though we cannot pin down anything as dynamic as learning in any way that is thoroughly satisfying, we can observe it, note its course and its character.

Part of the problem comes about because of the various uses to which the term *learning* is put. Kenneth Benne identifies three of the main uses:

- Learning may be thought of as acquisition and mastery by a person of what is already known on some subject.
- Learning may also be thought of as the extension and clarification of meanings of one's own individual experience.
- Learning is a process (in which) one tests ideas and generalizations relevant to some delimitable problems, and tests them in some more or less objectified and controlled experiences designed for the purpose.[6]

We have already stated that learning results in certain kinds of changes, the most common being the committing to memory of facts, the acquiring or improvement of a skill or process, the development of a changed attitude. Does the process of change in each case have enough similarity so that each can be termed learning without ambiguity? That is, is learning always the same thing? Let us suppose, for a moment, that in some foreign language separate words were used to denote each of these processes, for example:

Xing—facts and information.
Ying—the forehand drive in tennis.
Zing—to live and work with people of another color.

This might lead to clearer understanding. But then, of course, we should be obliged to seek relationships between the three notions and words. So we might as well stick to English!

Controversy in Learning Theory

One can organize learning in many different ways. During this century learning theory and practice have been expressed by psychologists who are grouped, or have grouped themselves, in three broad categories. Many, despite differences among them, would accept the general classification of *behaviorists*. Others stress cognitive processes, and a third group are usually considered or labeled *humanists*. Thorndike was just one of many behaviorists, and B. F. Skinner is another; psychologists such as Jerome J. Bruner, David Ausubel, and David Hunt have been giving major attention to cognitive learning; and men like Carl Rogers, Abraham Maslow, and Fritz Perls are identified in the humanistic position. In recent years, as the second and third groups have gained strength; books, journals, and the conventions of psychologists have abounded with controversy, with claim and rebuttal. It has been a scene lively in the extreme, although the clamor of conflict has sometimes obscured a broadened understanding of the object of all this attention, namely the learner himself. Gradually, however, as the enquiries have been carried forward, and tested again and again in the field, the anticipated syntheses and larger agreements are beginning to emerge. In several chapters, but notably Chapter 7, we will note some of these developments and what they mean for learning theory and practice.

We will also be concerned with the views and contributions of scholars other than psychologists: to the extent that they have something practical to say about learning, with historians and economists, sociologists and anthropologists, biologists and physiologists and philosophers.

This is not a book about educational philosophy except that every word in it is marked or marred by the author's understanding and beliefs about the nature and purpose of education. Long ago a well-known teacher was asked, "Where in your timetable do you teach religion?" "We teach it all day long," he answered. "We teach it in Arithmetic by accuracy. We teach it in Geography by breadth of mind. We teach it in Astronomy by reverence. We teach it in the playground by fair play. We teach it by kindness to animals, by good manners to one another, by truthfulness in all things." Just as one's philosophy is expressed, is worked out in every educational activity, so one cannot consider any aspect of learning without considering the ends of learning.

However, as indicated earlier, the purpose of this book is a *quest,* a *search* for a body of ideas, theories, and experience which will guide practical workers in many fields of adult learning. It is probably no longer necessary to justify the importance of theory. Theory is usually the result of the distillation of practice. Nothing is so practical as good theory. Put in the words of the old saw—theory without practice is empty, and practice without theory is blind. What we shall try to do constantly is to show the balanced relationship between learning practice and learning theory. Our effort will also be to discover agreement and integration of views wherever these exist or seem to be possible. We shall not evade or gloss over the real and important differences of view. But all these issues we shall treat as questions for further speculation and investigation, rather than as matters of faith or ideology on which we must now take a stand or "break a lance."

One can identify at least a dozen distinct philosophical points of view held by practitioners in adult education. For our purposes though, we shall deal with three major tendencies or emphases. Note that they are just that, *points of emphasis*; they are not fully articulated philosophic schools or theories.

One such stress is upon the development of the *intelligent, rational, humane individual,* who becomes so in large measure through intensive study of certain forms and fields of knowledge. Some urge that this result is achieved through vigorous study of mathematics and sciences. For others, like Sir Richard Livingstone, the heart of the study is history and literature. For Mortimer Adler it is in the "Great Books."

> The program of adult learning must be something that will sustain learning through 20, 30, or 40 years; something that treats adults as adults, not as children in school, something they can do voluntarily; something that fits them as adults or mature persons. . . . The Great Books deal with the basic problems, both theoretical and practical, of yesterday and today and tomorrow, the basic issues that always have and always will confront mankind. The ideas they contain are the ideas all of us have to think about. The Great Books represent the fund of human wisdom, at least so far as our culture is concerned, and it is this reservoir that we must draw upon to sustain our learning for a lifetime.[7]

Others would hasten to add, while possibly in agreement with the goal as stated, that *means* must be considered at the same time as goals. S. M. Corey of Teachers College, Columbia University, once said, in an address:

> Students who spend a great deal of time reading and discussing Great Books are learning primarily how to read and discuss Great Books. They are not necessarily learning how to behave in harmony with the principles elucidated in the Great Books. . . . If students get a great deal of practice following directions which members of the faculty give them, these students primarily are learning better how to follow the directions given them by members of the faculty. They are not necessarily learning to be resourceful and to stand on their own feet and to identify problems as well as methods of solutions of these problems.

Another kind of emphasis is upon *effective functioning*, not just upon a man of ideas or knowledge or humane principles but one who is equipped and able to take his part as father, workman, voter, or, if necessary, soldier. He achieves this, most would urge, through disciplined study and practice based upon his roles in the family and community. Some stress the community as a starting point for this development; others, as in the Antigonish Movement in Nova Scotia, start with his economic interests, and broaden out from there.

A third kind of emphasis is on the special demands upon an adult *in a democracy*. Robert Hutchins once stated this notion in striking form: "The foundation of democracy is universal suffrage. Universal suffrage makes every man a ruler. If every man is a ruler, every man needs the education that rulers ought to have." [8] Here such characteristics are favored as concern about the common weal, ability to take self-initiated action, responsibility for choice and direction of action, ability for critical observation and thinking, capacity for adaptation and application of what has been learned.

However, since this is a book primarily for practitioners, we will try to keep in some perspective the entire process of learning. This will include the establishment of goals and objectives, by the learner and by the teacher, or in collaboration. Much of the most important work in recent years by Robert F. Mager, C. O. Houle, and Malcolm Knowles has concentrated on these practical questions of goal identification, and this is taken up in some detail in Chapter 11. We shall deal also with the development of curriculum or program, establishing the requirements and conditions and environments for effective learning, and evaluating the changes in behavior that constitute learning.

Some Issues to Be Considered

A number of practical questions have arisen on which there are differences of opinion. These have sometimes grown out of philosophic inquiry or sometimes out of the practical day-to-day problems of those engaged in adult education. We shall state some of them here, without comment, simply to anticipate and open up some of the central problems affecting adult learning. In succeeding chapters considerable information about each of them will be presented. Here the extremes are stated in sharp contrast for the sake of clarity, but this does not necessarily represent positions that are actually held.

This list is not exhaustive. The reader will want to place some of his own queries here in this context:

The needs of the individual *contrasted with* the needs of society?

Is adult learning concerned primarily with the clarification of ideas and intellectual processes   *or* preparing the learner for action in community or society?

Emphasis upon the group: *or* does this pose any threat to the individual?

Should the curriculum satisfy what the adult says he wants	*or* what he ought to have?
Should the curriculum be selected, organized, and evaluated by a "teacher"	*or* by those taking part in the educational program?
Are the requirements of the *adult* learner significantly different	*or* the same as those of the child?
Should stress be placed on the content and subject matter of adult education	*or* upon the methods of adult education?
Should the primary content of adult education be based on the humanities	*or* the social sciences?
Should the teacher of adults have a "permissive" philosophy	*or* seek to bring about changes in the adult student?

Does the investing of many social agencies and social processes with education spoil spontaneity, destroy enthusiasm, and inhibit action? [6]

The Plan of This Book

We have already stated that our purpose is to assist an inquiry by practitioners in adult education leading to the organization of a body of theory and experience to guide their practice.

First of all, we shall deal with the learner himself, his personality, his physical changes, intellectual development, and the role of motives and emotions in learning.

Next, we shall select from the wealth of theory some of those formulations which seem to help us understand the learner and learning.

We shall also sample a number of fields of practice, where learning *about* learning is taking place. Attention will also be given to the forms and arrangements for learning, how organization and administration may condition and modify learning. In summarizing, we shall review some of the main features of the teaching-learning transaction—and finally, the particular role of the teacher or practitioner.

REFERENCES

1. Wilfred D. Gillin, *Toward the Liberally Educated Executive* (White Plains, N. Y.: Fund for Adult Education, 1957).
2. Robert J. Havighurst, *Social Roles of the Middle-Aged Person* (Chicago: Center for the Study of Liberal Education for Adults, 1955).

3. Robert Peers, *Adult Education* (New York: Humanities Press, Inc., 1958).
4. E. L. Thorndike, *Adult Learning* (New York: The Macmillan Company, 1928). By permission of Teachers College, Columbia University, New York, copyright owners.
5. UNESCO, *Learning to Be* (Paris: UNESCO, 1972).
6. Kenneth D. Benne, "Some Philosophic Issues in Adult Education," *Adult Education* (Chicago: Adult Education Association, hereafter designated as AEA), Vol. 7, No. 2.
7. Mortimer Adler, *Adult Education,* a lecture reprinted by the Great Books Foundation, 1952, copyright owners.
8. Robert M. Hutchins, "Education and Democracy," *School and Society,* 1949, Vol. 69.

SUGGESTED READING

Bischof, Ledford J. *Adult Psychology.* New York: Harper and Row, 1969.

Cotton, Webster. *On Behalf of Adult Education: A Historical Examination of the Supporting Literature.* Syracuse: Syracuse University Publications in Continuing Education, 1968.

Gagne, R. M. *The Conditions of Learning.* New York: Holt, Rinehart and Winston, 1965.

Grattan, C. Hartley, ed. *American Ideas About Adult Education, 1710–1951.* New York: Teachers College, Columbia University, 1959.

Houle, C. O. *The Design of Education.* San Francisco: Jossey-Bass, Inc., 1972.

Jensen, Gale, Liveright, A. A., and Hallenbeck, Wilbur. *Adult Education: Outlines of an Emerging Field of University Study.* Washington, D.C.: Adult Education Association of the U.S.A., 1962.

Johnstone, John W. S., and Rivera, Ramon. *Volunteers for Learning, A Study of the Educational Pursuits of American Adults.* Chicago: Aldine Publishing Company, 1965.

Kidd, J. R. *Education for Perspective.* Toronto: Peter Martin Associates, 1971.

Knowles, Malcolm S. *The Adult Education Movement in the United States.* New York: Holt, Rinehart and Winston, 1962.

Knowles, Malcolm S. *The Modern Practice of Adult Education.* New York: Association Press, 1970.

Liveright, A. A. *Study of Adult Education in the United States.* Brookline, Massachusetts: Center for the Study of Liberal Education for Adults, 1968.

Smith, Robert, Akers, G., and Kidd, J. R. *Handbook of Adult Education.* New York: Macmillan, 1970.

Verner, Coolie, and Booth, Alan, *Adult Education.* Washington, D.C.: Center for Applied Research in Education, 1964.

2

The Adult Learner

We have already discovered that the term *learning* is used in several different ways and that our central question, *"How do adults learn?"* is not one that can be answered directly. We shall now begin to get further understanding of the term by paying particular attention to the *learner*.

What do we know about the adult learner that helps us to understand him?

At first glance it seems not very much. We noted in Chapter 1 that the middle years of adulthood are *terra incognita,* that they have rarely been studied systematically. Any chart of the middle years is likely to be somewhat like that described in a verse by Lewis Carroll:

> He had bought a large map representing the sea
> Without the least vestige of land
> And the crew were much pleased when they found it to be
> A map they could all understand.

And about as useful for predicting the shoals and hazards or safe passages of life.

However, we need not be too pessimistic. A good deal is known even though it has not all been brought together. For example, a growing number of studies have come out in the past few years about the adult student.

Many institutions, university extension departments, colleges, and boards of education have begun to collect information much more systematically about the age, sex, occupation, previous educational experience, and achievements of their adult students. So have government departments, particularly those responsible for manpower training or adult basic education. Until recently such facts could not be obtained in any uniform way. Rarely, if ever, was even the effort made to find out much about such important matters as the previous educational experience of students. Even now follow-up studies of adult students after they finish their courses are relatively uncommon, and so it has been difficult to trace their record of progress. However, the situation is changing. There is now more attention to evaluation because administrators and those who make decisions about fund allocations are asking hard questions about results. Institutions now employ many more adult educationists and others who are capable of carrying out research. Yet, delegates at the World Conference on Adult Education in Tokyo in 1972 reported that a lack of such studies and a paucity of data about adult students still constituted a major problem in planning for adult education.

One difficulty is the lack of agreement about what information should be collected. And there is even a lack of agreement about terms. Efforts have been made by UNESCO to produce a glossary of terms and to obtain some agreement, across nations and in different languages, on what terms will mean. A *Manual on the Collection and Analysis of Adult Education Statistics* has been published for national statistical purposes. Authors of the manual wrote: "One of the most difficult tasks in preparing the Manual was to cut through the jungle of adult education terminology." [1]

Two kinds of information are needed: information about individual adult learners and about the number of adults in the total student population. The latter information is becoming much more complete. The number of adult students in the United States is very high indeed and growing rapidly, although some differences of opinion still exist about the totals. One observer estimated that there were 15 million in 1924, 22 million in 1934, 30 million in 1950, and 50 million in 1955. Recent estimates are probably more accurate since they are based on better data sources and research measures. *Volunteers for Learning* [2] by John W. S. Johnstone and Ramon Rivera, published in 1965, is regarded as a milestone study in reporting on the numbers and characteristics of adult learners.

Moreover, the average age for leaving school is still rising. We shall see in Chapter 4 what an important effect this has upon the ability of the adult to perform academic tasks, the kind measured on an "intelligence" test. Adults of all ages are "going back to school," the increase in total number is more noticeable than that in any particular age group. Of course, at any particular time this distribution may be affected by a special event, or circumstance. For example, provision of education of all kinds for veterans raised appreciably the number of men and women in their twenties and thirties taking full-time or part-time studies. Over the next two decades it is certain that the percentage of older people enrolling will markedly increase, due both to the increasing proportion of older people in the total population and to the number of new opportunities for education and recreation being planned specially for older people.

In a book entitled *Classrooms in the Factories* [3] the authors pointed out that corporations have educational programs for workmen and executives that in many ways rival those in colleges and universities. Thousands of men and women are enrolled in technical and academic classes and, in many cases, undertake advanced work in the natural sciences and sometimes in the social sciences and humanities.

For at least two decades studies have attempted to understand the motives which prompt adult students to enter upon a course of study. Robert Love [4] found that these are often highly complex. Two factors, at least, were present before adults enrolled in his institution: the student had an awareness of education as a positive value in solving problems and, at the same time, a belief that education is somehow equated with happiness and success. This and similar studies begin to explain some of the mistakes and failures that can occur, because the student may have an unrealistic view of the possibilities and values of his planned course of learning. Bernard James [5] has written that adult students who came to his class in "creative writing," ostensibly to learn how to write, in reality felt that they already knew how, but hoped to obtain some gimmick or acquire a slick style so that they could sell their wares.

The author once was interviewing a student who was registering for a course in calculus. In the conversation that ensued, the prospective student reported that he had gone only as far as the third grade in public school. When asked why he was enrolling for a course in higher mathematics he said, "You see, I used to work in the fifteen-cent store. I could figure prices and things pretty well. But now I am in a wholesale grocery and I have to multiply things like 37½ dozen eggs times 57½ cents. Hell, that's higher mathematics, ain't it?"

Studies in more recent years have increased in number and in rigor. For example, Stanley M. Grabowski completed "Motivational Factors of Adult Learners in a Directed Self-Study Bachelor's Degree Program" [6] in 1971, revealing many predisposing factors. Annual inventories of research in the United States report an increasing range of research problems, with the following examples investigated in the year 1973.

- Evaluating adults for further study
- The prediction of college-level academic achievements in adult extension students
- The older adult as a university student
- A study of perceptual and attitudinal change within a course on adult education methods
- An experimental study designed to test the relative effectiveness of a multi-media instructional system

• A study of the major reasons for adults beginning and continuing a learning project

In 1965, when the *Review of Education Research* [7] concentrated on adult education, Howard McClusky noted that the main studies in the field were concerned with rigidity and set, and attitudes, emotions, and changes in personality with aging. McClusky's conclusion contained his view that adult learning still requires a special focus and attention:

> First, one is impressed with data showing the great range of individual differences that increase with age. So extreme are the differences that one must be very cautious about the kind of claim he makes for the validity of his generalizations. Second, data from various sources are providing a growing case for a differential psychology of adults. Already it is clear that the pattern of abilities increases in difference from adolescence through early adulthood and on into the middle and late years. Third, more research is greatly needed but it must be conducted with concepts and instruments that are most relevant to the unique features of the adult condition. For example, more work needs to be done on an appropriate criterion of adult intelligence, on "age fair" tests, and on devices that get beneath the surface of the adult personality. Fourth, there is a serious lack of research dealing with the lower class adult. . . . Fifth, the problem of adult psychology is in part a problem of conservation of human resources. Already the limits of the productive years are moving upwards in both theory and practice.

What about achievement of the adult student? Knowing as we do that there is a widespread belief that adults do not learn well, one might expect that this belief would have been based, in part at least, on poor class performance. One might even have assumed that in comparison with daytime college students, adult students would not show up well when tested on the same examinations. However, *such is not the case.* In almost every single example where comparative results have been obtained, the adult student has obtained equal or better results than the daytime student.

Such studies have been available for at least four decades. In 1933 Herbert Sorenson made a thorough study of adult ability, and reports as one of his main conclusions:

> The evidence indicates that the measured abilities of extension and non-extension students are essentially equal. In some universities the extension students have higher abilities and in others the full-time students are slightly superior; but the differences are not very large at any university. They do indicate, however, that any existing superiority is found within the adult group. [8]

Nearly twenty years later John Dyer [9] reported that the superior adult student is as good as, or better than, the superior day student, and the average students in both classifications are about equal.

Data are also available from Eastern European countries where, on the whole, special attention and place are given to mature students who have experience in production on the farm, in industry, or in service roles. All the evidence seems to confirm that such persons can and do perform well, never forgetting, of course, that there are enormous individual differences in capacities and motivation. There exist considerable data, as well, from the United Kingdom and countries in Western Europe, concerning the attainments of part-time students, particularly where the rhythms of work and study are worked out in some appropriate way. The conclusions are supported with data from the various examples of education interspersed with life experiences in those colleges and universities in North America where "cooperative" plans have been followed. Evidence continues to mount, particularly from university extension departments, that the marks of mature students in university courses are as high and often higher on the course examinations than the average of "regular" students, although, as one might expect, "part-time students" obtain fewer places in the top one percent of marks than do "full-time" students. We note that this evidence continues to come in, that it is consistent, yet, despite such studies, many educational administrators continue to think of part-time students, or mature students, as incapable of doing or unlikely to do academic work of quality. Some assert, against all evidence, that such students are inferior in ability; others, that part-time students never have enough time or strength to do justice to academic work.

As we shall see later, the adult student tends to do better in some subjects like history or literature than he does in subjects like mathematics or physics. Although studies of this sort are limited to university and night-school fields, it is, however, already clear that adult performance on academic tests warrants the fullest opportunity for adults to enter any field of scholarship.

As far as the evidence goes there do not appear to be significant differences between the sexes at any time during adulthood, either in achievement on tests or in learning capacity.

It has long been known that adults will read the books that are accessible to them much more often than those which they claim that they want to read. Similarly, some studies have indicated that adults will take part in educational activities that are close at hand more often than those in which they claim to be interested but which may be more difficult to reach.

Evidence from research has appeared to support the contentions by sociologists such as W. C. Hallenbeck [10] that adults will readily engage in learning activities associated with certain major social goals, such as obtaining improved housing. As we have noted in another context, this is the basis for much adult education associated with "community development" all over the world.

Much recent research has started with the questions: Why are some adults blocked in their attempts to learn? What are the chief barriers and difficulties?

It is now considered almost an axiom that the economic and social position of a child may determine decisively how well he will progress in education and what he will become. The child who is undernourished in body and understimulated makes slow and shambling progress as a learner. Unfortunately, environments that deter learning in children seem also to have a serious effect upon adults. A man or a woman who has learned to accept or live with a detrimental environment is not a person who will readily undertake another learning experience. He foresees only one more painful step on the long trail of failure and shame.

One kind of evidence shows up both with remarkable clarity and consistency: that is, that social attitudes vary directly with the *amount* of education. Adults with less education tend to have less regard for civil liberties, less tolerance for groups other than their own, and to hold more authoritarian attitudes.

Some efforts have been made to diffuse results of these studies. Collaboration by ERIC and the Adult Education Association in the United States has resulted in several reviews of research abstracts, which now appear annually. There are annual inventories published in Canada, and abstracts and research reports appear regularly in the United Kingdom, Holland, Germany, Czechoslovakia, and Yugoslavia. Before long it should be possible for practitioners and institutes to receive research abstracts from any part of the world.

One area of scholarship has developed rather late; namely, Comparative Studies in Adult Education. Adult Education, more than any other educational field, has been marked by international associations and by the diffusion of such ideas or programs as the Folk Highschools originating in Denmark, the Workers' Educational Association of England, and Agricultural Extension from the United States. But systematic, comparative studies have only begun to appear and the first postgraduate course in this field was offered in 1967. However, recent progress has been rapid and there are universities in many countries giving such courses. Programs of research are being designed based on such concepts as "cultural diffusion," developed by Coolie Verner.[11] As more comprehensive learning theories are developed it will be possible, as in no other field of education, to test them simultaneously in several countries at once.

The Adult—In What Ways Different From the Child?

In quoting Howard McClusky we noted his opinion that "data from various sources are providing a growing case for a differential psychology of adults."

There are an increasing number of adult educationists, in the United States and abroad, who believe that there is a strong case for a different "science of teaching"—*andragogy* to distinguish it from *pedagogy*.

For Malcolm Knowles,[12] this change in title and emphasis derives from three propositions:

1. Where adult education has been a kind of luxury and secondary activity in our culture, the education of adults is rapidly becoming a central concern, a central need of our civilization.
2. Adult education has underdone an enormous growth both in the number of people it is touching and the number of institutions that are identifying adult education as a primary activity.
3. Up to this point adult education has been relatively ineffective in accomplishing its mission.

Knowles reasons that improved effectiveness will not arise simply from an extension of schooling as it now exists. He starts with an analysis of the differences between children and adults, a difference that begins in the concept of self.

A child first sees himself as a completely dependent personality. He sees himself in his first consciousness as being completely dependent upon the adult world to make his decisions for him, to feed him, to change his diapers, and to see where the pin is sticking. During the course of his childhood and youth, that dependence is reinforced as decisions are made for him in the home, at school, in church, on the playground, and everywhere he turns. But at some point he starts experiencing the joy of deciding things for himself. . . . To be adult means to be self-directing. Now at the point at which this change occurs, there develops in the human being a deep psychological need to be perceived by himself and by others as being indeed self-directing. This is the concept that lies at the heart of andragogy. Andragogy is based upon the insight that the deepest need an adult has is to be treated as an adult, to be treated as a self-directing person, to be treated with respect. Andragogy is student-centered and problem oriented.

And then Knowles concludes: "when you get right down to it, that's the way the education of children should be too."

Knowles and the educationists in Europe who also emphasize the differences that arise or must be reflected in dealing with adults face a dilemma, one that adult educationists have always faced. Should they stress differences due to age and experience or continuities? They do not want to do violence to their appreciation of the continuity of living or the belief that the learner can and must be seen as one developing personality all through life. It has been the adult educationists who have fostered the notion of *education permanente*, of lifelong learning,[13] of coherence and continuity throughout the life span.

Schools and colleges have traditionally planned with needs of children or youths in mind. Accordingly, if it was assumed that what was being offered was *education*, then if an adult wanted education he ought to take what was offered. Actually for years many adults seeking an education not only took a curriculum designed for children, were taught by teachers whose only experience was with children, but were obliged to sit at desks built for children.

Now most educationalists agree that curriculum and methods should be related both to the goals of education and to the needs of the student.

Are adults different only in that their bodies cannot easily be crammed into children's desks? Or are their needs and their experience so varied that there should be special provision of facilities, curricula, teaching style, texts and study materials, methods of instruction?

(In making these references to the differences between adults and children or youth we are not forgetting the truly enormous changes that have been occurring in the education, experience, life style and values of young people. In some respects the differences have been lessened but in others they have been accentuated.)

More and more evidence has been accumulating that justifies a special attack on adult learning. We shall not present this evidence here because much of it will come out in the subsequent chapters. Instead, we shall simply illustrate this whole problem by selecting four of many ways in which an adult learner may have a different perception or understanding of what he is learning than a youth has, or the ways in which he feels differently about it.

No "correct" answer. Most of the significant problems faced by an adult do not have a "correct" answer in the sense that the answer can be verified to the point that doubt or uncertainty is removed. This uncertainty usually characterizes problems in business or marital relations or politics. On the other hand, for most classroom problems of children there is a "correct" answer, in the back of the book or elsewhere.

"Correctness" associated with traditions or religion. The situation for the adult learner may be further complicated because for many problems,

though there may be no answer that will stand up to rigorous rational tests, some answers are regarded as being "correct" in terms of tradition or cultural habits or religion or an institution. The adult, more than the child, is bound by these stereotypes of what is "correct" and though modification is always possible, such modifications may have to run the gauntlet of rigid internal and external pressures to the contrary.

Solutions have effects! Any solution that an adult gives to a problem is likely to have its immediate effects upon other individuals. In the case of personal problems or labor-management discussions, what he decides to do will implicate others and he must take these possible implications into account. Many social problems might be "solved" theoretically, but a real-life solution may not seem immediately possible because of the human personalities involved. However, it should not be forgotten that one of the most important purposes of adult education is to give adults the opportunity to work out solutions free from the high, perhaps dangerously high, cost of error. By using role playing, for example, the learner may investigate the kinds of feelings that are associated with deeply disturbing emotional or social conflicts such as the "integration of a school" and try out actual solutions of these conflicts under conditions in which real life is simulated, but where the effects of a "mistake" are not disastrous.

Expectations of the "student" and "teacher" may be different. The child comes to school more or less to learn what the school is teaching. The adult may and often does bring quite different views to the classroom from those held by the teacher. This may result in conflict. The teacher may perceive this difference as undesirable: for example, as a failure by the adult to appreciate the subject or the worth of high standards. The adult learner may even feel guilty about his expectations. But the tension set up between the expectations of the teacher and learner is not necessarily undesirable; it can be the basis for effective learning by *both*.

Exploring Useful Hypotheses About Adult Learning

Any search or inquiry must proceed in part through the examination of certain hunches, guesses, notions, or hypotheses. Since, by many, adult learning was considered only as *remedial*, the number of conceptions designed to guide or challenge observation and reflection have not been plentiful. However, a change is also coming in this respect. We shall now summarize a few of these ideas simply to note the light they cast upon learning, the objectives they raise to be tested or evaluated and the critical questions they suggest. Again we have not included here all the notions worthy of attention but have selected a few for illustrative purposes.

The usefulness of such concepts can be illustrated negatively as well as positively. For example, take a trait such as intellectual curiosity. It is often said that every child is born with curiosity and that it is basic to much of learning, to man's intellectual progress, and to the advancement of science. Ordway Tead once wrote that a central purpose of college is to encourage "the student's sense of the wonder and mystery of life and reverence for living it. . . . His sense of curiosity and his grasp of the operating meaning of rationality should be fostered in every course." [14] But some people charge that the schools damage or destroy this priceless gift. Adult education is supposed to rekindle the fires of curiosity which somehow have been quenched. Now if we knew what curiosity is, or how it manifests itself, how it is cultivated or stunted, it might be of great value. In recent years more work bearing on the concept of curiosity has been done by psychologists in Toronto, D. E. Berlyne, H. I. Day, and others.[15] Their findings are interesting and promising for the future. Professor Day has developed a test of "curiosity" as a means of identifying adults who are lacking in formal education but may do well in further academic courses. However, the achievement thus far in defining what curiosity is in terms of behavior has not reached the stage where it is of much practical guidance to adult educators.

These are some of the concepts that have yielded useful hypotheses for investigation:

- the life span
- changes in role
- "studentship" and "membership"
- maturation

- adult experience
- the self-learner
- the significance of "time"
- "old age"

THE LIFE SPAN

It is not a strange or radical idea that, if we are to have much understanding of the nature of human beings, we ought to consider the whole span of life, the growth or development of man through all his years. However, it is a surprising fact that except for a few life insurance tables, and some isolated research reports, there are scarcely any such studies or organized bodies of data.

We have hundreds of studies of the child; the child of one week, the child of two weeks, the child of six months. There are also innumerable books about personality changes in children, about health, intellectual development, and hundreds of other aspects. We also have scores of studies about various phases of adolescence. In recent years there have been an increasing number of studies of older people, particularly those of advanced years. For the middle years there is a handful of highly specialized reports. But there is practically nothing which deals with the full-life development of man in any comprehensive way, at least as it affects learning. It is almost as if we assumed that all of adulthood was identical; that it progressed at the same pace, in the same directions, on the same plane.

But what a denial this is of human experience! Every minister, historian, poet, or novelist knows better.

In recent decades some scholarly texts have begun to deal with the same understanding that religion and literature have always had. The successive editions of the medical text *Problems of Aging* [16] have been organized to reveal development over the life span. Books by Raymond G. Kuhlen, *Life a Psychological Survey* and *Psychological Development Through the Life Span*,[17] both in collaboration with Sidney L. Pressey, followed later by *Psychological Studies of Human Development*,[18] edited in collaboration with G. G. Thompson, represent a major contribution. Books about the life span continue to appear, and since each has added a layer of information, much of it important in the understanding of learning, some are noted at the end of the chapter. Development psychology has become one of the most important subfields of this science.

The results of these development studies are certain to have their effect on the curriculum, the facilities planned for adults, and methods and techniques. As we shall see in Chapter 3, the variations in sensory capacity over the years are of surprising magnitude.

Students of the life span are greatly concerned with whether or not adults are less able intellectually, less capable of learning in older than in younger years. The very questions asked usually beg a negative answer: they are questions about decline. Decline is a fact of life, but where it is found is seems to be a compound of three factors—the three D's of adult decline—*disuse*, the failure to use one's capacities; the onset of *degenerative diseases* that sap vitality and cloud performance; and *disinterest*—the lack of strong motivation. The general question will be faced in each of the next three chapters.

CHANGES IN ROLE

We have already identified some of the important changes in role that may happen to any adult such as:

- Reaching the peak of one's work career
- Setting adolescent children free and helping them become responsible adults
- Working out a satisfying relationship with aging parents
- Creating a home which has a new focus as the children leave

People sometimes confuse roles with status (one's place in the order of things) or with social class (one's position on a social economic scale). Arising from this confusion and the changes that occur in role, status, and class, there has come a demand for a taxonomy that takes into account both roles and related competencies. A list suggested by Malcolm Knowles at a UNESCO Seminar in Hamburg in 1972 begins with the following:

Roles	Competencies
Learner	Reading, writing, computing, perceiving, conceptualizing, evaluating, imagining, inquiring
Becoming a self (with unique self-identity)	Self-analyzing, sensing, goal-building, objectivizing, value-clarifying, expressing
Friend	Loving, empathizing, listening, collaborating, sharing, helping, giving feedback, supporting
Citizen	Caring, participating, leading, decision-making, discussing, acting, having perspective
Family member	Maintaining health, planning, managing, helping, sharing, buying, saving, loving, taking responsibility
Worker	Career planning, technical skills, giving and using supervision, getting along with fellows, cooperating, planning, delegating, managing
Leisure-time user	Knowing resources, appreciating, performing, playing, relaxing, planning, risking, reflecting

Changes in role may also, of course, be directly related to changes in personality and the growth of the self. This extremely important subject is taken up in Chapters 5 and 6.

There are those who claim that, since change itself is the only constant, and change usually results in stress, one of the most important of all competencies is learning to relax, learning to man the defenses and marshal the energies that each person possesses.

Most people face many changes of role and circumstance. It is a cliché to say that the only common element is change. It would probably be more accurate to say that everyone faces stress as a result of change. Increasingly experts in physical education, medicine, and psychiatry are all saying that one of the most important things any person can learn is how to handle tension and stress.

STUDENTSHIP AND MEMBERSHIP

In a provocative paper, Alan M. Thomas [19] has argued that the role of *member* rather than that of *student* makes a significant difference in the behavior of a learner. Since so much of adult education goes on with *members* of various organizations, the result of this role difference is a matter of considerable importance. Of the two the role of student is much better understood.

> The outstanding characteristic of the student role is that it is completely dependent. This characteristic is established early because the child in the school systems is dependent in every sense, just as he is dependent outside of school.

Thomas suggests that the role of *student* affects adults as well as children.

> The dependency continues long after the individual's emergence from compulsory attendance and dependence on his parents. In fact, it continues right to the end of graduate school and after. The authority of parents and paternal school systems is replaced quite unobtrusively and almost (at least until recently) painlessly, by the authority of knowledge, competence, and skill. It is replaced also by the institutional control of rewards and accreditation, that is, of access to employment and prestige.

While dependence is the badge of the *student*, mutual agreement is of the *member*.

> The member role occurs when adults associate in a group of any size in order to achieve a specific goal. The goal can be completely internal to the group of associates, such as providing an activity in which they engage to their own satisfaction, for example a chess club or a sports club of some kind; or it may be a goal which involves influencing the community at large, such as a charitable or political group. The association occurs because of a mutual agreement about the importance of the goal, but it also includes satisfactions in the association itself which may be personal, professional, or of some other kind.
> . . . The member is neither dependent upon institutional authority nor particularly self-conscious about the engagement in learning. . . .
> Finally the member is not, except temporarily, aware of a sense of preparation or isolation. The need for learning emerges from action and is part of it, however interesting the periods of teaching and experimentation in learning may be. The physical venue of this experience is almost always the learner's familiar action-bound setting—the union hall, the conference room, the community centre—and the teacher comes to him rather than he to the teacher. . . .

Thomas maintains that both roles are important but should be brought into balance.

. . . it is apparent that there is now a major attempt on the part of individuals normally conceived of as predominantly *students* to become *members,* and conversely of members to become more like students. . . .

. . . The balance between the calm, controlled, bureaucratic, rational student learning and the more spontaneous, explosive, membership learning will be much more difficult to maintain in the future. Yet it is exactly that balance, risky as it is, on which the learning society must be built.

MATURATION

A most useful conception in adult education is that of *maturity* or *maturation.* The word "maturity" has been used so often, so loosely, and to cover so many ideas, that for a while, it appeared that it might lose most of its meaning and usefulness and become a spineless synonym for "good." Fortunately, it now seems to be becoming invested with new 'meaning, giving forth a number of hypotheses which are being studied.

A number of writers such as Angyal [20] and Snygg,[21] have pointed out that the human organism develops in certain predictable ways. It seems to move toward greater independence and greater self-responsibility. The tendency is in the direction of increasing self-government, self-regulation, and autonomy, and away from reliance upon control from external forces. This seems to be true equally when we are speaking of organic processes that are not conscious, such as the changing amount of water content in the body, or such intellectual functions as choosing what a person will do with his life. The human organism does not become highly specialized as does that of most animals. Becoming mature, for the human species, means a greater differentiation of organs and of function, through extending itself by the use of tools. It seems, also, that man develops in the direction of socialization. Robert Blakely has aptly described this human condition:

Man is the most highly adaptable form of life. . . .

Man makes the tools and machines that make further physical evolution unnecessary. Does he want to hunt like the bear? He invents the spear. Does he want to dive like the fish? He invents the submarine. Does he want to fly like the bird? He invents the airplane. There is no end in sight: yet he himself remains unspecialized. He takes on and puts off at will the specialized organs and capacities that encumber the bear, the whale and the eagle.

To do all this man had to become social. This meant language and culture. Language and culture meant something astoundingly new—the transmission of experience and knowledge. What one man discovered, all men could learn. What one generation accomplished, the next could build upon.[22]

Many writers, such as David Riesman, have noted with concern the tendency for modern man to become "outer-directed," to conform, to lose his autonomy. *The Lonely Crowd* [23] describes in detail the pressures exerted on all of us. The dangers are real enough. But what is equally real is the human tendency to resist, the will to grow. In a memorable sentence, Karen Horney writes: ". . . the ultimate driving force is the person's unrelenting will to come to grips with himself, a wish to grow and leave nothing untouched that prevents growth." [24] Carl Rogers has summarized the same tendencies, based on his practice:

> I find that the urge for a great degree of independence, the desire for a self-determined integration, the tendency to strive, even through much pain, toward a socialized maturity, is as strong as—no, is stronger than—the desire for a comfortable dependence, the need to rely upon external authority for assurance. . . . Clinically I find it to be true that though an individual may remain dependent because he has always been so, or may drift into dependence without realizing what he is doing, or may temporarily wish to be dependent because his situation seems to be desperate, I have yet to find the individual who, when he examines his situation deeply, and feels that he perceives it clearly, deliberately chooses dependence, deliberately chooses to have the integrated direction of himself undertaken by another. When all the elements are clearly perceived, the balance seems invariably in the direction of the painful but ultimately rewarding path of self-actualization or growth.[25]

These writers assert that it is part of the nature of man to grow toward self-direction, self-discipline, autonomy. Some call this tendency *maturation.*

One well-known statement of this view is that of Overstreet in *The Mature Mind.*[26] In this book the author brought together findings from psychology, sociology, anthropology, and psychiatry, attempting to fuse them into a harmonized view of what makes for maturity in human behavior. The mature person, he says, is one "whose linkages with life are constantly becoming stronger and richer because his attitudes are such as to encourage their growth rather than their stoppage." These attitudes are directed toward knowledge, social responsibility, vocational adjustment, skill in communicating, and social relationships. Overstreet believes that maturing in respect to any one of these has an influence on development over all the others.

Another useful formulation of maturity, applied to reading, has been developed by William S. Gray and Bernice Rogers. In their study, reported in the book *Maturity in Reading,*[27] the authors distinguished a number of characteristics of the mature reader:

- A genuine enthusiasm for reading.
- Tendency to read (a) a wide variety of materials that contribute plea-

sure, widen horizons, and stimulate creative thinking; (b) serious materials which promote a growing understanding of one's self, of others, and of problems of a social, moral, and ethical nature; and (c) intensively in a particular field or materials relating to a central core.

- Ability to translate words into meanings, to secure a clear grasp and understanding of the ideas presented, and to sense clearly the mood and feelings intended.
- Capacity for and habit of making use of all that one knows or can find out in interpreting or construing the meaning of the ideas read.
- Ability to perceive strengths and weaknesses in what is read and to detect bias and propaganda, and to think critically concerning the validity and values of the idea presented, and the adequacy or soundness of the author's presentation, views and conclusions.
- Tendency to fuse the new ideas acquired through reading with previous experience, thus acquiring new or clearer understandings, broadened interests, rational attitudes, improved patterns of thinking and behaving, and richer and more stable personalities.
- Capacity to adjust one's reading pace to the needs of the occasion and to the demands of adequate interpretation.

This list raises a number of questions which can be refined, tested, and evaluated.

If people are to undertake learning at any stage in their lifetime it will be necessary to develop much more precise diagnostic tools than are now available to help the learner make a sound judgment of his own possibilities and thus to plan ahead for his next stage of learning. It is too simple merely to have one set of criteria at the elementary or adult basic level, and another set at a level of "maturity." But these attempts to identify behavior that is mature may suggest to the adult educator ways through which he can assist adult students to appraise their own level of performance.

We will return to the concept of maturation in Chapter 6.

ADULT EXPERIENCE

We have already noted the danger of so emphasizing the changes associated with growing older that we lose sight of the underlying continuities in life.

Nevertheless, a principal factor—for some *the* principal factor [28]—in adult learning is the comparatively richer experience of the adult and what use is made of this in the learning transaction.

There are three related notions here:

- Adults have *more* experiences
- Adults have different *kinds* of experiences
- Adult experiences are *organized differently*

These points seem self-evident. An adult's sexual or social experiences are of a kind that mark him off from the world of children. The same can be said of his experiences of a job, or politics, or war. But this point has not always been understood or accepted. We have noted that it is forgotten or explicitly denied in the many cases where a curriculum for adults is simply a "warming over" of something that had been designed for youth.

In the adult years, despite all tendencies to conformity, the range of experience from adult to adult is greater than among children. Moreover, adults generally have dealings with individuals of all ages; in some societies this used to be true of everyone, but at present children outside of their own family meet individuals of other ages in rather formal ways.

Inquiries are going forward to examine these differences quantitatively, to discover their qualitative aspects, and to identify the kinds of experience that may dispose the adult toward effective and continuous learning. Past experience provides a basis for expectation. It may be that the *emotional tone* of those experiences will increase resistance to learning. Such hypotheses are being developed and tested; for example, that adults have an ability superior to young people in learning *relationally*. That is, they have more capacity, not just to memorize facts or understand ideas but to perceive how these facts affect themselves or others.[29]

In addition, there has been considerable research in regard to the effect of experience upon perception itself. This can be best illustrated from the results of a single ingenious experiment. The experimenter put a blob of red on a card and flashed it before the eyes of the adult students for a fraction of a second, and asked them what they saw. All of them said that they saw *red*. Next he took an identical card, with an area of red of the same number of square inches, but appearing in the shape of the ace of spades. After exposure of the card the subjects were again queried about what they saw. Now no subject reported that he saw red: some reported they saw *gray*, or *brown*, or *purple*, or nothing at all they could identify. Past experience in seeing a "spade" as black caused them to perceive any spade-like shape not as red, but as other colors; or the experience was so confusing that nothing identifiable was perceived. Past experience may block, modify, or it may affect perception, as well as how we solve problems and make decisions.

Of course, the most important aspect of experience and learning is the way that the learner perceives his own experience as unique and private.

This significant matter we shall consider in part in a later discussion of the self.

THE SELF-LEARNER

Throughout recorded history there have been men and women who continued to pursue learning with vigor until the end of their days. This was so in the Greek, Roman, and Renaissance periods in the Western world: Asian literature and history have many more examples. Henry Adams was far from being the most distinguished of these, but he will be remembered for suggesting that his education went on all through life and then for detailing in what manner this happened.

It has often been said that the purpose of adult education, or of any kind of education, is to make of the subject a continuing, "inner-directed," self-operating learner. "The primary task of an education," said Sir Arthur Currie, formerly principal of McGill University, "is to make men alive, to send them out alive at more points, alive on higher levels, alive in more effective ways. The purpose of an education is not the mere getting of the ability to sell your efforts at a higher figure than unlearned men do, but to make you a thinker, to make you a creator, with an enlarged capacity for life."

One can come upon the autonomous learner in novels, in plays, most often in memoirs, biographies, and autobiographies.

Relating the concept of self-learner to that of "social roles" may also have useful consequences. A number of studies have identified many social roles, such as parent, or spouse. With each such role there are associated tasks which the individual must learn to perform. At the point in his development when an individual must quickly be prepared within a limited time to fill such a role, occurs what Havighurst has called the "teachable moment." Much of parent education is based on the heightened motivation that occurs in the earliest months and years of parenthood. How such "teachable moments" may be utilized for other kinds of learning and how they may be related to continuing self-learning are very important questions which have not yet been explored.

One of the most interesting and protracted studies of the adult learner was launched at the University of Chicago under C. O. Houle about 1960. Starting with a short paper entitled "An Exploratory Study of the Self-Educating Person," [30] Houle and a number of colleagues and students went on to explore a whole series of questions. At first these were simple: Does a self-educating learner differ in any marked way from others? Are his interests wider, or deeper; are they found only in certain fields, or are they distributed? Does he participate to a larger or to a lesser extent in group and community activities than is common? Is he more intelligent? Has he had more extensive formal education? Do his habits display more perseverance and sustained effort?

One of Houle's students, Allen Tough, as a professor of adult education at the Ontario Institute for Studies in Education, has been continuing the enquiry throughout the 1960's. It has resulted in a very significant concept—the *self-directed learner*.[31] This we will take up in Chapter 11.

It has often been mentioned that in our culture we do not have the same conception of history, the same feeling that we are living in a great continuum with men and women who have gone before, or those who will come after, as do some other peoples. In general, our culture places more emphasis upon youth than do others. This fact influences in important ways what people will try to learn, or whether they will make the effort. If they accept the notion that life is mostly over at thirty-five or forty-five why bother to learn?

TIME

For an adult learner *time* is of very great consequence. This is true in several different respects—physically, culturally, emotionally.

Adults tend to perceive time differently.[32] The child or youth lives not only in the present but in the future. Time seems endless to the youth, but if he is obliged to postpone gratification of certain wants, the wait may seem unwarranted.

Adults have more stable interests and a different perception of time. They are able to internalize long-range goals and work toward them over a period of time. On the other hand, many adults as well as youth live in the here-and-now and will seldom work toward distant goals unless they themselves have a commitment to these goals. To the old what time is left may appear very short, and to be valued, perhaps even to be hoarded, rather than spent. Howard McClusky [33] has pointed out that the adult's view of himself—his self-adequacy—is very closely linked with his view of time. "I am too old," "If I were twenty years younger," may be ways in which the adult is not only talking about his chronological age but also stating what he feels about his own capacity.

For an adult, more than for a child, the investment of time in an activity may be as important a decision as the investment of money or effort.

Time may take on a new meaning as there is more leisure for more people. The problems sometimes associated with "leisure" grow out of the perceptions that adults have about time, and the somewhat limited experience they may have known of having large amounts of time under their own direction.

Hypotheses about the meaning of time, its relation to such notions as continuous learning, or to a concept like self-adequacy, are beginning to be investigated.

GROWING OLD AND THE ACCEPTANCE OF DEATH

Since more and more people live to experience old age, learning to accept the opportunities and exigencies of aging is a task for most of us. This is true of males, but particularly true of females who, on the whole, live about a decade longer as adults. Moreover, many of them live alone as widows a significant span of that time. Most men have no equivalent period of aloneness. In several of our chapters there will be references to aging and its consequences, particularly in Chapter 6.

It is self-evident that learning is something that happens to *a* person, it is an *individual* thing. It is equally true that one cannot have much understanding of learning unless he sees how the "self" is engaged in the changes we call learning. But it would be wrong to conclude that there is no more to learning than internal changes. How then could we explain the role of the teacher? Or the fact that much learning comes about through what transpires in a group? Or such phenomena as that in some societies extraordinary adaptations are made much more rapidly than in other societies? For example, we note the astonishing speed by which industrialization occurred in Japan, with all the learning that was entailed in that immense social revolution.

The self is never isolated; it takes part in various social situations, and is found in various social roles. "I am a part of all that I have met," sang the poet. Gardner Murphy puts it another way. "Paradoxically," he says, "it is often through the creation of the right group atmosphere that individuality can best be released."

The concept of the isolated individual as sitting behind a book or listening in his study to a radio or watching TV strips off the social clothing which gives context and meaning to the learning process. The individual learns as a member of a group, shares with others the goal of learning, interprets the material as something with respect to which he agrees or disagrees with others, constantly gauges for himself the implications of the knowledge or skill for his own action or place in the group. The types of investigation done long ago by Thorndike with reference to individual learning ability are important, and there must be much more study of what the adult can learn and how his learning depends upon constitutional factors, age, sex, experience and motivation. It is however, time for a broader view which considers the whole person and his social context as the subject matter for research in adult learning. Everything in clinical and social psychology should ultimately be made useful.[34]

This is the view of learning that one may expect from a social psychologist. Others, like Allen Tough, report that most learners alternate between individual and social kinds of learning experience.

In our inquiry we shall consider these factors and also what can be learned by other students of man, both social scientists and artists—at least so far as space will allow.

REFERENCES

1. John Bowers and E. A. Fisher, "The Search for a Terminology of Adult Education," *Convergence,* Vol. V., No. 4.
2. John W. S. Johnstone and Ramon Rivera, *Volunteers for Learning* (Chicago: Aldine Publishing Co., 1965).
3. Harold F. Clark and Harold S. Sloan, *Classrooms in the Factories* (New York: New York University Press, 1958).
4. Robert Love, "The Use of Motivation Research to Determine Interest in Adult College-Level Training," *Educational Record,* July 1953.
5. Bernard J. James, "Can Needs Define Educational Goals?" *Adult Education* (Chicago, AEA), Vol. 7, No. 1.
6. Stanley M. Grabowski, "Motivational Factors of Adult Learners in a Directed Self-Study Bachelor's Degree Program." Reported in *Continuing Education for Adults,* Syracuse University. No. 179.
7. American Educational Research Association, *Review of Educational Research,* Vol. XXXV, No. 3.
8. Herbert Sorenson, *Adult Abilities* (Minneapolis: University of Minnesota Press, 1933).
9. John P. Dyer, *Ivory Towers in the Market Place* (Indianapolis: Bobbs-Merrill Company, Inc., 1956).
10. W. C. Hallenbeck, "New Needs in Adult Education," *Teachers College Record,* May 1947.
11. International Counsel for Adult Education, *Convergence* theme issue on Comparative Studies in Adult Education, Vol. III, No. 3.
12. Malcolm S. Knowles, *The Modern Practice of Education* (New York: Association Press, 1970).
13. J. R. Kidd, *The Implications of Continuous Learning* (Toronto: W. J. Gage, 1966).
14. Ordway Tead, *College Teaching and College Learning* (New Haven: Yale University Press, 1949).
15. H. I. Day, D. E. Berlyne, and D. E. Hunt, *Intrinsic Motivation* (Toronto: Ontario Institute for Studies in Education, 1971).
16. A. I. Lansing, ed., *Problems of Ageing* (Baltimore: Williams & Wilkins Company, 1952).
17. Sidney L. Pressey and Raymond G. Kuhlen, *Psychological Development Through the Life Span* (New York: Harper & Brothers, 1957).
18. G. G. Thompson and R. G. Kuhlen, eds., *Psychological Studies of Human Development* (New York: Appleton-Century-Crofts, 1963).
19. Alan M. Thomas, "Studentship and Membership," *Journal of Education,* University of Alberta, Summer, 1967.

20. A. Angyal, *Foundations for a Science of Personality* (New York: Commonwealth Fund, 1941).
21. Donald Snygg and Arthur W. Combs, *Individual Behavior: A New Frame of Reference for Psychology* (New York: Harper & Brothers, 1949).
22. Robert J. Blakely, "What Is a Free Society?" *Adult Education in a Free Society* (Toronto: Guardian Bird Publications, 1958).
23. David Riesman, Nathan Glazer, and Reuel Denney, *The Lonely Crowd* (New Haven: Yale University Press, 1950).
24. Karen Horney, *Self-Analysis* (New York: W. W. Norton & Company, Inc., 1942).
25. Carl R. Rogers, *Counseling and Psychotherapy* (Boston: Houghton Mifflin Company, 1942).
26. Harry Overstreet, *The Mature Mind* (New York: W. W. Norton & Company, Inc., 1949).
27. William S. Gray and Bernice Rogers, *Maturity in Reading* (Chicago: University of Chicago Press, 1956). Copyright 1956 by the University of Chicago.
28. John Schwertman, *I Want Many Lodestars* (Chicago: Center for the Study of Liberal Education for Adults, 1958).
29. James B. Whipple, *Especially for Adults* (Chicago: Center for the Study of Liberal Education for Adults, 1957).
30. C. O. Houle, "An Exploratory Study of the Self-Educating Person," reported in *Adult Education* (Chicago: AEA), Vol. 8, No. 4. .
31. Allen Tough, *The Adult's Learning Projects* (Toronto: Ontario Institute for Studies in Education, 1971).
32. Robert J. Havighurst, *Social Roles of the Middle-Aged Person* (Chicago: Center for the Study of Liberal Education for Adults, 1953).
33. Howard McClusky, "Central Hypotheses About Adult Learning" (Lafayette, Ind.: Commission of the Professors of Adult Education, 1958).
34. Gardner Murphy, *Psychological Needs of Adults* (Chicago: Center for the Study of Liberal Education for Adults, 1955).

SUGGESTED READING

Anderson, Darrel, and Niemi, John A. *Adult Education and the Disadvantaged Adult.* Syracuse, New York: Syracuse University Publications in Continuing Education, 1971.

Cleugh, M. F. *Educating Older People.* London: Tavistock Publications (Associated Book Publishers Ltd.), 1962.

Cartwright, Morse A. *Ten Years of Adult Education.* New York: The Macmillan Company, 1935.

DeCrow, Roger. *Ability and Achievement of Evening College and Extension Students.* Syracuse: Syracuse University Publications in Continuing Education, 1959.

Havighurst, R. J., and Orr, Betty. *Adult Education and Adult Needs.* Syracuse: Syracuse University Publications in Continuing Education, 1956.

Houle, Cyril O. *The Inquiring Mind.* Madison, Wisconsin: University of Wisconsin Press, 1961.

Johnstone, John W. C., and Rivera, Ramon. *Volunteers for Learning, A Study of the Educational Pursuits of American Adults.* Chicago: Aldine Publishing Company, 1965.

McGhee, Paul A. *A School for Optimists.* Syracuse: Syracuse University Publications in Continuing Education, 1953.

Morton, J. R. *University Extension in the United States.* Birmingham: University of Alabama Press, 1953.

Neugarten, Bernice L., ed. *Middle Age and Aging.* Chicago: The University of Chicago Press, 1968.

Rogers, Carl R. *Freedom to Learn.* Columbus, Ohio: Charles E. Merrill Publishing Company, 1969.

Anthropological Backgrounds of Adult Education. Syracuse: Syracuse University Publications in Continuing Education, 1968.

3

Physical and Sensory Capacity

In this chapter we shall consider the relation of physical and sensory capacity to learning and note the changes in capacity that go on throughout life.

Nowhere have these changes in human life been more forcefully described than in a memorable passage from Shakespeare's *As You Like It:*

> And one man in his time plays many parts,
> His acts being seven ages. At first, the infant,
> Mewling and puking in the nurse's arms:
> Then the whining schoolboy, with his satchel,
> And shining morning face, creeping like snail
> Unwillingly to school: and then, the lover,
> Sighing like furnace, with a woeful ballad
> Made to his mistress' eyebrow: Then a soldier;
> Full of strange oaths, and bearded like the pard
> Jealous in honour, sudden and quick in quarrel,
> Seeking the bubble reputation
> Even in the cannon's mouth: and then, the justice;
> In fair round belly, with good capon lin'd,
> With eyes severe, and beard of formal cut,
> Full of wise saws, and modern instances;
> And so he plays his part: The sixth age shifts
> Into the lean and slipper'd pantaloon;
> With spectacles on nose, and pouch on side;
> His youthful hose, well sav'd, a world too wide,
> For his shrunk shank; and his big manly voice,
> Turning again toward childish treble, pipes
> And whistles in his sound: Last scene of all,
> That ends this strange eventful history,
> Is second childishness, and mere oblivion;
> Sans teeth, sans eyes, sans taste, sans everything.

This sounds a trifle bleak and threatening, but it is a reasonably accurate description.

To many people the fact that there is change and the fact that there is death is enough evidence that the powers in the later period are not equal to those during youth. In a society such as ours in which the attributes of youthfulness are highly esteemed, anything that is different from the quality of the young is inferred to be inferior. It *may* be of less value, but it is also possible that it may be of a *different* value.

Not all societies in the past, and not all cultures today, place the same premium on youthfulness as we do. For example, the largest number of our teachers are comparatively young, and we tend to think that this is an appropriate arrangement, perhaps even an inevitable one. But in some societies only those of the richest experience and ripest judgment are ever allowed to have any part in the teaching of the young.

We have no intention here to discuss the comparative advantages or disadvantages of the different stages in life. It is important, however, that as we study changes we try to do so with as little bias as possible. We should see these as changes that may have desirable *or* undesirable effects, depending in considerable measure upon the person himself; not as inexorable loss and decay. Browning was as accurate a student of the changes in human life as any psychologist and his findings are expressed in the lines:

> Grow old along with me
> The best is yet to be.

Accordingly, we are going to try to look calmly at the effect of the changes that occur during human life. This is no attempt to glorify what are sometimes referred to as "the golden years" of middle and old age. Nor is it a dirge or requiem, simply a search for understanding. We shall try to see what happens to the learner and in what way, if any, the changes that occur within him affect the amount and quality of his learning.

The Process of Aging

Nothing is so certain as "death and taxes," or so they say, except aging. There are three kinds of aging—biological, psychological, and social. J. E. Birren has written:

In a general way it would appear that many biological or physical characteristics show earliest maturation and decline, that psychological capacities mature and decline later and that social processes are slowest to reach full development and plateau and show least late-life decline.[1]

Biological aging has to do with an individual's present position in relation to his potential life span. Accordingly, while it may closely parallel chronological age, it is not identical with it. There are many factors that affect the length of life, and it used to be said that inheritance was the chief one. There are aphorisms in every language which claim that if one wants to live long he should choose well his mother and father. And yet there is mounting evidence to indicate that, respecting longevity, environmental factors may equal or surpass in importance the inborn potential.

In North America, with the present rates of life expectancy, about three-quarters of life is lived as an adult, and one-quarter in development toward adulthood. Females not only mature about two years earlier on an average; they also outlive the males.

In aging there are changes in structure, composition, and functioning of the basic bodily cells, and in every kind of physiological and sensory performance. While considerable amounts of information have been accumulating in recent years, it is still true that knowledge about aging and about the middle and later years is incomplete.

There is no longer much mystery about the way that a baby grows, changes, and develops, before birth and through childhood and adolescence. Millions of children have been carefully observed directly and by camera, studied, measured, tested. They have been under the scrutiny of thousands of patient, trained observers, in every country in the world.

The main fact about this stage in life is that almost from the moment of birth there is a rapid upsurge in every capacity and this continues throughout childhood, though at differing rates. At puberty, for example, there is an acceleration of bodily growth and around the ages of eighteen and twenty there is a general leveling off in most capacities.

When we come to study the development beyond the twentieth year, what a contrast! Here, there is no mountain of books, films, studies, reports. Since World War II there has been more attention paid to the last years of life, and gerontological studies are now considerable in number, though but a tiny fraction of those associated with the child. But, as noted earlier, the middle years still constitute a desert.

Middle age is unknown territory to the social scientist. Although he is thoroughly familiar with the length and breadth and depth of childhood and adolescence, and he has made intensive explorations into the domain of old age, his knowledge of middle age is limited to a small amount of highly specialized knowledge gained from marriage counselors, psychiatrists, and social workers, about small and nonrepresentative groups of middle-aged people.[2]

What we do have is not very well organized nor is it readily available. It consists of charts about average height and weight, and insurance tables. These are useful guides if we want to predict what may happen to a few thousand people in a much larger population, but not very helpful in counseling a single individual. There is much additional data in some medical journals and reports of medical research, and more is beginning to be generally accessible. One of the increasingly difficult problems for the teacher of adults is to keep up with, and arrange in some pattern, what is coming to him from many different sources.

THE BODY

The activities that we call learning take place in a total organism. It is a common view that the mental and emotional attributes of a human being are highly complicated and unstable but that at least one can count on some stability in regard to the body. However, as Walter B. Cannon once pointed out, any constancy in the body itself is a kind of miracle:

> Our bodies are made of extraordinarily unstable material. Pulses of energy, so minute that very delicate methods are required to measure them, course along our nerves. On reaching muscles they find there a substance so delicately sensitive to slight disturbances, that, like an explosive touched by a fuse, it may discharge in a powerful movement. . . .
>
> The instability of bodily structure is shown also by its quick change when conditions are altered. For example, we are all aware of the sudden stoppage of action in parts of the brain, accompanied by fainting and loss of consciousness, that occurs when there is a momentary check in the blood flow through the vessels. We know that if the blood supply to the brain wholly ceases for so short a time as seven or eight minutes certain cells which are necessary for intelligent action are so seriously damaged that they do not recover.
>
> When we consider the extreme instability of our bodily structure, its readiness for disturbance by the slightest application of external forces and the rapid onset of its decomposition as soon as favoring circumstances are withdrawn, its persistence through many decades seems almost miraculous. The wonder increases when we realize that the system is open, engaging in free exchange with the outer world, and that the structure itself is not permanent but is being continuously broken down by the wear and tear of action, and as continuously built up again by processes of repair.
>
> Here, then, is a striking phenomenon. Organisms composed of material which is characterized by the utmost inconstancy and unsteadiness, have somehow learned the methods of maintaining constancy and keeping steady.[3]

Some of the most important research affecting learning has been about bodily functioning and the influence of diet on ability to learn. The results are of direct practical application in many developing countries where decisions must be made about major food supplies. It is now generally known that absence of protein in the diet seriously affects human growth in the young and human functioning at all ages. Experimentation is continuing. This is one area of research, important for adult education, that is often disregarded. Nor should it be considered that the problem of diet is one only for developing countries or undernourished children. Many emotional disorders, indeed many learning difficulties can be traced, not just to an absence of protein or vitamins, but to a diet which is not suited to the rate of metabolism of an individual. Differences in the rate of oxidation of food are substantial, and a diet adequate for one will result in dullness or distractedness or impaired efficiency in another. Indeed, when a learning difficulty exists, and there seems to be no rational basis, a check on diet and metabolism should always be made.

As one might assume, the health and efficiency of the body affect profoundly the quality of learning. What about physique? The studies of L. M. Terman [4] have demonstrated quite conclusively that the gifted and superior children tend to be somewhat larger and heavier than those who are dull. However, correlations between physique and intellect are so low, and there are so many exceptions, that no inference is permissible in regard to a single individual child. Is this equally true of adults? Studies are inconclusive, but all of them point in the same direction. There is some evidence to show that people in positions of authority tend to be somewhat larger and heavier than the average. In one study it was found that bishops were two inches taller and almost twenty pounds heavier than rural ministers in the same denomination, and that university presidents and school superintendents tended to be greater in physique than men on their staffs. Still, too much ought not to be made between the correlation of positions of prestige and the physical superiority of the incumbent; the exceptions are so numerous. Yet, on the other hand, there is very little support for a commonly accepted stereotype, that a man of intellect invariably has a weak flabby body. Brains and brawn are as often, more often, found together than separately.

It has also been found that in elections, or in appointments where the characteristics and qualities of the various candidates are not fully known to those making a decision, factors such as height, appearance, carriage, vigor, are given much more significance than if all factors are established.[5]

One of the ways that physical capacity is expressed is physical fitness—or more properly, psychomotor fitness. There are really two ways of assessing fitness: the capacity to engage in a particular activity and the ease and quickness of recovery of equilibrium after the strain of that activity. Physical or psychomotor fitness is very much a function of age. For example, in one review of rejects from the American armed forces, it was found that the rate of rejects among men aged eighteen to twenty-four was 29.3 and of men thirty-eight to forty-four the rate was 64.7. These are startling discrepancies. However, one must remember that there are considerable differences typically in the use of physical energy by individuals at twenty and individuals at forty. Women who expend energy running a home and caring for children do not show such striking deficits at least until much later years.

We shall see later that such environmental factors as family, social position, economic and social status have an equal or greater influence on learning than does physique.

Early Studies of Growth

We have already noted that artists and writers often choose as their field of interest the kinds of changes that occur in human beings, particularly in such critical stages as puberty, at the time of choosing a mate or establishing a home, and when growing old. One might almost claim that the novel in literature was created as a special form for dealing with the changes and continuity of living, rather than just with moments of high dramatic tension which are likely to be the theme of poetry and drama. Conscientious artists like Leonardo da Vinci left many records of growth changes; diarists such as Pepys and Boswell also left faithful written accounts of growth and change. Still, most of this information was piecemeal and had little order or system. Atoms of experience were preserved, but these had insufficient meaning in isolation and there was little permanent gain in understanding.

One of the most notable accretions of knowledge about growth came through the work of a gifted and inquisitive amateur scientist, Sir Francis Galton, whose curiosity and interests ranged over many fields. Galton was not a man to speculate while lolling in an armchair; he developed a knack for testing out his hypotheses in many ingenious ways. He had no captive audience in a school or institution, and so he devised a human "laboratory" at a great national fair, a health exhibition held at South Kensington, England, in 1884. Galton set up his observations and experiments in a tent booth at the fair. He had collected various gadgets and measuring devices which would measure aspects of physical performance. Where no gauges existed he invented them. He must have been very persuasive, for, despite competition from all the other booths, more than 7,000 individuals offered themselves or were enticed to submit to measurement of seventeen different characteristics such as height, sitting height, weight, vital capacity, visual acuity, auditory capacity, strength of pull, strength of hand grip, span of arms, and swiftness of blow.

Galton wrote extensively and published the results of his measurements. Stimulated by his results and his speculation, other men began to observe similar phenomena. The most impressive use of such information was achieved by insurance companies who soon had quite reliable tables to guide them in the prediction of length of life and thus a more accurate estimate of the premiums to be paid for insurance protection.

On the average the female reaches physiological maturity around the twelfth or thirteenth year, the male about two years later. She reaches maximum height at about sixteen years; he, at about eighteen years. Of course, individual differences are enormous, and there are cases of some individuals of twenty-one who are not physiologically "of age." The female may lack the full strength of the male, but her strength per body weight may be greater, and her general health is often superior.

From maturity on, it is *normal* for the human organism to undergo the following kinds of changes, most of which occur *gradually*:

- Cell tissues become dryer, they do not grow so rapidly and the repair of cell tissues proceeds more slowly.
- Bodily cells become somewhat less elastic.
- The rate of basal metabolism is lowered.
- There is some decrease in strength.
- There is a decrease in the speed, intensity, and endurance of neuro-muscular reactions.
- Vision and hearing become impaired.

Other factors that may affect both learning and job performance are:

- While the heart increases not decreases in size and weight, in persons past sixty its capacity to increase in rate and strength of beats during intense physical work is usually diminished.
- Injuries to the skin may require five times as long to heal; all injuries take longer to heal, and convalescence after an injury or operation is prolonged.
- The old saying that a person is "as old as his arteries" can be accepted as partially true; there is some decreased elasticity and increased calcification of arteries.
- Bones become fragile and less elastic and therefore more exposed to fracture.
- The strength of the biceps declines, on an average, and in the sixth decade is about half of what it was in the third.
- There appear to be lessened reserves for stresses and reduced tolerances for heat, cold, overeating, dehydration, and salt depletion.

Yet, while these deficits are real, and age-linked, the differences that are found between people suggest that environmental factors as well as training and individual response and adjustment to decline may be more important than chronological age.

STRENGTH

There are many measures of strength—the weight a subject can pull, press, lift, or jerk, the grip of the hand measured in pounds, the thrust of the legs. Galton's data, supplemented by more recent observation, shows that the maximum performance in these motor abilities comes relatively late, close to the thirtieth year, and the decline thereafter is gradual. But we must remember that these are averages. In one study two men over sixty-five registered scores for strength that exceeded any of those in their twenties.

JOB PERFORMANCE

A few studies exist concerning the capacity of people to do "hard" physical work. Considerable research has gone on at the Fatigue Laboratory at Harvard. The curves of decline vary somewhat, but the loss until age seventy is gradual. At seventy or seventy-five, however, capacity for such work may be half of what it was at thirty-five or forty.

What is equally clear is that several nonphysical factors influence output markedly, particularly the amount of skill and experience a man has for a given task, and his motivation. For many tasks that are rated as "light" physical work, his output may not show any decline.

In one investigation in England where the task was sorting blocks, the men over sixty-five took much longer *on their first attempt* than those under twenty-five. But as the work continued the oldest group increased their output. At the conclusion of the study their production was only slightly lower than the youngest group and the men of forty-six to sixty-four had the best score of all. One man well over seventy was the third quickest in the entire group. It is obvious in this test that dexterity is a more important consideration than strength or endurance. And most studies indicate that losses in dexterity are negligible up to seventy and over, and that these losses can be retarded by training and practice.

It is still possible to find evidence of discrimination in employment related to age. But it is now better understood and accepted that, unless there have been cumulative injuries or a history of bad health, worker performance in most job skills, up at least till age sixty, is little influenced by physiological changes in aging. Dramatic changes are found, but they can usually be traced to injury or disease or excessive use of alcohol with accompanying neurological damage. Accidents, particularly at home, but also at work, show some increase with age; accidents are the sixth largest cause of deaths over the age of sixty.

As people grow older they slow down. This bald statement is somewhat ambiguous and it may seem trite and obvious. From our own observations we know that it is true. Yet the failure to recognize its importance has led to many misunderstandings and misinterpretations about people as they grow older.

Slowing up seems to take many forms. One is in regard to the speed of the flow of blood in the veins and arteries; others have to do with the passage of "messages" through the nervous system, the reaction of both voluntary and involuntary movements, and the time necessary for damage in the body to be repaired. The older person may also be more concerned about the correctness of his response and therefore not as quick to respond in an unfamiliar situation or when exposed to ambiguous stimuli. For all these reasons he apprehends and perceives more slowly, he acts more slowly, he thinks more slowly. His *learning rate* may have decreased, but not necessarily the number of correct responses and therefore his *learning efficiency*. There is another interesting difference between older and younger people, other than the slowdown that comes with age. With a young man, the speed of response or performance varies with the task and his familiarity or practice. With an older person, who has well-developed personality traits, relative quickness or slowness is a characteristic pattern of his response to stimuli and will be consistent in all his activities.

Ours is an age and a culture which is very "time conscious." When it is said of us that we are always "in a hurry" we take this as a compliment, whether it was meant so, or not.

The medieval man, or many a man in Asia today, would not be so prone to equate speed with quality of performance; they would be much less likely to measure "efficiency" in units of time.

Psychologists have also contributed to this practice. In their studies of children they found that for many tasks, the child who performed correctly, also performed quickly. In their publications and through the results of timed mental tests that some of them devised, the notion was circulated that there is a close, direct relationship between speed of response and correctness of response.

This is true, within limits, when applied to children. It is *not* true about adults, particularly the older adult.

Accordingly, in every activity in which people participate, attention needs to be directed to the factor of speed and its importance.

For example, studies of automobile driving have shown that a driver of age sixty travels many yards farther before taking action after receiving a warning signal than a driver of twenty. The increased time necessary for stimulus to reach his brain center and for him to respond by applying the brakes can mean an appreciable distance in a car traveling at a high speed. Galton published some observations about reaction time by calculating the swiftness of a blow, and expressing it in a series of comparisons, using age twenty-five as one hundred—as in the following table:

age 15= 84	age 35=99
age 20= 98	age 40=98
age 25=100	age 45=96
age 30=100	

We shall discuss more fully the factor of speed in estimating mental ability in Chapter 4, but it is equally important in learning new skills involving dexterity, or sight and hearing.

Sensory Acuity, Sensation and Sensory Processes

With aging there are sensory impairments which result from deterioration in the sensory apparatus itself, or in the central nervous system, and both of these may be affected by disease. One can speak of a simple form of sensing as awareness—awareness of noise, light, dark, touch, taste, odor, vibration—or a more complex pattern which is usually termed perception. For each kind of awareness, there is a threshold, the minimum stimulus to evoke a response, and on the whole these thresholds increase with age. Put another way, age produces increased interference with the stimuli. In the case of vision, this results in what is called the "dark glasses effect," a situation in which there is a lessening impact of the stimulus.

CHANGES IN VISION

Traders in horses will invariably examine the animals' teeth with the utmost care to determine age and health. Probably the best index of the soundness of the human animal is the health and capacity of the eye. There are more substantial changes associated with aging of the eye than in almost any other characteristic. Walter R. Miles [6] has stated that visual function is a clear measure of physiological age, and others have used visual acuity as a basic index for bodily aging. Growth in function is very rapid in early childhood; there is a slow but continuous gain between the thirteenth and eighteenth year. This is followed by a gradual decline until the fortieth year. After forty there is a sharp decline till age fifty-five and continuous decline at a decreased rate beyond fifty-five.

This decline of function is not only general but there also seems to be a steady decline in efficiency in specific visual functions. There is increasing density of the eye tissues, loss of water, accumulation of amounts of inert material in the eye tissue, as well as loss of fat and elasticity. With advancing years the pupils become smaller and react feebly, the cornea tends to lose in luster and transparency, the eyelids become thin and less elastic. In terms of function, older eyes suffer a greater proportionate loss of visual acuity when the illumination is dim. There is also a narrowing of the field of vision, and a slow-down of the adaptation to dark. There is an increasing incidence of cataracts and of defective color vision, the latter reaching as high as forty per cent of men over seventy.

However, as noted in the table, the greatest amount of decline occurs in the years forty to fifty-five. Studies have shown that over the age of thirty-five there is a marked preference for more illumination for reading than in earlier years. Beyond the age of twenty every person shows some decline in visual acuity; beyond age forty the decrease is considerable. That visual regression is a characteristic of normal healthy people is illustrated by one study of industrial workers:

Age group	Per cent with normal vision
below 20	77
20-24	68
25-29	61
30-34	60
35-39	55
40-44	50
45-49	35
50-54	25
55-59	18
60 and over	6

The measure of vision is usually stated as what can be perceived at a range of twenty feet. The familiar term 20/20 vision means that a person is able to perceive and identify letters as small as the average normal person can perceive at twenty feet. Vision in young children does not reach this standard. As visual loss increases in the later years, many individuals develop useful ways of accommodating, relying more on auditory cues, making upward adjustments of levels of illumination, and changing some of their habits, such as driving less at night. Unfortunately, people who are unprepared for what is a "normal" decline may become very perturbed. However, as in most circumstances in life, when people know what may be expected, their adjustment may be accomplished with dignity and without damaging misapprehension.

We shall summarize, at the end of this chapter, some of the practical common-sense procedures which to a considerable extent can minimize the effect of losses in sight and hearing, as far as learning is concerned.

CHANGES IN HEARING

In no capacity except sight are there greater changes at different stages in life than in hearing acuity.

In most people the peak of performance seems to be reached before the fifteenth birthday, and there is gradual but consistent decline until about sixty-five.

Auditory disability sufficient to create difficulties in understanding an interview or a telephone conversation increases from about five per cent in children under fifteen, to about sixty-five per cent in adults of sixty-five or over. Older people tend to slow up in their reaction to sounds. That is, not only do we decline in our ability to hear sounds but we are slower to hear— to translate the meaning of the sound, and to act in response to it.

In the years after twenty the nerve cells in the ear gradually seem to atrophy and there is a gradual loss of acuity for all tones, particularly high tones.

In older people there is considerable loss at the highest frequencies, beyond 10,000 cycles per second, and also of very low frequencies of 125 cycles per second or less.

It seems clear from the evidence that women lose acuity for lower pitch and men lose acuity for high pitch. An interesting consequence of this fact is that older women can, in general, communicate more readily with women and older men with men. Some attention has been given to this factor as a case of disharmony among older married couples, but no conclusive results have been found. People over sixty-five have somewhat less sensitivity to the richness of complex tones in high fidelity recordings.

In terms of the effect upon one's behavior, the psychological implications may be more significant than the physical. Hearing loss can have a marked influence upon an individual's confidence or insecurity. It may increase his feeling that he cannot learn new things. He may be more reluctant to venture into a new situation because of the apprehension that he might not be able to cope with it, particularly if the activity occurs in a setting of crowding and confusion.

Hearing loss may have other effects. A man who doesn't hear well may feel left out, isolated, cut off from his associates. He may even come to believe that people are whispering about him. Some who have suffered losses in hearing have developed symptoms of a kind of paranoia. Others display the reactions of people who are isolated, they withdraw into themselves, or retreat. The querulousness which, in literature, has often been associated with old age, so far as this charge is true, may be caused in part by a decline in hearing.

There is another loss associated with hearing, or rather with the receptor situated close to the cochlea in the ear. This is the vestibular apparatus that governs balance. Unlike some others, this sensation seems to be at its maximum effectiveness in the middle years between forty and fifty. But it is subject to decline which, in older persons, results not only in physical injuries but in considerable loss of confidence in their ability to cope well with new situations and activities.

OTHER SENSATIONS

There are some changes in older people in sensing sour, sweet, and bitter tastes, but they seem to be slight and more affected by such habits as smoking and drinking than by chronological age. Such changes may affect one's attitude to accepting new experiences of food and drink. Sensitivity to pain is also affected, but the chief changes in this "warning system" seem to occur after seventy. Discrimination in touch and vibration shows some gradual decline. However, for most people it seems that age seventy-five is typically the age when sensory processes per se may become a limiting factor in the behavior of the individual. We will note in Chapter 4 that the age of seventy-five is also regarded as an approximate borderline for intellectual capacities. In the years before, disease, training, habits, and other unique circumstances are more relevant than intrinsic age-related change.

ACHIEVEMENT IN WORK

We have already summarized the results of some studies of the success of older workers compared with younger. If strength is an important factor, or speed is at a premium, the older worker is at a disadvantage. But if these are relatively unimportant, he can expect to perform well. If there is emphasis upon such significant though hard–to–measure attributes as judgment, steadiness, reliability, the older worker usually outstrips younger workers.

There are few if any jobs the learning of which will not be possible if his attention is gained and if he is given sufficient time. During World War II many older men and women were trained or retrained for a wide range of jobs.

ACHIEVEMENT IN SPORTS

In a later chapter we shall consider in a general way the development of special abilities of all kinds. Here we shall note briefly physical performance in sports.

Many of the world's records in swimming have been held by young people before their eighteenth birthday, and teen–age world's champions have been known in women's tennis and figure skating. Activities which require energy in bursts place a premium upon youthfulness. Sprinting champions, both in running and swimming, are usually youthful; achievement in middle distances and long distances is common by those who are older. Most boxers are finished by thirty or thirty-five, but professional wrestlers may continue to perform night after night well into their forties or even fifties. The most consistently able performances by baseball players in the big leagues are given by athletes in their thirties but in all probability a baseball player attained his best batting average for a single year before he reached thirty.

Golfers rarely reach their peak in tournament skill until after thirty, one four–time winner of the American national championship, Walter J. Travis, did not take up the game until he was thirty-seven. Billiard championships are usually won by those in their late twenties, but many fine billiard players have continued to excel at ages forty, fifty, or even sixty. Winners in curling are found in all ages; "skips" are usually men in their later thirties or older.

In such activities as checkers or chess there are far more cases of success by the elderly than by youthful prodigies. One hears of only a few examples of older people mastering musical instruments, but this seems best explained by the small number of those who try. Here, as elsewhere, the belief that one cannot succeed results in refusal to try.

Sports championships are won by people who range in ages from fifteen up to forty or forty-five, but most championships are won at the ages of twenty-five to thirty-five. However, if experience and dexterity are the main requirements, the employment of all physical resources rather than the quick release of nervous or physical energy, excellence may be maintained throughout most of life. Games and other physical activities can also be learned relatively late, but we shall see later how success in learning a new game or physical skill may depend on the degree of interest in that skill.

Common-Sense Practices for Minimizing Losses Associated with Age

In Chapter 11 we shall deal with many implications of the findings for the teacher or leader. Here we wish to list only a few "rules of thumb" which, if followed, can help to eliminate most of the effects of physical and sensory losses, particularly with respect to sight and hearing. We do not mean to suggest that learning can happen as a result of a few simple changes in the environment; it is much more a matter of motivation than that. But such shifts can offset what some have regarded as serious deficits.

We need to modify conditions to overcome the limiting factors. This may be accomplished in a number of ways:

- By increasing the level of stimulation (such as illumination)
- By giving the subject time to anticipate or preview the new conditions as stimuli
- By allowing the subject to choose his own pace
- By giving immediate knowledge of results
- By eliminating or reducing environmental factors that produce discomfort, fatigue, and stress
- By reinforcing his successful behaviors
- By encouraging the individual to become increasingly self-managing

PRACTICES FOR OVERCOMING SIGHT LIMITATIONS

Illumination. One generalization may seem obvious enough, the need for adequate illumination. It is still common to meet the attitude that although good illumination must be provided for children, any old corner, no matter how dim, is good enough for adults. This is to put things backwards. Older people need better illumination than younger. Where premises are used for both children and adults, the best rule is to provide sufficient illumination to suit any adult member and the children will be well served. Not only should the illumination be sufficient (if in doubt consult any lighting engineer) but it should be constant, without flicker. Do not have your audience face direct light.

Glare. Have you ever noticed in how many conferences or meetings some members of the group are compelled to face glare, either direct or reflected? Usually a simple change in seating will reduce or eliminate this. Glare will cut down the total efficiency of your group; it is usually unnecessary and is an insult to your audience.

Blackboards. Have you ever made a census of blackboards used for adults? You may be astounded to note how many of them are shiny (glaring) or, even more common, are "tattletale" gray in color. Dirty chalk or dingy boards give you a result like automobile plates in one state during a particular year when the colors were described as "blur on blur." Chalk boards, or large paper pads which allow maximum contrasts should *always* be used; white on black, yellow on black, white on green make useful combinations.

Other Factors. Arrange seating so that people are close to speaker or demonstration. Use sharp color contrasts. Enlarge—if you use mimeographed material, choose pica type (at least) and double-space. Simplify—use simple words or phrases on chalk boards. Where possible avoid use of abbreviations. If possible remove everything from the board or chart except the relevant items.

PRACTICES FOR OVERCOMING HEARING LOSSES

Much can also be done in classes or conferences, to offset hearing losses:

Organization and Atmosphere. People with hearing loss will respond better and feel less isolated or threatened in small groups than in mass groups. In a face–to–face, informal group some hearing loss may not seriously matter. The conditions which are usually prescribed for effective small group discussion have even greater relevance for older people.

The Teacher or Leader.
- The teacher or leader should stand still in a position to be observed by all, so that the listener can adjust to the source of sound and also watch face and gesture which may provide him with visual cues to meaning.
- He should speak slowly, clearly, distinctly, loudly.
- He should talk directly to the group, using conversational manners and avoiding a monotone.
- He should use simple, clear, and meaningful words or phrases.
- He should use blackboard, wall paper, flannelgraph or other means to provide supplementary visual cues whenever new, unusual, unfamiliar words or numbers, titles, or ideas are introduced.

Additional Checks for the Teacher or Leader.
- Note and try to eliminate outside noises that may distract or interfere with the hearing of the group.
- Watch the faces of the group members to see if they are hearing.
- Ask someone in the back of the room to call attention when any members cannot hear.
- Questions directed to the teacher or leader by members of the group should be repeated for the benefit of the others.

It may take a minute or two for people to get used to the acoustics in a room or hall. Producers of training films do not put their important message in the first three minutes of the film; they allow time for people to "warm up" as it were and become accustomed to the acoustics. This is equally important in a class or meeting in which older people are present.

REFERENCES

1. J. E. Birren, *The Psychology of Aging* (Englewood Cliffs, N.J.: Prentice-Hall, 1964).
2. Robert J. Havighurst, *Social Roles of the Middle-Aged Person* (Chicago: Center for the Study of Liberal Education for Adults, 1953).
3. Walter B. Cannon, *The Wisdom of the Body* (New York: W. W. Norton & Company, Inc., 1932).
4. L. M. Terman and M. H. Odin, *The Gifted Child Grows Up* (Stanford, Calif.: Stanford University Press, 1947).
5. Alvin W. Gouldner, ed., *Studies in Leadership* (New York: Harper & Brothers, 1950).
6. W. R. Miles, "Psychological Aspects of Ageing," *Problems of Ageing*, A. I. Lansing, ed. (Baltimore: Williams & Wilkins Company, 1952).

SUGGESTED READING

Check, Donald B. *Human Growth.* Philadelphia: Lea & Febiger, 1968.

Donahue, W. *Education for Later Maturity.* New York: William Morrow & Company, Inc., 1956.

Hand, Samuel E. *A Review of Physiological and Psychological Changes in Aging and Their Implications for the Teachers of Adults.* Tallahassee: Florida State Department of Education, 1956.

Kuhlen, R. G. *Studies in Educational Psychology.* Waltham: Blaisdell Publishing Co., 1968.

Lansing, A. I., ed. *Problems of Ageing.* Baltimore: Williams & Wilkins Co., 1952.

Lidz, Theodore, *The Person, His Development Through the Life Span.* New York: Basic Books, 1968.

Pressey, Sidney L., and Kuhlen, R. G. *Psychological Development Through the Life Span.* New York: Harper and Brothers, 1957.

Welford, Alan T. *Aging and Human Skill.* Published for the Trustees of the Nuffield Foundation. London: Oxford University Press, 1958.

4

Intellectual Capacities

Most people are prepared to grant that a *few exceptional* men and women continue their intellectual pursuits until very late in life: Goethe, Robert Bridges finishing his greatest poem at age eighty-five, Tennyson's last volume coming out when he was eighty, Verdi composing sacred music when eighty-five, Wundt completing his memoirs at eighty-six. The performance of a Churchill or an Adenauer in mastering complex political and international problems is his latest years is also remembered.

But what of ordinary people? Is there a decline in intellectual capacity through life as there is in physical capacity? Many people think so. We have noted that this belief is firmly rooted in myth, fable, and proverb.

If capacities respecting psychomotor performance decline, why not capacities respecting cognitive performance? In asking this question, however, one should remember that the physical decline which does occur with aging does not begin seriously to affect performance until somewhere around the seventy-fifth birthday, although it used to be assumed that serious impairment came much earlier. It seems probable, as well, that with an elimination of disease and accident, the improvement in the standard of living, the strengthening of motivation—all factors that are not determined by biological aging—the serious effects of decline might be delayed even later.

Does one find evidence of comparable decline in intellectual capacities? This question has been a matter of controversy all through the century. Many serious students of the human condition believe so, and most used to do so. Some have been so convinced that even when their research data were negative and contradictory they fitted the data to conform with their pessimistic assumptions. Much of the evidence from earlier researches did seem to support the view that there was substantial loss. However, in many respects the growth, maturation, and decline of intellectual powers is markedly different from that of physical and sensory powers.

Increasingly through recent years, and by increasing numbers of psychologists and other students of the learning process, the second notion has been gaining ground. This is the view that age, in and of itself, does not significantly affect the ability of adults to learn. One needs to keep an open mind in regard to this matter, since able, conscientious scholars are divided in their interpretation of the data, but this latter position seems to be well supported by research and experience.

In this chapter we are concerned primarily with intellectual capacities, or intellectual potential and intelligence. One can make a distinction between intelligence and intellectual capacity and the ability to learn: in practice these concepts are often treated as if they were synonymous. We will review a number of related subjects: the nervous system as the underlying structure for most kinds of learning, intelligence and learning, cognitive learning, and particularly the attempts to measure learning through intellectual tests of various kinds.

The Nervous System and Intellectual Capacity

A psychologist is as dependent upon knowledge of the biological underpinnings of human behavior as he is upon scientific understanding of behavior itself. So is the educationist.

The nervous system is the co-ordinating center of the human being. It is composed of the brain, encased in a protective skull, the spinal cord, and a variety of peripheral nerves. The brain itself contains about twelve million individual cells, some specialized for *excitation* and some for *conduction*. Every cell normally maintains an electric charge between its interior surface and the bodily fluids just outside its cell membrane. The wave of electrical energy that is discharged by these cells is the basis for cell functioning, resulting in a pattern of nervous excitation that may be communicated from one part of the body to another. These impulses can be and are measured by very sensitive amplifying equipment, called the Electroencephalogram, or more commonly the EEG.

Traditionally the nervous system has been described as having a *sensory* portion concerned with detection and preliminary analysis of environmental stimuli, a *motor* portion which activates muscles and glands, and a broad group of *associative* cells that intervene between sense reception and motor functions. The system is a highly sensitive device for the detection and processing of environmental information and the initiation of appropriate action.

It is the complexity of this system, the incredible efficiency of the electrochemical apparatus, and the possibility of extraordinary numbers of associations or units or episodes of learning that mark man off from the other animals. The brain waves are affected by many kinds of stimuli: foods, level of blood sugar, drugs, feelings, and emotional associations. For example, on the EEG it is possible to note differences in the pulsation by having the subject think pleasure, or think pain.

Each part of the brain appears to have a highly specific function, not all of which are well understood. Efforts to locate the locus of various functions have been proceeding rapidly in recent years: this knowledge has implications both for repairing damaged brains and for the stimulus of normal learning pursuits.

Research on the nervous system goes on continuously, and much of it may be applicable to a better understanding of learning. Unfortunately, much of this research is carried out by specialists with whom educationists rarely interact; it is reported in language and in journals hardly accessible to educationists. And yet it will become increasingly important for those engaged in adult education to keep in touch with major findings and conclusions. Here we shall indicate only some of the experimental work that suggests important applications to adult learning.

We will review later the evidence about learning deficits with aging. But one fact seems fully established. The human brain enlarges throughout life; it does not atrophy. However, if not used, there seems to be loss both of neural connections and in the functioning of individual brain cells. This is why some physiologists have said that most senility may be unnecessary, caused, it is alleged, in almost 85 per cent of cases, by a lack of intellectual effort. Provided there is no tissue damage, if this decline can be interrupted by a change in motivation, the negative process can be reversed.

Extremely important results can be expected from the combined efforts of scientists (biologists, psychologists, pathologists, zoologists, neurologists, and technologists) who individually and in teams have been studying the nervous system. The most extravagant claims are being made, some of them by sober, careful scientists. It is alleged that a "breakthrough" in brain research is imminent, that developments in the past ten years—which overshadow those of the previous half-century—will in turn be dwarfed by those of the next decade or two. Scientists working in the field claim that brain research is about to catch up with space research, and that the greatest unsolved problems of the 1970's and the 1980's will not have to do with wars and economics but with how to utilize the new knowledge about the brain and the mind. In a televised interview given at the Medical Center of the University of Illinois, a leading neurologist, Dr. Fredric Gibbs, warned:

Man abuses knowledge. We may be lucky that our understanding of how the brain operates has been deferred as long as it has. . . . What we know about the machinery of the brain is peanuts compared with what we are going to know in the near future. . . . It is the kind of knowledge that involves ethics and morality and raises fundamental questions with far-reaching implications.

Many of the implications have to do with the learning of so-called normal people, as well as of those who have suffered some damage or deficiency.

The brain is not only the seat of the intellect but also the dwelling place of conscious and subconscious experience, of emotions, creativity, and thought. Specific locations of the cells affecting these behaviors are being found. So are the pleasure and pain centers. The use of mood-changing drugs and electrical stimulation of the brain (ESB) have brought about some understanding of the electrochemical changes that cause mental deviations. Dr. Wilder Penfield was the first to establish that electrical stimulation can resurrect subconscious memories of past events which the conscious mind has forgotten. These patients under local anesthesia do not lose contact with the present; they know they are in an operating room, but they seem to have two concurrent existences, one in their present situation, and one in that portion of the relived past. The phenomenon is called "double consciousness." It is also predicted that the so-called memory code will soon be broken, and thus an important part of learning will be better understood.

Research has already established that some behavior problems and psychoses have a physiological base and may be corrected or improved through biological procedures, some of them relatively simple, such as diet changes, to ensure an improved balance of proteins and vitamins, leading to improved metabolic processes.

Hypnosis and autohypnosis are already being utilized by some educationists as well as therapists. One application that sometimes employs hypnosis, but other techniques as well, is cognitive desensitization, used in situations where learners are tense and anxious about an examination, to relax them and free them to do their best.

Dr. Leroy G. Augenstein, in an interview at the Biophysics Center at Michigan State University, indicated another potentially valuable and potentially dangerous method for some kinds of learning.

Hypothetically it might be possible for someone to put information into the brain via the pressure cells while you are asleep. The information would go through the subconscious, so to speak; the facts would be stored away in the proper pigeon holes in the brain; they would be recalled at the suggestion of the person who put them there. This would be a fine and easy way to obtain an education but an unscrupulous person could wreak havoc.

He concluded: "Science and technology are far ahead of the general public's knowledge of the potentialities and problems involved." This state of ignorance may also be true of most adult educationists, and it is ignorance that should not continue. We will return to some of these subjects again in Chapter 7.

Intelligence and Learning

Interest in mental ability or intelligence has been continuous throughout the centuries; this era has been one in which attention became organized and systematic. Research has focused around a number of topics:

- The contribution of heredity and of environment to intelligence
- The distribution and extent of individual differences
- The relationship between physiology and the nervous system to the behavioral characteristics of intelligence
- Extremes: mental deficiency and genius
- The effect of social class and cultural environments on the development of mental abilities
- The relationship of education and training to mental abilities
- The growth and possible decline of mental ability

These factors are all interrelated, but it is primarily the latter two that will concern us most. However, questions of social class and individual difference are related intimately to the general question of loss or gain in intellectual quality through the life span. As we will see at many points, an environment rich in intellectual stimulus provides the setting in which intellectual capacities are maintained and perhaps extended; a deficient environment and the disuse of mental abilities results in impairment, decline, and in older people in the premature onset of senility.

Some definitions of intelligence have featured learning, others memory, others adjustment and accommodation, others conceptualization and abstraction. By the uncritical use of "intelligence tests," the gross example of circular thinking—"intelligence is what is measured by an intelligence test"—was fostered. This was amusing enough if not taken seriously, but it led to circumscribed views as well as definitions: intelligence was seen almost as a single quality. The growing realization that there are many capacities or abilities: mechanical, social, verbal, abstract, spatial-perceptual has also led to an appreciation that there are *intelligences*, not just *intelligence*. J. P. Guilford's [1] formulation of the varieties of mental abilities has attracted wide attention:

- *Intellectual abilities* classified according to operation (cognition, memory, production, and evaluation)
- *Intellect* classified in terms of content (figural, symbolic, or semantic)
- *Intelligence* classified according to product (classes, relations, systems, or implications)

Guilford writes: "Present IQ scales fall far short of covering the potential list of abilities, but it can be recognized that some of these abilities are indicated by certain components of these scales. The contribution of these abilities to measurement is all but lost in the composite scores usually in use." It is this analysis that caused Guilford to develop his "structure of intellect." If such an analysis is accepted, it becomes clear that an intelligent quotient or IQ is not unitary and could not be a measure of an innate or immutable inherited characteristic. It is a measure or numerical representation of performance on selected tasks, a measure that is related to the performance of other individuals on the same tasks. Regarded in this light, it can be anticipated that the scores of individuals will vary with different tests that are themselves measures of different tasks, and will also change over time. Studies of achievement on these tests over time bear out this expectation. What is noteworthy is that the earlier interpretations of data derived from adult performance on mental tests seemed to support the notion of constant decline after age twenty, but much evidence in recent years supports the contrary view that many of the abilities are maintained or enlarged at least up to the sixties and seventies.

Other tests used with adults as well as with children are "scholastic aptitude" and "achievement" tests. The implications of these tests for understanding intellectual capacities have not added much to what is known from analysis of intelligence test results, and our discussion will give much more attention to the latter forms of measurement.

In general, measures of intelligence have been used in education as estimates of expected achievement in academic pursuits. There are mental abilities that show little or no relationship to academic success, and most of these are abilities that are features of adult roles. The quality called *judgment* is an example. One of the research problems for adult education is to identify and develop forms of measurement that will predict the success of adults in all kinds of intellectual problems and roles, not simply academic performance. Moreover, if increasing numbers of adults are to undertake study appropriate to their needs and roles, and at any time of life, much more adequate diagnostic measures will be needed than now exist so that the adult learner can place himself appropriately respecting the skills and content he will study. It is also clear that if educational institutions are to be "relevant" they will need to offer educational experiences that do relate to most or all of the intellectual tasks and roles that people actually face, not just to a narrow range of tasks related to academic progress.

Implications From Results of "Intelligence Tests"

One cannot see or perceive learning taking place, although as has been noted it is possible to record electrical impulses on the EEG that seem to be generated during the activity of learning. One can also measure performance and make some inferences about learning. The most common kinds of performance measurement involve academic problems or the tasks selected for use in the so-called intelligence tests. Accordingly, much of the evidence that we will review has to do with performance on intelligence tests and the sometimes conflicting inferences that have been drawn.

There is much more consistency in the evidence than appeared to be the case even two decades ago. However, certain difficulties still remain.

Most of the difficulties arise from the nature of the tests, the subject matter of the tasks, the basis on which the test has been validated, the factor of time, and the adequacy of the motivation of the adults in performing these tasks. The tests measure performance at some selected moment. Performance of one individual is compared with a large sample of individuals and is usually expressed as an "intelligence quotient" or IQ. It was once assumed that a person's IQ would be constant, at least throughout childhood and youth. But this could be established only if the same individual were tested again and again, as he grew older, on identical or similar tests. Such a testing program of the same individual at different stages in his life is usually called "longitudinal."

There are very few "longitudinal" studies, although such a study is a most reliable way of noting actual changes in intellectual performance or capacity. Instead, most of the studies we have are what are called "cross-sectional" studies.

In the "cross-sectional" study, there is no measure of the change or growth in learning ability or intellectual capacity of a particular individual throughout his lifetime. What we have are the scores of one group of people, achieved at one point in their lifetime, compared with the scores of an entirely different group of people at a single point in their lifetime. For example, the scores of men and women of twenty-five are compared with the scores of different men and women of fifty. This comparison will be meaningful only if the compared groups are closely alike in *all* significant details. But in many important respects these groups may not be alike. For example, we can expect that the younger group will have had considerably more schooling since the average school-leaving age has arisen considerably since the fifty-year-olds left school.

Fortunately, however, some psychologists like L. M. Terman [2] began to observe or test the same individuals a second or third time during their life span. We shall note the significance of such "follow-up" studies and the increased knowledge concerning the persistence of the ability to learn that they brought.

Sometimes the scores and the "norms" of tests have been based upon the performance of a special group of adults, a "captive audience" as it were, men and women who are available to the experimenter in such places as prisons or hospitals. The experience of such people, to say the least, is atypical. However, more evidence has been accumulating from observations and tests of people who are *living ordinary lives* rather than as a patient or inmate.

In addition to the reservation that one may have about "intelligence" tests because of the sample of adults on which the results of these tests are based, there are some significant limitations in the tests themselves. This is in no way to suggest that such tests are valueless. Undoubtedly they have been of considerable importance in education, clinical work, and personnel management. However, they need to be used for adults with the most rigorous care because of a number of characteristics.

- Many of them are based on tasks associated with school rather than with real-life situations.
- Many of them rely on a motivation that is characteristic of youth, but not necessarily of adults.
- Many of them are based on the experience or performance of children and adolescents rather than upon the study of those who are adults.
- Many of them measure performance in units of time, which is an inevitable handicap for an older person.

With these reservations, we shall now review some of the evidence that has come from various studies that employed "intelligence tests." We begin with the period during and immediately following World War I because, while most conclusions reached in studies at that time do not stand up to scrutiny, they have materially affected or reinforced the attitudes of psychologists and educationists ever since.

THE CONRAD AND JONES STUDY

One study that received considerable attention in those years was that of Harold E. Jones and Herbert S. Conrad, reported under the significant title "The Growth and Decline of Intelligence." [3] We are mentioning it here not because we accept the assumptions on which it was based or the conclusions reached, but because the results have been quoted so frequently, what we believe is a misinterpretation of the data has been so widely believed, and because the study raises clearly some fundamental issues. The tests were administered with considerable ingenuity. In selected New England communities a free motion picture was offered. During the intermission members of the audience were invited to take some tests. Individuals who did not attend the movie were visited in their homes and also invited to take part.

In this way the *Army Alpha* tests of mental ability were administered to 1,191 selected subjects who ranged in age from ten to sixty. When the scores were plotted against chronological age the results seemed to show rapid intellectual growth to about sixteen years, some growth to about eighteen to twenty years, and a gradual but steady decline thereafter. At about fifty years, performance matched that of sixteen-year-olds. Performance on all the subtests was not uniform, and scores on "information" and "vocabulary" *did not reveal any decline*. However, deficits on such subtests as "numerical completions" were considerable. On the basis of these findings, the authors stated that tests of vocabulary and information were the *least* valid indications of intelligence and that speed was a factor of major consequence in the measure of intelligence. As we shall see, these two conclusions, or assumptions, are perhaps the two most important aspects of the whole problem. The authors acted on one other important assumption: namely, that all adults could be considered equivalent in all respects. This was despite the fact that, at the time of testing, the twenty-year-olds had had considerably more formal schooling than had the sixty-year-olds. The close relationship between success achieved by a person on an intelligence test and the amount of his schooling will be noted later.

We shall see below that the interpretation given by the authors no longer seems an adequate explanation and that with the same data one will probably arrive at a completely opposite conclusion.

THORNDIKE STUDIES

The studies of learning carried out by E. L. Thorndike and his associates were so substantial in result, were conducted over so many years, and were so ingenious and varied in design that they have been the subject not only of serious inquiry but also of fable and anecdote. How Thorndike progressed from the studies of fowl and animals to the human animal; how he arrived at Columbia with a taxi load of chickens ("the best-educated hens in the world, every one a graduate of Harvard"); how the chickens roosted on the Columbia University running track until a laboratory was built for them; how chickens, mice, snakes, football players and co-eds were all instructed in fascinating combinations in a series of experiments—these are now a rich part of the record and the folklore of psychology.

Thorndike's conclusions were based on the performance of people from fourteen to fifty years old in tasks of many kinds, such as learning to write with the nonpracticed hand, to translate a message into code, to acquire an artificial language, to judge weight, to memorize poetry, to perform disagreeable tasks, and many others.

One used to hear these experiments described as the "foundation stone" for adult education. With great care, and in considerable detail, Thorndike showed that the age of a person is *not* a very significant factor in regard to learning; that *all* men and women can learn.

Thorndike made three general observations about adult learning:

1. The most advantageous period for learning is between twenty and twenty-five years of age.
2. There is a decline in capacity for learning from this period to about forty-two years of approximately one per cent per year.
3. The influence of intellect upon the curve of ability to learn in relation to age is slight. The ablest man and the ordinary man show very nearly the same curve.

Another psychologist, W. R. Miles, summarizes these studies, and his own, when he says that "age has no veto power over learning, for any period in the natural life span." [4]

But while Thorndike's work had refuted those who believed that all the years after twenty were a slide downhill, the first effect of his work was to replace a ceiling of twenty years with a ceiling of forty-five years. But he had done more: he had helped stimulate colleagues to reject traditional views and formulas and study the problem itself. However, his own conclusions were influenced and limited by the very concepts and assumptions on which they were based.

- The results were based on *rate* or *speed* of performance. Efficiency was calculated according to the amount produced per unit of time, not on number of correct responses.
- Subjects of different ages were selected on the assumption that they were equal in all respects save chronological age.
- The tasks selected were laboratory or schoolroom tasks, not those of "real life."
- Thorndike's studies seemed to assume that learning is primarily a matter of practice regardless of the quality or character of the teaching.

A Shift in Opinion

Thorndike's own work was carried forward by a number of associates (notably Irving Lorge), and Lorge and others made substantial modifications, both in assumptions and in approach. Data are still incomplete, and differences of opinion still exist about how well adults learn, but since that time much of the research has steadily advanced the age at which excellent performance can be anticipated. If there is an upward limit of performance before the concomitants of aging exert a strong negative drag, it is more likely to be about age seventy-five than age forty-five, or that age in which most functions of the body begin to break down. Again, as in biological aging, the checking of accident, disease, higher standard of living, and enlargement of motivation may further extend such a ceiling.

One of those who have continued to represent learning capacity as a process of maturation and significant decline is David Wechsler,[5] who developed the Wechsler-Bellevue intelligence scales that have been used so extensively in most subsequent investigation. The Wechsler Adult Intelligence Scale (WAIS) is an individual intelligence test for adults; the Wechsler Intelligence Scale for Children (WISC) is an individual intelligence test for children. The adult scale contains several subtests. Some of them are timed and some untimed. The collection of test results in aggregate provides important information about human capacity and growth. In the earliest publications of the results, based on evidence collected in the 1930's, Wechsler interpreted the data as evidence that intelligence was at its maximum on or near the twentieth year, but from this point it declined steadily. However, upon a recheck of results of his own test in 1950, the Psychological Corporation (which distributes the test) revised information indicating that the *total score increases steadily from the teens to about age thirty-five years* and that subsequent decline is very much less than Wechsler had predicted. He himself revised conclusions, but contended that intellectual ability as a whole follows the same general pattern of decline as does physical ability, and that such individual abilities as vocabulary, memory, and so forth, which he claims enter into general intelligence, must also partake of this decline, although not necessarily at the same rate.

In the past two decades there have been scores of studies which have employed the WAIS, and the results are somewhat conflicting. Wechsler himself had reported that adults would *maintain* their ability on the subtests of vocabulary, information, and comprehension, while there would be a decline in scores on Object Assembly, Digit Symbol, and Block Design. There is the significant difference in the time factor between the first group and the second. In general, scores on performance tests do show a loss, but not on the verbal tests. The reasons for these somewhat confusing results are not fully established, or at least not finally accepted, but many more researchers now believe that the verbal, untimed scores are much more indicative of intelligence and of learning ability than the performance sub-tests.

Most test results over the years have followed the same trend; namely, they tend to show that intelligence or learning aptitude does not, or need not, decline in the years of adulthood. But this is a generalization. Test results for any individual are affected considerably by a number of variable factors which we shall now consider. These include previous schooling, speed, vocabulary, and attitude of adults to learning.

EFFECT OF SCHOOLING UPON ACHIEVEMENT IN INTELLIGENCE TESTS

As we have seen, it was once assumed that an "intelligence test" measured something that was constant and unchanging. It was supposed to be an index of "native" capacity regardless of experience or training, and it was assumed that a person would have the same IQ throughout life. The IQ, or Intelligence Quotient, was computed by taking the score that was made on an intelligence test and comparing it with the scores made by others of the same age. If this assumption were correct, the amount of schooling would make no difference to the IQ. However, no such claim would now be made. It is quite clear that there is a direct and intimate connection between education, experience, *and practice* in the development and maintenance of intellectual capacity. Second, most of the tasks employed in intelligence tests are based on school experience. The performance of any individual on such tests is demonstrably affected by the amount of schooling he has had.

A number of studies bear out this general contention. Lorge had the records of boys and girls tested in the eighth grade, and was able to test them again at age thirty-four. Those of equal mental ability as measured in the eighth grade, but who had continued longer in school, performed very much better at thirty-four than those who were equally "bright" but had enjoyed less schooling. He also found a high correlation between scores on the Army General Classification Test and "the highest grade completed." [6] John W. Tilton has published results showing that adolescents now do significantly better on intelligence tests than those of the same age in the 1930's, the difference being that on an average boys and girls now go to school longer.

Read D. Tuddenham showed that the poorest group of American soldiers in World War II did as well on the same tests as the average soldier in World War I. The middle score in 1943 would have ranked 88 per cent in 1918. Troops in World War II had an average of ten years of schooling, those in World War I had an average of about eight years. Tuddenham concludes: "The present population is superior in mental test performances to the population of a generation ago . . . a large proportion of this superiority is a consequence of more and better education for more people." Alas for him who claims that adults have a low mental age, basing his findings on test results in World War I. If he will check the data he will be confounded to discover that the "mental age of the average adult" jumped at least two years between the wars!

In appraising the results of any studies of the capacity of adults, one needs to have precise information about the amount of schooling of the individuals. It is significant to note that when this factor is taken into account, most of the data pointing to decline in the mental ability of adults ceases to have any point.

SPEED

We have already seen that as people grow older their reaction time, speed of perception, and speed of task performance all decline. In regard to performance a number of studies have shown that the decline is not solely for physiological reasons. It has been found, for example, that older people may be more concerned about accuracy than younger subjects and thus inclined to take more time for the task.

But whether for physiological or psychological reasons—*speed does decline.*

Most of the earlier tests of mental ability were based on the view that there is a very high correlation between speed and power. Thus if you tally the number of correct responses per minute or hour you will have an index of capacity. We have seen that there is general agreement that this is a valid assumption in regard to normal children. Many of those who, as in the Jones and Conrad study cited earlier, have measured the "intelligence" of adults likewise, seem to assume that for adults, as well, speed and power are also closely related.

Of course, if one assumes such a relationship one is forced automatically to accept the consequent view that the mental *power* or *capacity* of adults declines, since it is clearly established that slowing down occurs.

But suppose one lays aside such an assumption for a moment. Suppose one sets out to measure power or capacity separately from speed by giving subjects sufficient time needed to complete the tasks.

This is substantially what Lorge did in a series of experiments. He selected four tests—one *untimed* test of performance, and three *timed* tests of speed *and* power. The subjects were laborers of various ages. On the *timed* Otis Tests, subjects of twenty–twenty-five years scored on an average 44.4; subjects of twenty-seven-and-a-half to thirty-seven-and-a-half years scored 39.3; subjects of forty years and over scored 33.4. The scores for the same groups on the *timed* Army Alpha were 149.6, 142.3, 128.7. But on the *untimed* CAVD test *there was little or no change*.

One can see from these results that a test conducted with a time limit supports the conclusion that there is a steady decline with age. But when a test is employed where time is *not* a factor there is *no* significant decline associated with age. This kind of study has been repeated on many occasions with similar results. Lorge [6] concludes that there is a decline in the rate of learning as age progresses, *but that intellectual power in and of itself does not change from twenty to sixty*. Lorge attributes the decline in rate of learning to losses in visual acuity, auditory acuity, and reaction time. He also refers to such factors as increased fear of failure, desire to be "correct," retardation in the face of unfamiliar stimuli or setting, and as a generalization, an altered attitude of adults to learning. Note that all these factors were also encountered in Chapter 3 with respect to psychomotor learning. Lorge went on to point out that if a correction is made in the Jones and Conrad data of an amount of .780 a year (for loss of speed) their results are consistent for all age groups in their study.

We have already noted the different ways in which younger and older people may view "correctness." The matter is of some importance, worth an additional reference or two, even though this anticipates to some extent what will be discussed in Chapter 5.

A. T. Welford summarizes results from a large number of studies of job performance conducted in England:

> It appears that the older subjects' performance tends to be slower and more deliberate than that of the younger, but subsequently to be more accurate. . . . If we are interested in the total amount achieved regardless of any other consideration, then the younger subjects must be regarded as better, though not markedly so. However, the older subjects achieved their results with much less effort wasted on small errors, so that their performance can at least be said to have been more *efficient*. Finally if we are concerned with accuracy, as we should be if every error represented waste of valuable industrial material, we must regard the older subjects as, on the average, clearly superior. . . . Although speed may decrease among older people, this deficiency is often more than offset by gains in quality and accuracy. . . . Also, it seems, there is a substantial number of individuals who maintain performances comparable with those of people in their twenties or thirties.[7]

But this is performance, in the main, on industrial activities. What about those of a more "academic" kind? Robert Peers has reviewed a number of studies of tests of "reasoning," where older people seemed to perform less well than younger:

The statements from which the groups were required to make logical deductions were involved and questionable in themselves, so that the older subjects, with their greater range of experience and stronger convictions, were inclined to question and comment on the statements rather than make the logical deductions required by the instructions.

A quotation from one of the older subjects (aged 57) seems to make this clear: "I find this work more difficult because I am inclined to question several of the statements, instead of accepting them and drawing the conclusions, if any, which may justly be derived from them." It is difficult to see how, in the circumstances, the results can be regarded as demonstrating any less ability on the part of the older subjects to make logical deductions; it may merely indicate their unwillingness or even inability to do so from hypotheses which are not justified by their experience or which conflict with emotional and moral "sets." [8]

The factors which are usually expressed as the "rigidity" of older people will be discussed later. It is quite clear that measuring intellectual performance in time limits without taking such factors into consideration creates an added difficulty for the older person.

Some psychologists believe from the evidence so far that although with increasing years "slowing down" happens, the loss is considerably less significant in activities with which the individual is already familiar. There is also some evidence to suggest that loss of speed may be less for people of higher mental ability and for those who continue to employ fully their intellectual powers.

VOCABULARY

Many people seem to lack confidence about their speech and vocabulary. In part at least this may result from the widely advertised claims that some new book, or encyclopedia, or training scheme will increase vocabulary, give "word power" and bring about vocational and social success. One result of such clamor is confusion and insecurity. We may have a vague fear that we are lacking the rich, selective, comprehensive kind of vocabulary that everyone should have. In addition to these fears we are all conscious of how often we forget. We forget names of people, we can't think of the right word when we want it, we no longer remember the French or Spanish we learned at school. What we don't use regularly we tend to forget. For all these reasons, our feelings about our own capacity regarding vocabulary are often quite negative.

Consequently it comes as a surprise, almost as a shock, when we hear that *in capacity to use vocabulary*, adults do not show the decline that is characteristic of many kinds of capacity. If anything they tend to improve throughout life, right up to the later years.

We have already noted that in the Jones and Conrad study adults of any age continued to do well in vocabulary although other scores were down. This was explained by the assertion that vocabulary is *not* a reliable test of intelligence.

Studies by Lorge and others all show some improvement with age in scores on vocabulary. In one such test given to over 2,000 industrial workers in Scotland, the thirty-plus, forty-plus, fifty-plus, and sixty-plus all had better scores than the twenty-plus group. In another study of university professors, one of the eighty-year-olds made the highest score, and the older men had better scores than the younger on synonym-antonym tests and equaled the younger men on a test of word meanings. Now, if Jones and Conrad are right in asserting that a vocabulary test is not a useful index of intellectual capacity, the results above would be interesting, but not very important to our discussion. But if capacity in using vocabulary *is an important aspect* of mental ability, the persistence of this capacity throughout life is of the utmost importance.

On this particular point, there really isn't much difference of opinion. One might assume that the mastery and use of one's mother tongue would be as valuable an index of intelligence and ability to learn as it has proved to be a guide in the understanding of personality. And so most psychologists believe it. As a matter of fact, many of them regard the vocabulary test as the *most significant single test of intelligence*. If possible, psychologists will use a battery of subtests, rather than a single one, when they attempt to assess mental ability. But if one is compelled to choose one single test as a measure of intellectual capacity, the most satisfying is that of vocabulary. And it is on this supremely important kind of test that adults perform successfully throughout their life span.

Of course, as we might expect, performance is related to *practice*. In one study, for example, it was found that professional persons progressively increased vocabulary through ages sixty to seventy years, and that persons for whom language was not a major factor in daily living showed an opposite trend.[9]

ATTITUDE OF ADULTS TO LEARNING

Most of the comparisons that have been made of the performance of young people and adults on mental tests have not only assumed equal school preparation, but also equal or similar motivation. But the attitude of an adult to a test may differ markedly from that of an adolescent. It may be stronger or weaker. He may take the test seriously, with indifference, or even with hostility.

It can be predicted, however, that such tests do not always engage the fullest effort of an adult. Will a banker, or housewife or garage mechanic respond with much effort or enthusiasm when he is asked to learn Esperanto or the fact that K x G = Z? Contrast this with the attention that one sees being given to a complicated mathematical problem at a horse race, or stock market, or the capacity of a political agent or recent convert of a church to master extraordinary amounts of complex information.

Being able to see results has a positive effect upon performance. In tasks where men and women have been informed that they will be given the results of their work, they tend to achieve more, more quickly. As we have noted earlier, being aware of the purpose of a task is likely to increase efficiency. Where work seems to be without aim, output is less and fatigue seems to be greater. If the subject knows or suspects there is no possibility of accomplishing the task, there is a decline in the amount of effort.

The direction and intensity of the adult's motivation will markedly affect his success. Any resuts of adult performance on mental tests cannot be appraised without reference to the seriousness with which the adult undertook the tasks. We shall deal with this in greater detail in the next chapter.

Evidence From Follow-up Studies

We have noted that there are few *longitudinal* studies of mental ability where the performances of individuals on the same or similar tests were noted regularly over the entire life span. However, there have been a number of valuable "follow-up" studies in which individuals were retested at least once after a period of intervening years.

As mentioned earlier, Dr. Terman was able to test the same men and women at different ages. All the subjects showed gains in test scores. Using one of Terman's tests, psychologists N. Bayley and M. H. Oden obtained scores from a group of men and their wives, all about forty-one years of age, who had taken the same test twelve years before. Scores on the second test were consistently higher.[10]

It is relevant to our earlier discussion that, even with this select sample, the more schooling taken, the greater gain in test score.

Another investigator, W. A. Owens, has been able to test the same sizable group of 127 males on three separate occasions. His subjects had originally taken the Army Alpha test as freshmen at Iowa State College. In 1950, when his subjects averaged about fifty years of age, they were retested. Eleven years later, when his subjects were sixty-one, he administered the same test a third time. Thus, the intervals between the administration of these tests were thirty-two years and eleven years. At age fifty, the subjects showed a slight but positive gain over their performance as freshmen, and at sixty-one, they maintained the level they had attained at fifty, although with some decline in tests of numerical ability. It is relevant to our earlier discussion that, even with this select sample of university graduates, the more the formal education, the greater the gain in test scores.

Bayley's longitudinal studies are also of growing importance. Beginning in 1933, she has studied her original subjects over a span of four decades— 74 babies, now reduced to 54 adults. Some of her findings:

> Female mental abilities stabilize at an earlier age, while the male exhibits greater stability later. Early emotional experiences do make a difference in performance if the experiences occur at critical periods.

> Verbal scores are more stable than performance scores for both sexes; and are more efficient in the prediction of personality variables and mental ability. The data after 36 years were very little different than after 18 years.[10]

A second report of a major study involving larger numbers of people was published in 1971 by S. Granick and R. D. Patterson, which offers further evidence of persistence of many capacities.[11]

Most of the follow-up studies of Terman and others have had subjects of high intelligence. Would there be different results with average or below average adults? No conclusive answer can yet be given to this question. However, what evidence exists is again positive.

A few follow-up studies have dealt with people who had previously received low IQ ratings.

In one study the same battery of tests was given to a group of adults who had taken them eighteen years before. All showed gains, the average increase in IQ amounting to 15 points. Similar results were achieved in another study. Two groups of elderly males aged sixty-five to seventy were tested on the WAIS scale and retested over an average interval of eight years. Some decline was reported for all subjects; the *greatest* at the highest level of IQ. But this result is not confirmed in other studies of aging subjects. For example, the Fels Institute reports no decline over seventeen years in testing 72 women and 59 men of modest IQ with an Otis Mental Ability Test. In reviewing his own studies, as well as those by other investigators, Owens concludes:

> Thus far, it has been a rather generally accepted view that age is kinder to those gifted few. The present results, on the other hand, suggest that this is not the case, and that increments and decrements in test scores from age 20 to age 50 are roughly comparable at all levels of initial ability.

However, data sufficient to draw conclusions are still lacking for the years after age fifty.

Cognitive Learning and Thinking

This chapter is concerned with intellectual capacities and therefore with their utilization in cognitive learning and thinking. The field of cognitive learning has recently attracted the talents of the foremost psychologists, such as, Jean Piaget, J. S. Bruner, David Ausubel, and many others. We will be dealing with some of their views later, particularly in Chapter 7, and are concerned primarily in this chapter with the relationship of language and cognitive development, and with memory, forgetting, and problem solving, because surrounding each of these subjects there is evidence that bears on our concern with the emergence and development of intellectual abilities.

Are thought and speech inseparable? There are still conflicting views concerning this question which can be grouped around three positions. There are those like behaviorist John B. Watson who equate thought processes with motor habits in the larynx. There are a much larger number who take an intermediate position (for example, the Russian physiologist Ivan M. Sechenov) that language and thought are closely linked in childhood, but that as maturation proceeds during adulthood, thinking can and does become free of language. Thirdly, associates of Piaget maintain that cognition follows its own maturation patterns beginning in the youngest children before the development of language. This is an interesting problem, but of less moment for adult education than the relationship of language to memory acquisition, storage, and retrieval and how these latter processes may be altered through the life span. As we have discussed, the ability to use language well seems to improve, not diminish, up until the latest years, particularly if the ability is in continuous use. Learning that is associated and dependent upon a rich vocabulary, thinking that employs linguistic or symbolic constructs can mature and increase in quality throughout life. Another puzzling and significant question is the effect of different languages on cognitive processes. Does a Hindi-speaking man in India learn and think differently from an English- or French-speaking man? Are some languages more adapted to maintaining learning and thinking at a high level, and, if so, what are the reasons? Can effects desirable for maturation and maintenance of intellectual powers be transferred from one language to another? Answers to these questions are not clear, but the possibility lends interest and value to comparative studies in adult education.

Psycholinguistics, which brings together the theoretical tools of linguistics with the empirical tools of psychology in the study of mental processes in the acquisition and development of language, may become an important field for application to adult education.

The act of learning new material can be identified with the successful organization, acquisition, storage, and retrieval of information. Much of the content in manuals that offer advice to teachers is really about effective and systematic means by which such a communication system can be developed.

Memory is an electrochemical process: it may be evoked by conscious thought or subconscious recognition or even by stimuli closely associated with nonconscious centers such as a group of muscles. An athlete who has been injured may recall the act of injury when he receives a blow to the same muscles. There are both short-term and long-term memory systems. It seems probable that new learning goes first into the short-term system and may later enter the long-term memory system. This occurs as the result of a process in which one neuron excites another across the space between them which is known as the *synapse*. As the connection gets stronger less energy seems to be needed to repeat the crossing. (There is some evidence that unlearning—that is, blocking this crossing—requires considerable energy: this may be a partial explanation for the familiar difficulty of unlearning in the process of relearning.) Rote learning, stated most simply, is the effect of repetition until there is a well-established route across the synapse. Studies of memory by D. O. Hebb [12] and others emphasize the synapse as the locus for remembering and learning. Some physiologists and biologists emphasize not the location but the molecules involved as the basis for learning and memory—DNA (deoxyribonucleic acid), a giant molecule found in the chromosomes which is the primary hereditary material; RNA (ribonucleic acid), a molecule with somewhat similar structure to DNA, and certain protein molecules.

Both *recognition* (the selection of something that has been learned from among other possibilities) and *recall* (which is more difficult) are involved. Practice is usually required if there is to be memorizing. Small amounts of information may be memorized easily with alternating practice-rest-practice, but more complex information, let us say the lines of a play, needs to be organized in relation to knowledge already acquired and over a longer period of time. Many have experienced the phenomenon of remembering complex material better several hours or a day or two after receiving the stimulus than they did a few moments afterward: it seems that the brain is occupied in processing such material immediately after receiving it. This also has implications for communications research, particularly the phenomenon of "communications overload," when the brain receives more stimuli than it can process.

Some of the earliest treatises on education were concerned with remembering. The classical study of memory by Ebbinghaus was first reported in 1885. Studies have also been made about forgetting, studies based on either of two assumptions, or both. The first is that forgetting takes place over a passage of time because the memory trace that is formed in the brain when a fact is learned will decay and eventually disappear; the second that forgetting results because of interference of other material. Regardless of the reason, while many older people claim that they are no longer able to memorize, there does not seem to be actual impairment in learning complex material if it is meaningful, but some decline in the ability to learn isolated facts. The ability of older people to remember selectively, including details from very early years, is well established.

Human memory seems to operate in ways quite different from mechanical storage by computer. Adults, in particular, store material in ways related to their own experience; recall or retrieval is an act of re-creation and synthesis, not automatic recall. This is a partial explanation for the traditional unreliability of the testimony of witnesses to an accident or a crime. However, with training, adults can store and retrieve material with much greater fidelity.

For many, the test of intellectual capacities is in performance—in the rationality and precision of the mind as it solves problems. Thinking has at least two meanings—to think *about*, or problem solving, and to think *of*, or attend to some subject, "thinking of a person."

There are four distinguishable activities in the process of problem solving:

(1) *awareness* or knowing a problem exists
(2) *preparing* to find a solution
(3) *attempting* to produce a solution, and
(4) *evaluating* the adequacy of the attempted solution

These are steps found in any research project and in many forms of cognitive learning. They can be learned and made systematic, and adults who become capable of taking them seem able to maintain a high level of competency throughout the life span. Processes such as this do not seem to be eroded by age, as such, although the presence of apprehension, fear, or lack of confidence may have a strong negative impact.

Interest and Learning

One of the curiosities of human growth is that power in the use of verbal symbols persists throughout life, but there seems to be considerable decline in the use of mathematical symbols. When, for example, the scores of adults taking college courses are compared with those of younger undergraduates, the adults invariably tend to do better work in literature, philosophy, and history and less successful work in mathematics and physics. The problem itself is a complicated one. The less favorable scores could be substantially affected by lack of practice, lack of interest, or even the resigned acceptance of older people that they cannot do mathematics.

One of the reasons that adults continue to learn well, according to W. R. Miles, is that they concentrate their learning in the areas of experience in which their interests also lie. Thus their motivation is substantial and, as everyone knows, wanting to learn is the greatest aid to learning. During childhood, varied learning is common; in maturity, active learning is usually practiced in areas defined in terms of interest.

We shall examine these factors of interest and motivation in much greater detail in Chapter 5.

Some differences of opinion still exist in regard to the maintenance or decline of intellectual capacity, or learning aptitude, throughout life. But there has been a dramatic reversal in the trend of interpretation. Increasingly evidence is coming in to support the view that adults of all ages can learn effectively—"that age has no veto power over learning." In respect to tests of *vocabulary*, adults, if anything, show improvement, not decline. In giving the *same* tests taken earlier to adults a decade or so later (in follow-up and longitudinal studies) the individuals have usually registered a better performance when older. This seems to be true for individuals of slender as well as of excellent intellectual ability. The amount of schooling modifies considerably the performance in such tests. Indeed, a critical factor in many tests of ability seems to be the amount of practice of the particular task. When people "keep in training" in intellectual as well as physical tasks, their capacity is maintained.

Motivation of the adult undertaking the test is a major factor in performance. Also of importance is the development of well-defined goals for any program of studies, of clear statements about the difficulties or possibilities of succeeding in these objectives, of planning the enterprise in clear stages that can be attained, and involving the learner in some process of appraising his accomplishments.

Of all the human abilities, judgment and reasoning ability seem to reach a peak latest in life. These attributes are expressed both in intellectual and in social processes. There seems to be substantial evidence to support the view that the greater the individual's intellectual endowment, the less are deficits that come with aging. Such deficits, if and when they appear, are often or usually associated with disuse of powers. Exercise of the mind seems to retard deterioration. The older adult can continue to learn meaningful and difficult things, although there is a decline in ability to remember isolated facts.

REFERENCES

1. J. P. Guilford, *The Nature of Human Intelligence* (New York: McGraw-Hill, 1967).
2. L. M. Terman and M. H. Odin, *The Gifted Child Grows Up* (Stanford: Stanford University Press, 1947).
3. H. E. Jones and H. S. Conrad, "The Growth and Decline of Intelligence," *General Psychological Monographs,* XIII, 1933.
4. W. R. Miles, "Psychological Aspects of Ageing," *Problems of Ageing* (Baltimore: Williams & Wilkins Company, 1952).
5. David Wechsler, *The Measurement of Adult Intelligence* (Baltimore: Williams & Wilkins Company, rev. ed., 1955).
6. Irving Lorge, articles in *Review of Educational Research:* XI (December 1941); XIV (December 1944); XVII (December 1947); XX (June 1950).
7. A. T. Welford, *Skill and Age: An Experimental Approach* (London: Oxford University Press for the Nuffield Foundation, 1951).
8. Robert Peers, *Adult Education—A Comparative Study* (New York: Humanities Press Inc., 1958).
9. C. Fox, "Vocabulary Ability in Later Maturity," *Journal of Educational Psychology,* Vol. 38, 1947.
10. Nancy Bayley and M. H. Oden, "The Maintenance of Intellectual Ability in Gifted Adults," *Journal of Gerontology,* 1955.
11. S. Granick and R. D. Patterson, eds. *Human Aging II: An Eleven-Year Follow-Up Biomedical and Behavioral Study* (Washington, D. C., National Institute of Mental Health, 1971).
12. D. O. Hebb, *The Organization of Behavior* (New York: Wiley, 1949).

SUGGESTED READING

Ausubel, D. P. *The Psychology of Meaningful Verbal Learning.* New York: Grune & Stratton, 1963.

Bergevin, Paul, and McKinley, John. *Participation Training for Adult Education.* St. Louis: Bethany Press, 1965.

Birren, James E. *The Psychology of Aging.* Englewood Cliffs, New Jersey: Prentice-Hall, Inc., 1964.

Bischof, Ledford J. *Adult Psychology.* New York: Harper and Row, 1969.

John, E. R. *Mechanisms of Memory.* New York: Academic Press, 1968.

Klausmeier, J. G., and Harris, C. W. *Analyses of Concept Learning.* New York: Academic Press, 1966.

Kuhlen, R. G., ed. *Psychological Backgrounds of Adult Education.* Notes and Essays on Education for Adults, No. 40. Syracuse: Syracuse University Publications in Continuing Education, 1963.

Leagans, J. Paul, Copeland, Harlan G., and Kaiser, Gertrude E. *Selected Concepts from Educational Psychology and Adult Education for Extension and Continuing Educators.* Notes and Essays on Education for Adults, No. 71. Syracuse: Syracuse University Publications in Continuing Education, 1971.

Miller, Harry L. *Teaching and Learning in Adult Education.* New York: The Macmillan Company, 1964.

5

The Affective Domain

We have already made considerable progress in our search for understanding about adult learning. It is well established that the physical basis for learning is adequate, and we have just been noting that the intellectual capacity for learning is satisfactory. Adults can, and do, learn well all through life. But why does learning happen in some cases and not in others, if the physical and mental equipment is functioning? A typical answer is that the learner was not motivated. Many of the important factors in learning, such as motivation, can be grouped and considered as "affective." In the *Taxonomy of Educational Objectives* [1] these are described as:

> objectives which emphasize a feeling tone, an emotion, or a degree of acceptance or rejection. Affective objectives vary from simple attention to selected phenomena, to complex but internally consistent qualities of character and conscience. We found a large number of such objectives in the literature expressed as interests, attitudes, appreciations, values and emotional sets of biases.

Incidentally, the authors of the *Taxonomy* report that the "affective domain represented a more difficult classification problem than the cognitive domain."

In this chapter we will consider the interrelationships between feeling and other aspects of learning, and the effect of maturing and aging within this domain.

Feelings and Learning

There never was a time when it was not understood that emotions play an important part in learning. This has been expressed in a hundred aphorisms in various languages, "Spare the rod and spoil the child" just being the crudest, and the one with the widest currency. For centuries some people spoke and acted as if learning was not possible unless accompanied by pain and beatings. This is developed explicitly by novelists like Dickens and Marryat. Many a parent and teacher believed that a boy could not learn unless he was belabored with various kinds of weapons.

There are fewer people today who believe that physical beatings and various forms of corporal punishment are necessary for learning, although such ideas are slow to wither, particularly in some cultures. But there are many, perhaps an increasing number, of manifestations of learning psychology almost as crude: attempts to terrify people into acting in some different and improved fashion—to drive safely, or to give up alcohol or drugs, or to love their neighbor—all of them backed up with a naked or implied threat of dangerous or punitive consequences if they fail to comply. This phenomenon has not been sufficiently studied, but the results of most scare campaigns do not seem to be very impressive, and may often be negative.

The interests, needs, and motivations of any learner, child or adult, are primarily a matter of the emotions, not of the intellect. Any learner, in a classroom or elsewhere, brings to the learning transactions such feelings as self-esteem, fear, jealousies, respect for authority, need for status and prestige, and so on. While there has been much more attention to these factors in recent years, their importance had not gone unrecognized. For example, writing in 1924, J. Drever clearly identified the importance of nonrational factors:

> The fact must be emphasized once more that an individual's tendencies are educationally and socially more important than his capacities, however important the latter may be, and despite the contrary belief on the part of the man in the street. In school, and in life no less, it is the driving power that counts in the long run.[2]

But, while these factors were recognized by some, learning is often looked upon and spoken of as if it were entirely an intellectual exercise. Psychologist L. K. Frank said in an address:

> The dilemma of education arises from a belief in man as a rational being in whom emotion can be controlled by reason and intelligence. Educational programs shrink from any frank acceptance of the underlying personality makeup and emotional reactions of students as entering into the educational situation because to do so would bring widespread collapse of the whole educational philosophy and undermining of approved pedagogy.

This is not the place to argue about the consequences of not recognizing the place of emotions in learning. At any event, they are being given increasing recognition. Though psychologists differ in many respects, on a point like this there is general accord, even though the consensus may not yet be represented in educational practice.

We shall not, therefore, do much more than assert that feelings and emotions are to be found in any learning situation. The matter is discussed in considerable detail in the suggested readings. The reader can also gain further understanding for himself by observing or remembering his own learning behavior under such circumstances as the last-minute preparation before an exam, at the time of news of military victory or defeat, hearing about the fortunes of his favorite team during the World Series, the occasion of a death in the family, or by recalling his behavior in the classroom after receiving more than usual praise or rebuke from a teacher.

What is important, is to understand some of the main emotional influences on learning, to note the part that interests, attitudes, and motivation play in learning, and the way in which changes in these respects are brought about.

It is also worth noting not only that emotions influence learning, but that there are many similarities between the "field of emotion" and the "field of learning." Both learning and emotion are aspects of the same process of adjustment to environmental situations which the person must make continuously. Feelings are not just aids or inhibitors to learning; the goals of learning and of emotional development are parallel and sometimes identical and can probably be most conveniently stated as self-realization and self-mastery.

At the outset, it should be admitted that our knowledge concerning this is still rather embryonic. We notice the power and effects of the emotions even though we don't know too much about the causes, or precisely how they operate.

Feelings of Adults

It is a common view that the child is a "bundle of emotions," but some people seem to assume that the adult lacks feelings, or somehow "got over them." Of course, the reverse is true, as Gardner Murphy points out. "The adult has not *fewer* but *more* emotional associations with factual material than do children although we usually assume that he has less, because the devices of control are more elaborate and better covered in the adult." [3]

The adult carries one load or stigma from which the child is free. He is marked, for good or for ill (and it is mostly for ill), with the prevailing view that he and all other adults are not efficient learners. We have seen in the preceding two chapters that the facts contradict this assessment, but here we have an example of a case where the false assumption has just as much influence as if it were true.

The adult may bear one additional burden, that of failure or unpleasantness associated with learning during childhood. Adults in the future may not have so many negative feelings about their schooling. But many men and women, in the present day, though they might subscribe to the notion that "school days are the happiest days of life," still carry some feelings about the school they attended that range from mild dissatisfaction to hatred and loathing. If learning is associated with past defeats and failures, the adult will stay away, or be "too busy." After all, he has had a lifetime of experience in fabricating protective devices to protect his "self" from threat or defeat. Sometimes the first essential step is to make him feel that the new learning situation is indeed *new*, that it is planned for him, that it has no association whatsoever with failures in the past.

The common view about the weaknesses and failings associated with older people is very strong and is widely held. Irving Lorge and Jacob Tuckman once prepared a questionnaire employing such stereotypes as "Old people . . . are absent-minded." The questionnaire was presented to both children and adults. The results showed that as early as ten years of age children have a negative picture of old age, and that graduate students hold such a stereotype so tenaciously that even a course on the psychology of aging does little to remove the negative picture. Not surprisingly, older adults also have a similar view themselves.[4]

Few of us are fully able to understand or accept our own feelings. Often we don't understand other people or why we feel about them as we do:

> I do not love thee, Doctor Fell,
> The reason why I cannot tell.

Nor do we understand ourselves.

Most of us are capable of, and do have, what are sometimes called the "finer feelings." We like to think of ourselves as being kindly, reasonable, and loving. At times we may be shocked to find that we are also capable of being hateful, wicked, cruel, unreasonable. The inward struggle, the need to cover up our shortcomings from others, and particularly from ourselves, leads to a defensive behavior which deeply affects our freedom to engage in the adventure of learning.

For learning involves change. Who wants to change? No one really does. We all wish that the popular song "Just keep on doin' what you are doin' " could be our theme song. Newton's first law of motion is, "Every body persists in a state of rest (or of uniform motion in a straight line) unless compelled by external force to change that state." One need not accept this as a law to explain all human relationships, but human beings too, seek to remain in a state of equilibrium. No one wants to change but everyone must change. We must adjust to other people. We must take into account time and place and things. Change means disturbance, and a human being is ready to bear disturbance only under some conditions, and not at all under others.

This is not the place to attempt a catalogue of all the emotions. Moreover, they seldom present themselves in any simple form. They are nearly always mixed and complicated. The young man who has been summoned for an interview with his boss may feel—If-he-bawls-me-out-I'll-throw-his-job-in-his-face-I-hope-I-get-a-raise-I-wish-this-was-over. . . . Or the same young man on his way to see a young lady may feel—Will-she-go-with-me-to-the-dance-I-don't-care-if-she-doesn't-I'll-take-that-blonde-I-love-her. . . .

Constellations of Feelings

There are three, at least, emotional foci or constellations of feelings that are of constant influence on learning:

- Love and associated feelings such as respect, admiration, generosity, sympathy, friendliness, encouragement
- Rage, anger, and similar feelings such as outrage, sense of frustration, being thwarted and rejected
- Fear and such concomitants as suspicion

The first group in the many forms in which these factors are found, leads to calm, serenity, hope, joyousness, confidence, happiness. To the second and third the response is anxiety, withdrawal, despair, greed, hate.

As we have seen and will see further, the first constellation tends toward learning of quality and endurance and the second and third tend toward resistance to learning and to forgetting as a means of ending the tension, or threat or pain. One should not, of course, jump to the hasty conclusion that the feelings in the first constellation should be expressed and the others repressed. There are still wide differences of opinion, but most psychologists would now agree that all feelings should be expressed in some way and not simply bottled up, where they may work internally against the person. Books and group activities that encourage people to express every kind of feeling are now in vogue, such as *The Angry Book* by Theodore Rubin. The process of expressing feelings in ways that promote emotional health and do not injure the subject or those about him is not a simple one; it constitutes one of the most important objectives either for the teacher or the self-directed learner.

LOVE AND ASSOCIATED FEELINGS

In a book by Ashley Montagu the author takes a strong position about the place of affection in learning:

> . . . to teach is to love. And in the final analysis, as Goethe said, we learn only from those whom we love. . . . My greatest teachers have been great lovers. The very interests I have in this world I can trace directly, in almost all cases, to the moments when my teachers with love and reverence spoke to us of some great figure or event. . . .[5]

Or, as Carlyle wrote: "Love is ever the beginning of knowledge as fire is of light."

ANGER AND ASSOCIATED FEELINGS

Throughout life, of course, there are many changes in the kinds of situation or stimulus in which fear and anger are invoked.

Fear of the dark is characteristic of the child. But as his size and strength increase, and as intellectual maturity is reached, many fears simply "drop out" because the growing child becomes able to understand and to handle situations that had formerly resulted in fear. In later years declining physical or intellectual capacities may induce fear. There may be increasing anxiety about decline in sexual competence, or a new form of fear of the dark or of slippery streets on the part of a man or woman whose sense of balance is deteriorating. There is not yet much evidence about this, but it seems that anxieties are greatest in *anticipation* of the decline; that the adult *facing the fact* of decline is able to manage it with less actual stress than he displayed when he first began to be concerned.

There are also changes in the conditions that result in anger. Studies of college students have indicated that for them causes of anger usually come about from the thwarting of plans or wishes. Sometimes this happens as a result of the action of other people, sometimes through such institutional factors as college regulations, railroad schedules, and the like. Personal inadequacies and chance factors also make some contribution. As people grow older, there seem to be no fewer causes of anger, but most adults have learned something about the control of anger. However, anger resulting from a threat to one's values in areas like politics and religion seems to become of greater significance in later years. To put it another way, such attacks are seen as jeopardizing the "self."

Many studies and observations have reported that older people are rigid and inflexible. The word "set" is invariably applied to an older person. For anyone planning a program or curriculum with older people this is a factor which cannot be neglected. Views about politics, religion, morality, duty may be held fixedly; they are not subject to question or a review without displays of emotion. But there is enough evidence to question if this "crystallization" or "integration" happens invariably and inevitably, or results because of waning contacts with ideas or with stimulating social groups. The provision of educational opportunity for the old seems to inhibit somewhat the onset of such rigid behavior.

Many studies have shown that older people seem less self-confident than at an earlier age. Undoubtedly this is a result not only of decline in some capacity but because of their acceptance of the stereotype of loss to which we have already directed so much attention. In a recent study it was seen that a group of older professors made twice as many remarks belittling themselves when taking an "intelligence" test as did a group of younger professors.

FEAR AND ASSOCIATED FEELINGS

There are a growing number of studies that show the relationship between anxiety and tension and impaired learning. However, we ought not to expect that oversimple formulas, such as the advice often given to girls that, faced with any threat, they should "cry it out," will be effective in all situations. There are as many paradoxes in the field of learning as in any other area of human experience.

Accepting almost as axiomatic that most older students have suffered some loss in confidence, many programs of adult education plan for reinforcement of the learner—by helping him understand why he feels less confident, to realize that he can achieve by helping him relax and reduce tension, and by helping him improve in his study skills. In some recent programs for students of all ages, who were extremely tense before writing examinations, exercise was given to relax them and lower tension levels. Results suggest that much can be accomplished with learners of all ages in helping them utilize their potentialities and respond more effectively under stress.

But is there no learning at all if pain or fear is associated with the learning experience? Of course there is. For generations children and adults have learned some subjects, or lessons in life under the most threatening conditions. "The burnt child dreads the fire" and learns not to touch the stove. A child in fear of physical beatings may learn his arithmetic or irregular Latin verbs. But he may also—not always—learn to dislike or hate the teacher, to dislike or hate the school, dislike or hate the subject, dislike or hate studies in general. He may learn to defend and protect himself in the present and to avoid similar experiences at all costs as soon as he is able to escape. The adult whose honest questions are ignored or disregarded may learn that some foreman, or some professor, leans on and is circumscribed by his particular field of knowledge or his skill, or that such teachers are not really interested in learning. Such indifference is infectious.

Rogers has made a useful distinction between threatening conditions in life which result in learning directed to self-preservation, and learning under threat in the classroom:

> It may be objected that learning goes on in spite of, or even because of, threat. Witness the platoon which is likely to be fired upon as it goes into enemy territory, and because of this threat learns rapidly and effectively about the terrain. It is true that when reality provides the threat, the learning of behaviors which will maintain the self goes on apace. If the desired training has no other goal than to maintain the self as it is, then threat to self may not impede the progress of learning. But in education this is almost never true. What is desired is growth, and this involves change in the self. Whenever such a broader goal is envisaged, then threat to the self appears to be a barrier to significant learning.[6]

Motivation of Adults

Adults can learn, but do they want to? How can the attention of adults be secured for learning? How can they become effective and continuing learners? All people have *wants*, which they can acknowledge and articulate. They also have *needs*, but these are not always identified and the person may even need to be made aware of them or learn to identify them for himself.

First, we need to win awareness. In a world in which all conceivable means of expression are being employed to capture attention, how can those interested in learning succeed in the competition? The press, posters, radio, movies, television spray a kaleidoscope of sounds and images upon the individual. How can his eye and ear and emotions be gained for the purposes of education?

What people will, or can be persuaded to pay attention to, depends very much on their interests and attitudes. These, and motivation, have increasingly become the chief subjects of concern of the student of learning.

Early research about learning usually had to do with simple units of behavior like the "conditioned reflex" where a hungry dog who had been given meat, simultaneously with the ringing of a bell, would "learn" to display all the hunger signs whenever the bell was rung. But much recent research has been about social and human relations in which the primary attention is on motives and attitudes. Many writers have asserted that motivation will determine whether learning will happen at all, as well as the rate and the amount of learning.

We shall now consider and review some general propositions about motivation. A large part of our discussion will be given to interests and attitudes: how they develop, how they grow and change, how they affect learning. For illustration we shall note some recent studies that not only help us to understand attitude changes but that also suggest useful directions for education.

Perhaps the most curious and fascinating part about human beings is the drives and needs and desires and interests that make them what they are. In previous ages this was the field for speculation by the theologian, philosopher, and novelist. Now it has become a primary interest of the psychologist, other social scientists, and of the practitioner of the occupation known as "motivation research." Though a great deal more is now known about the motivations governing human action than heretofore much mystery still remains. But this need not daunt us. Alfred North Whitehead often said that he had a horror "about the teaching of inert or static ideas . . . that this is the correct thing to know! Once learning solidifies, all is over with it; when that happens, thought is dead." Fortunately, or unfortunately, there is still much more to be learned about motivation than is yet known.

VIEWS ABOUT MOTIVATION

The most-used term in adult education, and perhaps the most abused, is *motivation*. Motivation is a concept used to explain why organisms do what they do. It derives from a medieval Latin verb *movere* meaning "to move." One dictionary definition is "that which tends to move a person to a course of action." The interest that has been aroused in all fields of education is a form of recognition that learning is performed by the learner, a signal step in understanding and improving learning. Interest in motivation is found throughout adult education—in literacy programs as well as in the continuing education of doctors and managers. Both research and development projects concerning motivation in adult learning have been on the increase.

To simplify what is a complex field, it can be said that there are two main views of human motivation: "need reduction" and "positive striving." In the first, emphasis is placed on the need to satisfy bodily hunger and thirst and sleep and sexual appetites. It is asserted that the organism's motivation to perform a variety of activities arises from the necessity of fulfilling these basic needs. Some theorists have extended this view to include the need to avoid pain and discomfort or to minimize anxiety.

The "positive striving" view has many formulations, most of which claim that a potent motivating force is self-fulfillment (Carl Rogers and Erich Fromm) and the need for a human being to enhance his relationships within society.

These two views need not be seen to be in conflict or to be mutually exclusive. Indeed, as we shall see, Abraham Maslow's hierarchy of needs brings them into a single formulation since he maintains that man must satisfy his basic biological needs before higher order social needs will emerge. However, the two views may also be seen to be at opposite poles of a continuum.

Other theorists have postulated a need for comfort, or affiliation, within a welcoming social environment. This position may also be contrasted on a continuum which reaches to an opposite pole of achievement motivation. David McClelland [7] developed notions of achievement needs and achievement motivation, and these have been applied in industrial and business corporations and in developing countries. He has also pointed out that the expectation of achievement on the part of students and teachers affects the achievement of the learner. In a series of experiments, it was shown that when the teacher is informed that certain students are expected to do well and others less well, those for whom high expectations are held tend to do better than the others, regardless of the real ability of these students.

DEFINITIONS RELATED TO MOTIVATION

Definitions can obstruct and confuse as well as clarify, but it may be useful to have a brief look at some terms that are in common use, alas, sometimes with very different meanings.

Motivation is usually employed as the general term to designate the active kinds of relationships that an organism has with its environment.

Motives are "a state or set of the individual which disposes him for certain behavior and for seeking certain goals."

Sometimes *motives* are distinguished from *drives* where drives are used to denote such physiological needs as hunger or thirst, and motives to include interests, attitudes, and purposes.

Both wants and needs are included under motives. Strictly speaking wants are less forceful, they refer to desires, and may lead to action or may be accepted by the individual without his doing anything about them. Needs refer to demands and presumably always lead to some activity to satisfy or remove the tension.

Arising out of "need reduction" on the one hand and "positive striving" on the other, motivation seems to have two different though related effects—directing and selecting as well as reinforcing. Motives may lead either to approaching or avoiding behavior, and sometimes both. One writer was recently recalling his behavior during college days. He claims that he developed surpassing skill, when Saturday night was approaching, in lining up and extracting loans from new prospects and, at the same time, avoiding all those from whom he had borrowed in previous weeks.

A person who has developed a strong interest in opera or classic dramas may pursue these with great eagerness and avoid with equal passion the kind of music and drama which may have previously satisfied him.

Another distinction is between intrinsic and extrinsic motives. The first would be for the sake of the activity itself, such as the joy in playing tennis. The second might be pursued for some value associated with the activity, such as becoming club tennis champion.

It used to be commonly stated, though often denied in practice, that most extrinsic motivations were second-rate, if not downright harmful. Educational texts have been full of diatribes against special incentives even while educational practice placed an ever greater premium upon such incentives. The question is not quite so simple as some supposed. It is not always true that intrinsic motivation is superior in learning effect to extrinsic motivation. Thorndike noted long ago in his book *The Psychology of Wants, Interests and Attitudes*:

> In certain respects, intrinsic interests do possess greater merits. In so far as the task of education . . . is to develop or strengthen certain interests as more or less permanent features of a person's make-up, the more intrinsic the interest can be, the less dependent upon outside aids and circumstances, the better.[8]

But, he goes on to show, these advantages have often been very much exaggerated, at least as far as learning is concerned:

> If an educated adult for any reason is induced by any force, no matter how external, to want to learn a certain thing, no matter how remote learning it is from his other deeper, and more "real" needs, he can learn it provided of course that it is within his powers.

Riesman, in his book *The Lonely Crowd*, has discussed some of the ethical and practical issues involved in extrinsic motivation, in his discussion of "inner-directed" and "outer-directed" individuals.

PHYSICAL AND SOCIAL BASIS

Motives can be labeled internal or external depending on whether they develop within the organism or without. Hunger for food is an example of an originally interior drive but "hunger" for a good talk has an external origin. Sherif refers to the first as "unlearned biogenic motives" and to the second as the "learned, sociogenic motives." [9]

Primary Motives. There is the need of the body for food, drink, rest; for protection from threats in the physical environment (falling) and for elimination of waste products. For each of these there are characteristic intra-organic sources of stimulation, types of restlessness and tension, and characteristic acts which relieve tension and restore equilibrium. Of considerable importance, too, is the way that we experience some sensations associated with these drives as pleasurable and other as unpleasant. The strength of these drives varies in extraordinary degree throughout life. As a generalization it can be said that they seem to have greatest effect upon motivation and behavior in the early years of childhood and again in the very late years of life when physical losses may impose some limits upon behavior.

Secondary Motives. Beginning at birth there is also a complex of social motivations that are derived from biological urges, but that are equally based on the way a human being "gets along" with his family, in his school, in his job associations and on the way he manages the pressures of social living. These social motives are highly personal but at the same time are affected deeply by the culture in which the person lives. Some "cultural" needs are very powerful. This was seen clearly during the years of the depression when millions of people were out of work. As the Lynds reported in *Middletown*,[10] food sales declined nearly 50 per cent and sales of men and boys' clothing went down about 67 per cent. But gasoline sales declined only 3.6 per cent. The *secondary* need of gasoline, representing as it did social position as well as ability to see their friends, was actually a motive of extraordinary power in comparison with the primary needs of food and clothing. Both primary and secondary motives can be persistent or changing. Gardner Murphy once wrote that motivation

> . . . never "starts" or "stops." There are rapid or slow rises in tension level, and rapid or slow transmissions of the tension. . . . But the essential fact about motivation seems to be the continuous instability or restlessness, and the consequent interstimulation which characterizes all living systems.[11]

TIME AND MONEY AS KEY INFLUENCES AFFECTING MOTIVATION

Motivation, then, is influenced by the physiology of a person. But it is equally influenced by such nonbodily factors as time or money. A man or a woman who is consciously seeking a mate or a new job, or who is responsible for the care of children, has a very strong goal. Demands upon them in terms of time may result in actually reinforcing the motivation. Time is limited; if it is used for study, or for work, or for child care, this fact in itself acts to focus and intensify the motive. Other desired activities are forced aside, and, as this is done, the motivation associated with them may gradually be weakened and even replaced. When the person again has ample time for choosing a different activity this may be a time of bewilderment and frustration because the aims and appropriate motives necessary to fill the void may have become diffused or even have disappeared. A woman whose family no longer needs her attention at every waking moment, a man or a woman about to retire, is sometimes facing a critical adjustment, basically a crisis in motivation. The person who has acquired or developed many and varied interests, desires, and goals more readily meets these periods of increased freedom.

But time is restricted in another way. The adolescent has all the time in the world ahead of him, nothing seems impossible to do. But the woman at forty-five, the man at fifty, now realizes that it may already be too late for the expression of some deeply felt needs, and that all future objectives will depend upon how much time is left for their expression. The intensity of motives may deepen or lessen; a man may be determined to finish some task before it is too late, or he may become resigned to the likelihood that it will never be finished.

The influence of time upon what a man will desire to learn, or attempt to learn, is obvious. Equally obvious are the secondary effects upon personality and upon self-confidence, when various forms of frustration accompany the inability to pursue cherished goals.

One aspect of time that has had insufficient study is *span of attention*. The child stays only a short time with one activity, then shifts his attention. As he moves through adolescence the span lengthens until in adulthood there may be several hours of deep, absorbed attention. Much laughter is devoted to the absent-mindedness of some adults, such as professors, but this is recognition of what may simply be a misapplication of a highly developed and highly desirable capacity. The span of attention seems to be related far more closely to interests than it is to the facts of physiology.

Money, or the relative freedom of an individual to choose what he will do, by being able "to afford it," with all the emotional as well as economic consequences that it may bring, is also an influence of considerable intensity. To anyone it is of vital importance to have the money to prepare oneself for a chosen vocation, or to make a change in vocation, or to proceed or not, with plans for establishing a family, or to undertake chosen leisure-time pursuits. The possession or desire for money and the complex attitudes built around its possession and use are a major modifier of motivation.

Motives are also deeply affected by one's age, culture, and social group. In general, middle-class people are more likely to act in greater awareness of time than urban, working-class people. They have more of a link with the past and are more willing to postpone gratification of desires for the future. For the working-class person future rewards or sanctions are too uncertain to have much motivational value. There is a distinct difference between a man of fifty and a man of twenty-five in his attitude toward planning for the future, and toward such notions as saving and thrift. In general, the young man is prepared to use credit; the older man *may* do so but, perhaps, with some sense of impropriety or even guilt. Usually the older man will more readily accept the notion that saving is a good thing.

Learning to use credit is conditioned directly by one's experience and therefore by one's motivation. The young person in North America takes this easily in his stride. But a West Indian farmer, to whom his land is the symbol and guarantee of both freedom and status, and for whom the fear of the money-lender is very real, will try never to do anything which in any way threatens his title to his land. Great schemes for agricultural improvement may be held up because of widely held values, fears, and motives that may work against the proposed changes.

Some writers claim that educational motivations are quantitatively different from a buying decision or a choice of reading material, different not only in complexity but also in the length of time committed in the action. Entering a course or following some other educational venture requires a decision to accept behavior that is formalized, perhaps highly regulated, and covering more than one episode. The individual will make such a choice only as he has imagined for himself the satisfaction to be gained.

Some research has been made on why workers and farmers undertake study. For example, those in National Farm Radio Forum [12] in Canada overwhelmingly said that they were motivated by "neighborliness and community spirit" but they also referred to educational advantages, better understanding of farm problems, achieving a unity among farmers and preparing for social action on behalf of rural people. Ten per cent of the farmers and their wives reported they joined because they enjoy discussion. It is hardly *surprising* that "social" motives are often, or usually, present in most adult educational choices. Some people scoff at such motives as if they were unworthy, but they are to be anticipated and they provide as well an excellent basis for much learning.

Motivational Theories and Research

The sources of and power behind motivation, questions about what "instigates" it and what "energizes" it have long been matters of debate and controversy. For years argument raged about instincts—were they present in human beings as well as in animals; were they innate and unlearned; what and how many instincts did people possess. Some observers classified as instincts, fright, repulsion, pugnacity, self-abasement, self-assertion, sucking, spitting, smiling, sociability, and acquisitiveness. The number grew and grew until in 1924 sociologist Luther Bernard compiled a master list from 500 books by social scientists and found himself with a grand total of 5,759 separate instincts. This seemed so ridiculous that scholars began to look more and more for simpler explanations for motivation and behavior, particularly at social learning theory. The most celebrated statement about motivation, by Abraham Maslow, came about thirty years later and not only synthesized many of the contending formulations but has served as a stimulus for renewed theorizing and research.

MOTIVATION: A HIERARCHY OF NEEDS

Maslow went to empirical, theoretical, and clinical studies for the material for his conception. His focus was both on needs and human potentialities within the framework of a concern about human growth. He starts with the proposition that the human being is not an empty organism, or a *tabula rasa* on which society writes. Needs represent potentialities; they are not final actualizations: these come later. Some impulses are weak and can be inhibited or destroyed; there is no fixed sequence for obtaining gratification. Some are potent and found throughout the species, like the need for love. Some are specific to the individual—the need for expressing oneself in music or art. But if these needs find no outlets, the individual suffers various forms of damage.

Maslow has called these forces *organismically based needs* and has placed them in the well-known five stages:

Gratification of bodily needs
Safety insurance against pain and danger of life
Love, affection, warmth, acceptance, a "place in the group"
Self-esteem, self-respect, self-confidence, feeling of strength and adequacy
Self-actualization, self-fulfillment, self-expression, use of one's capacities "to be the most one is capable of being." [13]

Maslow did not state, as others have, that *literally* every aspect of expression on one level must be completed before the emergence of a second level. Indeed, expression at several levels may continue throughout life. But levels there seem to be. The more basic level must be relatively well satisfied before the organism is able to function on a higher level. The first level for Maslow, as for many other psychologists, are the physiological needs, including hunger, sex, and thirst as well as the need for sleep, relaxation, and bodily integrity.

When these needs are relatively well satisfied, the *safety needs* emerge that are centered around a predictable and orderly society. The human being seeks stability and protection, and, if these are denied, he may behave in a mistrustful and insecure fashion and seek various forms of support or escape. When such needs are comparatively well satisfied, the opportunity to possess and express affectionate relationships develops: *love* and *belongingness* needs. The fourth level are the *esteem* needs—including such matters as achievement and competence, independence and freedom, reputation and prestige and honor.

Self-actualization develops over time through the full employment of talents, capacities, and potentialities. It is implied in Maslow's concept that throughout his development and unfolding the individual directs most of his activities toward the needs not yet achieved or others that are frustrated, rather than toward those that have already been satisfied.

A NEW INTEREST IN INTRINSIC MOTIVATION

A book published in 1971 was entitled *Intrinsic Motivation: A New Direction in Education*.[14] *New* is relative; J. McV. Hunt traces the roots back to Plato and Aristotle, through Descartes and such classical educational theorists as Froebel and Pestalozzi, and would include the psychoanalytic theory of Freud and the "drive" theory by Hill, Miller, Dollard, and other psychologists. But the interest in intrinsic motivation is very much on the rise. The reasons are several. Exploration of creativity, on the one hand, and anxiety, on the other, lead back to motivations. There also seems to be a neurophysiological base: evidence from recent studies identifies the mechanism in the nervous system as a "feedback loop" and supports the contention that the brain behaves more as an *active* information processor and not so much as a *static* signal switchboard. Moreover, as we will review in Chapter 10, the interest in self-directed learning has multiplied, and motivational theory that relates to self-directed learning obtains consequent attention. Lastly, a number of theorists have been studying concepts such as *curiosity*.

In many of these studies the notion that the human being has a capacity for inquiring is advanced. For example, J. R. Suchman says of his investigations:

> At the outset of this work I regarded inquiry as an intellectual skill which had to be learned, and could be trained into people. In recent years I have come to reject this notion and to replace it with the view that man is by nature an enquiring creature, and that from birth he engages in a continuous process of inquiry into the characteristics of his environment, and his own relation to that environment.[15]

Suchman goes on to describe inquiry: "I see it as a natural, inborn, human process; the way people learn when you leave them alone, . . . as the pursuit of some kind of new meaning or experience. . . . It is free open, self-directed learning." Suchman adds, "Central to all these definitions must be the inquirer's sense of freedom and autonomy; freedom to pursue his own goals; freedom to transact with his environment in ways that he determines; freedom to form and test his own inferences."

The psychologist whose work has stimulated most interest in "curiosity" is D. E. Berlyne, particularly in his book, *Conflict, Arousal and Curiosity* [16] but also in many published papers. Prior to his work, the concept of curiosity was often the subject of rhetoric, but rarely of careful investigation. Since his book, studies are proceeding in many places. H. I. Day is concerned with *specific* curiosity related to a particular subject and leading to specific forms of exploration. He has also studied curiosity as "personality trait and looked at diversive curiosity." Day has found that *specific curiosity* can be measured on different operational scales (direction of attention, duration of exploration, physiological reactivity, verbal judgment of "like" "prefer"), and so forth. His test, OTIM (Ontario Test of Intrinsic Motivation) has been used to examine the relationship of specific curiosity to achievement in education, to mental health, to anxiety, to aesthetics, and to creativity. The results are extremely promising, even though far from conclusive. J. McV. Hunt has said: "We are still a long way from being able to spell out the educational and developmental aspects which create strong, informationally based motivational systems. In this connection, moreover, we must recall Maslow's hierarchy of motivational systems, for the irrational systems of pain, avoidance and hunger clearly appear to dominate intrinsic motives in the young and immature and may even prevent their development."

Berlyne has examined the power generated by *intrinsic* as against *extrinsic* motivation and acknowledges that the answers are not final or clear. But, he concludes, there may be more important questions.

> Perhaps more to the point is the likelihood that exploitation of intrinsic motivation may lead to different kinds of learning from other methods. If intrinsic reinforcement depends upon the establishment of congruence among neural processes, it seems plausible, pending rigorous verification, that it will above all impel the student to see connections, to form adaptive intellectual structures, and to recognize principles of wide generality and objectivity. Furthermore, since intrinsic motivation promotes questioning, exploration and productive thinking, it seems plausible that the student will be trained to examine statements critically before believing them, to be open to novel ideas and experiences, and to select both problems and ways of attacking problems shrewdly.

MOTIVATION IN BUSINESS AND MANAGEMENT

Much of the research respecting motivation for adult education has derived from studies of productivity and management. We have mentioned McClelland and his associates who have developed some practical measures of motivation. Some of the studies began during World War II, measuring the hunger drive and its changes during prolonged starvation. But research soon turned to appraising the need for achievement, which seems universal, but which also seems to be almost infinitely varied. For some, intellectual products represent the tokens of achievement, for others sexual conquest, making money, power, or displays of physical prowess or psychical insight. McClelland devised a system on which any sort of achievement would be tallied on an individual's score on need for achievement. He has used these measures with cultural groups outside the United States, as well as inside, but comparative measures of achievement have not yet been carried out with much thoroughness. McClelland has postulated ways of utilizing drives for achievement in education as well as in work situations.

Another psychologist who has worked on questions of motivation in the industrial arena is Douglas McGregor [17] whose conception of *Theory X* and *Theory Y* is often quoted and applied. McGregor said that two generalized theories underlie most forms of industrial organization. *Theory X* is based on the assumption that many individuals dislike work and will do anything they can to avoid it, that the average person prefers to be directed, has little ambition, seeks only security, and does not want responsibility, all of which means that the manager is forced to coerce people to do their work in any event. *Theory Y* is an alternative postulation, that the expenditure of energy is natural, that there are many ways of ensuring performance in addition to coercion, that commitment is related to the goals sought, that people like responsibility, that many of them are creative and that, unfortunately, in most industrial situations only a small portion of human potential is utilized. In management training these two theories are scrutinized in their application. The application of *Theory Y* in industry, training centers, correctional institutions, and schools has reinforced the view that the response of a man is related closely to what is expected of him and how he is treated. It has also led to the formulation of additional concepts and training designs such as the *Managerial Grid*, associated with Robert Blake.

A notion that has also commanded considerable attention is the contrast that has been made by Frederick Herzberg [18] between true *motivation* and what he terms *maintenance*. Herzberg asserts that many of the factors in a job that are often spoken of as motivation are really only *"maintenance"* factors and that *motivation* is something else. Factors such as salary, pension, recreation, and fringe benefits are important in maintaining the morale of managers and employees and keeping them satisfied, whereas, in the absence of such factors, the individual becomes dissatisfied and his work will decline. In other words, there are "industrial hygiene" factors. Maintenance seekers in work and education are concerned primarily with the nature of the work environment, with pay, working conditions, job security, policies, and relations with other employees or colleagues. They show less interest in the kind and quality of work, and, while they may succeed through the possession of talent, they do not develop professionally from the experience. They are usually "outer-directed" and are often highly reactive.

Motivating factors, on the other hand, are factors of achievement, responsibility, growth, and other matters associated with the self-actualization of the individual on the job. Motivation seekers obtain their satisfaction from achievement, responsibility, growth, advancement, work itself, and earned recognition. They often have a high tolerance for poor environmental factors. They seem to enjoy work, strive for quality, tend to overachieve, and benefit professionally from the experience.

Herzberg has looked at many kinds of workers, including executives, engineers, scientists, hourly technicians, assembly workers, and, he maintains, these distinctions between motivation and maintenance apply generally to all. Recently, there has been some attempt to consider the factors influencing good maintenance, and the factors influencing positive motivation, in voluntary societies and colleges.

BEHAVIOR THERAPY AND MOTIVATION

In recent years a substantial body of theory and practice has been developed that might fall under the label *behavior therapy*. This is the name usually given to techniques of psychological treatment which are derived from, or attempt to be consistent with, the findings of experimental psychology, particularly in the field of learning. The aim is to modify or eradicate symptoms or undesired behavior and develop more desirable behavior by the explicit use of learning processes which incorporate experimentally established learning principles. A whole literature has arisen under the term "behavior modification." As noted earlier, another subfield, "cognitive desensitization," is mainly concerned with the lessening or elimination of anxiety, for example, among learners who are undergoing an examination. Procedures are employed for achieving relaxation, sometimes involving role playing, or forms of hypnosis and autohypnosis, or a feedback system in which the subject is informed about what is happening to him and how he may gain some control over the situation.

In some of these activities *aversive conditioning* is utilized as a form of reverse motivation. For example, therapists working with alcoholics may use drugs such as Antabus so that the subject will be thwarted and blocked by discomfort from an "undesirable" kind of behavior; namely, further drinking of alcohol. Of course, the crucial problem remains of motivating him to undertake more acceptable behavior and to learn new kinds of responses to his problems and anxieties.

Interests

In discussing motivation thus far we have, for the most part though not entirely, been dealing with needs. Now we shall turn our attention to interests and attitudes. We shall not try to distinguish fully between needs and these other responses; they are not identical, but neither can they easily be separated. An interest is often the direct expression of a need, but sometimes it is a substitute. There are, for example, many interests that are some form of substitute for sex hunger. But most interests and attitudes would be included in what Sherif described as sociogenic motives, not internal ones.

We shall not try to make much of a point of the difference between interests and attitudes. If you will search the dictionaries you will discover some variation but there is far from complete agreement. Perhaps the most useful distinction is historical. That is, the earliest research was in what were called *interests*. The results were important, even though the methods used and the conclusions reached were relatively uncomplicatd. With refinement both of theory and method, the studies of *attitudes* have become much more subtle. A deeper understanding of what constitutes learning may be coming about through intensive studies of how attitudes are formed and modified.

Our own discussion of these responses will follow the historical precedent; we shall begin with interests and shift over into a consideration of attitudes.

INTERESTS AND LEARNING

Those concerned with learning have often speculated about the relationship between interest and learning. It has long been recognized that there may not be much learning of consequence unless a marked interest is present. The factor of interest was likened by early psychologists to a sentry at the gate, admitting certain stimuli and blocking out others. This is a rather mechanical metaphor; learning is much more dynamic than this interpretation suggests. Interests act not so much as sentinels as an impetus to seek out new experience, or as a favoring climate for change and growth.

Many writers on education, John Dewey for instance, have equated interest with discipline. Dewey often said that the price of self-discipline is the arousal of interest. Others have spoken of interest as an essential condition of responsibility.

A number of psychologists have studied the role of interests, the name of Edward K. Strong [19] being the most prominent. Usually the study has been of those interests relevant to education, vocation, or leisure time.

Changes in Interests. Most observers agree that although interests change radically during life, these changes do not occur in any capricious or inexplicable way. Changes of interests are an accurate reflection of such things as changes in abilities and energy, outlets for the sex drive, modifications of the personality, and shifts in vocational and cultural expectations as youngsters become mature, middle-aged, and elderly. His vocation is much more likely to affect a man's interests than will his chronological age. But changes do occur during life. Older people are just as likely to have strong likes and dislikes as younger. Activities which require well-developed physical or sensory skill, daring, or stamina show the greatest change of all. For most men scaling a cliff or walking along a precipice might be considered a "normal" interest in the twenties, but exceptional thirty years later. Team sports, strenuous tests of endurance, driving a car, performing conjuring tricks may also decline, but bird watching or visiting museums may persist or increase. The older man is likely to be much more resistant than the younger to acquiring interests that interfere with established habits or customs.

One study suggests that a man's hobbies, which often require greater physical activity than those of women, are more likely to have to be given up in the later years. Thus a man who is limited to such hobbies may lose these interests at about the same time as he retires from work, constituting a serious double loss.

Interest in physical activity declines, but it should not be considered that older people ought never, or will never, take part in activities making some physical demands. Walking and visiting friends may be very pleasurable activities. An eighty-year-old widow recently received a power saw and lathe and has learned quickly how to make her own furniture. This is uncommon, but is far from an isolated case.

However, interests and recreations that have to do with talk, writing, reading, and that are carried on at a modest pace, are most likely to survive and even increase in intensity with the passing years. This means that most of the interests associated with most forms of learning endure or even intensify throughout life. However, some studies seem to indicate that there may be a lessening interest in linguistic skill and in efforts requiring writing. The older person, much more often than the younger, prefers interests that are carried on individually rather than in company. However, this finding ought also to be accepted with some caution. It may simply be related to the fact that at present many older people in our society lack congenial social groups. There seems to be a slight decrease in the total *number* of interests as one gets older chiefly because of the decline in those involving physical activity. But most observers agree that interest span, that is, variety and quantity of interests, is closely related to "intelligence."

For interests associated with reading of books and magazines there are considerable individual differences. But we have already seen that interest in reading tends to persist, perhaps to grow. So, in general, does attention to radio and television, though this is more likely to be done individually than in company. Attendance and interest in movies declines sharply after age twenty-five. In the over-sixty group 75 per cent of people never attend a movie.

The changes in interest do not take place at a uniform rate. E. K. Strong stated that at least half the changes are likely to occur between twenty-five and thirty-five, about 20 per cent in the next decade and about 30 per cent between 45 and fifty-five. On the whole, as we noted earlier, the older adult seems to be more resistant than the younger if what is to be learned seems useless or meaningless. Moreover, the older person seems to apply stricter tests of relevancy than does the younger.

Interests and Emotions. The older person seems to suffer more anxiety as the result of poor success while following up an interest. He also seems to do less well than the younger where learning is carried out under conditions of mild bodily discomfort.

The generalization that breadth of satisfying interests goes along with happiness seems to be justified for all ages. One writer who has studied the lives of older people maintains that of the three factors that seem essential in a satisfying old age (namely economic security, freedom from physical hardship, and varied interests) the factor of interests is most important. Another who interviewed a large number of teachers concluded that those who were able to carry on wide, varied activities were much better "adjusted" than those whose interests were restricted to work. One does not have to accept the view that "adjustment" is invariably desirable to feel a sense of sorrow and pity for one whose interests have never ranged beyond his job.

Perhaps the most striking single fact about interests is that they are well established at an early age. Most observers believe that if an interest is to have much intensity it must have been established, with satisfaction, before the age of twenty-five. To put it another way, if a man or a woman is to take a rewarding interest in the fine arts when he or she is fifty, the beginning for this activity should have developed in the teens or twenties. If he has had no exposure to this interest, or has gained no satisfaction from its expression, he is much more likely to resist, to feel it is not for him, that he "has no time."

It should be pointed out, however, that people tend to read the books that are accessible to them more often than the books in which they say they are interested. This phenomenon seems to be paralleled by their choice of learning or leisure-time pursuits. In part at least, this is determined by what is easily available, not just by what they say they want.

Interests are very much a matter of culture and social position. The game of squash is played by those who belong to social clubs in which there are courts; polo is played by those of wealth and social position, as well as by a handful of cowboys. Some sports like bowling are played by everyone, but predominantly by wage earners. Playing cards is available to all, but the number of people playing poker, or bridge, or whist, is determined in considerable measure by the social position of the players. Interests in opera, symphony concerts, ballet, drama, libraries, used also to be very much a matter of social class, but there has been an expanding participation in these activities by all social groups.

Attitudes

Probably in no other field of human activity has there been more speculation and research than upon attitude formation and change. Attitudes are learned. They have been defined as "patterns of response which predispose the individual to rather specific behavior." Gordon Allport once said that the common element in all attitudes is "readiness for response." [20] Ideals, prejudices, and beliefs are often found together. They seem always to have well-defined objects or values, of either a favorable or an unfavorable nature.

Attitudes have cognitive, affective, and action components. If one is concerned about an attitude toward communism, for example, one would inquire about how much the subject knows about communism (cognitive), whether he dislikes, hates, approves, or is enthralled by communism (affective), and whether his feelings are expressed directly or covertly in action.[21] The origin and development of attitudes depends on a range of factors: genetic factors, physiological state of the subject, his direct experience, the social groups to which he belongs, and the kinds of communication to which he is exposed. Certain diseases have been associated, at least by novelists if not scientists, with attitudes and it has been alleged for example, that tuberculosis and optimism have a closer relationship than would occur by chance. The effects of disease, surgery, loss of certain functions, and the use of drugs may drastically affect attitudes as well as behavior.

AGE AND CONSERVATISM

As we have discussed before, one respect in which the older adult may differ from the younger is that he is more conservative. Or at least this is the claim. It is worth noting the reasons that are usually cited for this tendency:

- He was reared at an earlier time when, in general, attitudes were not so "liberal" as at present, and he has persisted in these attitudes.
- He learns more slowly.
- He has a more restricted social life, attends fewer movies and public meetings and may choose books, friends, and learning experiences to conform with well-established biases.
- He has a particular social role. The older adult has a position and is more apt to defend that position, and to maintain the attitude associated with it, than the youth who has no particular status.
- He has suffered some losses in sensory and physical capacity, with lessened self-confidence and therefore may feel that it is more necessary to cling to habitual patterns of behavior and display more tenacity in the face of threatened change. He finds the old ways more comfortable and less threatening.

CHANGES IN ATTITUDE

In general, changes in attitude can be brought about by lessening the tension and the conflicts with which the person is affected. For example, providing jobs and housing for older people will probably have considerable effect upon their attitudes. Much can also be done by increasing the number of opportunities through which older people will continue to read, hear lectures, see films, take part in study-discussion groups. A major goal is to help them keep up with and take hold of life rather than sit back and submit to inevitable decline. Older people who have maintained an active interest in affairs rarely become the conservative or reactionary influences that sometimes act as a block to progress.

Indeed, so many exceptions appear to the association of maturity and old age with conservatism and resistance to change that the subject is once more under review. It has been noted frequently, for example, that some of the most unusual concepts are developed or encouraged by people who no longer hope to hold or win a position or status, people who have time to reflect and have no great stake in the present, except to improve it. In the author's own experience, there has never been a time in his life when he so consistently rejected new or unpalatable ideas, when he was so convinced he was right, as at age seventeen and eighteen. As in so many areas. it seems that chronological age, compared with other factors, is of little utility in understanding or predicting attitudes.

Changes in attitude have been a subject of research of increasing importance. Much of the work has been concerned with communication, and these studies will be reviewed in Chapter 10. From time to time medical scientists have reported, or have warned, that dramatic attitudinal changes can be induced through surgical procedures such as by lesions, by implanting chemical agents, by altering diet, or by electrical stimulation. Changes in attitude associated with hypnosis and suggestions are frequently reported. But the greatest attention has been directed to the effects of drugs. These chemical agents can be used and have been used for many purposes: to relax, to perk up, to go to sleep, to stay awake, to deaden our sensitivities, to heighten our consciousness, to enliven our thoughts and enhance our awareness of obscure realms of experience. Each can be used to manipulate the attitude system: for example, varying the level of hostility or affecting the person's openness to outside stimuli, or enhancing his readiness to respond in certain directions. These developments, for good and for ill, parallel the equally significant current developments in brain research. No adult educator can possibly keep up with all the research that may affect his work, but he cannot remain aloof and ignorant of occurrences that affect so many lives.

A good deal has been found out about attitudes through studying the ways in which people have approached certain situations, as illustrated in several experiments. Two of these have been selected for illustrative purposes: one in which women learned new food habits and one in which the subjects learned to do something that had previously been distasteful.

CHANGE IN HABITS

Stimulated by some extraordinary research projects conducted by Kurt Lewin [22] and his associates during World War II, there have been a number of studies of the way women learn about and change their habits of serving food. The experiments were conducted somewhat as follows. The immediate object of the project was to teach the *facts* about nutrition, and the desirability of serving certain kinds of foods while cutting down on the use of other kinds. The content was presented according to two plans. In the first, the women in a large group were taught by excellent instructors who used charts, films, and demonstrations. Under the other plan the women covered the same content but under the guidance and direction of discussion leaders. In each case an effort was made to provide the best possible instruction for the same amount of time. At the conclusion of the course, the women were tested to determine *what facts they had learned*. The results were about the same in the two cases. All the women learned a good deal.

As far as facts were concerned it seemed to matter not at all whether they were taught in a large or a small group. But after an interval of weeks or months, the women were tested once more. This time they were not asked to recall *facts*, but to report on changes in *practice*. Did they now serve less starches and more vitamins, or did the course produce little or no change in their behavior? Now it was found that the women in the small groups who studied the same content and learned the same facts, *had changed their practice* demonstrably more times than those taught in large groups.

Several explanations have been offered for this variation in behavior. Most observers who have studied the results conclude that the significant factor lies in the attitude that is encouraged and developed through a *different quality of participation* in the small group. For some of the women in the large group the class was interesting enough, but it remained a *government* or *university* class. For most or all of the women in small groups, the group soon became *our group*, and the women developed a bond of relationship with other members. Accordingly, they began to assume some obligations to their fellow members, and to the leader. They seemed to feel that they must do something about what they had learned. Attitude change often seems to accompany the acceptance of responsibility or an obligation to oneself and to others.

One needs to be cautious not to extend too far the significance of these inquiries, but they have much to say about the ways in which attitudes of responsibility, as well as incentives for further learning, may be established.

ALTERING THE MEANING

We noted earlier that Thorndike and others conducted some experiments in which adults would "learn" to do things that at first were distasteful. Despite the supposedly universal aversion girls have for mice, women students were given white mice for pets to see what effect this might have on the girls (and the mice). It is amusing to note that this kind of experiment has often been thwarted because the students will refuse to give up their pets at the end of the trial period.

Other students have taken part in experiments designed to have them overcome their repugnance to snakes. This experiment has usually begun with a group of co-eds' being asked to handle snakes. All would refuse, even in the interests of science! Each day a similar attempt would be made but familiarity alone would bring slight, if any, improvement. Only a few girls would undertake to touch the snakes after many trials. At this point a number of *changes in the situation* would be introduced. Instead of "snake" the reptiles would be given names, chosen from movie stars and college football heroes. Second, the snakes would be tied with ribbons, and would be thoroughly saturated in perfume. As these successive changes were introduced, more and more, finally all the girls were able to handle the snakes without any outward show of distaste.

A pleasant story. But it has a very important lesson which goes far beyond the experiment itself. Notice what the changes introduced really were. At first glance they seem amusing and trivial, but this is not really so. What has been done is that the *meaning* of a situation that has deep significance has been radically altered. At the beginning of the experiment the meaning is snake-ugly-dirty-dangerous-slimy-odorous. With the changes introduced, the meaning changes substantially. Accordingly there is also a chance for behavior to change.

For many kinds of learning it may be necessary to alter the meaning of the situation. Another example of the same principle occurred in a community center in a large city. The staff person felt that an excellent activity for high school members was square dancing. But when first suggested, the proposal was greeted by the young people with hoots of derision. The staff member bided his time. At a dance at the center arranged several months later, he brought in a group of eight men and women who were to put on the "floor show" (the activity of greatest prestige, for the members concerned). The featured dancers presented square dances. In introducing the dance, the program director emphasized vigor, and the demands upon skill and energy. The "floor show" then demonstrated dances which exhibited these traits. Next, eight boys and girls, selected because of prowess in dancing, were invited to take part with the visitors. By this time the staff member had accomplished his main purpose. Square dancing which had conjured up a meaning of country-hick-oldfashioned-slow now had meanings derived from floor-show-speed-agility-endurance. From that point on interest in the activity itself was enough to ensure support for it.

The information reviewed about needs, motives, interests, and attitudes is all very interesting. But, some people have asked, what does it mean in practice? Some books on learning make no reference to these matters. Yet, to anyone who has read this far, it must be obvious that the crucial questions about learning deal with the way in which the learner becomes deeply involved. The student of learning must be fully aware of the sources of motivation in needs, interests, and attitudes.

There will be effective learning when certain conditions are realized:

- Stimulus-and-security
- Dependence-and-independence
- Reorganization of previous experience
- Relevance of relationships
- Satisfactions in terms of the learner

Both security and stimulus are essential. Much that has been written or said about learning has concentrated on the stimulus. It has been argued that if you make the stimulus strong enough, or challenging enough, or threatening enough, it will produce good learning. Does it? Not always. The child that is to be punished in the event of mistake, the salesman who will be fired if he does not reach his quota, may be thrust down into failure due to fear and nervousness. The result of a strong stimulus without *something else* may be rebellion, withdrawal, rejection, or apathy. The something else needed is a condition of security. By this we mean that the learner needs to feel at home with himself, sufficiently confident that he can meet the challenge successfully, or he may make no effort at all. He must have enough well-being *and* enough challenge or he will not dare the pain or discomfort that, in little or in large, always accompanies any learning.

The learner has two opposite needs—dependence and independence. He wants to lean on the parent or teacher, or foreman or coach, to be guided by him. He would like to have the hard tasks done by someone else. At the same time he wants to assert himself, he is fed up with being a "yes man," he wants to dominate, to have people know that he is "quite a person." Sometimes one of these opposing tendencies is stronger, sometimes the other, but both are always present. The learner who understands that he has such counterpoised drives, is already in a better position to bring them into some kind of equilibrium. Conversely, neither the situation in which dependence is always penalized, nor the one in which independence is always punished, gives much opportunity for effective learning.

Learning depends on previous experience. Of course, you will say. But this is a qualitative matter as well as quantitative. It is much more than how much experience—it is what *kind* of experience and what *meaning* it has, how it affects the self. One of the earliest concepts of learning was that called the *tabula rasa,* in which it is alleged that a human being can be likened to a fresh and empty sheet upon which are to be written all the lessons in living. A second concept was that the human being is like a sponge, soaking up facts and skills, and releasing them (forgetting) under pressure or through aging. We know that the process of learning is not passive reception of experience, or passive absorption of facts. The human being is active, he reaches out, he seeks, he selects experience and relates and integrates new experience into himself. What that being is, how it has handled previous experience, what are its feelings from previous learning encounters —these are mattters of utmost significance.

Any student of any age brings his experience to the classroom or seminar. But the experiences of the adult may be extensive and varied. This may be the richest source of his learning objectives as well as a resource for testing out hypotheses growing out of the subject matter. To the extent that this is achieved, the adult is likely to take a responsible part in the learning transaction.

Learning depends upon the relevance of relationships. We have all heard that the "3 R's" have a central place in learning, and we know what they stand for. R might equally stand for *relevance*. We have seen that the human learner is not a sponge, soaking up all experience, but a subtler selector of experience. One of the principles of selection is relevancy. Children expect to have to learn things, whether or not they see any meaning in the learning; adults are much less ready to accept learning without clear relevance. It has been pointed out frequently that teachers of mathematics, diligent as they may be in teaching the steps or processes in mathematical problems, will not have much success unless they explain what is being attempted, what is the nature of the problem, and what is the purpose of the exercise. In addition, the way the proof of a problem is arranged makes a marked difference between success in understanding the problem. Otherwise here may be some memorizing (quickly to be forgotten) of certain mechanical steps.

Adults expect to find relevance both in the objectives and in the methods employed. For them, evaluation often means reassurance that what they are doing is relevant.

Continued learning depends upon the achievement of satisfaction. The satisfaction must be felt in terms of the learner's own expectations and needs. Satisfaction should obtain in his relation to the teacher or leader. Studies of "leadership" show that all successful leaders have at least one trait in common—that the followers attain satisfaction in the relationship. It should also come about in relation to the other participants and to the subject matter itself.

There will be effective learning when interests and attitudes are focused and expressed.

Both interests and attitudes are examples of learned motives. During a lifetime interests change significantly. In the main the shift is away from activities demanding strenuous physical effort, and toward those involving talk, reading, and similar pursuits. Interests and attitudes are closely linked with occupation, class, and culture; they may be influenced more by occupation than by chronological age. Many of the changes in interest as people grow older favor the conditions under which education is usually conducted. However, if experience in a particular activity did not occur, with satisfaction, in the first two or three decades of life, the development of that interest in an older person would be far from automatic. But interest can be created and can be changed, if the initiation of interest is undertaken with care.

Attitudes can also be changed. They are complex forms of response and they may serve many functions in the emotional life of a person. They are most likely to be altered when the person is not undergoing threat or tension; to solidify under overt or presumed attack. The tendency toward rigidity and conservatism that is often found in older people may have nothing inevitable about it. Where basic needs of older people are met, such as the provision of shelter and economic security, interesting employment, and the feeling that one is wanted, reactionary behavior is not common and more "liberal" attitudes can be expected. In changing attitudes, the *self* must be involved. This may happen through assuming responsibilities to oneself and to others. Change can also be achieved through modifying the *meaning* of the social situation.

REFERENCES

1. Krathwohl, D. R., ed., *Taxonomy of Educational Objectives: Affective Domain* (New York: McKay, 1964).
2. J. Drever, *An Introduction to the Psychology of Education* (London: Edward Arnold, Publishers, Ltd., 1924).
3. Gardner Murphy, "Social Motivation," *Handbook of Social Psychology* (Cambridge, Mass.: Addison-Wesley Publishing Company, Inc.), Vol. II.
4. Jacob Tuckman and Irving Lorge, "The Influence of a Course on the Psychology of Adults on Attitudes Toward Old People and Older Workers," *Journal of Educational Psychology*, Vol. 43, 1952.
5. Ashley Montagu, *Education and Human Relations* (New York: Grove Press, 1958).
6. Carl R. Rogers, *Client-Centered Therapy* (Boston: Houghton Mifflin Company, 1951).
7. David McClelland, J. W. Atkinson, R. A. Clark, and E. L. Lowell, *The Achievement Motive* (New York: Appleton-Century-Crofts, 1953).
8. Edward L. Thorndike, *The Psychology of Wants, Interests and Attitudes* (New York: D. Appleton-Century Co., Inc., 1935). By Permission of Appleton-Century-Crofts, Incorporated.
9. M. Sherif, *An Outline of Social Psychology* (New York: Harper & Brothers, rev. ed., 1956).
10. Robert S. Lynd and Helen M. Lynd, *Middletown* (New York: Harcourt, Brace and Company, 1929).
11. Gardner Murphy, *Personality: A Biosocial Approach to Origins and Structure* (New York: Harper & Brothers, 1947).
12. R. Sim, J. Nicol, A. Shea, and P. Simmins, *Canada's Farm Radio Forum* (Paris: UNESCO, 1954).
13. A. H. Maslow, "A Theory of Human Motivation," *Psychological Review*, Vol. 50, 1943.

14. H. I. Day, D. E. Berlyne, and J. McV. Hunt, *Intrinsic Motivation* (Toronto: Ontario Institute for Studies in Education, 1971).
15. *Ibid.*
16. D. E. Berlyne, *Conflict, Arousal and Curiosity* (New York: McGraw-Hill, 1966).
17. Douglas McGregor, *The Human Side of Enterprise* (New York: McGraw-Hill, 1960).
18. Saul W. Gellerman, *Motivation and Productivity* (New York: American Management Association, 1963).
19. E. K. Strong, Jr., *Change of Interests with Age and Vocational Interests of Men and Women* (Stanford: Stanford University Press, 1931 and 1943, respectively).
20. Gordon Allport, *Handbook of Social Psychology* (Worcester, Mass.: Clark University Press, 1935).
21. H. Brewster Smith, "A Study of Attitudes Toward Russia," *Public Opinion and Propaganda* (New York: Dryden Press, 1954).
22. Kurt Lewin, "The Relative Effectiveness of a Lecture Method and a Method of Group Discussion for Changing Food Habits," *Readings in Social Psychology* (New York: Henry Holt and Company, Incorporated, 1947).

SUGGESTED READING

Bischof, Ledford J. *Adult Psychology.* New York: Harper and Row, 1969.

Hamachek, D. E., ed. *The Self in Growth Teaching and Learning.* Englewood Cliffs: Prentice-Hall, Inc., 1965.

Harris, Irving D. *Emotional Blocks to Learning.* New York: Free Press of Glencoe, 1961.

Insko, Chester A. *Theories of Attitude Change.* New York: Appleton-Century-Crofts, 1967.

Kuhlen, R. G., and Thompson, G. G. *Psychological Studies of Human Development.* New York: Appleton-Century-Crofts, 1963.

Neugarten, B. L., ed. *Middle Age and Aging.* Chicago: University of Chicago Press, 1968.

Reese, E. P. *Experiments in Operant Behavior.* New York: Appleton-Century-Crofts, 1964.

Rogers, Carl. *Freedom to Learn.* Columbus: Charles E. Merrill Publishing Co., 1969.

Staats, A. W., and Staats, C. K. *Complex Human Behavior: A Systematic Extension of Learning Principles.* New York: Holt, Rinehart and Winston, 1963.

Thompson, C. H. *Counseling the Adult Student.* Washington: American College of Personnel Association, 1967.

6

Being and Becoming

In an old school reader, one of the stories "with a moral" which used to so delight the editors of such texts gives an account of the chief minister of the king who approached three stonemasons engaged in work on Saint Paul's Cathedral in London. The questioner asked each man in turn what he was doing.

"I am trimming and laying stones," said the first man.
"I am earning wages to care for my wife and family," said the second.
"I am helping Sir Christopher Wren build a great monument to the glory of God," said the third.

Whatever you think of such fables, there are at least three aspects in any learning transaction. And the cathedral that every learner is building is himself.

Everywhere in the world men and women have questions or serious problems about identity. They may be puzzled and distraught persons searching for a meaning in their existence, trying to come to terms with themselves, or they may belong to whole nations where the subject of national identity is being debated daily. Questions of being, becoming, belonging arise daily, and almost as regularly appear books with titles that reflect these concerns. The most prestigious international report on education is titled *Learning to Be*.[1]

One observer has reported, however, that there is a clear distinction in the behavior of people when they heard the title of this report. Some older educators, he discovered, invariably asked "learning to be—what?" While others accepted the title as being clear and precise. Whether younger people are more appreciative of the idea of education for being, it is true that educational theorizing for many years has been mainly about specific "atoms" of learning behavior—such as conditioned reflexes and connections

124

between a specific stimulus and a specific response. In earlier times, and in other countries, notions of being and becoming were well understood. In the Hebrew culture there is the familiar joke about the Rabbi who asked the young boy, as part of his religious training, "My son, who made you?" Expecting an answer that God had done so, he was completely taken aback when the young lad replied boldly, "I'm not finished yet." And there is the recollection of the wise old Rabbi Zushya, who said, "In the coming world they will not ask me 'Why were you not Moses?'—they will ask me, 'Why were you not Zushya?'" *Being* and *becoming* are not only what living is about, but also the chief object of learning.

This chapter is about being and becoming, about the self. It is really Chapter 2, part two. Chapter 2 was about the learner, and what he is like as a learner. This was followed by a review of cognitive, psychomotor, and affective aspects of learning. This chapter brings these aspects of learning back into focus. It is not about the characteristics of the learner, but is about his becoming a self, a person, a unique individual, a soul. It is also about the impact of his self upon learning and about the consistency and change in that self throughout life. It is about learning to live with stress and tension; it is about learning about life and learning about death. And it is about self-fulfillment, enlargement, self-actualization.

The sound practitioner tries to keep in touch with, and to learn from, those who spend their main energies in studying man. But the sciences of man can be confusing, to say the least. Gordon Allport said: "It is especially in relation to the formation and development of human *personality* that we need to open doors. For it is precisely here that our ignorance and uncertainty are greatest." Allport feels that both the methods used and the populations sampled can lead to error.

> Our methods, however well suited to the study of the sensory processes, animal research, and pathology, are not fully adequate; and interpretations arising from the exclusive use of these methods are stultifying. Some theories of becoming are based largely upon the behavior of sick and anxious people or upon the antics of captive and desperate rats. Fewer theories have derived from the study of healthy human beings, those who strive not so much to preserve life but to make it worth living. Thus we find today many studies of criminals, few of law-abiders; many of fear, few of courage; more on hostility than on affiliation; much on the blindness of man, little on his vision; much on his past, little on his out-reaching into the future.[2]

The Self

We have referred often to the development of self and the genetic and social factors out of which self is shaped. It could be stated that there are four selves, or, more correctly, there are four different aspects of self:

- What the person actually does and says
- How the person perceives and feels his own behavior
- How what the person does is perceived by others
- The ideal self (in Freudian theory the superego) which each of us carries, constant while constantly changing, throughout life

The differences, even the conflicts between these aspects of self have long been the main field of attention for the novelist and dramatist. The learner must cope not only with what emotions are released at the time of an action but with how others expect him to feel and how he idealizes himself as feeling. The housewife looking at contemporary paintings (or considering joining such a course as "Understanding Modern Painting") is the subject of a complex of feelings associated with the painting itself: what her friends or her husband will say about such painting, what she has read in a magazine or seen on television, what view she has of herself, what her understanding is of such terms as *culture*.

Finding a personal identity is a task for every person, and failure here may result in serious breakdown. People in many countries have a related problem—their identity as a national, a citizen of a particular country—not that of an individual. In many countries undergoing development one reads that there is a serious *crisis of identity*: you will find the same expression and debate in other countries such as Canada, which is relatively affluent, but where problems and doubts about nationality and groups or cultures within the national boundaries have not been resolved. A personal identity and a national identity are scarcely appreciated, if one has them, but deeply desired and missed if one is without. In his novel *Smith's Gazelle*, Lionel Davidson has an amusing comment about Hamud, seemingly an unlikely candidate for a hero.

> He didn't expect to see such things himself. He knew his own function was essentially interim, but he was very glad now that he knew what it was. It wasn't given to many to know their true function in the world. The number of one-eyed, one-eared, broken-backed shepherds with no roofs to their mouths, who knew why they were born, could probably be counted on the fingers of one hand. All this was a matter for blessing and celebration and Hamud did so fairly continuously.

People with many more advantages than Hamud lack an understanding of identity and function and the attainment of such is a major objective of adult education.

SELF AND PERSONALITY

Carl Rogers has developed a theory of personality in which the self is the major concept. There are two structural aspects in Rogers' theory, the *organism* and the *self*. The *organism* is the location of all experience, of everything that is potentially available as awareness, and this totality of experience constitutes the phenomenal field which is the individual's frame of reference and can be known only to the person himself. Gradually a portion of the phenomenal field becomes differentiated, becomes the self. The *self* is an organized and consistent whole: though constantly changing, it is specific at any moment. In addition to the real self, each person has an ideal self, which is what that person would like to be. When there is considerable discrepancy between the real self and the ideal self, there is dissatisfaction in the individual. This dissonance can, and often is, a prime source of learning stimulus, but it can become so abrasive and threatening that the person may take various unhealthy ways of relieving the tension.

Rogers believes that both the organism and the self possess strong tendencies to actualize, and are subject to strong influences from the environment, especially the social environment. Conflicts may arise between the self and the organism. To survive, for example, the organism may act in certain ways—snatching food from others when on the verge of starvation, let us say—that are at variance or abhorrent to the self which strives to operate with values, or to obtain social approval that has no direct relationship to mere survival. A breach between the organism and the self can be as stimulating to learning, or as potentially destructive, as the tension between self and ideal self. Rogers is a therapist as well as an educator and his *nondirective* or *client-centered* therapy offers a means by which the subject examines the incongruences between the organism and the self or the self and the ideal self, and brings these into some coherence.

Maslow's attention has been on healthy and creative persons, those who have been eminently successful in self-actualization.[3] In studying the lives and achievements of such men and women as Lincoln, Eleanor Roosevelt, and Einstein, he has identified a number of distinguishing personality characteristics:

- They are realistic: they accept themselves, other people, and the natural world for what it is.
- They are problem-centered, rather than self-centered.
- They have a great deal of spontaneity, but also a need for privacy.
- They are autonomous and independent.
- They identify with mankind; most of them have had mystical or spiritual experiences.

- They have deep rather than superficial relationships with a few loved people.
- Their values and attitudes are democratic.
- They do not confuse ends with means, and their honor is not hostile.
- They resist conformity: they transcend the environment rather than just cope with it.
- They have a fund of creativeness.

These are characteristics that may be potential in the child, but only develop over time and some of them relatively late.

Maslow speaks "of a self, a kind of intrinsic nature which is very subtle, which is not necessarily conscious, which has to be sought for, and which has to be uncovered and then built upon, actualized, taught, educated."

Many other theorists, Freud for example, have theories of personality that implicate education and learning, and some of these will be referred to in Chapter 7.

A Paradox: Self and Humanness

In education for selfhood the infinite variability of human beings is stressed, as well as the emergence of an unique, independent being, distinct and separate from any other. Yet, paradoxically, the same route takes one past idiosyncrasy, where one is different from everybody else in the world, to the place where one discovers his species, that he is human. Carl Rogers said: "How does it happen that the deeper we go into ourselves as particular and unique, seeking for our own individual identity, the more we find the whole human species?" and Maslow:

Discovering your specieshood, at a deep enough level, merges with discovering your selfhood. Becoming (learning how to be) fully human means both enterprises carried on simultaneously. You are learning (subjectively experiencing) what you peculiarly are, how you are you, what your potentialities are, what your style is, what your pace is, what your tastes are, what your values are, what direction your body is going, where your personal biology is taking you, i.e., how you are *different from others*. And at the same time it means learning what it means to be a human animal like other human animals, i.e., how you are *similar* to others.[3]

Maslow goes on to contrast two different, "almost mutually exclusive" conceptions of learning. One is extrinsic learning, teacher planned, oriented, and controlled, reflecting the goals of the teacher and ignoring the goals of the learner. The other is learner planned and directed. This second conception we will deal with in detail in Chapter 10.

We will now review some of the relationships between the learner and his emerging self. None of these statements, of course, is original with the writer: he has borrowed extensively, particularly from the field of counseling.

The learner reacts to all experience as he perceives it. The learner is at the center of experience; in a very real sense he occupies a "private world." No one but the individual himself can truly feel an injury suffered in a factory, or the approval of his shop steward, or appreciate the emotion resulting from a pay raise or a demotion. However, experience is only potential; he can deny it to consciousness, distort it, or modify it. One man can react to an identical experience in a way markedly different from another. For an American watching a Western movie on television, observing the familiar scenes, and the highly stylized characters and action, the symbols and events have one kind of meaning. But when the viewer lives in some Asian or Eastern European country the same happenings may support his belief that lawlessness, murder, and disorder are a commonplace in the United States.

The learner reacts to experience as an organized whole. Later we shall encounter theories of learning that suggest that there are minute and discrete units of learning behavior involving a restricted part of the individual— for example, a nerve-muscle combination. However, most of the evidence from research now indicates that the total organism is involved in almost any activity. We now know a great deal more about psychosomatic medicine. Medical research is full of cases such as that of a schoolteacher who dreaded the visit of the inspector and who would wake up with a paralyzed leg on the occasion of his expected visits, but would be free of such a malady on the following day. A corollary of this notion is that what leads to the *organization*, rather than the *fragmentation*, of the person tends to support constructive behavior.

Learning (and any other behavior) is essentially an attempt by the person to satisfy his needs as he perceives them. Learning happens readily where the individual perceives that his needs can be satisfied by certain courses of action. This is not to argue that there can never be learning unless the person is interested or is aware of the value of what is to be learned. The adult student may not know in advance how fascinating or difficult a particular study may be. But it does mean that effective learning depends upon the learner's being fully engaged. When this occurs the accompanying emotion tends to support the achievement of the action. The intensity of the emotion will depend upon how important the person feels the expected achievement to be in terms of his own development.

The behavior of the learner can be fully understood only from his own point of view. Many a teacher or reformer has been perplexed or scornful because an adult is resistant to learning something new. This action, or refusal to act, can be understood only in the individual's own terms. If a workman were to develop radically different interests in art or religion or politics, this might cut him off from the intimacy of his circle of workmates. Peasants in underdeveloped countries have been taught new agricultural practices that increased their yield and income. But sometimes they have reverted to old practices and accepted a lower living standard when they discovered that certain old and valued social customs were destroyed or jeopardized by the new practice.

Any teacher or foreman must always try to understand how the individual views the learning situation. What does it mean to him?

Gradually within a human being there is the development of the self, and this development is crucial for all learning. All through life, but particularly in the days of infancy and early childhood, a portion of the total world of the individual becomes recognized as "me, myself, and I." First comes simple awareness of experience; then likes and dislikes. "I experience cold, or wet, and I dislike it." Of course the infant is not able to verbalize, but this seems to be his response. Later the reactions of others are added— "I hit my brother, and my mother called me a wicked boy." The self is built up not just with what is experienced directly but with the meanings concerning that experience that one may accept from others. Here is the stage for the drama on which Freudian interpretation is based, the interaction of the *id*, the *ego*, and the *alter ego*. The self may be based upon the perception of actual experience or feeling, or upon distortions. For example, what has been termed a "rejecting" mother may have built up a picture of herself as being loving toward her child. With this concept she is able to accept and live with the sensations of affection which she feels toward her child. However, the organic experience of dislike, distaste, or hatred toward her child is something which she must deny to her conscious self. Yet her need may be to express these feelings of distaste or worse by some aggressive act. She must search for some act which will bring release from intolerable tension, but her action must somehow conform to her view of the good mother. If a good mother in her view can be aggressive to her child only if the child has been *bad* and merits punishment, much of his behavior is seen as bad and punishable. This behavior is found beyond the parent-child relationship. One famous banker used to claim that he never foreclosed unless the man was given to dishonesty and dissolute habits. But it was also said of him that he found a surprising number of men who were thus afflicted!

All new experiences for the learner are symbolized and organized into some relationship to the self, or are ignored because there is no perceived relationship, or are denied organization, or given a distorted meaning be-

cause the experience seems inconsistent with the structure of the self. We are all aware of how selective is our attention. A friend recently joined a committee which is planning educational projects for the North American Indian. In the first week after beginning this work he was conscious that the radio and newspapers seemed to be full of references to the Indian, but he had never noticed these references before. One listens, sees, perceives selectively. Many sensory experiences are ignored until they are required to give meaning or content to some need of the individual. The seaman perceives meanings not seen by the landlubber; the Australian bushman can follow tracks imperceptible to anyone else.

Much is ignored and some experiences are even rejected and distorted. Notice that what is rejected is what is *inconsistent*, not just what is unflattering. The person whose self-concept is of failure and inadequacy cannot accept praise as being true or honest. He may need to be helped to a different picture of self before he is able to accept or assess either praise or blame.

Out of this condition flow many of the opportunities for both the teacher and the therapist.

Perhaps the most important task in learning is the development of a self that can deal with reality. The learner is able to move toward maturity, as discussed earlier, only when the self is able to perceive experience for what it is—not as threatening, or not in distorted symbols. This is not so obvious as it may seem. Many a person seems unable to deal with the subject of communism, or homosexual behavior, without employing distorted symbols. Or there may be outright rejection. The condition for effective learning is a self that is so constituted, and so *self-understood*, that even changes or a reorganization of that self can be faced without fear or flight.

Changes in Role

We have already referred to the importance of role, and role can be discerned along both vertical and horizontal axes.

Vertically, roles can be charted in relation to social-economic position. We have noted that the learning of children is vitally, sometimes drastically, affected by the economic position of the family and the kind of intellectual and sensory stimulus that is offered, even the kind of diet that is available. One's social-economic position in the later years is often related directly to one's expectations, and one's willingness to learn. People in the "poverty cycle" do not easily engage in learning activities, particularly if such activities are considered not for them, or useless, or an arena in which the poor are bound to fail. But as a man or woman may move upward, on the social-economic scale, he or she may see education as a prime means of upward mobility and be more ready to utilize it for this purpose as well as for other needs.

Horizontally, roles change as people age, women no less than men: student, wage earner, family member, husband or wife, grandparent, widow, or widower, pensioner. A number of psychologists have been contributing major papers in conceptualizing development stages and role changes, writers such as R. G. Kuhlen and Erik Erikson. For both sexes, there are many more vocational changes than used to be common. Each such change in economic or social role requires learning. At earlier and middle ages, it seems, people are readier to resort to education for help in role changes: older people seem more resistant at least to formalized learning activities. But this is clearly more a matter of personality than of age.

In one respect, many older persons do have a different self-concept. It is traditional to think of children and youth in the role of learner. However, it is still true that society in general, and most adults conceive of the older adult as a *nonlearner*. Howard McClusky says:

> Our theory is that this failure to internalize the learner role as a central feature of the self is a substantial restraint in the adult's realization of his learning potential. Or more positively stated, if and when an adult thinks that studying, learning, and the intellectual adventure is as much a part of life as his occupation and obligation to his family, he will be much more likely to achieve a higher level of intellectual performance.[4]

In all these vertical or horizontal changes, the human being is growing as a self, and his identity and special characteristics determine how readily and well he undergoes change.

McClusky has developed an ingenious formula S-O-R to indicate these shifts. He starts with the traditional S-R (Stimulus-Response) formula:

> The S-R formula is essentially a more recent version of antecedent association or connectionist theories of learning. . . . The S-R scheme works fairly well as long as learning is confined to simple kinds of learning. But it encounters several difficulties when learning is much more complex and the learner is more mature. Consequently, it is a much better explanation of the quasi-mechanical learning of early childhood than it is of the more complex learning of the adult years. The difficulty lies chiefly in the fact that the raw physical properties of the stimuli are not sufficient to account for individual differences in response. Something more, called the "intervening variable" is required. In terms of our formula, the intervening variable is the person -O-, the one stimulated and the one responding.

Then, referring to pedagogy, McClusky writes: "The neglect of the person (-O-) as learner explains why telling (-S-) is not necessarily teaching and why listening (-R-) is not necessarily learning. Both Input (-S-) and Outcome (-R-) must be anchored in the person who is supposed to be learning. This point is specifically relevant in the adult years when experience becomes more and more cumulative and behavior increasingly differentiated."

Some factors have special significance for learning and becoming. The "level of aspiration" and "social class" are two, and "time" and "money" are other factors that affect being and becoming. "Peaks" that happen in the lives of many people and the fact of decline are also significant.

LEVEL OF ASPIRATION

Much that has been said about the "level of aspiration" is now being comprehended under such notions as "self-image." We shall not deal with these related concepts fully, but they are very important for learning. What does the learner feel that he might achieve? How far does he think he can go? On the whole is he "optimistic" or "pessimistic" in his view about his own potentialities? Does his view about his possibilities correspond with reality?

We can see many examples of the way that "level of aspiration" modifies feelings and behavior.

It used to be thought, for example, that all people in tropical areas are indolent because of the heat and the ease of living. This is far from true. Some are, and some are not, as in other parts of the world. Indolence is not unusual in the tropics, but where it is found it may be a matter of inadequate diet and is frequently associated with the "self-image."

Our own culture is one in which there is quite general acceptance of such slogans as "The sky is the limit," "The incredible we will do now, the impossible will take a little longer." "Any man may become a millionaire," "Anyone may become president." But, though holding such notions in part, the adult may also have deep-seated feelings of personal inadequacy, all the more poignant because they conflict with what he feels he ought to be able to accomplish. After all, if you lived in another country and belonged to a restricted class, expecting always to live in that class and in that manner, you would not be assailed by guilt feelings for not doing better. In our relatively open society, such feelings are more common. Class and social position have much to do with anyone's level of aspiration.

EFFECTS OF SOCIAL CLASS

A number of studies have shown that the factor of social class may have as much to do with success in school as "intelligence." Boys and girls from certain homes tend to do better schoolwork and stay in school longer than boys and girls with the same aptitude, who come from other homes. Farmers of a certain kind make full use of agricultural extension services, others do not. By class we mean simply what Morris Ginsberg described in the *Encyclopedia of the Social Sciences:*

> . . . groups of individuals who, through common descent, similarity of occupation, wealth, and education, have come to have a similar mode of life, a similar stock of ideas, feelings, attitudes, and forms of behavior, and who, on any or all of these grounds, meet one another together on equal terms, and regard themselves altogether with varying degrees of explicitness, as belonging to one group.

It used to be commonly believed that there was no such thing as class in the equalitarian society of North America, that such things had been left behind in Europe. Robert and Helen Lynd, in their two books on *Middletown,* have many references to this. They observed:

> To most of its people in whatever group, "class differences" and "class consciousness" are vague, unfamiliar, and, if recognized, unpleasant and sinister terms. . . . Any talk about "class differences," a "class struggle," and similar unpleasant things are attributed to "reckless outside troublemakers." Officially Middletown scoffs at the "class struggle." [5]

This attitude went so far that anyone who was concerned about class differences was considered somewhat unreliable; he might have had some contact with subversive ideas. However, with the publication of early social studies, such as those of Lloyd Warner [6] and his associates in the 1940's this situation began to change. Nevertheless, a public opinion poll question employed not very many years ago which asked, "To what social class do you belong—the middle class, the upper class, or the lower?" drew the following answer:

- willing to identify themselves with upper class   6%
- willing to identify themselves with middle class 88%
- willing to identify themselves with lower class   6%

Where people place themselves may not be so accurate but is just as revealing as where they are placed by an outside observer. Warner's famous classification is:

Upper-upper	1.44%
Lower-upper	1.56%
Upper-middle	10.22%
Lower-middle	28.12%
Upper-lower	32.60%
Lower-lower	25.22%
(unknown)	.84%

This discrepancy between how people class themselves and where Dr. Warner placed them is exceedingly interesting. Of the utmost significance is the feeling of people in the different classes both about each other, and about other groups. One can and does hear such remarks as "All the people on this street are a nice class of people," "They are honest enough, but nobodies," "I would rather not have my daughter go to a party on that street," "Boy, are the kids in that school a bunch of squares," "They are too rich for my blood," "Down in that section they live like animals."

In the past decade and particularly among younger people, the notion of "social class" has been much more widely discussed. If invidious statements are made, it is usually the middle class, or "middle-class morality" which is the subject of scorn or criticism, most often by those who exist in or come from that class. But while "social class" appears and reappears as the subject of speeches, papers, and broadcasts, and more is known about it in a general way, many of the behaviors of people toward each other have not changed as much as some had hoped.

One is influenced in making or resisting changes in behavior by the very strength of one's group or cohesiveness of one's neighborhood. For example, James Duncan and Burton Kreitlow found that where the bonds of religion and ethnic societies are strong, the men are less likely to adopt new attitudes and new techniques.[7]

Where and how one lives has a crucial effect on feelings about events and activities. When adolescents become men and women they may change their economic and social position since mobility is one of the main features in our society. But whatever their social position, it markedly affects their feelings about participation in such activities as violin playing, golf, going to races, kinds of music that one listens to, art, reading or discussing philosophy, choice of magazines, courses in parent education, and so forth.

It is quite possible to conduct activities in most of these fields for people in most social positions. But the way in which they are approached and encouraged to take part must take into account their present feelings about such matters and the light in which that participation will be viewed by others around them.

Their social position will therefore also influence the satisfaction that they may receive from an activity, although other factors also modify satisfaction.

SOURCES OF SATISFACTION

We pointed out earlier that the individual will tend to persist in a task, no matter how difficult, if he is getting enough satisfaction from it. To continue may cause him physical pain, as in practicing rowing when his hands are covered with blisters, or boredom as he struggles to master a multitude of new words and constructions when he is preparing for a fellowship to study in another land. But if he is not gaining satisfaction on his own terms, he will tend to reject, to forget, to excuse himself. This is all part of "normal" behavior. The abnormal person may develop the ability to blot out whole scenes and episodes from his experience if, instead of satisfying, it is threatening or painful to him.

Satisfaction, whether it is in physical or intellectual activity, is itself an emotional matter, not an intellectual one. We *feel* satisfied, *and* this gives us some release from tension or we *feel* the discomfort of dissatisfaction.

In a class, or learning group, there are three sources of relationships in which satisfaction may or may not show itself. First, there is the relationship between student and teacher; second, the relationship between student and other students; and, third, the relationship between the student and the subject matter of the course.

In his relationship to the teacher, to his fellow students, and to the subject being studied, the student, consciously or unconsciously, always hopes to demonstrate his worth and to feel enlarged. Accordingly, if he perceives that he is under attack by the teacher, or threatened by his fellow students, or certain to appear in an unfavorable light in his handling of the subject matter, his mind and his energies will be engaged in covering up and protecting himself, not upon opening himself up to change and growth. How much can he be himself? Will the teacher accept anything he may bring to the discussion? Will his fellows think him queer if he really says what he thinks? These are questions he wants answered even before he permits his curiosity in the subject matter to be displayed.

In his approach to subject matter, whether as individual student or as class member, the student is an explorer, a discoverer. If he finds that there is no adventure, if the teacher is weary of exploration, or always has some *truth* up his sleeve to play if the student is not following a prescribed pattern, if the student is denied any opportunity for discovery, much of the satisfaction of learning is dissipated. Most of us have seen an older brother spoil a great adventure for a younger by revealing its climaxes too soon, or by belittling, by saying that all this is "old stuff." This can also happen in the classroom or laboratory.

Fellow class members can be seen as colleagues, collaborators, allies in a joint undertaking. If so, the class is a place where one can try out ideas—even though to try means to risk failure. But if class members are perceived as competitors or critics, as hostile, one will not venture much, or one may become aggressive in attacking them or in defending one's present position.

It is also possible, of course, that relationship with the class members may become so supporting, the attitude and experience of all class members may become so much alike, that little learning is possible. But such an eventuality will happen only if the teacher abdicates *his* responsibility and if the subject matter is not used with judgment and effectiveness.

There must be some dissatisfaction, unrest, desire for something else, if there is to be learning. It is in the balanced relationship of these three factors, that learning is made effective and enduring.

Strong feelings may also be associated with different subject matters. An engineer may get a sense of completeness, symmetry, well-being, delight in solving a difficult but orderly mathematical problem. When he is studying modern history or economics and at the end of a session there seem to be more unanswered questions than when he started, he may have feelings of actual alarm and pain, rather than well-being. In both cases the learning may be substantial and significant, but in the latter condition the result may be a conflict in feelings. And as we have seen, the presence of these feelings may sharply influence whether he will undertake a further learning experience in such a subject.

Maturity

We have considered the concept of maturity in an earlier chapter, but what was said is also relevant here. For some, maturity is an attitude, but for many others it is a ripening, a developing state. Several attempts have been made to measure maturity in general, in addition to measuring such attributes as "maturity in reading." Erikson [8] has postulated eight stages of ego development:

1. "Trust versus distrust" (early infancy)
2. "Autonomy versus doubt and shame" (later infancy)
3. "Initiative versus guilt" (early childhood)
4. "Industry versus inferiority" (middle childhood)
5. "Ego identity versus role diffusion" (adolescence)
6. "Intimacy versus isolation" (early adulthood)
7. "Generativity versus ego stagnation" (middle adulthood)
8. "Integrity versus despair" (late adulthood)

To measure maturity at any stage, therefore, one would try to assess to what degree the individual has reconciled the conflicts of duality in each stage. Buhler and Havighurst have developed notions of maturity as "ful-fillment." Allport lists six criteria for judging maturity in a person:

> The mature personality will 1. have a widely extended sense of self; 2. be able to relate himself warmly to others in both intimate and non-intimate contacts; 3. possess a fundamental emotional security and accept himself; 4. perceive, think, act with zest in accordance with outer reality; 5. be capable of self-objectification, of insight in humor; 6. live in harmony with a unifying philosophy of life.[9]

Buhler believes that there are four basic tendencies in life: (1) toward need satisfaction; (2) toward adaptive self-limitation; (3) toward creative expression; and (4) toward upholding internal order. But Havighurst raises questions about *when* fulfillment is probable or possible.

> Fulfillment is likely to come well before the end of life. In this case, how is a person to make a meaningful use of time in his later years? Most men and women in western cultures aim their life at a goal which is located in the middle years. Women feel fulfilled when their children are grown up and well started on their adult life. A working class man feels fulfilled when he has raised his family and paid for his house. A middle class man feels fulfilled when he has reached the peak of his work career and has assumed a place of civic or professional leadership.[10]

Men and women in other cultures may seek fulfillment in other ways and into older age: they tend to welcome, not dread, the later years. To the extent, in Western culture, that people achieve fulfillment early, the later years represent a decline and perhaps a severe anticlimax. We will deal later with learning associated with the fact of peaks, decline, and death.

The Notion of Becoming

Gordon Allport is the psychologist, and *philosopher*, who is most often associated with the concept of *becoming*. Allport starts with the potentialities in man as distinct from other animals. "Man alone," he reminds us, "has the capacity to vary his biological needs extensively and to add to them countless psychogenic needs reflecting in part his culture (no other creature has a culture) and his own life-style (no other creature worries about his life-style). . . . Immense horizons for individuality are added to the meagre neural equipment of lower animals. Man talks, laughs, feels bored, develops a culture, prays, has a fore-knowledge of death, studies theology, and strives for the improvement of his own personality."

Allport believes that the outlines of a psychology on *becoming* can be found only by looking within man as he develops over time. He is deeply concerned with changes that occur throughout life.

> In this intricate process of growth we encounter the puzzling question: What is the relative importance of earlier and later stages of development. We know that there are layers in each person that are archaic and composed of relatively isolated earlier systems. Yet there are also layers in which a man is fully adult, his psychological maturity corresponding to his age. The drama of human life can be written largely in terms of the friction engendered between earlier stages and later stages of development. Becoming is the process of incorporating earlier stages into later; or when this is impossible, in handling the conflict between early and later stages as well as one can.[9]

He discerns another continuing tension between that which makes a man unique and that which pushes him toward conformity. "All his life long this being will be attempting to reconcile two modes of becoming, the tribal and the personal; the one that makes him into a mirror, the other that lights the lamp of individuality within." Becoming, for Allport, is a fusion of many things, and it is always future oriented. "Personality," he says, "is not what one has but rather the projected outcome of his growth." It is this view, and this achievement in Allport, which makes him such an example of a continuing learner, open always to new concepts and possibilities, not to be adopted and then relinquished as fads, but to be tested for truth and utility.

Transactional Analysis

From time to time new systems or popularizations of treating stress in human beings are developed. One of those that has gained wide attention and application in North America is called *Transactional Analysis,* literally to analyze the transactions that occur between people. Transactional analysis is therapy, but it is not necessarily group therapy, although the group is often utilized as a setting. It involves people learning new relationships and ultimately each developing a reorganized self. Its directness and pragmatic flavor was once summed up by its founder, Eric Berne:[11] "Get well first and analyze later."

In transactional analysis there are four possible life positions, all of them involving a relationship with someone else. In the colloquial language favored, they are termed:

1. I'm not O.K.—you're O.K.
2. I'm not O.K.—you're not O.K.

3. I'm O.K.—you're not O.K.
4. I'm O.K.—you're O.K.

It is based on a conception that each of us is capable of displaying three ego states: parent, adult, and child. (Comparisons are often made with Freud's id, ego, and superego, but these are not at all identical concepts.) The *child* is fun-loving, expressive, and conscious of sex; the *adult* is rational and reasonable; the *parent* is critical, judgmental, the epitome of what used to be called the "Presbyterian conscience." A healthy person is one who has learned to keep the rational *adult* in control, but in league with and indulgent toward the lively *child*, while keeping at bay and under control the nagging *parent*.

This brief description, of course, does not do justice to an important movement of therapy and learning about the self, and the interested practitioner should review the growing number of published books and papers.

Transactional analysis is not without its critics. Some dislike the colloquial style of Berne and Thomas A. Harris, coauthors of the best-selling book *I'm O.K.—You're O.K.*[12] But their charges go deeper than dislike. They claim that transactional analysis is simplistic and distorting in its explanations of such a complicated phenomenon as the human mind. People, they claim, are not helped to deal with more serious problems and may develop unfounded confidence, which can lead them to error and later stress. However, others disagree, and there are thousands of people who claim they have been helped, not just to better health, but in learning to understand themselves and to develop a stronger, more integrated self.

Identity Crisis and Peak Experience

Earlier we quoted Havighurst as he described people who achieve "fulfillment" many years before the end of their lives, and for whom the rest of life is anticlimax.

Fulfillment and peak performance, for some, comes much earlier than the middle years. The lives, rarely triumphant and often sad, of "youthful prodigies," or the more common example of young people who before the age of twenty win adulation in sports or entertainment, and are destined never to have the same level of attention again, are well known. For other people, however, the highest point in performance comes later; it is no more than a rise on a plateau, and they continue to obtain satisfaction, if not public acclaim, from several or many activities.

The phenomenon of peaks and crises in life has been studied by novelists, poets, and dramatists as well as by social scientists, but it's still an area where there are few certainties. One of the most difficult and fascinating problems is the *crisis of identity* that affects people, often in the middle years—people who have advanced through earlier stages with poise and sureness. Some cases have been celebrated: King David, Saint Augustine, and in more recent years, Freud and Gandhi, but it has happened to thousands or millions of others lesser known. It is Erik Erikson who refers to and describes the *identity crisis* that may arise in life; others have termed it, a "destination crisis." Whatever the term, the adult educator is frequently in touch with learners who are agonizing or groping through such crises and hope that education may help them reach self-understanding and achieve a more coherent identity or self. In programs of continuing education for doctors, engineers, and other professional personnel, this crisis is often referred to as "midcareer slump" and it is stated that a significant objective for continuing education is reducing the likelihood of the depression appearing or eliminating it if it does appear. This is a matter which is receiving more attention generally, the problem and need are widespread and affect most people at least on some occasions. Unless the learner is able to pass through this crisis to a new self, much of the learning offered by adult education agencies may be of little use.

Some people have said that the most effective test of a human being is how well he adjusts to the changes of living; indeed, some have defined personality as: "The characteristic way in which an individual responds to the events of adult life." There is stability and persistence of the self, but there are also substantial changes. When Neugarten [13] reviewed research about stability of personality over the lifespan, she noted that some traits (like relative masculinity or masculine interests and attitudes) tend to persist. By contrast, evidence indicated that certain children who were hostile and dependent became friendly and outgoing as adults. Birren summarizes the data: "While there is measurable continuity in personalities from early childhood onwards, continual evolution of the personality over the life-span would seem to characterize the healthy, adaptive adult." [14]

Recently, a number of psychologists have been studying a range of changes in older people. For a while the concept of *disengagement*, that is of the older adult cutting himself off from family and society, was widely discussed, but it now seems clear that this does not happen, at least in gross forms, to even a majority of adults. It has been claimed, however, that personality changes are more variable over the adult years than are mental abilities. Even these changes are not uniform since, for example, it seems that personal values and vocational interests remain stable, whereas self-regarding attitudes change markedly. It is possible that health and energy, and what some call ego energy, constitute the chief determinants.

Everyone faces the fact of decline, some with sorrow, fear, or resignation, others viewing it simply as an altered state and not a lesser one, a time when they are not compelled to do some things and are freed to do others. Some not only live well in their older lives, but have a more benevolent picture of the past, as if they have been glad to shed some unattained, perhaps irrational goals. In one study of men entering and undergoing retirement, the older men presented a more benign picture of their early family lives than the younger. The investigator reported: "The pre-retirement period is characterized by a sense of insecurity and instability. It seems that after retirement the individual has less need to be defensive in his relations with others."

"Successful" adjustment to aging has been studied, and there are both inner, psychological criteria (i.e., self-regard and contentment) and outer social or behavioral criteria. On both counts, some of the persons who have been described as "self-actualizers" meet these criteria well.

The concept of *peak-experience* [15] is usually associated with Abraham Maslow. By *peak-experience*, Maslow means not just the apex of the curve of performance in any behavior, but something much more specific. He is talking about the finest achievements of "self-actualizing" people. They include parental experiences, "mystic or oceanic experiences, nature, aesthetic perception, the creative moment, the therapeutic or intellectual insight, the orgasmic experience, certain forms of athletic fulfillment. . . . These and other moments of highest happiness and fulfillment, I shall call the peak experiences." In his memorable book and papers on this subject, he included many experiences which are usually referred to as religious. In developing a psychology of the fully functioning human being, Maslow did not see any opposition to a psychology for the average, but one that "transcends it and can in theory incorporate all its findings in a more inclusive and comprehensive structure which includes both the sick and the healthy, both deficiency, Becoming and Being." Maslow makes the point that what may be common in the experience of exceptional people does happen at peak times in the experience of the rest of us and should therefore be recognized. He describes certain common attributes of self-actualizing people and attributes of other people at their highest moments:

- They are more able to perceive the world as if it were independent not only of them but also of human beings in general. They can more readily look on nature as if it were there in itself and for itself, and not simply as if it were a human playground put there for human purposes.
- Repeated expression makes the perception richer; it does not lead to boredom, loss of attention, or familiarization effects. (Repeated exposures to a great painting brings increased enjoyment, repeated exposure to bad painting will make it look even less beautiful.)
- Lovers can see potentialities in each other that other people are blind to. "Love is not blind"; it is probable that love is more perceptive than nonlove.

- Perception can be unmotivated, impersonal, desireless, unselfish; it can be object-centered, not ego-centered; it can have an independent reality of its own not dependent upon the beholder.
- The peak-experience is felt as a self-validating, self-justifying moment which carries its own intrinsic value with it.
- The peak-experience is felt as good and desirable and is never evil or painful or undesirable.
- The emotional reaction in the peak-experience has a special flavor of wonder, of awe, of humility before the experience.

If peak-experiences affected only a few great persons, one could admire and pass on. The fact that, at least on some occasions, many people reach them suggests that one aim of an education for being is the development of people and environments in which peak-experiences can be expected and encouraged.

Learning to Die

On his last tape Abraham Maslow said: "I've just finished a revision of my *Motivation and Personality*." It wasn't published until he could say, "This is complete, this is the way I want it to be." His book had become a summary of his lifelong struggle to prove that "wonderful people can and do exist—even though in very short supply and even though having feet of clay." The first copy reached him the day before a massive blockage stopped his heart.

Maslow could not have known the hour, but it is probable that, had he the choice, no other activity would have suited him so well to occupy his last days. It is not given to everyone to close out his life so triumphantly, but everyone has the chance, and perhaps the obligation, to learn how to live well and approach death well.

At an even earlier age, Maslow had been well prepared: "I had really spent myself. This was the best that I could do, and here was not only a good time to die but I was even willing to die." This was not resignation; for him it was completeness.

Others aren't prepared for death; they fear it or rage against it. They echo Dylan Thomas: "Do not go gentle into that good night. . . . Rage, rage against the dying of the light." And, except for the clergy, most professional literature used to exclude significant references to death, as until very recent times it excluded talk about sex. Nothing was certain but "death and taxes," but you only talked about taxes. Death would come, but it was not a subject for conversation, research, or education. The subhead "Learning to Die" only a few years ago would probably have evoked outrage in some, nervous or scatological humor in others, and fear in still more. But the fact of death, attitudes to death, preparation to cope with the death of others and with one's own death, these are now subjects for research and educational courses in more and more places.

The past decade has been an age of youth; it has also been an age of death: by accident, by senseless killing, by one's own private act, by slow decay. Soon the median age of the living will be in the fifties; older people in numbers and percentages will continually rise; and the certainty of death will mark our times. But people before us always lived with death's shadow or certainty, nor could they expect to live very long. The fact and inevitability of death need not be more fearsome than the dread that it might come, perhaps less so.

One of the findings of research about men and women dying is that, unless they are drugged or in a coma, in the process people are themselves: the interval of dying is psychologically consistent, sometimes an exaggerated extension of the individual's personality and life-style. The ways in which he has always coped, defended, adjusted, and interacted remain with him, coloring his inner life and characterizing his behavior.

University or college courses and seminars on death were a rarity, attracting few participants, but both the number and size of the seminars are growing. In the university programs that he offers, Edwin Schneidman [16] tries to bring about an understanding of death in all its aspects, and to de-romanticize it. He notes that all deaths can be placed in three categories: (1) intentioned (2) subintentioned, and (3) unintentioned. He believes that a better understanding of the intention of the person vis-à-vis his own death is a foundation that all should have and one that is essential for full growth of the self, as well as rational behavior toward cessation of the self. Among the *intentioned* he includes those individuals who play a direct and conscious role in effecting their own demise. For the *unintentioned* death happens, it is neither willed nor hurried. The *subintentioned* he believes is characteristic of a majority of deaths. The decedent plays some covert or unconscious role in hastening his own demise. There are a variety of behavior patterns such as poor judgment, imprudence, excessive risk-taking, neglect of self, disregard of health regimen, abuse of alcohol, misuses of drugs. Such persons *might* benefit from programs of education or therapy that face directly and squarely the fact of death.

Most observers about death point out that it touches those who go and those who remain, and that the burden of the survivor may be the greater. Arnold Toynbee's reflection has often been quoted:

I guess that if, one day, I am told by my doctor that I am going to die before my wife, I shall receive the news not only with equanimity but with relief. This relief, if I do feel it, will be involuntary, I shall be ashamed of myself for feeling it, and my relief will, no doubt, be tempered by my concern and sorrow for my wife's future after I have been taken from her. All the same, I do guess that, if I am informed that I am going to die before her, a shameful sense of relief will be one element in my reaction. . . . This is, as I see it, the capital fact about the relation between living and dying. There are two parties to the suffering that death inflicts; and, in the appointment of this suffering, the survivor takes the brunt.

While Schneidman does not disagree with such a conclusion, he does feel that death ought to be faced literally and not romanticized. He takes the position that only when so faced can the genuine self develop, and that, *perhaps* (and he makes no strong claim), *perhaps* such real, rational views of life and death will act in subtle ways to deter the suicide and perhaps some of the evil deaths by murder, violence, massacre, and genocide.

Other educational programs about death, often carried out in short intensive seminars, also concentrate on the real, rather than on the mythical. Some of these courses take a comparative approach and show how men and women in others ages, or in other cultures, go about living and dying.

Some of them use word games, set problems for discussion, such as

A society that denies life ends by accepting death.
A society that denies death begins to accept life.

True or romantic?

How ought a person to die? What is the proper response to our own mortality and the loss of friends and enemies? Does "dignity" require that we maintain life against all consequences, or that we assist men to die on their own terms?

Usually matters such as bizarre and costly funeral arrangements, and such ethical problems as, if a person has become a "human vegetable" should life be sustained by every possible means or should it be terminated are considered.

Objectives of these courses seem to be similar: to enlarge the concept of self in its full dimension and prepare people for cessation.

REFERENCES

1. UNESCO, *Learning to Be* (Paris: UNESCO, 1972).
2. Gordon Allport, P. E. Vernon, and G. Lindzey, *Study of Values* (Boston: Houghton Mifflin, 1960).

3. Abraham Maslow, *Religions, Values and Peak-Experiences* (Columbus: Ohio State University Press, 1964).
4. Howard McClusky, "An Approach to Differential Psychology of the Adult Potential" in *Adult Learning and Instruction* (Washington: Adult Education Association of the U.S.A., 1970).
5. Robert S. Lynd and Helen M. Lynd, *Middletown* (New York: Harcourt, Brace and Company, 1929).
6. W. Lloyd Warner and Paul S. Lund, *Social Life of a Modern Community* (New Haven: Yale University Press, 1943).
7. James Duncan and Burton Kreitlow, "Selected Cultural Characteristics and the Acceptance of Educational Programs and Practices," *Rural Sociology*, December, 1954.
8. Erik Erikson, *Identity and the Life Cycle, Psychological Issues*, Monograph No. 1, 1959.
9. Gordon Allport, *Becoming* (New Haven: Yale University Press, 1955).
10. Robert Havighurst and Ruth Albrecht, *Older People* (New York: David McKay, 1954).
11. Eric Berne, *Games People Play* (New York: Grove Press, 1964).
12. Thomas A. Harris, *I'm O.K.—You're O.K.* (New York: Harper & Row, 1967).
13. Bernice Neugarten and R. J. Havighurst, *Society and Education* (Boston: Allyn and Bacon, 1962).
14. J. E. Birren, *The Psychology of Aging* (Englewood Cliffs, Prentice-Hall, 1964).
15. Abraham Maslow, *op. cit.*
16. Edwin S. Schneidman, *Psychology Today*, Vol. IV., No. 3.

SUGGESTED READING

Bandura, A., and Walters, R. H. *Social Learning and Personality Development.* New York: Holt, Rinehart and Winston, 1963.

Bloom, Benjamin S. *Stability and Change in Human Characteristics.* New York: John Wiley and Sons, Inc., 1964.

Erikson, Erik H. *Childhood and Society*, 2nd ed. New York: W. W. Norton and Company, 1963.

Erikson, Erik H. *Insight and Responsibility.* New York: W. W. Norton and Company, 1969.

Glasser, William M.D. *Reality Therapy.* New York: Harper and Row, 1965.

Krasner, L., and Ullman, L. P., *Research in Behavior Modification.* New York: Holt, Rinehart and Winston, 1965.

Maslow, Abraham H. *Motivation and Personality.* New York: Harper and Row, 1954.

Maslow, Abraham H. *Toward a Psychology of Being.* Princeton, New Jersey: Van Nostrand, 1962.

May, Rollo. *Love and Will.* New York: W. W. Norton and Company, 1969.

Schutz, William C. *Joy: Expanding Human Awareness.* New York: Grove Press, Inc., 1967.

7

Theories of Learning

It was traditional in the older textbooks to start with an historical sketch because scholarly works were expected to begin that way. But in this book we have attempted to eliminate everything that is not directly useful to the practitioner. It is our view, however, that some knowledge of learning theories is essential for every practitioner so he can understand why certain methods or techniques can be applied, and can understand, apply, or reject new proposals that are made to him.

In this chapter we will not sample all educational theories, but just a selected few which are most applicable to adult education, and which the practitioner will encounter frequently in his reading. We will review the evolution of theory during the entire century, emphasizing a few theoretical contributions that are receiving greatest current attention. Some of them, such as *cybernetics*, are not so much theories of learning as ways of describing a process so that we may better understand what is occurring.

Use of Theory

The research worker needs a set of assumptions as a starting point to guide what he does, to be tested by experiment or to serve as a check on observations and insights. Without any theory his activities may be as aimless and wasteful as the early wanderings of the explorers in North America, or one's attempts to find one's way, without a street map, around a city he is visiting for the first time.

A well-conceived system can encourage both study and action, as noted by Edna Heidbreder in her book *Seven Psychologies*:

Systems of psychology are to be regarded not as statements of psychological knowledge but as tools by which psychological knowledge is produced; not as accounts of scientific fact, but as a means of acquiring scientific fact. . . . For scientific knowledge does not merely accumulate; it is far more likely to grow about hypotheses that put definite questions and which act as centers of organization in the quest of knowledge. . . . Frequently the victories of science are won through the use of conjectures that become the basis of active and ingenious research especially directed toward the particular body of evidence which will prove or disprove the point of issue.[1]

Most of us are ready to concede that a research worker ought to be guided by theory. The librarian or night-school teacher needs it, too. He also is dependent upon sound theory if he is concerned in the slightest degree with the improvement of his own work. Let us start with an obvious example: A diving coach has a student who is learning to do the one-and-a-half forward somersault. The coach gives careful instruction; perhaps he demonstrates correct form. The student tries it once, twice, three times, ten times, thirty times, without any noticeable improvement. He doesn't have the feel of it. Then, perhaps on the thirty-seventh attempt, his body rolls and opens out at the precise split second and he makes a tolerable entry into the water. Much more important, from that time on he is always able to perform this action. He can improve the grace of the act, but he never again needs to learn the combination of muscular-sensory actions necessary for its execution. Now, how does the coach go about teaching another boy to do the same thing? By the same long series of trials? But a coach who knows even the rudiments of *Gestalt* theory will understand that for some kinds of learning, being told about performance or even thinking about performance is not enough; the senses and muscles must actually try out, trace out, "learn" the pattern of performance. Understanding this, even in elementary fashion, will assist the coach to devise means by which the young athlete can go through the movement until his senses and muscles learn the pattern, while he is protected somewhat from the consequences of failure. This is why a "safety belt" is used for teaching many athletic skills. Protected in this way, the body is put through the correct motions and acts.

Some knowledge of theory always aids practice. It also may stimulate new forms of practice, just as the alchemists' theory that baser metals could be transmuted into gold stimulated the development of chemistry. The theory that the earth was round stimulated exploration, trade, and the opening of the new world. Practitioners are sometimes wary of theory, because, since it is an attempt to explain what is not yet fully understood, it frequently contains (is almost certain to contain) some error. Beware of the theorist, so we say, because later on he will be proved wrong in some of his speculations. But wrong theory is not necessarily destructive in its results. Nor does the lack of theory guarantee against undesirable consequences. Naturally one needs to approach any theory, particularly any new theory, with caution. To what extent does it seem to fit the facts? But in terms of its main effect, whether or not a theory is correct in every particular has little to do with the possible value of that theory in practice. It is possible that much of what Sigmund Freud once hypothesized as the basis for human behavior will be found in error. But the effect of Freud's work has been that most or all of us think or act in a different way than we did before; it has had enormous consequences for practice.

Just as we need not be upset because time may prove that there were errors in a certain theory, we do not need to reject one hypothesis that may appear to be contradictory. There is not *one* theory of learning, there are *several* theories of learning.

We have noticed earlier that the word *learning* is used to cover a wide variety of experiences, such as memorizing a poem, acquiring a vocabulary, finding out how to use a typewriter, becoming more able at reasoning and deciding, acquiring the skill of swimming, acquiring preferences or prejudices, changing one's behavior or attitude toward other people. These activities are not all alike; indeed, we may be making an error of some magnitude in including all of them under a single term "learning." One psychologist, E. C. Tolman, has suggested that there may be as many as seven different kinds of learning. So our dilemma in gaining a theory of learning that will withstand critical inquiry may in part be one that we ourselves have created. Until we can reach more agreement about what constitutes learning we ought to expect that there will be more than one theory to explain all that is meant by the term.

Actually, most of the theories, though they show discrepancies and conflict, tend to be supplementary and complementary rather than antagonistic. Often it is really a case of *both and* or *yes but* rather than this-cannot-be-so-because-the-opposite-is-true. And most of the theorists draw closer together when they are formulating implications for the teacher or practitioner. Indeed, one of the gains that the practitioner studying the theories of learning may make is that he will find many of the *same* principles and practices emphasized from different points of view. As time goes on these theories seem to be tending toward reinforcement rather than mutual destruction, or the kind of stalemate or paralysis which is sometimes the result of conflict.

Our plan, then, is to look briefly at some characteristic theories of learning, note both their similarities and their differences, see how they help us to build generalizations from what we have ourselves experienced, and how they answer our questions or pose some fresh ones. With patience we may be able to struggle to some kind of formulation for ourselves that will not only give us better footing for our present work but help us keep up with the explorations going on all around us.

The main source of good theory is good practice—the best theory is a distillation of practice. Accordingly, Chapter 8, which deals with some major fields of practice, should be considered as a complement to this chapter.

Most of the scholarly disciplines also contribute to theory. We are accustomed to speak of psychology as if it constituted learning theory, as if learning were a subfield, or "belonged to" psychology. Indeed for C. L. Hull [2] and many other psychologists, learning and behavior were hardly to be distinguished. But many disciplines have contributed to and do contribute to learning theories, particularly sociology, anthropology, psychiatry, history, economics, and also physics and chemistry. And learning theory first emerged from philosophy and theology. What one thought about the nature, origin, character, and destiny of man determined what one postulated about how he learned.

Philosophers and Learning

In his introduction to the book *Modern Philosophies and Education*, John S. Brubacher wrote:

> The study of educational philosophy has flourished in the twentieth century as never before in the whole history of education. Earlier centuries, no doubt, produced a fair share of famous essays on education, but relatively few of these essays were philosophical in exposition and intent. . . . The twentieth century, by contrast, has produced almost a plethora of publications on philosophy of education.[3]

We shall attempt here no systematic treatment of any major philosophic points of view, but instead shall simply single out some examples of philosophical positions that have specially affected learning theory and practice for adults.

One such group is the Catholic philosophers, men like Etienne Gilson and Jacques Maritain, and a long line of Catholic educationalists. Maritain has summarized the central Thomist position on education:

> Knowledge is a value in itself and an end in itself; and truth consists in the conformity of the mind with reality—with what is or exists independently of the mind. The intellect tends to grasp and conquer being. Its aim and its joy are essentially disinterested. . . . There is no other foundation for the educational task than the eternal saying: It is the truth that sets men free. . . . Education is fully human education only when it equips (the learner) for truth and makes him capable of judging according to the worth of evidence, of enjoying truth and beauty for their own sake, and of advancing

toward wisdom and some understanding of those things which bring him to intimations of mortality.[4]

Some Catholic teachers, such as Dr. M. M. Coady of the Antigonish Movement in Canada, have emphasized that adult education "must begin with the economic." Unless learning is imbedded in man's everyday pre-occupations, it may neither take hold nor move forward. But this does not mean that materialism occupies the entire field or sets the limits for adult learning. For Coady, learning is to make men "masters of their own destiny":

We have no desire to create a nation of shopkeepers, whose only thoughts run to groceries and to dividends. We want our people to look into the sun, and into the depths of the sea. We want them to explore the hearts of flow-ers and the hearts of their fellow-men. We want them to live, to love, to play and pray with all their being. We want them to be men, whole men, eager to explore all the avenues of life and to attain perfection in all their faculties. Life for them shall not be in terms of merchandising but in terms of all that is good and beautiful, be it economic, political, social, cultural or spiritual. They are the heirs of all the ages and of all the riches yet con-cealed. All the findings of science and philosophy are theirs. All the crea-tions of art and literature are for them. They will usher in the new day by attending to the blessings of the old. They will use what they have to secure what they have not.[5]

A second group, sometimes referred to as "Aristotelians," is best repre-sented by Mortimer Adler. Adler's speaking and writing are distinguished by two characteristics: the directness, forcefulness, certitude of his credo and assumptions, and his emphasis upon the learning of adults. No one need be unaware of his position for long:

The *ultimate* ends of education are the same for all men at all times and everywhere. . . . They are absolute and universal principles . . . absolute in the sense that they are not relative to contingent circumstances of time and place, universal in the sense that they are concerned with essentials.[6]

One may be attracted by such claims, or repelled, but they are not easily ignored. About method he makes the same absolute claims as about aim:

Similarly, it can be said that educational means in *general* are the same for all men at all times and everywhere. If the *ultimate* ends of education are its first principles, the means *in general* are its secondary principles and the scope of the philosophy of education goes no further—*to know these first and secondary principles in an absolute and universal manner.*[7]

Adler is equally insistent that learning is for the mature, and for developing maturity:

> In America today we are blinded by a romantic adoration of the child. We thus come to suppose that the most important problems of education concern the rearing of children, and we exaggerate the importance of the educational institutions which deal with children. But clearly the beginning of anything is not as important as the end, and the beginning can only be well thought about in terms of the end. The end of education is one of overcoming the deficiencies of immaturity.[8]

His insistence upon rigorous logic in the formulation of ideas about learning has been a spur to all—alike for those who believe as he does and those who are opposed—to state their positions clearly. The best-known example of an adult activity influenced by Adler is the Great Books program with its characteristic form of study based on the examination of "fundamental" problems and principles, employing a Socratic questioning style. (It should be added, of course, that although this program has been much influenced by Adler, many with a different philosophy participate in it.)

But if the "Aristotelians" have prodded and provoked friends and foes alike to further efforts, a similar claim can also be made for Dewey, Kilpatrick, and other experimentalists (or instrumentalists or pragmatists, for all these terms have been applied). Brubacher in the introduction already quoted asked, "What is the reason for this greatly augmented interest in educational philosophy?" and answered his own question, "Perhaps the simplest answer is the rise of 'progressive education' as a *cause célèbre.*"

In sixty years or more of prodigious scholarship, demonstration, and teaching, John Dewey achieved enormous influence over the theory and practice of education. Author of some of the most important books written on education (for example, *Democracy and Education, How We Think, Human Nature and Conduct, The School and Society*), author in his very last years of such a wide range of papers as "Democratic Faith and Education," "Authority and Resistance to Social Change," "Liberty and Social Control," "The Relation of Science and Philosophy as the Basis of Education," Dewey has both so many followers *and* critics that a balanced assessment of his achievement is hardly possible at present. But of his influence there is no doubt, in rethinking educational goals, in reshaping curricula, in underscoring the social context of thinking and learning, in bringing about shifts in method, in emphasizing science not only as a subject but as method and ethic:

The sciences had to battle against entrenched forces to obtain recognition in the curriculum. In a formal sense, the battle has been won, but not yet in a substantial sense. For scientific subject matter is still more or less segregated as a special body of facts and truths. The full victory will not be won until every subject and lesson is taught in connection with its bearing upon creation and growth of the kind of power of observation, inquiry, reflection, and testing that are the heart of scientific intelligence. Experimental philosophy is at one with the genuine spirit of scientific attitude in the endeavor to obtain for a scientific method this central place in education.[9]

Like Adler and Catholic theologians in this one respect at least, Dewey often emphasized the importance of adult learning:

Education must be reconceived, not as merely a preparation for maturity (whence our absurd idea that it should stop after adolescence) but as a continuous growth of the mind and a continuous illumination of life. In a sense the school can give us only the instrumentalities of mental growth, the rest depends upon an absorption and interpretation of experience. Real education comes after we leave school and there is no reason why it should stop before death.[10]

William Kilpatrick had also had an impact on theory and practice in learning. Kilpatrick's emphasis was always upon living, upon a curriculum based on living, upon a school that provided rich experiences of living. "In a democracy," said Kilpatrick, "it is self-directing personalities that we try to build, the kind that can carry forward life ever more successfully in a developing world. Such a world calls for the experimental outlook and an experimentally directed education." The child "learns only and exactly his *own* responses."

I learn what I learn as I accept it. I learn it in the degree that I live it, in the degree that I count it important to me, and in the degree that I understand it and can fit it in with what I already know. And what I learn I build at once into character—that, in fact, is what to learn means.[11]

This is a philosophy and practice deeply concerned with living, morals, ethics, and character. His talk and writing were usually about the child, but there are many applications of his thinking to adults. One example of many is that in his description of how the school "must be a place where living goes on, the best and finest type of living we can help people create," he set down many of the conditions essential for an adult residential school.

Kilpatrick wrote often about individuality or selfhood and how it developed as the result of interaction with other selves, in a social process.

How one becomes aware of self, how one knows about it, the values of the self—these are all social in origin. The self, from one point of view, is an expanding organization of experience and thought.

Education conceived in this way does not end at any prescribed period. It is as meaningless to say that a person has finished his education as that he has finished his experience of art. "I don't need a book, I already have one," is a very old joke; it is not a view of education that is satisfying in any respect.

Eduard Lindeman, through his teaching and writing, had an effect both upon the practice of social work and of adult education. Lindeman was deeply concerned with the relationship of study and action, and with the function of education in a democratic society.

> Learning which is combined with action provides a peculiar and solid enrichment. If, for example, you are interested in art, you will gain much more if you paint as well as look at pictures and read about the history of art. If you happen to be interested in politics, don't be satisfied with being a spectator: participate in political action. If you enjoy nature, refuse to be content with the vicarious experiences of naturalists; become a naturalist yourself. In all of these ways learning becomes an integral part of living until finally the old distinction between life and education disappears. In short, life itself becomes a perpetual experience of learning.[12]

A society that neglects education, for all people of all ages, runs a great risk, for action may thus be governed by expediency or worse. Education for adults is not just a pleasant conceit; it is an imperative if democracy is to survive, Lindeman believed.

> The key word of democracy is participation. It is at this point that education enters the equation. Social action is in essence the use of force or coercion. The use of force and coercion is justified only when the force is democratic and this means that it must be derived from intelligence and reason. Adult education thus turns out to be the most reliable instrument for social actionists. If they learn how to educate the adherents of their movement, they can continue to utilize the compelling power of a group and still remain within the scope of democratic behavior. When they substitute something other than intelligence and reason, social action emanates as sheer power and soon degenerates into habits which tend toward an anti-democratic direction. Every social-action group should at the same time be an adult-education group, and I go even so far as to believe that all successful adult education groups sooner or later become social-action groups.[13]

Perhaps the most eloquent of educators in this century was Sir Richard Livingstone. He did not produce a systematic body of theory, but his ideas about adult learning have been widely quoted and practiced. One idea he advanced frequently is that only in adulthood is it possible for some kinds of learning to happen. Children and youths have not the requisite experience on which learning must build. In this he follows Aristotle's "A boy cannot be a philosopher," and Newman, writing in *An Essay in Aid of a Grammar of Assent*, who said:

> Let us consider, too, how differently young and old are affected by the words of some classic author, such as Homer or Horace. Passages which to a boy are but rhetorical commonplaces, neither better nor worse than a hundred others which any clever writer might supply, which he gets by heart and thinks very fine, and imitates, as he thinks, successfully in his own flowing versification, at length come home to him, when long years have passed, and he has had experience of life, and pierce him, as he had never before known them, with their sad earnestness and vivid exactness.[14]

Learning that is necessary for good citizenship has a special importance for the mature, Livingstone believed:

> What lovers of paradox we British are! Youth studies but cannot act; the adult must act, and has no opportunity of study; and we accept the divorce complacently. But action and thought, living and learning, naturally belong together and should go hand in hand. Instruction in civics at school, if you will. But when the children are adults and have votes, let such instruction be available so that their votes can be used with intelligence.[15]

A central idea for Livingstone was the necessity of the study of the "first rate." He quoted Whitehead: "Moral education is impossible without the habitual vision of greatness." This is true of *all* education, adds Livingstone:

> The way to acquire a good taste in anything, from pictures to architecture, from literature to character, from wine to cigars, is always the same—be familiar with the best specimens of each. Knowledge of the first-rate gives direction, purpose and drive; direction, because it shows what is good as well as what is bad; purpose, because it reveals an ideal to pursue; drive, because an ideal stirs to action. . . . The sight of goodness in life or in literature or history gives a standard and a challenge.[16]

A philosophy that gained attention during and after World War II and that has had some impact on education is usually termed *existentialism*. This philosophy is concerned with the unfolding of the individual, as a whole, *in the situation in which he finds himself*. It is learning directed to the whole man, for the whole of life. And it is about existence, omitting nothing that bears on existence. The existentialist, like the psychiatrist, aims to free man from his isolation, from his anonymity, to free his mind from confusions that prevent him from accepting himself and releasing his own powers. Every man, it is urged, should try to learn what it is to be a man, including all the limitations as well as the potentialities. In the end, as one writer has put it, what counts is "education for character, for the habits that enable a man both to remain free and to remain with the truth when he finds it."

These are meager samples of what men are writing and saying about educational philosophy. But they suggest what can be found in this field. It is exceedingly rewarding for a teacher of adults to probe deeply into the speculations of such men and to make detailed comparisons of the main claims of each.

In recent years more of the issues have been identified and studied, as *subjects* or problems and not so much as the *credos* of conflicting ideologies. An example of such thinking was the publication of the Adult Education Association of the U.S.A. entitled *Seeking Common Ground in Adult Education.*[17]

Most of the recent debates about education have been largely philosophical in nature—that is, they have been more about values than about techniques.

As strong "new" disciplines such as psychology are developing, the uniqueness and special qualities of each are inevitably emphasized. In this way, psychological learning theory becomes separate and distinct from other learning theory. However, the counter-trend is now appearing with the realization that no discipline—particularly an isolated, insulated discipline—can have or hold all truth. The insights from many fields of knowledge about learning and how each may reinforce or stimulate speculation in other fields are beginning to be appreciated. This trend may be leading toward a science —the science of Mathetics, to which we referred in Chapter 1. One distinction of Mathetics is that all relevant disciplines in the natural sciences, social sciences, and humanities that have anything to say about learning theory are utilized.

New Voices

Much theorizing and many concepts are arising outside of North America. This is not a recent phenonemon; early in the century, men like Rabindranath Tagore and Gandhi in India developed formulations that have affected practice in many countries. The difference today is the possibility of diffusion, the fact that such influences may be heard or monitored in many foreign countries almost as soon as they are current in the home country.

An influential voice in Africa is Julius K. Nyerere, President of Tanzania, whose vision of education "for self-reliance" has been studied for possible application in many other countries both inside and beyond Africa.

Two men who have worked in Latin America have also received general attention. Ivan Illich [18] was born in Europe, but that part of his career in Puerto Rico and in Cuernavaca, Mexico, has won attention. Illich is primarily an analyst and critic, not a theorist. He has been incensed at the negative power exercised by some institutions and has been concerned particularly about the institution of schooling, its exorbitant costs in some countries, as well as the control of the school over entrance to jobs and upward social mobility.

Illich has frequently emphasized the need for alternatives to the present system without advocating many, although his own work has shown that adults who are well motivated make as much progress in a year as might be accomplished in six years of elementary school. If resources are pitifully scarce it may be the most sensible practice to provide basic education for some persons when they are adolescents or adults. He has advocated the use of a basic *educredit* so that all human beings, at any age, can utilize the credit to "purchase" an education, rather than be obliged to take a prescribed portion in their earliest years.

One cannot find many places where Illich's proposals are worked out in practice, but few planners or organizers of educational systems are likely to operate without at least listening to his basic critique or considering his recommendation that more autonomy be given to learners.

Paulo Freire [19] is a Brazilian educator whose ideas have been worked out in several countries in Latin America. Freire is much more than an analyst or critic: he has developed a pedagogy for adults, a pedagogy for *free* men. Freire says that education can be planned to result in self-affirmation or to result in oppression. He distinguishes what he calls *conscientization* which leads men to freedom, and control over their own destiny, from a "banking" concept of education that ends in conformity. One is based on human dignity and enhances that dignity; the other, Freire says, uses men as instruments, and tools. The "banking" concept of education is highly structured, with the goal of dominating:

- The teacher and the students are taught
- The teacher knows everything and the students know nothing
- The teacher thinks and the students are thought about
- The teacher talks and the students listen

Education for freedom, Freire says, is problem posing; it strives for the emergence of consciousness; it attempts to achieve a critical intervention in reality; it employs the method of dialogue; and it ends not in talk but in action.

Conscientization, therefore, goes beyond the possession of a few basic skills of learning. Becoming literate, to Freire, means much more than acquiring technical skills in reading, writing, and mensuration; instead, it becomes a process based on and implying values, and it leads to social and political acts. Adults in Brazil, and later in Chile and Bolivia, who became literate in programs with which Freire was associated, did not stop when they could decipher a few words or sentences; instead, they moved on to try to grapple with their adverse human conditions. The words selected by Freire for beginning study are not just simple words or frequently encountered words, they are words that have a high "valence" of emotional power calculated to arouse the learners.

Freire also distinguishes between a magical or unreflective approach to the world and a critical vision of reality. Through study, the learner modifies his basic perspectives. It is a critical, active process through which habits of resignation and feelings of pessimism are overcome. Starting with concepts about the problems and aspirations of the learners, key words are selected, "those most charged with existential meaning, and thus major emotional content, but also the typical expressions of the people."

Selection of words is based on three criteria:

1. Words that include the basic sounds of the language.
2. Words that enable the trainer to move from simple letters and sounds to more complex ones.
3. Words with a potential capacity to confront social, cultural, and political realities.

This is an oversimplification of what is a pedagogy of depth and profundity, but it does indicate that basic strategies are involved and that the first and most important act of the teacher is to *learn from the students,* learn about their condition, wants and needs, and the very concepts and language that they use.

Other Disciplines

Sociology is another discipline from which theory and practice applicable to adult learning have been derived. In particular, studies associated with social class, dynamics of groups, associations and organizations in communities, studies of professions and the ways in which members of the professions are prepared and educated, studies of the social environments in which much learning occurs, and forms of control of mass communications have all been useful for learning theory. More and more universities have been recruiting sociologists for Adult Education Departments, and their contribution to learning practice is certain to continue to enlarge.

Programs in the developing countries and for the "under-educated" learners at home have benefited from insights first developed in anthropological research. Since anthropology deals not only with the impact of culture but also the ways in which cultures are modified, there are direct applications to learning theory and practice. In the past decade or so, as anthropologists and psychiatrists encountered each other and associated themselves in cross-disciplinary studies, some extraordinary insights have begun to appear. Applications can be found in the functional literacy programs and particularly in the training of personnel who will work in other countries.

The traditional disciplines of history and philosophy continue to contribute hypotheses for testing. As historical research about the way men and women have learned in previous epochs (in the Athens of Pericles, for example) and what seemed to motivate the learner, is undertaken, some useful ideas surface about motivation respecting education for citizenship, or about beauty, or about how curiosity is aroused and nourished.

It is in some of the applied fields, particularly when there is interaction of several disciplines, that new theory seems to be created. When economists, econometricians, and political scientists have combined forces in educational planning, novel procedures have been devised. Both systems analysis and cost-benefit studies for adult education have been utilized. On the other hand, there seems to have been less attention to research in aesthetics and creativity than might have been anticipated.

We shall now turn our attention to the endeavors in learning theory contributed by the psychologists:

- Developments in psychological theory during this century
- Some of the more important psychological theories of learning
- Implications for the practitioner

The rapid accumulation of theory since World War II parallels the accelerating growth of educational research. Readers will, of course, be aware that considerable skepticism still prevails about the value and application of much educational research, particularly that carried out under special laboratory conditions far from the places where most learning is happening. Considering the huge size of the learning research effort, the largest single area of study by experimental psychologists, there have been remarkably few applications and a much smaller impact upon education and training than might have been expected. Theoretical and basic research feeds largely on itself with little influence from the real world, even from the results of practical research. But, even so, the practitioner has much to gain from a close examination of learning theories derived from various fields.

Developments in the First Half of This Century

The first psychological theories concentrated attention on relatively simple units of learning, and were often based on observation of animals. Laboratory techniques borrowed from physics and biology were employed, and the learner was treated as if he were an empty organism, responding to outside influences in ways that were more or less automatic or even random. Usually a specific stimulus was assumed to be connected to a specific response and the observer would attempt to study the kind of stimulus and the kind of response S → R. The latter could be varied by rewards or punishment. Hungry rats or hungry dogs could be placed in one part of a maze and food in another. When the animals made a *correct* response they were rewarded with food or punished by not receiving it or even by loud noises or electric shocks. The same procedure could be followed with human beings as subjects. Soldiers learning a signaling code would make certain motions until they had achieved the correct response whereupon the sergeant would bestow approval or even extra privileges for good performance. Out of this kind of experimentation came what were sometimes called laws of learning.

It should be pointed out that the rudimentary nature of the mechanism studied, and of the explanation offered, was not just because psychology was at a much more primitive state than at present. In part, *connectionist* and *behaviorist* theory now seems oversimplified because the advocates of these theories were in rebellion, were reacting against sophisticated explanations of learning based on religious or philosophical interpretations and upon an assumption that an individual was possessed of certain properties and faculties. In attempting to overthrow theories that depended upon mystical explanations of human nature and conduct, an attempt was made to find explanations for man's behavior in the fact that he is a *human animal*.

But neither the so-called laws of learning nor the theories of connection and association could explain all phenomena. For example, lines presented in this fashion | | | | were perceived as four separate lines, but in this fashion ☐ as *one* square. Four circles presented in this form O 0 o o would be perceived as four circles, but arranged as two eyes, a head, and a body might represent a man. Or, on a standard test, a boy of ten might perceive a number of circles as just so many circles, whereas for a soldier these forms might symbolize woman. *Arrangement* of things could give an additional meaning to things.

Theories were now developed and given widespread circulation in which the arrangement or pattern of units was considered significant. Learning was no longer perceived as a simple relationship of experience-stimulus-response, but of ordering and structuring experience.

But it soon became apparent that learning was even more complicated than mere patterning. If an instructor was talking about some mythical social system in which men and women shared the possession of all goods he could expect one kind of interest and attention. But if, in describing the same kind of social arrangements, he were to state that this was a *Communist* system, he could expect a radically different kind of response from before. Not only would the quality of attention alter but if he were to test his students the following day he might find that some remembered considerably more, some remembered considerably less, and some remembered things which he had not said! Learning, then, is something more than pattern: there are emotional factors that can markedly affect what is learned and what is recalled. As a result of studying the effect of emotions upon learning, the teacher became more interested in the needs of students, what experience the student brings to his study, and what is his social position. All these matters were seen to predispose the student to accept, reject, or distort material presented to him.

It was also observed that a man in one kind of group is awake, active, cooperative, participating; and in another he is silent, opinionated, or critical. Not only his behavior but how much he will learn is affected. A man who is a member of one work team cannot seem to master the technique of assembling a radio component after two full days of trial. But when shifted to another team, he becomes proficient and speedy in the assembly work within a matter of hours. Learning for him may depend in large measure upon his associates. Considerable study is now going on about the group as a place where learning happens, about motivation, cognitive processes, and reinforcement.

We shall now make brief reference to a few of the psychological theories of learning that continue to receive attention and that have some implications for adult learning. Since there is space here to identify only a few of the leading psychologists, there will be inevitable distortion in the presentation. At a recent international conference in Paris, one teacher who is not at all a dogmatic person was able to use only the declarative form of the French language. After two or three statements she would pause, smile, and say "peut-être?" ["perhaps?"]. In using these summaries the reader is warned to punctuate them with a few "peut-êtres"! Better still, he should study the actual statements made by the writers referred to at the end of the chapter, as well as criticisms of these theories.

We noted in Chapter 2 that three general theoretical formulations have received the most attention—behaviorism, theory derived from psychoanalysis, and theories of the humanistic psychologists. However, we will try to relate other contributions that do not fit neatly into these categories.

Connections (Trial-and-Error)

For at least half a century there was one widely accepted explanation about learning called by the rather clumsy term *connectionism*. As early as 1898, E. L. Thorndike, in his book *Animal Intelligence*,[20] asserted that the basis of learning is an association between sense impressions and impulses to action. The association became known as a "bond" or "connection," thus the name. Sometimes it was also referred to as the stimulus-response or S-R psychology of learning, and much of it had to do with learning through trial-and-error.

Tolman, who was often critical of Thorndike, once said: "The psychology of learning has been and still is primarily a matter of agreeing or disagreeing with Thorndike, or trying in minor ways to improve upon him. All [psychologists] seem to have taken Thorndike, overtly or covertly, as our starting point." There were a number of reasons for the predominance of the views of Thorndike and his associates, in addition to the brilliance and versatility of the man himself. His position was established early, and his theory, more than any other was linked directly with classical *association* and thus with the learning theories of scholars going back to Aristotle. Thorndike, however, carried association far beyond the rather crude formulation known prior to 1900 by such men as John Locke, Thomas Hobbes, and John Stuart Mill.

All people are familiar with the idea of learning by association—"once burned, twice shy." To many boys of all ages the month of October always suggests "World Series." Long ago John Locke had written in his *Essay on the Human Understanding*:

> The ideas of goblins and sprites have really no more to do with the darkness than light: yet let a foolish maid inculcate these often on the mind of a child and raise them there together, possibly he shall never be able to separate them again so long as he lives. Many children imparting the pain they endured at school to their books they were corrected for so joining these ideas together that a book becomes their aversion and they are never recovered to the study and use of them all their lives after.[21]

Thorndike's was a view of learning that seemed to be well grounded in physiology; its experimental methods and use of mathematics also won respect. It dealt with a unit of learning—a stimulus, an organism, and a response—that could be comprehended. It was established just at the time when teacher-training was being developed on a much wider scale than ever before and Thorndike's psychology became almost the *official* psychology in many a school system. He was often criticized but seemingly without much loss of position or prestige. It was as a result of no outside attacks, but a consequence of his own integrity that he strode to the platform of one great international convention to announce boldly, "I was wrong." Subsequently he made substantial corrections in many of his most important conclusions.

We noted in Chapter 3 that much that we know about the learning of adults started with Thorndike's investigation. His studies covered a wide range of learning situations and his ideas were stated in an extensive series of papers and books. The focus for much of his work was on the rate of learning. Thorndike did not develop a single, consistent theory; yet, considering the breadth of his interests and his courage in changing his opinions in the light of new evidence, there is a remarkable coherence in his position.

In addition to what came his way through traditional association psychology, Thorndike was influenced strongly by research on animals by the early experimenter Wundt and others. He himself devised many of the most typical and most used problem situations for studying animals, such as the maze and the puzzle box. Concern with individual differences which he derived in part from Galton was another factor in his development. For the rest there was endless experimentation, insatiable curiosity, and the ability to prize discovery far more than consistency.

Connectionism, as Thorndike developed it, links human behavior to that of lower animals. Thorndike's "laws of learning" were developed from animal experiments. He put it that *learning is connecting* and the connections have a basis in the nervous system. Those things which we call intellect and intelligence can be thought of as quantitative rather than qualitative—a person's intellect is the sum total of the bonds that he has formed, and the greater the number of bonds the higher is his intelligence.

A man's life would be described by a list of all the situations which he encountered and the responses which he made to them, including among the latter every detail of his sensations, precepts, memories, mental images, ideas, judgments, emotions, desires, choices, and other so called mental acts.[22]

One of the most influential, even though most criticized, activities of Thorndike was the stating of three "laws of learning." These are not laws in the sense that this term is used in physics but statements about the directions in which learning happens. These concepts were stated in language meant to be intelligible but not technical; they were aimed at helping teachers in the classroom and did not attempt the precision favored by the psychologist in his laboratory. We have already noted they were modified somewhat in the last years of Thorndike's life.

> *Effect.* The bond between a stimulus and a response is strengthened or weakened because of the satisfaction or annoyance that accompanies the action.
> *Exercise or frequency.* It is often said that practice makes perfect. But it *doesn't* matter how much we practice something that pains us deeply, we may never attain much skill in it. Repetition by itself does not produce effective learning. But repetition with meaning results in substantial learning.
> *Readiness.* If the organism is ready for the connection, the result is pleasurable (therefore enhances learning); if not, the result is not pleasurable and learning is inhibited.

Thorndike was opposed to meaningless drill. "Arithmetic consists not of isolated unrelated facts, but of parts of a total system, each part of which may help to knowledge of the other parts, if it is learned properly. . . . Time spent in understanding facts and thinking about them is almost always saved doubly. Drill and practice are necessary but only when employed with meaning." Another problem in which his influence was shown was in regard to "transfer of training." Does the learning of Latin improve one's ability to learn English? This was a common enough assumption. "No," said Thorndike, "improvement in any single mental function need not improve the ability in functions commonly called by the same name." At first this denial resulted in acrimony, but it helped teachers and psychologists to study the conditions under which there might be transference—when Latin was taught in such a way that learning English would be improved. In the profitable observation and study that was touched off in this way, much of the nonsense that once had been believed and solemnly asserted about the value for learning of certain forms of discipline was undermined or washed away. One still hears some teachers and others aver that to do something distasteful, because it *is* repellent, will result in strong character and effective learning, but such talk is rare indeed. Of course we are not here concerned with its possible ethical effect, but its relevance, if any, to learning.

Most critics of Thorndike charged that his theory is too mechanical, oversimple and atomistic. In his later years Thorndike himself talked more and more of broad patterns of response. A colleague, R. S. Woodworth, rejected the notion that the connections were one-to-one:

> Either S or R may be as big and complex as you like. Such a performance as lifting a heavy weight by the co-ordinated action of arms, legs and trunk

is properly regarded as a single response. And such an aggregate of stimuli as is presented to the eye on looking out of the window works as a single combined stimulus when it arouses the response "What a beautiful day." [23]

Thorndike was well aware of the importance of purpose even though he seldom emphasized it:

The influences which co-operate with the situation to determine their response are as complicated, variable, purposive and spiritual as the learners themselves are. The chief role in the drama of learning is not played by external situations, but *by the learner*. The reason why I have said so much about frequency of connections, satisfyingness of connections, identifiability of situations, availability of responses and the like, and little about the purposes or mental sets or total minds which direct and organize them is not that I belittle the latter. It is rather that the general importance of the latter is obvious.[24]

Thorndike laid great stress upon rewarding—stating that a reward acts directly upon the neighboring connections and thus strengthens them. Punishment is much less effective in his view. Punishment does not have a direct weakening effect although it may cause the learner to do some other act which, if rewarded, will attain the effect. This aspect of Thorndike's work has had considerable influence. The evidence he adduced from his experiments had some effect in banishing or limiting some of the more brutal or futile uses of punishment in schools and training situations.

PURPOSE AS A CENTRAL FACTOR IN LEARNING

Most of the men who are concerned about some form of association have tried to explain learning in ways that did not depend upon cognition or purpose. Thorndike did not repudiate such aspects of learning, but he felt that he could explain what happened more satisfactorily in other ways. The Gestalt psychologists showed the place that purpose and goals have in the selection of responses that an animal would make in a particular situation.

Edward C. Tolman took the conception of purpose a little further. He chose *Purposive Behavior in Animals and Men* [25] as the title for his most important early book. Tolman found many affinities between his own system and other schools of psychology, including psychoanalysis.

Tolman insists that behavior is directed in relation to goals. It is always moving toward something or away from something. What is significant about what an animal or a man is doing is *what he is doing it for*. The learner selects the means or tools for achieving his purpose and he chooses what he will learn in relation to some purpose; learning doesn't happen by chance. For him there is also a principle of least effort: the learner tends to select the means which will most easily and most quickly achieve his purpose. Because this is so, Tolman believes, people are teachable; they make good learners.

Instead of believing that the learner is being goaded by stimuli to choose certain responses and having them stamped in by repetition and rewards, Tolman believes that the subject is learning not specific responses but a *map or path*, is learning not just to move but the meaning of the movement. Tolman placed considerable emphasis upon the use of creative inference in learning and upon all aspects of cognition.

Tolman's second contribution to learning has been to bring into some common exchange theories from several fields of psychology. By calling attention to purpose, he cleared away much that was sterile about behaviorism. By attempting to study and describe how it works, he devised some means of observing some of the subtler kinds of human experience.

Most of the humanistic psychological theories of learning, and most investigators interested in motivation, have stressed purposive learning.

Conditioning (Behaviorism)

Perhaps the simplest way to describe some aspects of learning is *conditioning*. This is also based on association. Conditioning theories were first developed in the laboratory, where animals were forced to salivate, or escape from electrical shocks. This seems far removed from human life and yet theories derived in this way have not only been influential but continue to be employed in learning activities for adults.

To those who based their theory on conditioning, it was not necessary to postulate a purpose for either learning or conscious thought. As in connectionism the drama of learning is played by the organism, the stimulus, and the response.

It is now customary to distinguish between two emphases in conditioning—*classical*, or *respondent*, conditioning, for which I. P. Pavlov is the outstanding name, and *operant*, or *instrumental*, conditioning, for which the chief name is B. F. Skinner. Much of the theorizing and development work that went into programmed learning was initiated by Skinner. He started with interests akin to those of Thorndike, and like Thorndike has influenced education at many places, including writing a utopia, *Walden II*.[26]

From experiments on dogs by Pavlov, the resulting notion of the *conditioned reflex* or *conditioned response* was chosen as the significant unit of learning. In training by conditioning one starts with a response already well established that is related to a stimulus or cue, and then proceeds to fix the same response with a different cue, or produce a different response to the same cue. Thus, in an anecdote told by psychologist E. R. Guthrie, the horse of a village parson had been properly trained to halt at the cue word "whoa." Alas, the village boys began to prod him with a pitchfork as they shouted the word "whoa," and before long the horse would bolt and run, instead of halting at this command, thus producing a calamitous result. Boys have also taught parrots to swear in a similar way. Conditioning has been used not only to fix desirable habits but also to break undesirable ones. Several of the cures for alcoholism are based on the use of various drugs that, in the presence of alcohol, make the patient violently ill. After exposure to this cure for a while, the patient is supposed to reject alcohol itself. Of course, attempts are made simultaneously to help him gain new satisfactions in life and not be forced to rely upon some addiction or substitute.

No theory of learning has received more attention in the past decade than *operant conditioning* where the response of the subject or organism is instrumental in obtaining reinforcement. Here the behaviors are somewhat more complex. For example, a person learns quickly that money can be used to obtain many things that are enjoyable or help to avoid other things that are not enjoyable. Behavior that results in obtaining money tends to be repeated. It isn't that money produces the behavior that will obtain it, but that the behavior that is *instrumental* in obtaining money tends to persist and will be attempted again and again. Responses, simple or complex, that are rewarded, or *reinforced*, therefore tend to persist. Accordingly, in a particular situation, the most likely response is one that has previously been rewarded or reinforced. In his first few years, a child learns that to obtain what he likes or to avoid what he dislikes is dependent on behaving in ways that are considered "good" by his parents. Similarly an adult entering a new country, or going to work in, for him, a new industry, will soon find that certain behavior, even a certain kind of dress, is approved and therefore reinforced.

Skinner, with his black training box and the carefully controlled environment for reinforcing or impeding the behavior of pigeons and rats, has been able to take a relatively simple theory and show its endless variations and applications to many forms of learning. The number and amount of reinforcers has been calculated for a variety of stimuli. A major reinforcer used is money.

The ingenuity and control exercised by Skinner in his research has not only influenced educational practitioners in schools, corporations, and corrective institutions but has also served as a model for many other kinds of research. His writing has been easy to understand, and his theories have seemed applicable to many situations for children and adults. Nevertheless, his theories have also been subjected to strong criticism by those who feel they are oversimple or are utilized in inappropriate situations.

As well as being concerned with rewards, Skinner investigated *aversion* —the factors that distress people, such as pain or loss of affection or friendship—and has contributed significantly to aversion therapy; for example, where the problem is to lessen smoking or drinking by employing chemicals that make smoking or drinking unpleasant. *Behavior modification* is now a procedure utilized in many classrooms but more often in various forms of treatment institutions. The *morality* of such procedures, as well as their long-term effectiveness, is a matter of discussion and debate.

Two earlier influential psychologists whose work was based on conditioning are John B. Watson, who has been best known for the theory called "Behaviorism," and E. R. Guthrie.

For Guthrie, learning is primarily the alteration of behavior that results from experience. Responses are of at least two kinds—the *outward act*, such as reading, writing, speaking, sitting, rising, and the *inward bodily reaction* such as increased supply of oxygen in the blood or glandular secretion. Emotions are also of two kinds—those that *excite* and lead to the altering of behavior and those that *depress* or hinder the alteration.

For Guthrie association happens because the pattern of stimuli at the time of a response tends on the recurrence to be followed by the same response. What could be simpler? The only elements are stimulus and movements. No mention of goals, of drives, of many repetitions. No mention of either reward or punishment. According to Guthrie we learn only what we do, not what we accomplish. That is, we learn specific responses. These can be errors or bad habits, as well as good. Responses can be associated or disassociated from the stimulus. Forgetting, Guthrie says, happens not because of the passage of time but because disassociation has taken place for one or more reasons:

- The correct response is blocked by an inhibitor such as fear or disgust, e.g. in the treatment of alcoholism.
- The response is blocked by fatigue—applied particularly in the training of horses (also in some modern applications of "brainwashing").
- The stimulus is repeated with such slight intensity that it is soon associated with a different response—such as getting the horse used to the saddle by starting with a light blanket.[27]

Guthrie also believes that learning occurs at once (in a single association episode), but if it is to be strengthened, the correct response must be attached to a whole series of stimuli. Accordingly a skill is not a simple habit but a collection of habits. Practice, Guthrie pointed out, can be wasteful in time and result unless it is the correct response to a number of cues. Practice should be in the specific situation where we expect the response. If a man or a group is to perform in a variety of places or situations, the practice should take place in all these situations.

Guthrie does not believe, with Thorndike, that punishment has an effect which is much less significant than reward. Punishment can be influential, depending upon the circumstance.

Sitting on tacks does not discourage learning. It encourages learning to do something else than sit. It is not the feeling caused by punishment but the specific action caused by punishment that determines what will be learned. To train a dog to jump through a hoop, the effectiveness of punishment depends on where it is applied, front or rear. It is what punishment makes the dog do that counts, or what it makes a man do, not what it makes him feel.

Guthrie's ingenious statements help us to understand some phenomena of learning, but fail to account for others. Still, their lucid presentation and their practical application to many training problems have won attention by teachers and trainers who have tended to reject other psychologists because the latter have used language or symbols that are difficult to follow.

In many learning situations the subject makes some initial gains, then there will be a period of no gain, followed by further progress, punctuated by periods of no gain. The record of the practice of the skill or knowledge can be charted and the occasions on which the subject's performance levels off or shows actual decline are called *plateaus*.

There are as many practice curves as there are subjects and kinds of learning. But, in the main, these curves follow two fairly general patterns. In one, the initial learning is rapid and the plateau does not appear in the early stages. But when it does appear it tends to be wide, and this phase can be exceedingly frustrating to the learner. In the other pattern, the early gains are slow, but after a certain stage is reached progress is rapid and the plateaus may be of slight dimension. Type A is found in learning of some relatively simple subject matter where the principles can be readily grasped, or some physical skill which is like the skills that the subject has already learned. Type B is found (a) where the principles are difficult to grasp (b) where the skills are of a different order from those already experienced (c) where, as in the learning of a language, there must be a certain amount of learning of words and ear training before any real progress is possible (d) or where extensive unlearning is necessary to remove old habits that interfere with the new, such as changing the hand grip in golf.

Why should anyone go to the trouble of charting one's progress in this way? The answer is plain. The curve is one of the most effective means, not of teaching, but of helping the teacher or the learner to sense when "something must be done." If the performance of a subject is steadily rising one might assume that the learning is proceeding in satisfactory fashion. If, however, a plateau has been reached it may be the signal for a change in the learning practice. The curve warns the teacher about this; it can also give the subject a much better understanding and awareness of his progress.

Of course, it may be essential to continue for a time at the plateau if, as some psychologists argue, the plateau represents the period in which the person is integrating the new experience. But the plateau need not be unduly protracted. How can the learning plateau be interrupted? There are many possibilities. It may be accomplished by increasing the motivation. It may be done by improving some of the methods of working. Another means is seeking to see the problem *whole* in order to understand where the particular information or skill is related or by a better distribution of practice with shorter periods of activity repeated more often and with greater relaxation between. The curve is the guide to improvement. With no attention to it, the learner may begin to feel he has reached his limits, that he has achieved "good enough." As one writer put it, "If John Bunyan had written a *Learner's Progress* he would have noted Mr. Faint-Heart and Mr. Fairly-Good stopped here."

The most common use of conditioning is in animal training, such as by a cowboy who is breaking in an untamed and fearful horse. To the wild horse a man, noise, the bind of the harness or the saddle are all equally stimuli that will bring about a response of fear and flight. Accordingly, the horse is given time to become used to having the man touch and fondle him, so that the cue *man* does not bring the response of *fear* or *run*. Next the horse is saddled, and additional time is allowed until this act no longer brings about a negative response. Finally, the man climbs astride the horse. Each step in the conditioning, where different responses are learned, is accompanied by support and reassurance to the animal, while the doses of fear-producing stimuli are slowly increased. The impatient or clumsy trainer, who gives too little support or who allows the tension cues to come too quickly, may jeopardize the training, for if the horse is again frightened the original strength of the fear cues may be reinforced.

Gestalt Psychology

Those who emphasized conditioning were often criticized because they were concerned about atoms or particles or pieces of learning. The group of men who were particularly concerned about the *whole* rather than its parts, and about *patterns* of learning rather than a single incident, have been called *Gestalt* from the German word meaning "shape" or "form."

Much of the research of the early Gestalt psychologists Max Wertheimer, Wolfgang Kohler, and Kurt Koffka consisted of studies of movement or rhythm, and of the properties or configurations or patterns of action. Kohler carried out much of his work while he was interned in the Canary Islands during World War I. His book *The Mentality of Apes* won immediate attention. The stories of animal behavior were themselves impressive, and there always seems to be widespread curiosity about the great apes. Moreover, this represented the first forthright attack on the then well-accepted position of Thorndike and others who were within the general framework of association psychology. It is easier now to see complementary relationships between these theories; at first, all that was noticed was the conflicts.

Research by the Gestalt psychologists is almost as well known as that of Pavlov or Thorndike. Frequently apes or gorillas were employed as subjects. A typical kind of experiment would go something like this: A hungry ape is placed in a cage, and on the roof of the cage is a stalk of bananas. In the cage are a long stick and a heavy box. For a while the ape paces around eying the bananas. Then he jumps and tries to reach them. He may jump again and again, failing each time. After a while he may take the stick and try to knock down the bananas, try and try and try, but he fails each time. Up to this point there has been no step-by-step learning that could be charted on a practice curve, no apparent gain and plateaus; there has been only failure. But suddenly, all at once, the ape grabs the stick, climbs to the box, leaps up swinging the stick, and knocks down the bananas. He has grasped *the pattern of action* required and from that time on he can repeat the pattern. He may improve his performance in climbing or hitting with the stick but he is always able to co-ordinate the parts of the whole. These experiments took many forms such as reaching through the cage bars with a stick, piling one box upon another—even, on one occasion, joining two sticks together, which seems to have happened by chance but continued to be repeated thereafter.

Note three attributes here:

- The solution seems to come abruptly as a flash of insight.
- The solution seems to be permanent and to carry over into other experiences.
- The solution seems to come about because the learner perceives the relationship of the different factors in the scene rather than responding to isolated stimuli.

The Gestalt descriptions and explanations differed most from those of Thorndike in insisting that the trials of the learner were by no means random. . . . One might describe their earlier behavior as trial-and-error but, as one writer put it, the apes "made clever errors." Changes in spatial relations would alter the nature of the problem: a stick placed out of sight and out of reach might not be employed at all, or only very late in the process; but a stick placed close to, or in line with, the food was resorted to relatively early. Once the relationship was seen, the stick could be moved away or hidden, and the animal would search for and use it. Kohler maintained that this happened because the object had become endowed with new meaning, that a stick which before was just something to bite upon now took on the character of thing-to-get-fruit-with. According to Kohler:

> What the animal has actually learned is to make an irrelevant object relevant to the situation. . . . only one conception of the performance is possible; that the animal has acquired an ability to introduce "tool" into certain situations. Nor is this ability limited to the particular thing with which it was acquired; on the contrary, it is an acquisition of a much more general nature.[28]

The emphasis at every stage is upon perceiving relationships, rather than responding to isolated objects or stimuli. Factors which hinder the understanding of this relationship are these:

- The animal may lack sufficient motivation. (Gestalt psychologists put special emphasis upon motivation.)
- The elements of the situation may be scattered too widely for the relationship to be perceived—for example, when the stick is out of sight.
- The organism may have insufficient experience to be able to master the skills needed.

A fourth factor occurs when old habits block the acquiring of new. The context is important. An ape which had been using one box to get food would not employ another when the familiar one was in a corner and another ape was lying upon it. The second box was apparently perceived not just as something-to-aid-in-getting-food but as having a different meaning. Context is even more important with human beings and, as we noted in Chapter 5, learning may happen only as, and when, the social context is given a new meaning.

Gestalt psychologists have not explained with complete satisfaction how insight happens. But they have contributed considerably to learning theory and practice. Theories such as conditioning and trial-and-error explain, with some success, the learning of animals, but they do not begin to comprehend human learning, particularly of mature and experienced people. For notions such as insight and the role of motivation the Gestalt ideas are more relevant. Gestalt theory emphasizes that problems are to be solved sensibly, with concern about structure and organization. Learning does not happen mechanically, they insist, or simply by repetition or drill. The subject will behave as intelligently as he can under the circumstances. There may be fumbling and trial-and-error but only when the problem is too difficult, and only till a solution can be achieved. Gestalt theory also stimulated considerable speculation about whole learning which soon became a part of the theory and practice of many teachers and trainers. It is now a commonplace in the teaching of reading or tennis, or a foreign language, or the use of a micrometer, to begin with meaningful wholes while watching for the points at which practice is needed on specific aspects, whereupon these acts are worked back into broader wholes. The attack is on the larger patterns first, even if they seem to be complex. For example, in teaching badminton an attempt is made to give some impression of the whole game, its ebb and flow, its strategy, whereupon specific attention is directed to teaching the serve or footwork, or the forehand smash. Sometimes the learning may seem slower at first if this method is followed; actually it is only the performance that is slower. Eventually, before very long in fact, there is accelerating achievement.

Another lesson, useful for athletic coaches and others who teach physical and motor skills, has been described earlier; namely, that some kinds of skills can best be learned, perhaps can only be learned, by tracing out the desired action in such a manner that the muscles and senses become familiar with the desired pattern. As we have noted, with a complicated bodily skill such as a somersault dive from a springboard, the body may be put through the action several times while the person is protected by a safety belt from harm, fear, or the development of repugnance. When one hears a coach talk about "the feel" of an activity, this is what he is referring to.

Gestalt psychology also played some part in stimulating an approach to learning which is usually referred to as "field theory" and which we shall deal with later.

GESTALT THERAPY

The work of Fritz Perls and others who think of themselves as Gestalt therapists is not so much a break with early Gestalt theory as an application in depth of some notions that affect human behavior under stress.

Gestalt therapy is the most prominent of a large number of group approaches to therapy that have developed in midcentury. Early work by Kurt Goldstein and J. L. Moreno in Europe has been followed up in the United States, with some critics claiming that such methods as "encounter marathons," groups oriented to touch and sensation, addiction groups, and so on, derive their significance from certain conditions in the urban middle-class culture of the United States and would have little application outside that culture. No name as prominent as Sigmund Freud is associated with group forms of therapy, but Fritz Perls has made contributions that go far beyond his own practice. Gestalt therapy emphasizes the *whole* situation, "that the whole determines the parts" as can be expected. At its beginning Gestalt psychologists and existentialist philosophers (Martin Buber, for example) were working together; the therapy is one of *How* and *Now*. Perls has said:

> There are two legs upon which Gestalt therapy walks, *now* and *how*. The essence of the theory of Gestalt therapy is in the understanding of these two words. *Now* covers all that exists. The past is no more, the future is not yet. *Now* includes the balance of being here, is expressing involvement, phenomenon—awareness. *How* covers everything that is structure, behavior, all that is actually going on, the ongoing process. All the rest is irrelevant.

Gestalt therapists are not interested in the clients' history, have very little interest in past experience or in dreams (except as they apply to the *now*), and are not much concerned with future growth or long-term processes. The objective is awareness and understanding of the present in all of its implications.

Group therapists, any more than individual therapists like Freud, are not centrally concerned about learning. But there are applications, positive and negative, from therapists to learning. T-groups, encounter groups, sensitivity-training, and such formulations as the "Blake Grid" for analysis of decision-making, have been adopted by adult education institutions and in management training. On the other hand, critics claim that these therapies tend to be anti-intellectual, that they eliminate all perspective gained over time and all those processes which, for implementation, must continue over time.

Field Theory

A number of psychologists have been contributing to what is generally called "field theory." The most influential has been a German, Kurt Lewin, who spent his last years in the United States. At an earlier stage in his career he had been associated with Wertheimer and the other Gestalt psychologists, but he was more interested in motivation and personality than in perception and learning.

We shall deal with the application of some of Lewin's principles to group development in a later chapter. Much of what is often termed group dynamics grows, directly or indirectly, from his speculations and early experiments.

Lewin has identified four kinds or aspects of learning:

- Change in cognitive structure (knowledge)
- Change in motivation (learning to like or dislike)
- Change in group belongingness or ideology (example: an immigrant coming to terms with and integrating into a new culture)
- Achieving voluntary control of body musculature (example: speech skills) [29]

At the beginning of his work, Lewin was not interested in learning as such. Part of his approach to the study of psychology was borrowed from physics. Quite early he set himself to the analysis of the actual situation, what was happening, rather than the result. He developed the concept of the *life space*, the totality of facts that determine the behavior of a person at a given time. For example, he would not be particularly concerned with measuring the difference in achievement between a housewife and an actress in memorizing poetry. The usual means of measuring performance would reveal that each was learning so many words or sentences per hour of time, as though each task were identical. His more subtle analysis showed that what each was doing is really very different, so different it can hardly be compared. The housewife is mainly searching, she is groping, beset with fears and anxieties which inhibit learning. On the other hand, the actress has a well-developed technique for the study of words; with her the whole process is almost mechanical. What interested Lewin was always what was actually happening to a subject, with *his* experience, in a particular social setting. What forces were at work upon the individual? What stresses were there for him?

It is interesting to note the relationship between field theory as applied to learning and the now famous speculations of Dr. Hans Selye about *stress*. The implications of this have been alluded to by Professor Marshall McLuhan:

Selye has come up with the first non-visual disease theory since the Greeks introduced the image of the skin as an envelope enclosing organs. His *stress* theory is entirely a *field* view of disease. The body is part of a total field.

The Greek view of the body as a package of organs and humours got cut down, at the Renaissance, to the view of the body as a pumping station. Then with the rise of chemistry in the nineteenth century the body became a chemistry factory. Everybody was loaded with germs. But the rise of field theory in physics now has its medical counterpart in Dr. Hans Selye's stress view. He rejects the idea that each disease has a specific cause which must be found and isolated in order for cure to occur. In a word he regards as unreal and outdated, the lineal view of disease as a specific target for which a specific shot is indicated.[30]

Lewin in describing his own work has said that he used a "constructive" method rather than one of classification. By "constructive" he means studying an individual case rather than an abstract one, but studying it with the aid of such concepts as psychological tension. Second, he chose a dynamic approach, one that attempted to get to the depths and not be satisfied with superficialities. Third, he chose a psychological rather than a physiological approach—he showed very little interest in the minutiae of what happened in the nervous system or the glands, or the blood pressure. Two other characteristics were the attempt to analyze the system as a whole, not in separate parts, and, like Hull, the attempt to make a mathematical representation of the field of inquiry. He tried to represent some of these dynamics by borrowing concepts from mathematics and physics. The accuracy of his formulae, as well as the suitability of using such analogies, has often been criticized; but this theory does not depend upon the analogies he used or upon his mathematical presentation.

For Lewin the chief area of attention is the psychological field, *the life space*. The life space is where the person lives psychologically, as seen from his own viewpoint. Some famous *New Yorker* cartoons show a man in the real world seeing some reality, usually an attractive blonde, in his own special way. This is not a dream or a delusion; the man is not withdrawn from reality but is living in a real world and responding to it rationally while, at the same time, perceiving in his own characteristic fashion. A man interacts with the real world, and this produces some changes in his psychological world. The teacher, says Lewin, must never forget both realities—the real world and the life space of the child. He must try to understand the psychological world of the child. If, instead of dealing with the world of the child, he substitutes the world of the teacher or of anybody else, "he is not being objective, but wrong."

The life space is influenced and altered by the physical and social environment but is not identical with that environment. The most interesting psychological problems, therefore, have to do with the person in his life space. The person may be attracted by an object, and Lewin described this attraction as showing *valence*, of course borrowing the term from chemistry. This provided him with a means of describing and observing different kinds of conflict:

- Two positive valences, e.g. a student must choose between basketball and going to a dance.
- A simultaneous positive and a negative valence. A workman is offered double-time for overtime when he wants to go to a ballgame.
- Two negative valences. A man is threatened with the loss of his job if he doesn't report the negligence of his work partner.

Using the concept of valence, adding to it concepts of direction, distance, and time, Lewin was able to identify and describe many kinds of social problems in terms precise enough so that they have been studied experimentally. One classical investigation was conducted by associates of Lewin on the effect of three kinds of leadership upon learning and character changes.[31] This experiment has many implications, but we shall describe it briefly as it relates to learning. Groups of boys in a clubhouse are learning to use carpentry tools. They are subjected, in turn, to three different kinds of leadership. In one—*autocratic*—the leader decides what will be done and what will be learned, assigns all the tasks, instructs in considerable detail, and gives praise or blame according to his own standards. In a second—*laissez-faire*—the leader leaves all decisions about what is to be done, what is to be learned, how it is to be done, up to the boys. In the third—*democratic*—the leader and the boys discuss and reach decisions about the ways in which their tasks will be carried out. All the boys are organized in small groups and in turn are subjected to each kind of leadership. Their behavior and how it is altered, what they do, how they react to each other and to the leader, was recorded by observers and by a moving picture camera focused through a one-way glass screen.

The research team was thus able to study the behavior of the boys and make inferences about changes in what they did, how they felt, how they acted toward each other, how much they accomplished, how much they learned. It was found, for example, that the productivity in the craft activity was greatest in the early stages by the boys under authoritarian leadership, and least under laissez-faire, but that at a later point the boys under democratic leadership outstripped the others in things done, as well as in learning how to deal effectively and wholesomely with themselves, their fellows, and their leader.

Some psychologists claim that Lewin's theories have little or no relevance to learning. This seems far from correct. And even if this were so, it is still true that the experimental work which he originated, and the "small group theory" with which we shall deal later, have made a substantial impact upon adult education.

Psychoanalysis

It is not possible, of course, to deal with the many applications of psychoanalysis to learning theory because the subject is so vast. Though Sigmund Freud was not especially interested in learning as such and made no systematic attempt to understand or write about it, his dynamic conceptions have influenced every nook and cranny of human behavior.

A number of basic concepts of Freud have direct application to learning, for example:

- Pleasure principle—the law of effect
- Fear and anxiety as a drive or inhibition
- Unconscious influences upon word association, recall, and forgetting of names and events
- Fixation—either meaning an arrested development in which an adult may continue at an adolescent level of behavior or meaning fixed habits
- Regression, where a person returns to earlier modes of behavior
- Learning as an aspect of psychotherapy

Freud's work gave a considerable support to all who place primary attention upon the emotions and motivation in learning. Despite his preoccupation with the irrational, his suggestions with respect to learning all play up the rational, cognitive aspects of learning and play down simple or irrational elements. The aim of psychoanalysis is to get rid of the blocks to rationality and, therefore, to rational learning. An important step on the way to rationality is self-understanding, which in itself, as we have seen, is a powerful aid to education. Most of all, psychoanalytic thinking has opened up the entire field of human behavior to scrutiny. Learning is not relegated to a portion of life, not even bounded by such a distinction as what is *neurotic* and what is *normal*. The range of subject matter for students of learning now includes symbolism, repression, and the factors which tend to change and distort perception.

Many other psychoanalysts—Horney and Fromm, for example—have also made several applications of therapeutic principles to learning.

In a larger way so have some men whose work is more closely identified with Jung than with Freud. One of these, Otto Rank, has had a marked influence on both theory and practice in school, particularly in nursery and infant schools. Another, W. R. Bion, has made many contributions to group therapy and understanding the small group, with some practical applications to education. He postulated that, in a group, the learning activity is always influenced to some extent by certain emotional stakes. The drive toward learning may be purposive; the emotional preoccupations are nonpurposive and not under conscious control. In understanding the behavior in a group the interplay between task and feelings must be noted. Behavior by members of the whole group which, on the surface, appears contradictory, may thus appear to have consistency. Bion's theoretical concepts have been tested out systematically by Herbert Thelen and Dorothy Stock and reported in a book entitled *Emotional Dynamics and Group Culture*.[32]

Cognitive Learning

Most learning theorists have been interested in problems of cognition, but it is only in recent years, through the work of such men as Piaget,

Bruner, and Ausubel that cognitive learning has received major and direct attention.

Lacking sufficient contact with Europe, adult educationists are coming rather late to any appreciation of the possible contributions of Jean Piaget. It is true that Piaget has focused his attention on children, particularly younger children, and the ways in which their intelligence develops. In identifying the successive stages of development of the intelligence of a child, Piaget claims that the child's intelligence is "qualitatively" different from that of an adult, and, in so doing, he helps establish what is most characteristic about adult intelligence. Moreover, the stages which a child goes through *may* also prove to be analogous to stages in the development of some new literates or some handicapped or retarded adults.

Piaget's views about knowledge and the development of logical operations may also have application to adult education. In an address given in North America, he said:

> To understand the development of knowledge, we must start with an idea which seems central to me—the idea of an operation. Knowledge is not a copy of reality. To know an object is to act on it. To know is to modify, to transform the object and to understand the process of this transformation, and as a consequence to understand the way the object is constructed. An operation is thus the essence of knowledge; it is an interiorized action which modifies the object of knowledge. For instance, an operation would consist of joining objects in a class, to construct a classification, or an operation would consist of ordering, or putting things in a series, or an operation would consist of counting, or of measuring. In other words, it is a set of actions modifying the object and enabling the knower to get at the structures of transformation.[33]

And the four main factors by which Piaget explains the development of operational structures are useful concepts for adult education. They are: (1) maturation, the continuation of the development of the body, the nervous system and mental functions; (2) the role of experience as the person reacts to his successive environments; (3) social transmission including language and education; and (4) self-regulation.

There is insufficient space here to summarize those aspects of Piaget's work that merit attention by adult educationists. But he will serve as an example of what is available to those who will look around them and not be put off by labels that imply that So-and-So is a child psychologist or a rat psychologist, and therefore has nothing to contribute to adult education.

Many of those engaged in educational research are concerned with the learning of subject matter. From the days of Thorndike, this has been a preoccupation of many in adult education. Most adults and many adult educationists suspect that their memory is regressing or could be vastly improved. They tell each other stories about men who have prodigious memories, and also of other men, more like themselves, in the wry and painful story:

> I think I'm losing my memory.
> How long has this been going on?
> How long has what been going on?

There is interest in memory span and problems of recall, in transfer of training, in association, in the utilization of habits, in distribution of practice, in meaningfulness, and particularly in uses of feedback and feedback systems.

Some attention has been given to the work of Jerome Bruner,[34] particularly to his views about discovery learning. Bruner claims that through the method of discovery:

1. There is an increment in intellectual potency.
2. Emphasis is placed on intrinsic rewards rather than extrinsic rewards.
3. The student learns how to discover, i.e. the student masters the ways and means of discovery.
4. Memory processing is facilitated.

Bruner holds, as do many others, that the mere storage of information is subordinate to locating and information retrieval in the conservation of memory. An effective memory results from improved organization; and organization, in turn, is likely to be most productive when there is interest in the content and what is learned is related to what the learner already knows.

Bruner takes issue with many common educational practices. He insists that the notion of readiness ("readiness to read") is a mischievous half-truth. One does not wait for biological process to produce readiness; one *teaches* it, since readiness comprises mastery of simple skills. He emphasizes that cognitive or intellectual mastery is itself rewarding. And he deplores the fact that much education is carried on without usable feedback, with evaluation only after the job or the course has been completed.

To Bruner, "education is experience reorganized," and knowing is a process, not a product. Learning is its own reward, and the sustaining energies for learning are "curiosity, a desire for competence, aspiration to emulate a model, and a deeply-sensed commitment to the web of social responsibility."

We shall make no attempt to summarize all the important contributions to cognitive learning theory. Instead, we will only note their importance. While some seem to have application only to young children, others have much to say that seems applicable to classrooms in colleges, universities, and other adult activities where meaningful learning of subject matter is the goal. David Ausubel is an example of a theorist whose work has become known by adult educationists. Ausubel contends that only meaningful verbal reception learning, a variety of cognitive theory, is central to the acquisition of subject matter. He deplores the fact that educational psychologists have been unduly preoccupied with such matters as measurement and evaluation, personality development, mental hygiene, group dynamics and counseling, and have neglected to study learning in the classroom. He asserts that there are substantial differences between rote-learning and meaningful learning, although the two are often confused.

> Rotely learned and meaningfully learned materials are represented and organized quite differently in the student's psychological structure of knowledge, and hence conform to different principles of learning and retention. Not only are the respective learning processes dissimilar, but also the significant variables in the two processes are different or have very different effects. Hence the extrapolation of rote learning theory and evidence to school learning problems perpetuated erroneous conceptions about the nature and conditions of classroom learning, led psychologists to neglect research on factors influencing meaningful learning, and thus delayed the discovery of more effective techniques of verbal exposition . . . It encouraged many teachers to perceive and present potentially meaningful materials as materials for rote learning, or to believe (since educational psychologists regarded all verbal learning as a rote process) that meaningful learning could only be achieved through the use of nonverbal and problem-solving methods.[35]

Ausubel also recommends how materials can be presented in meaningful ways and carefully examines modes of presentation, rates of retention, and so forth. In this examination he is led to differ sharply with those who advocate discovery learning as a general method.

Bruner and others have argued that discovery is necessary for "real possession" of knowledge, that it has certain unique motivational advantages, organizes knowledge effectively for later use, and promotes long-term retention. Ausubel denies some of these specific claims, although agreeing that the discovery method does offer some unique pedagogic advantages under certain conditions, as well as being necessary for the development of problem-solving abilities. But he contends that discovery learning "is not an indispensable condition for the occurrence of meaningful learning, and is too time consuming to be used efficiently as a primary method of transmitting subject matter content in typical classroom situations." Ausubel has developed a number of other inquiries that potentially have considerable significance for adult education. One example is a study of "closed-minded-ness"; it questions whether dogmatism in students may result in the rejection of certain viewpoints even before the evidence is presented and examined. This is a phenomenon long recognized in adult education, but the techniques for dealing with it and its impact on what is learned are not yet well understood.

There is, of course, considerable interest in "intrinsic motivation," as reported in Chapter 5. Many younger psychologists are investigating motivational variables and the role of the educationist in making education interesting and rewarding. Concepts of maturity, mental health, creativity, and curiosity are being developed, and all of these seem to have specific application to adult education.

The notion "learning how to learn" and the evolving of human abilities are frequently the subject of rhetoric in adult education, but they have also been the subject of careful investigation by such psychologists as H. F. Harlow, R. M. Gagne and G. A. Ferguson.

Concepts and Concept Formation

Writing in *The Structure of Scientific Revolutions* in 1962, Thomas S. Kuhn pointed out that at one stage in the development of a scientific activity a certain phenomenon may be considered as minor and therefore may be largely disregarded, while at another stage the same phenomenon becomes a central and organizing focus.

For adult education, a central concept is concepts! Adult education used to be lacking in large resonant concepts, but several have been added recently. Moreover, the utility of concepts in learning has begun to stimulate many forms of research and action.

a. *Concepts that have been established.* We shall refer to four concepts which affect not only the organization of adult education but also the learning processes especially.

(i) *Education-permanente*, or lifelong integrated education which comprehends all learning at whatever age into a larger harmony and establishes adult education as part of a larger whole. This notion, not at all new to North America, has been carried by UNESCO into the languages of all countries. Under this notion, while adult learning may require special attention and effort, it is seen as part of a process that begins when a child is born and continues until death. This concept makes some postulates about continuity in learning, as well as about the kinds of learning that should be developed during the years of childhood.[36] Thus far there has been little systematic research probing of the many implications of the concept, but one study by Leonard Shorey,[37] dealing with factors connected with the continuing education of teachers, has been completed.

(ii) *Self-directed learning.* The corollary of *education-permanente* is the notion that all people, at all ages, can be assisted to become increasingly capable of initiating and managing their own learning. We will deal with this concept later and review some of the studies that support its major premise.[38]

(iii) *The learning system.* There *is* a learning system, although it is not easy to discern or to understand what are the parameters. The learning system includes not only those organized educative experiences that occur inside institutions but also nonformal education and all the individual but purposeful learning by people of all ages that happens outside of schools and colleges. For such a melange of activities the word *system* may not seem appropriate. Yet the *learning system* is a basic concept, and with it one can begin to comprehend not only classes and institutions but also account for the individual learner, on the one hand, and the entire learning enterprise on the other, thus visualizing the relationships of learner and subsystems to the whole.

(iv) *The learning force.* The notion of a learning force is part of, or is the obverse face of, the "learning system." Here are included all learners of whatever kind or content. The *learning force*,[39] as Stanley Moses has described it, is very much larger than any estimate made previously about the clientele for adult education: it is the total public for education.

b. *The role of concept formation in adult education.* As any learner makes progress within a field of study he encounters scores of isolated facts and large collections of data, but more and more an order emerges, if the process is a rational one:

- A description of the field and its phenomea
- Definitions of the questions that arise
- Approaches that seem effective in tackling its problems
- Methods of enquiry that seem useful in gaining understanding
- Concepts that give order and meaning to objects and events
- Generalizations that are formulated to express relationships found among concepts
- Records and catalogs of facts, generalizations, concepts and methods

The importance of concept formation is beginning to receive considerable emphasis. Without concepts the learner is soon confused and lost in the welter of bewildering information. The rationale for emphasizing concepts is the assumption that a direct relationship exists between a person's possession and utilization of concepts and his performance either as a learner or as an educationist.

All practitioners need to acquire a set of concepts that make it possible for them to have minimum understanding of what is entailed in adult education. For example, a cooperative extension agent needs to learn some central concepts from sociology (examples are attitudes, social classes, ethnic backgrounds) so that he may understand the meaning of the situations he will encounter. Concepts can be used as "tools" for analyzing behavior, and in obtaining a perspective about emergent problems. Concepts are tools for thinking and understanding and learning.

CONCEPTS AND IMAGES—BEHAVIOR MODIFICATION

Many applications of concepts and concept formation might be cited but we will review one more application by David E. Hunt,[40] an attempt to adapt educational approaches to the needs of individual learners.

In the Conceptual Systems Theory originally stated by Harvey, Hunt, and Schroder (1961), a person is assumed to progress through a series of successive stages along a dimension of conceptual level. This conception was developed primarily for children and may need further refinements for work with adults, but it seems to be promising, particularly for adult basic education. To reduce the model to simplicity, a teaching method would be matched to conceptual level somewhat as follows:

Stage	Conceptual Level Characteristics	Ideal Training Conditions
Sub 1	Impulsive poorly socialized egocentric inattentive	Accepting but firm clearly organized with a minimum of alternatives
Stage 1	Compliant dependent on authority concerned with rules	Encouraging some independence within normative structure
Stage 2	Independent questioning self-assertive	Allowing high autonomy with numerous alternatives and low normative pressure

Some attempts have been made to introduce a Stage 3 and even to relate these stages to Maslow's hierarchy of needs.

It seems evident, even from a cursory treatment of the subject, that concepts and concept formation will become increasingly important in adult education. One reads and hears of new applications; for example, "concept therapy," in which the first step in modifying behavior is to have the subject or learner adopt a new image of himself and his role. More and more as learning is seen to be a matter of altered behavior, concepts will become the counters and instruments of these changes.

CHANGE THEORIES

Social changes, of course, involve groups and associations as well as individuals. We have quoted Alan Thomas about the effects on learning of *membership*, and we have noted that some educators work with whole systems in an effort to bring about changes. Practitioners in adult education need not only to know about certain activities of community development but about such matters as "community psychiatry," "milieu therapy," and "intervention theory." There is a difficulty, of course; none of these "theories" are yet well formulated or tested. We return again to these matters in later chapters and have included some references selected from the large number of books that have been appearing that deal with these theories.

Altered States of Consciousness

Some learning theorists have once more begun to interest themselves in the possibilities for learning as a result of altered states of consciousness. This is a difficult, controversial, and fascinating field which we cannot begin to understand or even review in a few paragraphs, but we will mention some sources for further exploration.

It is evident that many people who have used various forms of mind-expanding chemicals have done so in their desire to have new growth experiences. This real and compelling motive has often been misunderstood in the waves of controversy about the *drug scene*, about problems of law enforcement, because of the destructive impact of some chemicals on the person, and generally because of apprehension or even guilt that many people exhibit respecting society. Most of what might be positive, "safe," and valuable about use of chemicals for learning has been obscured or denied because of the violence of this argument.

The use of hypnosis for learning new behavior is also on the increase and is also a matter of controversy. Over the past century some doctors, dentists, and therapists have used hypnosis in healing, but only in the past decades have medical associations recognized these procedures as a legitimate port of health therapy. Many educationists either know little about the uses of suggestion or hypnosis or are alarmed at the very notion. The word conjures up vaudeville stunts or the dread possibilities of people being "brain-washed" or forced to change their behavior against their will. However, the use of suggestion can be self-administered and controlled; hypnosis can lead to *autohypnosis* where the learner is fully in charge of the process. Despite real, as well as fancied, difficulties, suggestion may become one of the useful methodologies for motivating people, particularly people whose educational experience has been one of recurrent failure, to undertake and persevere in an educational or training program of learning.

Most of these methods use, in one way or another, different states of human consciousness or awareness related to the rhythms of brain activity. All of these states are *normal*, but we tend to think that the *beta* state is standard and that others are in some way mysterious. The *beta* rhythm is associated with what is usually called "active" thinking, or active attention. In this state, the focus is on the outside world, or on solving concrete problems. During the *alpha* rhythm the mind is alert but not focused on external processes nor engaged in organized, logical thinking. The *theta* rhythm is usually associated with an unconscious or near unconscious state, slipping toward unawareness and often accompanied by dream-like images. The *delta* rhythm is commonly associated with deep sleep.

Now, why is this important? Because certain kinds of learning, such as laying down the sounds and rhythms of a new language or a creative insight in art or music, may happen more satisfactorily in the states other than the *beta*. It is argued, with considerable support from research, that language sounds and vocabulary are best learned in the periods just before sleeping or before full awakening when the subject is in an alpha state.

Hypnosis and autohypnosis may assist the subject to enter these other states of consciousness and therefore prepare him for the learning best fostered in these states.

Journals of popular psychology refer often to *bio-feedback*, which means simply that the learner is given information about how well he is functioning and thus better able to modify his behavior. The data may include information about heartbeat, blood pressure, temperature, muscle contraction, and brain rhythms. Knowing what happens to him under certain kinds of stress or stimuation and, therefore, more about the stimulus that "triggers" this behavior, is one means of helping the subject learn how to cope with such stimuli and prepare for changes in behavior that will be more productive.

Evidence is mounting from many sources about the relationship between alpha and theta rhythms and artistic or scientific creativity. To repeat just one example among thousands, Rollo May [41] tells of a scientist who dreamed of a sought-for formula, wakened and in his excitement, hurriedly scribbled it on a paper tissue, only to find he could not read it in the morning. Each night thereafter he concentrated on redreaming it and about a week later actually did so. This time he got up immediately, recorded carefully the formula, and it became the basis of work that was awarded the Nobel Prize.

L. E. Walkup, in a paper, "Creativity in Science Through Visualization," says:

> Creative persons appear to have stumbled onto and then developed to a high degree of perfection the ability to visualize—almost hallucinate—in the area in which they are creative. And their visualizations seem to be of a sort that lend themselves to easy manipulation in the thinking process. . . . If correct, this aspect of creativity suggests many research attacks and many potential changes in education for creative activity.

There are now many books and journal articles about these developments, a few of which are noted in the Suggested Reading at the end of the chapter.

Some Other Approaches

Any reader of science fiction knows that many problems in the physical world are first stated and solved by using the language of mathematics, before there has been any laboratory work or pilot projects. Can such methods be applied to the social sciences?

MATHEMATICAL MODELS

One of the earliest applications of this approach was in the field of learning theory when Ebbinghaus in 1885 found that the curve of forgetting of facts that had been memorized was roughly in logarithmic form. Accordingly he fitted a logarithmic equation to it.

$$b = \frac{100\ c}{(\log t)\ k}$$

where b = percent retained by the savings measure,
t = elapsed time, and c and k are arbitrary constants.

This may not mean very much to most of us, but it was highly suggestive to later psychologists as was work by C. L. Hull. We have also seen the attempts by Lewin to use mathematics to represent central ideas and relationships. Numerous attempts have been made to present learning curves in precise mathematical form and to employ the result in predictions of future learning. So far the results may have been disappointing but at least have been highly suggestive. An example of the use of mathematical principles in another field occurred when life insurance companies began making actuarial curves or tables and employing them in determining the likelihood of insurance risks.

Mathematical models, developed from success in games such as chess and from the study of communication, may still yield important data about learning.

As W. K. Estes [42] points out, information that is incorporated in such a model is in a form that is suitable for prediction, the results of different kinds of experiments are more nearly comparable when referred to such a model, quantitative analysis of data is usually facilitated by having such a model, and the very rigor associated with constructing the model itself leads to precise testing of any assumptions.

It may be that this mode of theorizing holds much for the future. Naturally it will not and need not replace other kinds of investigation. Mathematical models are far from foolproof; they are useful so far within a limited range of phenomena. Moreover, as E. R. Hilgard [43] reminds us, the most arresting theories are still, and may still be, made without benefit of mathematics, as were Freud's.

CYBERNETICS

The application of *cybernetics,* or feedback, have been many. The term was coined by Norbert Wiener [44] and is applied to part of the process of communication and of learning, an extremely important part. As in Lewin's work, which has served as a means to understand and describe complex processes of learning, *cybernetics* is not so much a theory as a way of describing and understanding. The language of feedback is useful for describing any kind of purposive behavior and therefore will often apply to situations in which two-way communication and learning are taking place.

Is a General Theory of Adult Learning Possible?

Many adult educationists have pointed out the need for some generalized theory of adult learning that would (1) provide a guide for developing curricula and selecting methods and teaching styles; (2) offer hypotheses for research; and (3) establish criteria for evaluation. This may sound somewhat like a search for El Dorado, and no such magical or scientific theory is likely to arise or be formulated soon.

Nevertheless, the need for generalized theory is real, and it may be that improved generalizations are already possible. At several points in this chapter we have noted possible elements or factors that might be combined within such a generalization.

One example is found in a paper by Josephine Flaherty.[45] Starting with general agreement that almost all human behavior is learned and that learning results in a relatively permanent change of behavior, she goes on to suggest an initial synthesis of learning concepts that might be brought together into a generalized theory, using both the concepts of "fluid intelligence" and "crystallized intelligence."

> Horn and Cattell postulate that the primary ability factors of Thurstone, Guilford and others, which are called intelligence, can be organized at a general level into two principal dimensions. These are: (a) fluid intelligence which is the result of the influence of biological factors on intellectual development, that is, heredity, injury to the central nervous system or basic sensory structures, and so forth; and (b) crystallized intelligence which is the result of experience, education and cultural background.
>
> Each of these dimensions has a profound influence upon the development of an individual's "abilities." The fluid dimension appears to determine how well an individual will perform in novel situations to which he cannot react on the basis of previous experience in a highly similar situation. Hence, fluid intelligence determines the extent to which a person can "transfer" his past experience to new situations. Crystallized intelligence reflects the extent to which an individual has mastered the skills and knowledge of his culture, that is, his store of proven "aids" to problem solving. . . .

Relating these two concepts, Professor Flaherty suggests:

> . . . that an individual solves a problem (or learns) by one of two methods: either he uses his fluid intelligence for reasoning, concept formation, perception and education of relations, or he calls upon his store of "aids" to problem solving (abilities) and applies these directly. It is highly unlikely that learning or problem-solving is accomplished by either of these methods alone; rather, an individual probably uses a combination of the two methods in order to arrive at a solution in the most economical (in terms of energy) way. Generally, one would tend to call upon his store of "abilities" or ready-made solution instruments, and when these fail, he would exercise his fluid intelligence. Thus, limits on learning or problem-solving are set by an individual's level of fluid and crystallized intelligence. . . .

Professor Flaherty notes that many theorists agree that learning results in a relatively permanent change of behavior, that it takes place within the context of experience, and that ease or rate of learning depends on the ease with which new information is integrated by the learner.

REFERENCES

1. Edna Heidbreder, *Seven Psychologies* (New York: The Century Co., 1933). By permission of Appleton-Century-Crofts, Incorporated.

2. C. L. Hull, *Principles of Behavior* (New York: Appleton-Century-Crofts, Incorporated, 1943).
3. John S. Brubacher, *Modern Philosophies and Education* (Chicago: National Society for the Study of Education, 1955).
4. Jacques Maritain, in *Modern Philosophies and Education* (Chicago: National Society for the Study of Education, 1955).
5. M. M. Coady, *Adult Education in Canada* (Toronto: Canadian Association for Adult Education, 1950).
6. Mortimer Adler, in *Modern Philosophies and Education* (Chicago: National Society for the Study of Education, 1955). Permission granted by The Great Books Foundation, Chicago, copyright owners.
7. *Ibid.*
8. *Ibid.*
9. John Dewey, *Problems of Men* (New York: Philosophical Library, Inc., 1946).
10. John Dewey, *Democracy and Education* (New York: The Macmillan Company, 1920). By permission of The Macmillan Company.
11. William H. Kilpatrick, in *Modern Philosophies and Education* (Chicago: National Society for the Study of Education, 1955).
12. Eduard Lindeman, *The Democratic Man,* Robert Gessner, ed. (Boston: Beacon Press, Inc., 1956). Used by permission.
13. *Journal of Educational Sociology,* September, 1945.
14. J. H. Newman, *An Essay in Aid of a Grammar of Assent* (London: Longmans Green, 1891).
15. Richard Livingstone, *On Education* (New York: The Macmillan Company, 1945).
16. *Ibid.* Cambridge University Press, copyright owners.
17. Adult Education Association, *Seeking Common Ground in Adult Education* (Chicago: Adult Education Association of the United States, 1959).
18. Ivan Illich, "The False Ideology of Schooling" from *Great Issues Today* (Chicago: *Encyclopaedia Britannica,* 1970).
19. Paulo Freire, *Pedagogy of the Oppressed* (New York: Herder and Herder, 1970).
20. E. L. Thorndike, *Animal Intelligence* (New York: The Macmillan Company, 1911). By permission of the publisher.
21. John Locke, *Essay on the Human Understanding* (London: 1775).
22. E. L. Thorndike, *The Fundamentals of Learning* (New York: Teachers College, Columbia University, 1932).
23. R. S. Woodworth, *Psychology* (New York: Henry Holt and Company, Incorporated, 1929).
24. E. L. Thorndike, *The Fundamentals of Learning* (New York: Teachers College, Columbia University, 1932).
25. E. C. Tolman, *Purposive Behavior in Animals and Men* (New York: Appleton-Century-Crofts, Incorporated, 1932).
26. B. F. Skinner, *Walden II* (New York: The Macmillan Company, 1948).
27. C. L. Hull, *Principles of Behavior* (New York: Appleton-Century-Crofts, Incorporated, 1943).
28. W. Kohler, *Gestalt Psychology* (New York: Liveright Publishing Corporation, 1947).
29. Kurt Lewin, *Resolving Social Conflicts* (New York: Harper & Brothers, 1948).

30. Marshall McLuhan, *Explorations 8* (Toronto: University of Toronto Press, 1948). University of Toronto, copyright owners.
31. Ronald Lippitt and R. K. White, "An Experimental Study of Leadership and Group Life," *Readings in Social Psychology* (New York: Henry Holt and Company, Incorporated, 1947).
32. Dorothy Stock and Herbert Thelen, *Emotional Dynamics and Group Culture* (New York: New York University Press, for National Training Laboratories, 1958).
33. Jean Piaget, *The Psychology of Intelligence* (London: Routledge and Kegan Paul, 1950).
34. Jerome Bruner and others, *Studies in Cognitive Growth* (New York: John Wiley and Sons, 1966).
35. David P. Ausubel, *Learning Theory and Classroom Practice* (Toronto: The Ontario Institute for Studies in Education, 1967).
36. J. R. Kidd, *The Implications of Continuous Learning* (Toronto: W. J. Gage Ltd., 1966).
37. Leonard L. Shorey, "Teacher Participation in Continuing Education Activities" (Toronto: The Ontario Institute for Studies in Education, unpublished Ph.D. Thesis).
38. Allen Tough, *The Adult's Learning Projects* (Toronto: The Ontario Institute for Studies in Education, 1971).
39. Stanley Moses, *The Learning Force* (Syracuse: Syracuse University Publication in Continuing Education, 1971).
40. David E. Hunt, *Matching Models in Education* (Toronto: The Ontario Institute for Studies in Education, 1971).
41. Rollo May, *Love and Will* (New York: W. W. Norton and Company, 1969).
42. W. K. Estes, *Modern Learning Theory* (New York: Appleton-Century-Crofts, Incorporated, 1948).
43. E. R. Hilgard, *Theories of Learning* (New York: Appleton-Century-Crofts, Incorporated, 1964).
44. Norbert Wiener, *Cybernetics* (New York: Appleton-Century-Crofts, Incorporated, 1956).
45. Josephine Flaherty "Some Thoughts on the Assessment of Learning Ability" (Toronto: The Ontario Institute for Studies in Education, 1971).

SUGGESTED READING

Bergevin, Paul. *A Philosophy for Adult Education.* New York: Seabury Press, 1967.

Blakely, Robert J. *Adult Education in a Free Society.* Syracuse: Syracuse University Publications in Continuing Education, 1966.

Bugental, J. F. T. *Challenges of Humanistic Psychology.* New York: McGraw-Hill Co., 1967.

Deinum, Andries. *Speaking for Myself: A Humanist Approach to Adult Education for a Technical Age.* Syracuse: Syracuse University Publications in Continuing Education, 1966.

Hilgard, E. R., and Bower, G. H. *Theories of Learning* (3rd ed.). (New York: Appleton-Century-Crofts, 1966).

Jensen, G., and others, ed. *Adult Education—Outlines of an Emerging Field of University Study*. Washington: Adult Education Association of the U.S.A., 1964.

Leagans, J. Paul, Copeland, Harlan G., and Kaiser, Gertrude E. *Selected Concepts from Educational Psychology and Adult Education for Extension and Continuing Educators*. Notes and Essays on Education for Adults, No. 71. Syracuse: Syracuse University Publications in Continuing Education, 1971.

Lengrand, Paul. *An Introduction to Lifelong Education*. New York: UNESCO Publications, 1971.

Powell, John W. *Adult Education Issues in Dispute*. Chicago: Adult Education Association, U.S.A., 1960.

Rogers, Carl R. *Freedom to Learn*. Columbus: Charles E. Merrill Publishing Company, 1969.

Silberman, Charles. *Crisis in the Classroom*. New York: Doubleday, 1970.

8

Some Fields of Practice

So far we have come a long way on our quest. We have looked searchingly at the learner and have seen how radically he changes, yet remains essentially the same, as he goes through life. We have examined his actions, interests and motives—how attitudes are developed and how they change. And we have had an all-too-brief look at some theories of learning, and considered how one can bring theory into some consistent pattern for oneself.

It does not seem possible to give a simple satisfying answer to the question "How do adults learn?" but we have observed many forms of learning in practice, and in consequence the very word *learning* is beginning to take on additional layers of meaning. We have not found it possible to fashion a single comprehensive theory of learning either, although the conditions for such achievement have at last been defined, and the rigorous preparation for such a formulation begun. We are more fully aware that the processes we call *learning* are not all of the same kind and are not easily comprehended in any single formulation.

But that is no new problem. It isn't easy, for example, to include all the principles and ideas that we usually associate with the notion *democracy* in one single system either. And yet enough agreement on principles and practices which, for all the limitations and ambiguities, serves fairly well, has been attained. This is what has been needed for learning. A review of the theories over which some men have quarreled and argued fiercely reveals more similarities and complementary relationships than irreconcilable conflicts.

We are now going to turn from these general observations and begin to review briefly (again risking the danger of oversimplification) what is being found out about learning in some practical fields of training, experimentation, and research.

193

In Chapter 7 we reviewed some theories of learning that illuminate the work of the practitioner. Now we consider some experiences from fields of practice out of which principles may be derived. This is not a manual for action or a collection of how-to-do-it tips, but an examination of practice which may well provide some guiding principles.

First of all, many disciplines are employed in these fields, and there are examples of interdisciplinary or cross-disciplinary practice.

Second, what has been called the "creative frontier," the growing edge, is just as often to be found in some practical field of work as it is in the laboratory. Ideas about learning are just as likely to come from an amateur scientist, like Galton, or one engaged in some pursuit other than that of learning, like Freud, than from those observing animals or men struggling with a problem box or problem. Whitman once talked about democracy itself as a great school:

> Political democracy, as it exists and practically works in America, with all of its threatening evils, supplies a training school for making first class men. It is life's gymnasium, not of good only, but of all.

Adult education is particularly rich in programs from which information, insights, and even models may be extracted. There is infinite variety in the scale of activities. Within the scope of adult education occur educational activities planned along a continuum that reaches from the self-study of a single individual through various kinds of small intimate group associations to very large aggregations. Many of these activities cut across lines of age, class, culture, and nationality, so the possibility of comparative studies is always present. Comparative studies not only provide information and concepts from other systems but also lead to evaluation and understanding of one's own system and oneself. A feature of many adult education activities is that they occur at a crossroads where several disciplines intersect.

In a television interview, Edward Murrow once asked scientist Robert Oppenheimer how ordinary people can ever keep in touch with the scientist who is forging ever farther ahead in his discoveries. Oppenheimer acknowledged that this is a perplexing matter. And he added, the difficulty is not one for the layman alone; it may be burdensome for the scientist, who, while he continues to cultivate his own tiny patch of truth, may be equally ignorant as other men, of all other fields of inquiry. It is in the places where the paths of such scientists intersect or cross; it is at the intersections of two fields of work or inquiry that the greatest amount of growth may be expected, he pointed out. We shall note some examples of these creative intersections in this chapter.

These are all positive advantages. But the favorable results do not arise by chance. If learning practice and theory are to be enlarged and deepened, it will be by practitioners and scholars who are on the alert, who develop systematic means for monitoring and evaluating experience, and for diffusing and sharing the results. These are tasks that need to be shared by universities, associations of adult educationists, and international organizations. But the process starts with the practitioner, who will remove his blinkers, scan and appraise his own work, and then take a step beyond his own job and agency to observe how learning occurs in other settings.

The numbers and kinds of educational activities for adults have increased to such an extent that only a computer can keep track. Indeed, one of the most useful innovations of recent years are computer-based information projects designed to provide learners with information about learning opportunities that are available to them. But one can easily be lost or suffocated by complexity, and it may be necessary to select certain activities and certain fields for special study, particularly those which seem to promise the largest returns. While the criteria for selecting activities as a source of insights or models for adult learning are still to be worked out with greater care, the following fields of practice can be cited because they have proved already to be productive sources. No consistent plan of presentation has been followed here. Another observer might have produced a different list. The selected experiences are examined briefly, not so much in terms of their intended purpose as for what they infer about learning. This is a suggestive, not a comprehensive, record of some of the fields of activity that anyone interested in learning should keep in sight. Of course it is no easy task to keep up. It's like "Wonderland." "Here," said the Queen, "it takes all the running you can do to keep in the same place. If you want to get somewhere else, you must run at least twice as fast as that."

Large-Scale Training Programs

Harold Clark [1] was one of the first observers to point out that there are really two systems of higher education, or three if one counts the community colleges as a separate system. In addition to colleges and universities there are the training programs organized and run by great corporations. In number of students, in size of teaching staff, in competence of staff, in library and research facilities, the *higher* education offered by business organizations is of considerable magnitude.

Training today is a very large enterprise. It is carried on under a great many and a great variety of auspices. We shall deal particularly with four fields of training because of the mass of the operations and because of the impact that these programs are having, and will have, on theory and practice of learning:

- in adult basic education programs
- in agriculture
- in industry
- in the armed forces

In each of these fields there is a substantial number of full-time teacher-trainers. For example, there are approximately ten thousand men and women engaged full time in some form of agricultural extension. In aggregate, the student body in these four fields must reach many millions every year. The training programs have budgets that usually exceed or at least compare favorably with that provided in schools and universities. Most of these programs can draw upon at least a small research staff which helps to plan and appraise the educational activities. Many of these agencies have had some opportunity for publishing and there have been voluminous reports, studies, pamphlets, and booklets dealing with some phases of the work. In sheer volume this is immense. It is difficult to judge quality, because there have been few attempts to apply rigorous evaluation. Nor will it be our task to do so, except in a very general way. We shall assume that a worker in any particular field is familiar with the writing in his field. Our purpose will be to derive general observations and principles from the three fields, and point to additional sources of information so that a teacher in one institution has a brief introduction to other related fields.

We shall make no attempt to deal with the origins or evolution of these training programs although this is a very large and fascinating topic of social history and one deserving much more serious attention by historians. In most fields training began with certain marked characteristics. Invariably it started in some form of apprenticeship, in which one man taught one man, usually in the manner of "Do like this." Later the skilled man was obliged to undertake the training of several. The *students* were obliged to copy the behavior of the *master*, with a heavy emphasis upon drill. Belief in the efficacy of repetition and the efficacy of punishment marked many training schemes, which also had to labor under the kind of assumption, current in the British Navy, but found in many forms elsewhere, that "what was good enough for Lord Nelson is good enough for you." Not all the training was poor; much of it may have been quite good. But it varied according to the insights and skills of individual trainers, there was no extensive body of knowledge about training to be passed on, and much of what was advocated was exceedingly limited or downright harmful.

The earliest fields for extensive application of what the psychologists were finding out about learning were large-scale training projects. The beginnings go back at least to the first decade of this century and the process was accelerated during World War I. In the twenties and thirties came an expanded program in agriculture and an increase in the number of industrial psychologists that were hired by industries. But the most rapid developments have occurred during and since World War II.

ADULT BASIC EDUCATION (FUNCTIONAL LITERACY)

In several countries during the 1960's the largest programs of adult education were some form of elementary academic education, called by many names but notably *adult basic education* or *functional literacy*. Here the numbers of learners were very large, many of the programs were not impoverished for resources, and the practitioners were able to utilize fully educational technologies. The field of functional literacy has attracted experienced adult educationists, as well as workers from other fields and disciplines. One finds programs based on the most traditional methodologies and materials alongside projects by apostles holding radical educational ideas. One major concept has appeared—*conscientizacion*, developed by Paulo Freire in his work with illiterate peasants in Brazil, and later extended and modified by his experiences in other countries.

Since 1967, UNESCO has given increasing attention to evaluation of the forty or fifty major national programs in functional literacy, and reports are becoming available, including efforts at cost benefit analysis. Crude though the early attempts of evaluation have been, they are being refined. Moreover, some of these projects are now preceded by preliminary studies which attempt to establish the most likely communities or environments for learning, and to establish favorable preconditions for learning campaigns.

In 1970, the report *Adult Basic Education* [2] was published in the United States, bringing together what had been established about learning theory and practice in ABE programs during the 1960's.

A phenomenon of the 1960's was the emergence of many kinds of social action projects for underprivileged people who were working for their own advantage or with the assistance of many kinds of social *animateurs*, including educationists, lawyers, doctors, and social workers. The extent and variety of these projects has increased, and there have been some examples of purposeful utilization of them for adult learning. The task of the *animateur* is to help people learn how to care and fend for themselves. The task of adult educationists is to utilize such programs not only for social goals but also for the increased understanding of learners about society and about themselves. There has been a spate of romantic rhetoric respecting some of these programs. It is not surprising that some have not lived up to what were unrealistic expectations, but they have offered and will continue to offer many opportunities for self-actualization. What has been lacking is a better understanding of the learning goals and methods to achieve such goals within a process where the emphasis is upon social action.

AGRICULTURAL EXTENSION

During this century the proportion of farmers in the total population of the United States has declined markedly, and thus agricultural extension is no longer the most prestigious subsystem of adult education. However, it is an example of extraordinary achievement, the practices of which are of considerable importance in most countries of the world.

Agricultural extension used to be regarded as "aiming to make two blades of grass grow where one grew before." It is now conceived as something very much broader:

> To assist people engaged in farming and homemaking to utilize more fully their own resources, and those available to them, in solving current problems and in meeting changing economic and social needs.[3]

The content may encompass the entire range of agriculture and home economics, yet centering on the interest or need of the individual. The goals are broad and various. They may include:

- Development of an awareness of the problem.
- Stimulation of a group to organize for co-operative action.
- Training of individuals in the skills of farming and homemaking.
- Obtaining the acceptance of the findings of scientific research in the production, marketing, and consumption of agricultural products.

The chief methods used by extension agents have been (1) individual contacts which include farm and home visits, office calls, telephone calls, result demonstration and personal letter; (2) group contacts such as demonstration meetings, leadership training meetings, lectures, tours; and (3) mass contacts such as bulletins, news stories, radio and television, mass meetings. Those responsible for this widely ranging program have put considerable emphasis upon appraising results. The techniques employed may have lacked somewhat in depth or subtlety, but they are rigorous in at least one sense. The usual procedure is to count the number of times there is an actual *change in practice*. It is not possible to deal with all learning on this basis but it has added something to our understanding about learning when its effects are tabulated in this concrete way. By choosing a unit such as a change in practice, one is then able to compare and contrast the kinds of factors which may have produced that change. We say *may have*, for although this research rests upon an assumption that the change is *caused* by a method, or a combination of methods, and the assumption may be valid, no final proof is possible because of the number of modifying influences.

There seem to be five stages to this process of adaptation as described in a special report entitled *The Diffusion Process*:

1. Awareness or learning about the idea or practice
2. Interest, being concerned enough to seek further information
3. Evaluation, weighing the merits of the idea or practice
4. Trial, seeing how it works in practice
5. Adoption.[4]

Studies have been conducted covering almost 50,000 separate changes in practice in over 15,000 farm families in 27 states. One of the most interesting findings is that changes in farm practice happen *indirectly* at least two times out of five—that is, farm people often learn from, or copy, their neighbor. For men, the figure is quite high: the neighbor is a source of the changed practice at least 25 per cent of the time. For women, about half of the practices came as a result of a meeting in which some new method was demonstrated. Covering both men and women, changes occur about 25 per cent of the time from individual contacts with the extension agent, about 33 per cent of the time by various kinds of meetings and group contacts, and about 23 per cent of the time through the mass media.[5]

There are other ways to look at these results. In addition to checking the kind of influence which seems to have produced the change, it has been possible to estimate what was the cost of the change. It was found, for example, that about 20 per cent of the total budget of extension workers was used for demonstrations of methods and leadership training which in turn produced about 20 per cent of the changes in practice. Farm and home visits cost about 14 per cent of the budget but brought nearly 16 per cent of the results. On the other hand, result demonstrations which took about 17 per cent of the budget produced 8 per cent of the result, or only one-half of what might be expected. The effectiveness of exhibits seems to have been less than one-fifth as much as the funds spent on it would warrant. News stories and radio, however, with one-twentieth of the budget, produced three times the result that might be anticipated.

The studies revealed other interesting facts. Efforts have been made to find out factors about the personality and the experience of the learner which seemed to be linked most closely to readiness for change. There is considerable evidence to show, for example, that some farmers can learn from almost any kind of stimulus—from neighbors, the agricultural agent, pamphlets, or radio talks. But others, usually those who have enjoyed much less formal schooling, are not able, or are not willing, to learn from reading or listening to the radio. They seem to require personal help; they can learn directly from the agent through demonstrations but seldom, if ever, from a pamphlet. In general, people with the least academic experience require the most personal attention. But the studies also revealed that many extension agents spend most of their personal time with the most able farmers (the farmers that could learn in all the other ways) and spend least time with those who do not learn easily except by direct contact. This seems also to be the experience of a number of other field services, operated by governments, universities, business corporations, and churches.

A factor which may result in resistance to change is the strength of the ethnic, religious, or social groups to which a farmer belongs. Duncan and Kreitlow [6] found that farmers who belong to groups or organizations that are cohesive adopt new practices less frequently and less readily than do other farmers of equal ability and experience, but for whom neighborhood or kinship ties are not so binding. We note elsewhere, that the strength of the bonds within the major groups to which one belongs will modify appreciably the perception of ideas or messages to which one is exposed. It is well established that new ideas are much more readily accepted (that is, learned) if they are or can be associated with existing values.

Considerable attention has also been given to the message itself, in print, radio, or picture—how readable, or how easily communicated, it is. Some of these findings will be summarized later under "communication research."

Most of the "training" for agriculture takes place in special colleges or in large-scale agricultural extension programs. Many variations can be found, from place to place, but it is all one system. There are a growing number of extension services operated by such private organizations as seed or farm implement companies, and there are also individual farm consultants. But nowhere in agriculture is there the variety of method and technique that is found in industry where the direction of training is largely in the hands of private companies.

INDUSTRIAL TRAINING

A growing number of people are engaged in full-time industrial training. Many of them now belong to societies of trainers and may thus be enabled to share in common exploration of philosophy and method of training. For some people "training" is beginning to be a profession, with an increasingly well-organized body of knowledge and skills. One now hears much more often the phrase "training the trainers," and this implies that there is a body of theory and practice which is becoming established and which is being taught or communicated.

The industrial trainers have several factors in their situation that are favorable for further advances in learning theory and practice. Theirs is a comparatively new calling from which one can expect some freshness and flexibility of viewpoint—necessary alike for exploration and for integration of theories. Their task is important and is recognized as such; they commonly have funds at their disposal that are more ample than most educationalists have ever had and which can be applied to research. Moreover, variety in "students" and in learning objectives is sufficiently broad to allow for flexibility. Some of the "students" may be top executives, others may be research scientists. Corporations in the United States now employ more than half a million research scientists, and such men may be obliged to go "back to school" regularly to keep up with radical advances in their own or allied fields.

At present training in industry covers many fields:

- Apprenticeship of various kinds.
- Skills taught and supervised by foremen in informal, on-the-job situations.
- Classes, training departments or schools organized in the company or by an industry-wide trade association for employees or management.
- Classes inside or outside the plant organized in some plan of relationship with an educational authority, such as a community college or school board, for employees or management.

Large-scale training programs in industry has been going on for most of the century. Research associated with training was given considerable impetus after the success of the so-called Hawthorne experiments.[7] The experimental approaches in human relations taken in the Hawthorne plant of the Western Electric Company are now referred to as "classic," and they have affected training and industrial organization ever since. The researchers and the company began, in a modest way, to investigate factors which influenced industrial efficiency. Most of the results were presented in terms of output of production because this could be expressed in quantitative terms and could be measured. But since the studies had to do with such matters as the aspirations of workers, and the way workers regarded, or frustrated, or supported each other, the results have had implications far beyond industrial production.

Executives of Western Electric had arranged for a relatively simple research project; namely, how an improvement in illumination affects the rate of output. Their next series of experiments were to have much wider significance. It all began in a little room in the plant, with six girls as subjects.

Before the investigation began, careful records had been kept and what each girl had produced over several months was already known, as well as a large body of information about production rates of all employees. The experiment was to study the output curve of the girls in the test for a long enough time and under various changes in working conditions, so that which conditions were most satisfactory in their effect might be determined.

At the beginning of the experiment the girls were kept for five weeks working under conditions very much as before, so that any changes in output brought about by the transfer would already be accounted for.

Over several months a series of changes were introduced, one at a time:

- increase in pay for piecework
- two rest pauses
- lengthening of rest pauses
- lunch provided in morning and afternoon
- shortening of work day
- shortening of work week

With *all* these changes the output improved. Moreover, when an attempt was made to return to previous conditions, output did not drop, it continued high and showed some improvement. No matter what was done, it seemed, the girls produced more. How could this be accounted for?

The explanations were provided most readily through talking with the girls themselves. The girls said they liked to work in the test room; "it was fun." Second, though they were under the constant surveillance of the experimenters, the absence of the customary supervisory control made it possible for them to work freely without anxiety. Conversation was allowed. It had formerly been restricted in principle and barely tolerated in practice; now it was allowed natural expression. Third, the girls realized that they were taking part in what was considered an important experiment, their work was expected to produce results which would lead to the improvement of working conditions for their fellow employees. Fourth, there was development within the group itself. Parties and social occasions were arranged, and the girls became attached to one another, and to the group. When one girl would have a good reason for feeling tired the others would "carry" her, working especially fast to make up for her lower output. Within the group itself leadership developed.

At about the same time a group of men were being tested in a "bank wiring" operation, under *social* conditions which tended to produce opposite results. The work routines established for the men seemed to deny all that gave work its value, the men were afraid of supervision and acted in the most ingenious ways to nullify it. Production and worker satisfaction were equally low.

These facts and these explanations are not so surprising as they seemed forty years ago. There has been a substantial shift in the attention of social scientists, from an exclusive concern with measuring the effect of physical and environmental factors upon behavior to never-ending investigations of the factors within a person, and his personal relations with others. Investigators such as David McLelland's assessment of the "achievement motive" and Frederick Hershberg of the distinction between "maintenance" and "motivating" factors in production to which we referred in Chapter 5 are just two examples that have been widely discussed. Most industries have given major attention to what constitutes "job enrichment" and similar questions have been investigated and debated by trade unions. The implication for learning institutions of "job enrichment" is better understood but not always practiced.

Research which was once characteristic of North America and the United Kingdom is now going on all over Europe and many Asian and African countries.

Circular Effect of Morale and Efficiency. During World War II ample opportunities were afforded to study the importance of similar factors. One such study,[8] for example, had to do with morale and efficiency in the shipbuilding industry. Two shipyards owned by the same company, were located in the same city, but were operated under different managements. The workers shared unsatisfactory housing conditions, a severe climate, and inadequate recreation for themselves and their families. One might therefore have expected similar output records. Yet in one yard a ship was turned out every 76 days; in the other it took 207 days, or nearly three times as long. The community environment and the physical working conditions were similar, and so was the work experience of the men, but some marked differences were found in other factors: The earning situation (overtime and back pay, as well as the basic wage) was much better at one plant. Poor morale in the other plant seemed to have been aggravated by broken promises. As one man put it, "If only they didn't keep promising these things! If they'd only keep the promises they make or didn't make any, maybe they'd get better work."

First, like other social processes, there is a *circular causal relation* between morale and production. Good production gives men a feeling of accomplishment and leads to increased effort. Low production reduces motivation, which in turn leads to reduced productivity. Instead of a one-way causal relation, most social processes show this circular interaction.

Second, worker morale is directly related to its immediate physical and psychological context. Moreover, under such circumstances most individuals can absorb considerable deprivation on the outside and still keep up their work morale. The inference should not be drawn, of course, that management has no stake in good living conditions for workers in the community. Rather the implication of these findings is that management should put its first emphasis upon making the job itself remunerative and psychologically rewarding.

Genuine participation. The employee needs an opportunity for expressing his ideas and making suggestions. This happens often in the higher ranges of management, but not always in the lower reaches. An example that can be repeated endlessly concerns the owner of a small plant turning out gymnasium and playground equipment. This was a family-owned industry; the owner knew all the workmen by their first names, and often worked beside them at the bench. When, in a period of financial difficulty, he called on the help of a management-consultant firm, the experts were able to tell him nothing that he did not know. Nevertheless the inquiry led to results that raised his production and sales in a substantial manner. The consultants talked with *all* the workmen seeking their advice and suggestions. Six of their recommendations were followed up, and these brought about the critical improvement in the situation. Naturally such an operation cannot proceed in identical fashion in vast industries, but the efficacy of active participation in bringing results of higher quality does not require further demonstration.

Responsibility. When subordinates have achieved security they are able to assume responsibility gradually and accept it with pleasure and pride.

The right of appeal. The growth of self-assurance and self-expression can be safeguarded only if a person feels that he can win approval for an idea and an action, if it is sound, regardless of views of an immediate superior.

We have referred in Chapter 5 to forms of management training, such as the *Managerial Grid* [9] by which managers work out a relationship between "production goals" and goals of good human relations.

In their book *New Understandings of Leadership* [10] Ross and Hendry discuss a number of other facets of "leadership" that affect learning in industry and elsewhere. Perhaps the most important of these is *empathy* or social sensitivity—that is, the accuracy with which one person is able to perceive another. How well the leader understands the follower as the latter sees himself has a marked effect on the leader's behavior and consequently, upon the response that the follower makes to that behavior.

One approach to management training was developed in the 1950's around the concept of *sensitivity*. When first proposed by Robert Tannenbaum it may have been novel but would now be accepted by many industries. Tannenbaum states three specific objectives for sensitivity training:

- a greater understanding of one's self
- an awareness of one's impact upon other people
- a deeper appreciation of what goes on between people when they interact in a social situation. [11]

An attempt is made to help the managers become better skilled at helping individuals in communicating more effectively, in counseling, and in dealing with situations involving tension and conflict.

In these studies all the factors mentioned are operating when the task is learning just as when the task is production. We shall deal with other factors that also affect both learning and production in industry, under such heads as group development and research in communications.

THE ARMED FORCES

The staggering task of training millions of men and women, in and out of uniform, during World War I and again in World War II provided new opportunities as well as new problems. We have seen how the use of psychological tests advanced tremendously during and after World War I, based in part on the fame of the army *Alpha* and *Beta* test scales. Until then, most observations of adults had been of very small samples, usually isolated in institutions. Now there were large numbers of men to test who were from every kind of background and with every kind of experience.

Research in regard to training and education went on continuously during World War II. There was, for example, an entire project devoted to the study of audiovisual training aids and the conditions under which learning with such aids is effective. Most of this work was carried out in universities by individual investigators, or teams. This was one of the first large-scale attempts by men from different disciplines to work together on basic problems. The problems of such collaboration are many, but we have noted before that many human problems cannot be tackled solely from the point of view of a single discipline. Learning itself is one of the best illustrations of this point. Because it is multidisciplinary, the research associated with the armed services may have much to contribute to general learning theory and practice.

Other Findings. During World War II there were many examples of new applications of learning theory as well as activities which deepened our understanding of learning. Much attention was given to such basic questions as these: How could men be trained for their forthcoming ordeal? What facts, skills, or attitudes were most important? These major inquiries were usually preceded by field studies conducted by social scientists, *in the battle situation.* Then training goals were formulated, and methods and materials devised. For fast and effective learning the *real* situation was reproduced for training (through maneuvers and exercises. Combat problems were presented, in film and in actual test. The use of equipment was taught with the actual equipment, or in mockups, or with films.

Of course, information and skills are not everything. There is also morale. Could morale be taught? Perhaps not; at least not directly. But some factors in morale could be studied. A Canadian professor of philosophy [12] had been making a thorough study of young men who were idlers and drifters during the depression years, apathetic, morose, angry, and sullen. Three years later some of these men, and others like them, were the heroes of the Battle of Britain. Their squadrons were considered to epitomize morale. What were the differences? There seemed to be many, but three in particular:

- The airmen were well-trained and knew they were well-trained—their equipment was the best obtainable.
- The job they had to do was of the utmost importance and was so recognized.
- They belonged to a small select group—each man felt himself responsible to the others as well as to and for himself.

Later studies have given support to these findings. A flyer valued first his own crew, then the squadron, next the group, the wing and finally the air force itself. Ideas he might have about justice or democracy were not without significance in his behavior, but the key factor was his belief in himself and his associates. Other studies were carried out to discover what kinds of traits or experience were most closely associated with certain tasks. Measures were devised by which it was possible to predict, with reasonable accuracy, which of them might learn one kind of task, which another. There has been some application of this knowledge since, in selecting men for universities, and men for training for special industrial tasks.

Considerable study was devoted to learning procedures. How are men helped to achieve the most in class or demonstration?

The adult who is made to feel responsible for his own education tends to achieve the best record. Instructional materials were most successful when they were based on the actual experiences and needs of the men and women for whom they were prepared. Army men learned fundamental skills of reading, writing, and arithmetic with far greater efficiency when the subjects covered in the exercise books were about army life and adult experiences; much less well when the instructional materials were about childish things.

Some Implications. Millions of men and women studied in the classrooms of the armed forces. What was learned from these projects of training in use of equipment, tactics, literacy, language, international affairs, mathematics, and skill processes? This question was given intensive study by C. O. Houle and others. They reported a number of findings:

- Interest in education among adults is very widespread.
- Far more people than ever before were exposed to education as part of their adult experience and are motivated to continue learning if suitable opportunities are provided.
- Educational experiences for adults should be introduced into the activities to which adults *choose* to belong.
- The more education people have the more they are likely to want.
- Participation in education will be increased if the activities are provided geographically close to the students.
- Programs of adult education must be directed toward the achievements of goals which the students feel to be real and significant.
- The success of an educational activity for adults is enhanced if it starts at the level of the students and then proceeds to more abstract things.
- The motivations of adult learning grow in part out of the social setting in which the learner lives.
- Almost all adults who lack the basic tools of learning can achieve them if the subjects are well taught.[13]

Other Schools. Learning no less dramatic and no less crucial than in the army was occurring elsewhere during the war. One key place was in camps for internees, such as the Relocation Camps for the Japanese in North America. Here there was a struggle between those who wanted to use stern discipline as a tried-and-true method, and those who felt that more rational measures were possible.

In one of the camps, sociologists and anthropologists were brought into the staff. Soon an occasion arose for a test of rational principles. An ugly strike developed, brought about almost by group hysteria. For a while it seemed that nothing could be effective but brutal shoot-'em-down measures. However, some of the administrators were prepared to risk a good deal for their principles. In the face of mob violence an Emergency Council was created. Both the real difficulties and those conjured up in hysteria were faced by the council and proposals of how tensions could be reduced and human dignity restored were studied. No one pretended to know all the answers, but camp inmates and staff agreed to try, *and try together.* Order was soon restored. As a by-product some hypotheses had been established for use in the tension problems to be faced in the future. As Alexander Leighton described it: "I am certain that in the Relocation Camp experience, my hands, groping blindly below the surface, touched here and there on a real body of constants and laws in human living." [14]

In places under the horror of bomb raids, there were other learnings of a grim and necessary kind. How did you help people prepare themselves for an attack? Not by talk, or by study about war; the anxieties created before the event often seemed harder to bear; seemed to be more crippling than the blow itself. Not by taking children away from parents; family groups tended to stand firm against the dangers if family members were able to give support to each other in mastering the lessons of survival in the midst of terror. Not by taking people from one environment or culture and thrusting them into another. City people forced to leave their homes and snatched up into comparative safety of the country often seemed to crumple and break down when taken from the life that they knew. It was found that the best chance for city people to learn how to cope was to seek shelter in a comparatively safe part of the city, the environment in which they feel at home. Above all, people must not be fed on lies and promises. In times of peril truth seems to serve best. As Alfred Noyes once wrote:

> It might be
> The final test of man, the narrow way,
> That he should face this darkness and this death
> Worthily, and renounce all easy hope,
> All consolation, all but the wintry smile
> Upon the face of truth.

These are tragic lessons and one can hope that they will not need further application in similar settings. But they have validity for the way in which men will strive with any disaster, whether man-contrived or not. And in the process something has been learned about man, his nature, and how he learns.

CONTINUING EDUCATION FOR PROFESSIONAL AND PARAPROFESSIONAL

During the 1950's and 1960's the greatest gains in numbers of new programs in adult education were those planned for the continuing education of professional and paraprofessional personnel, including executive officers in corporations and in government. The reasons are many—the explosion of knowledge, the effect of "future shock," the increase in the numbers who have been to university and acquired a taste for further study, pressures to improve the quality of service offered, the thrust of enforced control by government over the professions, the availability of public funds for this purpose—all of these have had their individual and cumulative impact.

One result was that hundreds of alert, intelligent men and women were caught up in adult education as learners, demanding higher standards of excellence, and scores of them brought their talents and experience to planning, organizing, and teaching. Practices that had been innovated in adult education institutions were quickly adopted, refined, improved, and extended. It has been a time when stimulation methods, use of games, many examples of reality learning, utilization of various kinds of groups, testing the use of new media communications have flourished.

Measures have been taken only recently for those engaged in continuing education in one profession to share experiences with other professions or with the larger field of adult education. But it is clear already that any practitioner may find many implications for his work in the examination of goals, methods, planning, program, delivery systems, and evaluation techniques—all developed or demonstrated in professional continuing education.

SYSTEMS ANALYSIS

One of the major research modes that triumphed in World War II, and in corporations since is *operations research*, or *systems analysis*. Analyzing *inputs* and *outputs* is one useful way of understanding complex procedures in very large organizations. Since the data must be rationalized, and presented in a mathematical form, systems analysis has been a means which some educators have used to describe their goals and processes with much greater precision. Slavish adoption by educational institutions of processes like systems analysis and "management by objectives" does not seem warranted. However, related fields of practice do offer hypotheses which can be tested in the educational setting.

So far we have been considering fields of practice that are part of, or associated with, large-scale training projects. We shall now turn to selected experiences from other fields.

Groups and Group Development

Future historians may ultimately refer to the second quarter of the twentieth century as the era not of depression and war, but of *the group*. It was in these years that interest in group life, and what happens to individuals in groups, broadened and deepened. As more and more attention was showered on the group, particularly the small group, there was the usual and almost inevitable reaction. Some people who were specializing in studying group processes, or were working with groups, made claims and statements that could hardly be supported, and a counter-reaction soon appeared from those who charged that interests and values associated with the individual, and experience in large-scale or mass movements, were being slighted, even endangered. Flurries of this sort accompany most social changes and they need not occasion too much alarm. What ought to happen is a thoughtful examination of the new development to see if application can be made of it.

Writing in 1969, Carl Rogers has given some impression of the scope and influence of small-group experience:

In the rich, wild, new tapestry that is intensive group experience, one looks in vain for valuable or familiar designs. . . . It would, in fact, be surprising—and perhaps worse—if we *were* all that sure all this soon about what they are, because the group experience is so new. It is a potent new cultural development, an exciting social invention, a truly grass roots movement that has grown out of personal, organizational and social mud. Unrecognized by any major university, without backing from foundation, or government enquiries until the last few years, it has grown until it has permeated every part of the country and almost every social institution.[15]

It would be incorrect and rather silly to say that there was no interest in groups in relation to learning before 1925. Nevertheless, the major developments have all happened since. Some of them were first associated with Mary Follett and propositions which she advanced in the late twenties in such books as *Dynamic Administration*.[16] In the thirties a few social workers in such agencies as YMCA's and community centers began to talk of their special field as "group work," and in 1934 Busch published a book using the words "Group Work" in his title.[17] Also in the thirties and early war years, efforts were made to apply group processes to certain kinds of therapeutic situations. Psychiatrists and psychologists in their treatment of bewildered boys, or adults who were emotionally injured by some wartime experience, used the life in a group as one experience for cure and relearning. This was also the time when Sherif, Asch, and others were studying experimentally the difference in performance of an individual, alone and in a group.[18]

From these several fields of inquiry some broad generalizations were established:

- Groups have certain characteristics, an existence and dynamics of their own, that make them more than a sum of the individuals who take part.
- Group characteristics such as size, atmosphere, flexibility, homogeneity, cohesiveness, leadership exist in an equilibrium so that changes in some characteristics may result in changes in others.
- Groups may therefore change and undergo processes through time.

The period in which the terms *group dynamics* or *group development* were generally employed began during World War II. A number of social scientists, most of them in some association with Kurt Lewin, began a series of experiments in training in which factors of human relations were emphasized. To one of these experiments we have already given some attention. That is the means by which women were taught facts about nutrition and how changes were brought about in the *practice* and *habits* of some of the women. We have also referred to another experiment, developed under Lewin's direction, on the effect of certain kinds of leadership or "social climate" upon learning and behavior. Late in Lewin's lifetime a Center for Group Dynamics was set up at the Massachusetts Institute of Technology and subsequently transferred to the University of Michigan with the name Research Center for Group Dynamics. In 1947 a National Training Laboratory in Group Development began to hold training sessions each summer at Gould Academy at Bethel, Maine. This Laboratory was established for the following purposes:

- to develop a body of people prepared to carry on human relations training throughout a wide range of social institutions and activities
- to accomplish through research a gradual improvement in the theory and procedures of human relations training
- to work toward the general improvement of group problem-solving and member skills in society.[19]

The laboratory training, research, and consultation have led to a wide range of activities. Among them are an annual training and research seminar at Bethel, a year-round consultation program, a series of research projects on human relations training, a number of regional and local "laboratories" and workshops, and the production of various training aids such as films, articles, and training manuals.

Accordingly, many of the activities that may be included under such a term as group development have been associated, directly or indirectly, with the National Training Laboratory. However, other developments began to emerge in California, first the notion of "sensitivity training" by Robert Tannenbaum, then a swirl of activities, usually making use of small groups, at places like Big Sur and Esalen, activities that associated education with therapy, with the arts and creative expression, with new forms of verbal and nonverbal communication.

The National Training Laboratory. The specific objectives of the Laboratory have been stated as follows:

- To increase one's own sensitivity to the factors in intra-group and inter-group relations.
- To increase ability to *diagnose* the significant factors in human relations situations.
- To develop *insight* into the effects of one's own behavior upon another's.
- To provide an evaluation of human relations training through the use of *research evidence.*

- To provide opportunities to exercise group *problem* solving methods in human relations.
- To provide opportunity to practice some *leadership skills.*
- To relate the learnings of the laboratory to *back-home* situations.

Three educational decisions were made when the Laboratory was established. First, it was decided that *changed behavior* as well as *knowledge* was a primary objective. Accordingly methods had to be devised where members would become more deeply involved in the project. Second, there was a concern that the changes would hold true when the member left the Laboratory and returned home. Third, it was agreed that training *and* research must both be present and be mutually reinforcing.

In the Laboratory, then, the concern has been for learning that results in change and in developing an understanding and skill in dealing with the forces that tend to promote or inhibit change. Procedures have been developed which display a number of novel features.

The Laboratory attempts to create, for purposes of analysis and practice, group situations where are present the kind of factors operating in other groups. The learner participates in a group and continues to study what happens to him, to the other members, and to the "culture" of that group. He hears lectures on theory, he studies and reads, but first of all he takes part in and studies his own group in action. He is aided to use rigorous methods of observation and analysis in respect to his group. Every attempt is made to create an atmosphere in which he feels free and able to examine his own and others' behavior and to accept help and criticism from others. Opportunity is provided for him to become better aware of problems of insecurity and resistance to change as well as to practice some of the group skills he has learned.

The Laboratory employs many training forms and devices:

- *The T group* or training group for achieving a greater sensitivity to what happens in the group and a better understanding of self in relation to groups. The T group may tackle such problems as style of leadership, overcoming group or individual apathy, and how to reach group decisions.
- *The S group* for practicing such skills as how to make decisions in a group. These skills are practiced, as far as possible, in actual reality situations.
- *Theory sessions* in which a background of information and theory is provided so that a member may relate his experiences in an organized way.

- Sessions on such practical problems as what methods to use in large meetings.
- *The C or community group* in which a member meets with others in a small intimate circle in which he can freely discuss his experiences under no pressure to make decisions.
- Counseling with staff members.
- "Back home" sessions for the study of what the learner will be doing upon return and the application of his training to his regular tasks.

Implications for Learning Theory and Practice. The National Training Laboratory and similar centers have made a number of contributions to learning theory and practice.

- There is a substantial body of research data about what constitutes training.
- There have been many and varied uses of *reality situations* in learning. (We mean by reality situation the establishment of a setting which has factors similar enough to those actually faced by the learner so that he can observe, and analyze, and actually test out his theory and method. We noted earlier that training in the armed services has increasingly been in "reality" situations—training maneuvers carried out under live bombardments, use of actual weapons, or carefully simulated conditions.)
- The attempt to combine training and research, though not uniformly successful, points the direction in which most satisfactory teaching must move.
- The concern not only with the learning of content but with changes in behavior that carry over into practice has resulted in much more thorough exploration of how change is brought about.
- Many practical devices useful in other learning situations have been demonstrated and refined, such as observation techniques and role playing.

The books, reports, journals that deal with T groups, encounter groups, sensitivity training, and group therapies number in the hundreds. One short and practical guide to some of these concerns is *Introduction to Group Dynamics* by Malcolm and Hulda Knowles.[20]

Research about small groups is now going on in countries other than the United States. It may deal with a comparison of individual achievement with that of individuals in groups, or the way that groups relate to one another, or productivity as the result of group interaction and support. For example, in countries like Norway and Germany, there have been measures of performance when small groups in a ship or a factory are given actual autonomy and responsibility for some major work function. In most such situations, production or performance is considerably improved.

One of the most interesting fields of research is that in which the productivity of the group is compared with that of the individual. For many tasks people achieve considerably more in groups. But for some others, particularly in intellectual tasks, they may do better alone. Lorge and Brenner [21] have reported the somewhat contradictory evidence that has accumulated from these studies. Though not yet conclusive in result, these studies should provide much guidance in the future for adult education.

There have been a number of studies which deal with the impact, the pressure of the group upon the individual's judgment. Both Asch and Sherif [22] report that individuals are influenced significantly by their associates, even in giving incorrect estimates of distance, or weight or volume. In early attempts to develop useful devices for film evaluation, it was discovered that it was essential to record the reaction to the film of the appraisers, *as individuals*, before any consideration within the group. Discussion was useful in bringing out subtleties, but it invariably resulted in some merging or polarizing of opinion, whereas both the individual impressions and whatever consensus was achieved were useful. If the group effort preceded individual appraisal fewer of the individual differences were displayed. The impact of groups upon "conformity" is of significance for educational practice; it is also a matter of great ethical importance.

Theories and Research About Leadership

We have already noted that some studies have been conducted about leadership in military situations. Gouldner and others have reported how leadership is expressed in such fields as industry, in a social institution, in athletics, in a committee, and in technical assistance projects abroad.

In their book *New Understandings of Leadership* [23] Ross and Hendry have brought together many of the findings from a multitude of separate studies. Leadership is seen in three aspects:

- as traits within the individual leader
- as a function of a group
- as a function of a situation

It is quite clear from the studies reported that certain factors that had been assumed to be intrinsic to leadership are found only in some situations, and not at all in others. Of the multitudes of lists of traits (appearance, intelligence, and so on) that observers claim are associated with leadership, no two lists have much that is common.

However, some factors seem to be present in most examples of leadership. One of these, we noted earlier, is *empathy*. It seems probable that the leader, to an exceptional degree, is able to identify with, and to respond to, the emotional needs of the members of a group. He seems to have an enlarged sensitivity to their needs for recognition, affection, adventure; or he is perceived by the group members as being sensitive to such needs. Another factor is to be, or to appear to be, *practically concerned* with doing something about these needs. In one industrial plant men in high-producing sections felt that their foremen took a more personal interest in them than did men in low-producing sections. Likewise more men in the high-producing sections reported that their foremen were helpful in training them for better jobs than those in low-producing sections reported. Another factor, sometimes called *surgency*, has to do with liveliness, cheerfulness, and enthusiasm. The leader seems to display more self-assurance and internal strength, notably at times of crisis, than do other men. He seems, also, to *want* genuinely to be a leader. It may be becoming for a leader to hesitate until he is asked or drafted, but most leaders seem to be men who draft rather easily! Ability to communicate at a level deeper than talk also seems to be an essential. It seems equally important that the leader facilitates communication among the members, and is able to bring some color and excitement, some meaning and importance, to the activity.

As far as these findings are true, it becomes apparent that leadership is something much more complicated than the few skills that are often the content of courses termed *leadership training*. Such training may include skills like group organization, or mastering certain kinds of subject matter— but none of these learning experiences, useful though they may be, are of themselves essential or guarantees of acceptance as a leader. The *qualities* of the leader do evolve and change but not in any simple way.

It appears that the way in which a person grows and changes and develops *as a leader* has many parallels with other kinds of learning. Accordingly, close attention to leadership theory may be expected to be rewarding for teachers and other practitioners.

Communications Practice and Research

Few words are used more often and more loosely today than *communication*. The possible exceptions are the words *democracy* and *leadership*. In a single day the author heard the following:

"They robbed our communications"—a boy of thirteen was complaining that the rival baseball team had become aware of the signals his team was using.

"We ain't communicatin' right"—a youth of seventeen was deploring the rift in relationships between himself and a young lady.

"There has been a serious breakdown in communications with the Capitol"—a radio news analyst was explaining that he had not been able to get certain information from Congress.

"That strike is a direct result of lousy communications by the general manager"—a labor leader was blaming management for causing an industrial impasse.

How men express themselves, how they talk with each other, how ideas are exchanged, how feelings are aired and shared, these are crucial matters for learning.

One of the reasons that the word *communication,* though long and clumsy, is heard from every lip, is that communicating is now possible through so many new and exciting forms, by the mass media of communication. Just having the means of communication is hardly enough, as Thoreau wryly pointed out a century ago:

We are in great haste to construct a magnetic telegraph from Maine to Texas; but Maine and Texas, it may be, have nothing important to communicate. . . . We are eager to tunnel under the Atlantic and bring the Old World some weeks nearer to the New; but perchance the first news that will come through into the broad, flapping American ear will be that the Princess Adelaide has the whooping cough.[24]

But such means of communicating as television are so visible, and so omnipresent, that they cannot be ignored. Another reason is the growing interest in the *practice* of communicating, of using these new and remarkable tools by business men, advertisers, pressure groups, and government. Study about how ideas or slogans are transmitted, and what effect they may have, is going on constantly. Anyone today who wants to be aware of all the ways in which people learn cannot fail to keep in touch with various forms of communications research.

There was no such thing as organized communications research before 1930. A mail vote of the sort that the former *Literary Digest* magazine used to send out was considered an ample means of assessing public opinion. In the years since there have been studies of many kinds:

- *Control*—who owns the instruments of opinion and who determines what shall be said.
- *Audience*—what kind of people buy books, read newspapers, listen to radio or watch television? What are the predispositions of the audience?

- *The communications message*—Readability: do people understand what they read? Do they "get the point" of the radio or television message?
- *Social effect*—What is the response and the result of the message in changes in behavior?
- *Responsibility*—Freedom and responsibility of the editor, critic, broadcaster, teacher?
- *Political consequences*—how the *form* of communication, and its control, provides the opportunity for or modifies the results of different forms of government as a democratic or totalitarian power.

Change in the form of communication, such as invention of the printing press or television, has results that can only be described as revolutionary. Aristotle was sharply rebuked by Alexander for putting down words in a manuscript; it might result in rulers' being obliged to share power. Plato was equally concerned about the spread of written communications:

This discovery will create forgetfulness in the learners' souls, because they will not use their memories; they will trust to the external written characters and not remember of themselves. The specific which you have discovered is an aid not to memory, but to reminiscence, and you give your disciples not truth but the semblance of truth; they will be hearers of many things and have learned nothing; they will be tiresome company, having the show of wisdom without the reality.[25]

When the press became a true mass medium with the spread of inexpensive books and pamphlets, men like Newman were alarmed. But the fact that the form of communication has been instrumental in political control and the evolution of political power has been only dimly perceived, right to the present day when the speculations of Harold Innis [26] and others have initiated a new approach to the study of its consequences. Innis was interested in the means of communication in different periods of history and the use of these means by elite power groups. He explored some of the effects of the printing press such as the breakdown of international communication, the impetus given to nationalism by the exploitation of all vernacular languages, the loss of contact between writer and audience, and the inhibiting and depressing effect of the press upon such other forms of communication as music, plastic arts, and architecture. Much subsequent speculation, by Marshall McLuhan and others, originated in these propositions by Innis. Karl Deutsch wrote about political influence achieved through the media in his book *Nationalism and Social Communication*.[27]

These consequences may, or may not, be desirable. They are of many kinds. McLuhan pointed out that a feature of the book is its "republicanism."

> The page of print is not only a leveller of other forms of expression; it is a social leveller as well. Anyone who reads has at least the illusion of association on equal terms with anyone who has written. And that fact gave the printed word a privileged place in American society and politics. The Duke of Gloucester could say caustically to Edward Gibbon on the completion of his *History:* "Another damned fat square book. Scribble, scribble, scribble, eh, Mr. Gibbon!" But there were no fox-hunters in America to put the literary upstart in his place.[28]

McLuhan, in his most famous aphorism—"The medium is the message"—makes a point which seems inescapable and yet has evoked vigorous debate and discussion, that various media communicate and have effects and importance "regardless of the content." [29]

Those who are concerned with the probity or aesthetics of what is communicated bridle at this emphasis on the process, and some have charged that the proposition has provided a cloak of respectability for those engaged in mass communication. It is, of course, a perversion of McLuhan to suggest that since power and influence reside in the process, it matters not how accurate is the content of the message and, therefore, the purveyor of mass communications has no more responsibility.

McLuhan has given several concepts or propositions to the English language: one of them, "the global village." He argues that the impact of the media is to *tribalize*, to provide common experience to all people, no matter where they live. The aptness of this concept can be discerned. At the same time the media, or at least some of them, such as oral and video cassettes, seem as likely to individualize, to offer messages that are local and are received by individuals, thus making possible almost everywhere expressions of education "where you live" such as the Open University. Before the advent of printing, manuscripts were often used not for individual study but in social settings. When writing was in manuscript, manuscripts were read aloud; and writer and learner were still in direct touch with each other. Manuscript readers memorized most of what they read because, in the nature of things, they still were obliged to carry their learning with them. Difficulty of access to the manuscripts made different habits of mind and study. Most learning was oral and so was teaching. The spread of the inexpensive printed page helped to bring about solitary learning and private study. Today's emphasis upon the seminar and the group is not so much a break with the past as it is a return to it.

The effects of the mass media upon freedom of speech are far-reaching, more so than has been generally appreciated. As McLuhan has pointed out:

The instantaneity of communication makes free speech and thought difficult if not impossible and for many reasons. Radio extends the range of the casual speaking voice, but it forbids the many to speak. And when what is said has such a range of control it is forbidden to speak any but the most acceptable words and notions. Power and control are in all cases paid for by loss of freedom and flexibility.

Learning From Mass Media

How well do people learn from the mass media? Research to answer this question goes on in most of the countries of the world: a 1971 UNESCO publication by Ignacy Waniewicz, entitled *Broadcasting for Adult Education*,[30] referred to research and application in at least seventy-two countries. As a generalization, educational level is useful as a means of predicting the behavior of the recipient of a communication. Studies have confirmed a general tendency toward higher selectivity, more critical thinking, and "better taste" in the use of the mass media as the years of schooling rise. As is true of books, the individual tends to select mass media programs that are accessible to him, sometimes, in preference to what he says he is interested in, if the latter is harder to come by. People seem to learn more of what is concrete than what is abstract through radio and television. And as we have seen in another context, a variety of media seem to have a greater effect than a single method. Another way of saying this is that the greater number of sensory channels used in the learning process, the greater is the actual amount of learning. Studies have confirmed that learning is more rapid and efficient when the learner is a participant rather than simply a spectator and that learning must be used to be retained.

There have been many studies of learning by pictures, by moving pictures, by radio, by television, by cassettes, and by combination of media. In the present chapter we have already noted some such studies in connection with training in the armed services. Schools and universities have also been at work, and the results have been frequently reported in such books as *Audio-Visual Methods in Teaching* by Edgar Dale.[31]

It would be difficult now, as Waniewicz discovered in preparing the report for UNESCO, for any one person to deal with or account for all the research that has been completed, in scores of countries, respecting learning associated with the media. Used in certain procedures, media can affect the learning of very large groups indeed, or of individuals scattered over vast areas. The message conveyed can be reinforced by a variety of means. The learning may be information, or skills or attitudes. Most people would no longer be concerned solely with educational radio, or educational films, or instructional television, but with the full range of the media of communication. One witnesses the creation of more departments of media services in institutions and school boards or agencies featuring many media and having multifunctions such as the Ontario Educational Communications Authority.

It is quite obvious even from this scanty review that a system of communication whose *content* and whose *form* can so deeply influence human life must necessarily have many implications for learning. We shall deal with only three such implications, (1) the notion of *readability*, (2) the problem of *two-way* communication, and (3) studies dealing with the *effects* of communication. We select these, rather than other investigations, because they have continuing and wide application in education for adults.

READABILITY

How effective is a given sample of writing? Is it readable? Two separate, yet connected ideas—*appeal* and *clarity*—are involved in this question. Is the material of sufficient *interest* that people will want to read it? Is it *comprehensible* so that they will understand?

The problem is an important one. Governments, corporations, voluntary organizations all try to inform, instruct, warn, and assist people through the use of printed material. In a great many cases still, and this used to be true almost invariably, the printed message is in a form that people either will not or can not use. In 1930, at a time when the adult population had gone to school on an average only six or eight years, most of the printed messages planned for their use were prepared at about the grade-ten level or higher. The disparity is not so great now, but the problem has not suddenly disappeared.

Readability is far from being a new problem. Writers in all ages have been confronted by it. Many have been quick to offer their favorite remedy, some useful, some not. There are about as many quack cures for the disease of nonreadability as for the common cold. Most of the attention has been focused on words as if all the difficulty were found in them. "Write in words of one syllable" is common, and very silly advice. We are told to use *familiar* words, select the *concrete* rather than the *abstract*, the *short* word not the long, and to employ the word coming from a *Saxon* root rather than from one of the romance languages. "Choose from the vocabulary which is common to all your readers" is another bit of advice. Ingenious ways of doing this have been devised. As long ago as 1875, a Russian professor studied several thousand letters written by farmers to learn what vocabulary and idiom he might safely use in writing agricultural and educational bulletins.

Linguists have been forced to study other factors than word difficulty. One of these is difficulty of concept. Much of the writing in science and philosophy is hard to understand because the ideas as well as the vocabulary are remote from our ordinary experience and everyday habits of thought. Nevertheless some rare beings have found it possible to write and speak about difficult and complex subjects in a comprehensible and interesting fashion. Is this a special gift, or can it be learned? We have noted that in the pedagogy of Paulo Freire the first task of the teacher (or writer or broadcaster) is to learn from the students the concepts that concern them and the very images and language they best understand.

In the 1930's investigation of readability was carried out in "reading laboratories," work of an analytical and experimental nature. Certain barriers to understanding were identified, such as the length of sentences, the number of prepositional phrases, the number of difficult words. Those that seemed to be most significant were selected and worked into a formula for predicting reading difficulty by Irving Lorge.[32] Using his ingenious system, one can assess the grade level for most writing and thus estimate how difficult the reading may be for a class or group. One can also derive hints about how to write with greater chances of being understood.

Other studies and formulas have also been published. The best known is by Rudolph Flesch,[33] developed in a series of books such as *The Art of Plain Talk* and *The Art of Readable Writing*. Flesch worked out his formula through a detailed study of popular magazines where he assumed he could find a key to reading comprehension. Flesch believes that in these media, and in ordinary conversation, we can find the best guide to comprehension. "The secret," he says, "is not difficult ideas expressed in easy language, it is rather abstractions imbedded in small talk. It is heavy stuff packed with excelsior." Gaining interest and attention is a large part of the answer. Flesch combined a somewhat different set of factors in his formula. He uses sentence length; he adds as a new and positive factor personal references (names of people, pronouns, or other words which are "easy," which are interesting, and "which give a breather" in tackling the more difficult tasks). He uses, in a negative way, the "gadgets" of language, the affixes which may shift the meaning back and forth—leading to errors as common as the use of *irregardless* meaning *regardless*. His formula gives a measure of difficulty ranging from *very easy* through to *very difficult*, or from the level of comic books to scientific and philosophic journals.

There has been expected reaction against such formulas, that the natural expression of writers is stultified, that concern for formula impedes the search for language and concepts, which Freire and others consider are crucial to learning.

However, these formulas do have a practical use in the preparation of material that will be at a level to facilitate learning. Used with judgment, they can help to assess or to get rid of much that is dull and useless as well as provide some tips in the preparation of study material. It is possible to write simply and lucidly, without writing down or primerizing. The latter is a very real danger. The adult student who feels insulted by the childish level or the substance of reading offered him will not be well motivated for further learning.

TWO-WAY COMMUNICATION

For many older people the very term "mass media" raises the same mental image—a picture of Hitler or Goebbels screaming into a microphone and forcing a single set of ideas upon millions of listeners. This is one-direction communication, and we often talk about the mass media as if it always happens this way.

But let us look at another kind of communication system from the same historical period. During the war, in London, certain men and women volunteered or were appointed to act as wardens. Their duties were to watch for fires and to rescue the injured. But as time went on, another role emerged. They began to be a means of transmitting news about how people on other streets were getting on, as well as reliable information from official sources to counteract the spread of rumor. Government now had an excellent means of distributing needed facts and maintaining morale. But this was not just *one-way* communication; much of its strength was in its *double* flow. The street warden reported back complaints, the fears that people had, their doubts and questions, as well as stories of achievement and heroism, and these were all used to modify policy. The officials now had an additional source of information, and a means of checking the effectiveness of policies, or—what may be of equal importance—how people perceived or felt about these policies.

There used to be considerable adverse criticism about monolithic, propagandistic policies in Socialist countries. If communication in these countries were all one-way, it is conceivable that there might long ago have been a serious breakdown. Actually, there is a highly effective oral-communication system in Russia, mostly one-way in direction, but not entirely.[34] Hundred of thousands of men and women hold an official position as a go-between from higher authority to cells or groups—the farm group, or block of neighbors, or a factory team, or a student class. It is their duty to bring information and to interpret decisions reached above to their group. But they are also charged with noting the questions and doubts that arise within their group and to estimate whether or not the group is prepared to act, or must be educated before the inception of a new policy. Russian political leaders accordingly receive an enormous amount of information back from local units, to guide them in policy-making and the timing of certain actions, or at the least, to know where to expect resistance.

These examples all deal with large numbers of people. What about two-way communication as applied to small groups or an individual learner?

There are many applications of two-way communication in the use of mass media such as the videotape recorder, with various results. The recorder or VTR has been used by *animateurs* and community development officers in villages in Tanzania and in impoverished mining communities in Canada: based on some techniques developed earlier by the National Film Board. The village people use VTR to record their own discussions about their problems—problems that may have been with them for half a century. Then they have a chance to see and hear themselves and to change or improve what it is they were trying to say. An extraordinary process of learning begins as people see and hear themselves—and see their environment—"as others see them" but also "as only they can see themselves." This process of self-discovery has usually been followed by a commitment to work together to change conditions. As a by-product, administrators and officials have received information about the lack of communication they have with village people, often a major part of the problem.

Results such as this have led to some examples where communication media such as mimeograph, low-range radio, VTR are given to people, for their own communication, instead of or in addition to beaming messages *at* people. In general, if material is presented with the opportunity for reaction and questions, the learning is more effective. You can talk at people, or talk *by* people, or talk *with* people. This can be tested by anyone through a simple experiment. Give paper and pencils to two classes or groups, who are separated. Now take a card on which there are half a dozen figures, triangles, squares or circles, of different sizes and in different positions. Have an *instructor*, yourself or a group member, describe verbally the figures on the card and their relationship to each other. Ask the members to draw the figures showing these relationships. Repeat the instructions as given until everyone has it approximately correct but do *not* allow the group members to ask questions or make comments. Now repeat the whole exercise with a second group. Only this time encourage questions and conversation about the test. You will find, almost invariably, the same kind of result. Many, though not all, of Group One will complete the assignment more quickly. But few of them, perhaps none of them, will understand the instructions perfectly the first time. Group Two will probably take longer to complete the assignment, but accuracy of all members will show considerable improvement over Group One. As a by-product, they may also take a much greater interest in the test.

This and a dozen other experiments all indicate that the learner should have an opportunity to raise his doubts, air his misunderstandings, become involved by verbalizing, if learning is to be accurate and effective. This principle, usually called "feedback," is discussed further in Chapter 10.

So important is this fact in its many ramifications that some psychologists, poets, and educationists have said that all learning is a dialogue—between learner-author, or learner-teacher, or learner-fellow-learners. It is when the conditions for this dialogue are not present that we may fear the consequences.

EFFECTS OF COMMUNICATION

Human beings are not entirely powerless, however, even in the face of one-directional communications. Recently a high school teacher was talking about a colleague who had argued that television would have little educational result because people could always turn it off. "I reminded him," said the teacher, "that I have a class of forty boys and girls all of whom were born with exceedingly precise instruments for turning *me* off at any time that suits them."

People are not just the innocent victims of anyone who controls the air waves. This is a problem that is serious enough, but not without its positive side.

Since World War II there have been an increasing number of studies that have dealt not just with the message transmitted but with the effect of the message upon the recipient. In particular, attention has been directed to the blocks, or the modifiers, of the message.[35]

People respond to a message selectively, depending on their own experience. S. I. Hayakawa illustrated this point with the account of a recent episode:

> The writer was driving a car at dusk along a western road. A globular mass about two feet in diameter appeared suddenly in the path of the car. My passenger in the front seat screamed and grasped the wheel attempting to steer the car around the object. I tightened my grip and drove right into it. In each case the behavior of the individual was determined by his own past and by his own phenomenal field. My passenger, an Easterner, saw the object in the highway as a boulder and fought desperately to steer the car around the object. I, native to the vicinity, saw it as tumbleweed and I devoted my effort to trying to keep the car on the road. But notice, at the moment of action, what the driver was trying to do made sense to the driver, but made no sense to the passenger.[36]

Not only does a man's experience condition his perception of a message, but he "chooses" messages he thinks will "reward" him or that conform with his present attitudes. We have seen earlier that students with different biases learn and retain with varying success facts about communism, depending on whether they are favorably disposed or antagonistic.

One important factor in the communication process is how reliable the recipient feels the communicator is. If there is disbelief the audience may not respond. In one celebrated presentation *Is Anybody Listening?* [37] the author warned business men that millions of dollars spent in providing information to their employees would all be wasted unless the employees had some trust, otherwise the words would fade away unheard and unread. One of the most alarming aspects of the many confrontations at universities involving students, faculty, and administration was the lack of trust, which endangered or impeded many attempts to bring about acceptable solutions.

Another factor is that of point of view. Is more than one presented? In research in the use of army training films it was found that although giving *one* side produced positive change, giving both sides of an issue usually produced more change in the intended direction. A man was more likely to accept a new point of view, opposed to his initial opinion, if the film made what he considered a fair presentation of the grounds for that opinion. A film that "seemed one-sided" was immediately judged to be propaganda, and therefore discounted. It was also found, as was assumed, that the greater the critical ability of the subjects, the less likely they were to accept an unsound interpretation. The book *Personal Influence* [38] by Elihu Katz and Paul Lazarsfeld summarizes much of the research about the effects of communication and advanced some stimulating propositions which continue to be studied. The book itself is an excellent example of what can happen when more than one stream of inquiry intersects. In this case, studies of the effect of mass media and studies of small groups were brought together.

In his introduction to the book Elmo Roper wrote:

As a result of my own research into public attitudes I have come to the tentative conclusion that ideas often penetrate the public as a whole slowly and—even more important—very often by interaction of neighbor on neighbor without any apparent influence of the mass media. . . .

Roper believes that the American public, in so far as the transmission of ideas is concerned, can be represented as six concentric circles:

- In the tiny inner core are the "great thinkers," a few in number in any age, and not necessarily widely known by their contemporaries, men like Plato or Marx whose ideas become distributed over continents and ages.
- A still tiny group of "great disciples" who are close to the source and become effective advocates. As examples, he lists Paul in religion and Abraham Lincoln in politics.

- The great disseminators—"as many as 1,000 or as few as 250 in American society today," the men and women who have a public for the ideas they talk about.
- The "lesser disseminators"—editors, writers, broadcasters, organization officials—people who have a particular forum, but a limited one.
- The "participating citizens"—people who vote regularly, work, and contribute to local and national campaigns and causes.
- The politically "inert" who are seldom active in their community.

Roper points out that these are loosely formed groups; that a "great disseminator" in one field may be "politically inert" in another. It is Roper's contention that the "politically inert" probably come to accept ideas more readily from their "participating citizen" neighbors than in any other way, and that these citizens are likely to be influenced in turn by the "lesser disseminators."

Studies of political behavior also have some implications for learning. In an early study [39] carried out during a presidential election, successive interviews were held with the same families each week or month over an entire year. The subjects were asked each time whom they intended to vote for, and what had caused them to make this choice. In this way extreme shifts in political attitude (such as when a man who was planning to vote Republican decides to vote Democratic, or vice versa) were thus identified. In such a case the man or woman whose opinion had changed was asked the reasons for the change.

It was while studying what had affected these major changes that a situation was discovered which had not been expected:

- Practically no one did so because of the influence from a speech, reading newspapers, a radio talk, or a movie.
- *Almost everyone* who made such a shift did so because of belonging to, and exposure in, a small face-to-face group—for example, the family, the women gathering each morning for coffee, the men dropping in at a tavern together after work.

When a man has made a radical change of view, the mass media do seem to affect his views; that is, they tend to support his new position. He now reads and hears and sees selectively. Impressions reach him that tend to buttress his point of view. The mass media have considerable power in reinforcing a decision already arrived at. With enough repetition they tend over a period of time to fix or weaken a choice. In a country like Nazi Germany, where there was little alternative to *official* messages, they would have a very strong effect. But the mass media are not so effective as *primary groups* as the source for *changing* opinions or attitudes. Their basic long-term effect seems to be a slow modification, or coloring, or infiltration upon the view of the world held by the individual, and therefore of the self. But it must be admitted that longitudinal studies of this influence are as yet few and incomplete.

Other kinds of studies have brought forth some additional evidence. In some subjects, like the study of international and public affairs, there is a greater tendency to accept "expert" opinion from people who have prestige. For such things as fashions, food, movies, even local public issues, attitudes are much more likely to be affected by the people in the primary groups to which one belongs.

In reporting on these and other studies, Lazarsfeld has made an important point about the people who exercise this influence:

> Some people seem to serve as personal transmitters for others. Without these relay individuals, messages originating from the mass media might not reach otherwise unexposed people.

Thus certain people, and certain primary groups may transmit, may block, or may modify messages.

This function of transmitting messages (not necessarily originating them) has often been identified as an ingredient in leadership. It is in this sense that Saul Alinsky in his early book *Reveille for Radicals* [40] speaks of the leader as one "who knows the telephone number of the people." Kurt Lewin used as a term for a somewhat similar function, "gatekeeper," meaning a person who can exercise control over the flow of information in regard to an activity. For example, in the case of food the mother is usually the "gatekeeper," and her attitudes and behavior tend to influence the family, while in the case of baseball the father might be the "gatekeeper."

These are only a few of the basic concepts dealt with in communications theory and research. Enough has been found to illuminate many learning principles and to convince practitioners of the necessity of trying to keep informed about this rapidly developing field.

Other Fields of Practice

We have reported, largely for illustrative purposes, a few fields of practice from which much new evidence that bears upon learning theory is being collected.

We shall now mention, in passing, a few additional fields which also provide excellent possibilities.

COUNSELING

Personal counselors are now found in schools, colleges, universities, corporations, trade unions, clinics, and social agencies, and in private practice. The significant task of counseling is not giving information or advice. Many counselors would say that it is never advice giving. The counselor's function is to bring about learning on the part of the client. The client may have information and skills to learn but above all else he must come to terms with himself, and accept not only himself, his strengths, weaknesses, capacity for affection and growth, but also begin to learn to be self-managing. This process is closely related to most aspects of learning, as we discussed in Chapter 2.

The parallel between therapy and education is so significant that some direct application of theory and practice from different therapies has been made to adult education. Developments of many kinds of individual and group therapies accelerated throughout the 1950's and 1960's and we have earlier pointed out applications derived from therapists such as Carl Rogers, Fritz Perls and Eric Berne. Any practitioner in adult education will wish to review from time to time the implications for learning from these therapies, and also from practice in handling drug and alcohol patients, or individuals in correctional institutions. Any good therapy or treatment is essentially a process in which new behaviors are learned and reinforced, and the patient-client-inmate is helped to develop understanding and acceptance of himself as well as new goals, loyalties, interests and activities.

TEACHING OF LANGUAGES

It is now thoroughly understood that the way one uses one's own language has a marked effect upon one's personality. We can assume, therefore, that the learning of language may have important implications for general learning.

This point is well exemplified in the debate which still continues between those who favor the teaching of a second and third language in early years of childhood and those who say it should be postponed until the child has a thorough grasp of the mother tongue. Neurologists, such as Wilder Penfield, claim that the brain cells of the young child are much more receptive, and more capable of managing several patterns of language sounds than in the years after eight or ten:

When a baby is born the speech areas of the cerebral cortex are like a clean blank slate, ready to be written upon. There is an optimum age within the first decade of life when these special areas are plastic and receptive. The method of teaching children their mother's own language has been the same in all lands and in all ages. It is extraordinarily efficient. It conforms to the changing capacities of the child's brain. . . . A child who learns three languages instead of one, early enough, learns the units of all three without added effort and without confusion. . . . During higher education it will always be desirable that some students take up new languages at a later period and there is a good deal of evidence that he who has learned more than one language as a little child has greater facility for the acquisition of additional languages in adult life.[41]

It is also true, of course, that the young child gets more satisfaction out of repetitive behavior and has less inhibitions about trying a new and difficult kind of behavior than does an older person.

Those who urge postponement often do so from a theoretical position. They claim that until a child has a firm grasp of his own language, an attempt to communicate in another tongue will confuse him and have an adverse effect, not only upon his ability to learn, but upon his entire personality development. This latter view is currently being challenged.

Early childhood seems to be the best time for the brain to store up sound patterns, but the cultural aspects of language, of course, are as possible for older people, as are other kinds of learning. There are examples of men and women well into their eighties learning to speak an additional language. However, as Penfield has pointed out, both interest and facility for this would have been increased by successful experience in the earliest years.

Learning a new language means to learn how to think, how to feel, and how to express oneself with the aid of new and different symbols. Students of language have been studying the ways in which this happens. All the major theories of learning are finding some application in the new language classes organized for men in the armed services, for people undertaking technical assistance assignments abroad, for immigrants, and for refugees. Moreover, in addition to learning theory, there have been valuable experiments concerning size and form of class organization. For maximum effect in learning in a language class, size should be small enough so that every student gets considerable individual practice, and just large enough so that there is some group support as well as an increase in interest and in motivation. Classes of five or six have been used with excellent effect. Results have also been obtained by subjecting a person to the sounds to which he must become familiar just as he is going to sleep and even while he is sleeping. This suggests interesting possibilities for other forms of learning, although it also opens up some new and difficult ethical problems, somewhat like those of subliminal advertising and other attempts to reach the individual beyond his conscious control.

Finally, the effort to teach languages is now a matter of considerable importance in most countries of the world. This is one field where advances that may be made in Israel, or Brazil, or elsewhere, may be of greater significance than any upon the American continent.

CROSS-CULTURAL EDUCATION

Substantial numbers of people are traveling these days. Many of them are doing it for one main purpose—business or pleasure—but have as a subsidiary purpose learning about another culture.

It has usually been assumed that travel is broadening and if people will travel they will grow in understanding of other people. In general this may be true. But it happens in no direct or certain way. There is nothing inevitable about good human relations. It is well to remember, for example, that most, if not all, of the political leaders in Asia and Africa who are leagued against the West, have visited and lived in one or more of the countries of the West. What kind of exposure did they have to Western culture? What did they learn?

There are also the people who travel but seem to be touched not at all by their experience, or who may actually have had all their prejudices confirmed. A character in one of John P. Marquand's novels "traveled all around the world but never left Boston." How can people be helped to learn about another culture? And what will this tell us about learning itself?

The goals of cross-cultural education and the goals of comparative education are similar: to help the learner systematically explore the values of another culture and better understand himself, his own values, and society. When looked on in this light, both fields are perceived not as esoteric or exotic but valid, perhaps essential, kinds of learning for any human being.

TECHNICAL ASSISTANCE IN UNDERDEVELOPED COUNTRIES

There have always been men and women who went out to other lands, for religious, political, humanitarian, or commercial reasons, to take some part in the direction of new activities there. But the scale of such activities has shifted, the numbers involved are many times greater. "Experts" are being supplied not from a few countries only, but from all countries, and many of these "experts" work together as members of an *international team*. How they learn from each other, how they learn to get along as colleagues, and how they learn to deal with the new culture in which all are working, is a matter of great fascination, and full of implications for learning practice and theory.

In such situations learning new skills or knowledge does not happen easily unless attention is paid not only to individuals concerned but to the culture in which they live. Even if a new skill or resource results in better health or income, it will not be accepted if it runs counter to cultural values. This is just a special example of the more general case that the new learning must enhance the self, or it runs the risk of rejection or distortion. Examples are many.

In some foreign lands it is easy to conclude that the village markets do not provide an efficient or economic means of distribution of products. But the people will not be prepared to accept some other form of distribution if the social life, the opportunity for men and women to exchange news and gossip, is thereby eliminated. It may be more efficient to replace the work gangs who sing and labor together on each other's fields with some other form of work organization but the people may reject this change, even if it means some improvement in the economy, if it is gained at the cost of enjoyable social contact. Men or women who have perfected some skill, and gain prestige for that skill, will not easily give it up to learn other skills even though there may be some monetary gain. One's culture always modifies *what* one will learn and *how* one will learn.

Perhaps the sharpest lessons from international development abroad are how often wrong advice has been showered on people in foreign countries, how many wrong or inadequate models have been recommended, and how self-critical any adult educationist needs to be about his own capacity and motives.

REFERENCES

1. Harold F. Clark and Harold S. Sloan, *Classrooms in the Factories* (New York University Press, 1958).
2. William S. Griffith and Ann P. Hayes, *Adult Basic Education: The State of the Art* (Chicago: University of Chicago Press, 1970).
3. L. D. Kelsey and C. C. Hearne, *Co-operative Extension Work* (Ithaca: Comstock Publishing Associates, 1949).
4. George M. Beal and J. M. Bohlen, *The Diffusion Process* (Ames, Iowa: Iowa State College, 1957), Special Report, No. 18.
5. M. C. Wilson and Gladys Gallup, *Extension Teaching Methods* (Washington, D.C.: U.S. Department of Agriculture, 1955), Extension Circular, 496.
6. James Duncan and Burton Kreitlow, "Selected Cultural Characteristics and the Acceptance of Educational Practices and Programs," *Rural Sociology*, December 1954.
7. Theodore M. Newcomb and Eugene L. Hartley, eds., *Readings in Social Psychology* (New York: Henry Holt and Company, Incorporated, 1947).
8. D. Katz and H. Hyman, "Morale in War Industry," *Readings in Social Psychology, op. cit.*
9. Robert R. Blake and Jane S. Mouton, *The Managerial Grid* (Houston: Gulf Publishing Co., 1964).
10. Murray G. Ross and Charles E. Hendry, *New Understandings of Leadership* (New York: Association Press, 1957).
11. Robert Tannenbaum, "Sensitivity Training for Supervisors." By permission of the author.

12. Gregory Vlastos, *Adult Education in Canada* (Toronto: Canadian Association for Adult Education, 1950).
13. Cyril O. Houle, Elbert W. Burr, Thomas H. Hamilton, and John R. Yale, *The Armed Services and Adult Education* (Washington, D.C.: American Council on Education, 1947).
14. Alexander Leighton, *The Governing of Men* (Princeton: Princeton University Press, 1945).
15. Carl Rogers, "Inter-personal Relations U.S.A. 2000" in *Convergence*, Vol. 11, No. 3.
16. Mary P. Follett, *Dynamic Administration*, Metcalf and Urwick, eds. (New York: Harper & Brothers, 1942).
17. Henry Busch, *Leadership in Group Work* (New York: Association Press, 1934).
18. S. E. Asch, "Effects of Group Pressures upon the Modification and Distortion of Judgment," *Readings in Social Psychology* (New York: Henry Holt and Company, Incorporated, 1947).
19. Leland P. Bradford, ed., *Explorations in Human Relations Training* (Washington, D.C.: National Training Laboratory in Group Development, 1953).
20. Malcolm Knowles and Hulda Knowles, *Introduction to Group Dynamics* (New York: Association Press, 1972).
21. I. Lorge and M. Brenner, *A Survey of Studies Contrasting the Quality of Group Performance and Individual Performance* (New York: Bureau of Applied Social Research, Columbia University, 1957), Technical Report No. 1.
22. M. Sherif, *An Outline of Social Psychology* (New York: Harper & Brothers, 1948).
23. Murray G. Ross, Charles E. Hendry, *op. cit.*
24. Henry David Thoreau, *Walden* (New York: New American Library, 1942).
25. Plato, *Phaedrus* (New York: Modern Library Edition, 1936).
26. Harold Innis, *Empire and Communications* (Oxford: Clarendon Press, 1950).
27. Karl Deutsch, *Nationalism and Social Communication* (New York: Dryden Press, 1956).
28. Marshall McLuhan, in *Explorations 4* (Toronto: University of Toronto Press, 1956). University of Toronto, copyright owners.
29. Marshall McLuhan, *Understanding Media* (New York: McGraw-Hill, 1965).
30. Ignacy Waniewicz, *Broadcasting for Adult Education* (Paris: UNESCO, 1972).
31. Edgar Dale, *Audio-Visual Methods in Teaching* (New York: Dryden Press, 1956).
32. Irving Lorge, "Predicting Readability," *Teachers College Record*, March 1944.
33. Rudolph Flesch, *The Art of Plain Talk* and *The Art of Readable Writing* (New York: Harper & Brothers, 1946 and 1948, respectively).
34. Alex Inkeles, *Public Opinion in Soviet Russia* (Cambridge: Harvard University Press, 1950).
35. Wilbur Schramm, ed., *The Process and Effects of Mass Communication* (Urbana: University of Illinois Press, 1955).
36. S. I. Hayakawa, "Success and Failure in Communications," *Journal of the American Association of Training Directors*, Vol. 12, No. 7.

37. W. H. Whyte, *Is Anybody Listening?* (New York: Simon and Schuster, Inc., 1952).

38. Elihu Katz and Paul F. Lazarsfeld, *Personal Influence* (Glencoe, Ill.: The Free Press, 1955).

39. B. Berelson, P. F. Lazarsfeld, W. F. McPhee, *Voting* (Chicago: University of Chicago Press, 1954).

40. Saul Alinsky, *Reveille for Radicals* (Chicago: University of Chicago Press, 1946).

41. Wilder Penfield, "We're not giving our children a chance to learn a second language," *PR in Canada* (Toronto: Canadian Public Relations Society), Vol. 2, No. 1.

SUGGESTED READING

Anderson, G. Lester, ed. *Education for the Professions.* Chicago: University of Chicago Press, 1971.

Bennis, Warren G., Benne, Kenneth D., and Chin, Robert, eds. *The Planning of Change.* New York: Holt, Rinehart and Winston, 1961.

Berelson, Bernard, ed. *Reader in Public Opinion and Communication,* 2nd ed. New York: The Free Press, 1966.

Biddle, William W., and Biddle, Loureide J., *The Community Development Process: The Rediscovery of Local Initiative.* New York: Holt, Rinehart and Winston, 1965.

Bradford, Leland P., Gibbs, Jack R., and Benne, Kenneth D., eds. *T-Group Theory and Laboratory Method.* New York: John Wiley and Sons, 1964.

Collins, Barry E. and Guetzkow, Harold. *A Social Psychology of Group Processes for Decision Making.* New York: John Wiley and Sons, Inc., 1964.

Glaser, William S. and Sills, David L., eds. *The Government of Associations.* Totowa, New Jersey: Bedminster Press, 1966.

Gleaser, Edmund J. *This Is the Community College.* Boston: Houghton Mifflin Company, 1968.

McKenney, James L. *Simulation Gaming for Management Development.* Boston: Harvard Business School, 1967.

Miles, Mathew B. *Learning to Work in Groups.* New York: Columbia University, Teachers College Press, 1970.

Ohliger, John. *Listening Groups: Mass Media in Adult Education.* Syracuse: Syracuse University Publications in Continuing Education, 1967.

Rogers, Everett M. *Diffusion of Innovations.* Glencoe, Illinois: Free Press, 1970.

Rosenberg, B., and White, D. M., eds. *Mass Culture: The Popular Arts in America.* New York: Free Press, 1957.

Schein, Edgar H., and Bennis, Warren G. *Personal and Organizational Change Through Group Methods: The Laboratory Approach.* New York: John Wiley and Sons, Inc., 1965.

Smith, Robert, and others, ed. *Handbook of Adult Education.* New York: Macmillan, 1970.

Zahn, Jane C. *Creativity Research and Its Implications for Adult Education.* Syracuse: Syracuse University Publications in Continuing Education, 1966.

9

Environmental Factors in Learning

It should be quite clear that learning cannot and should not be identified with gimmicks and devices, or special forms of organization. Yet there are many factors of the setting, the emotional climate, and the ways that learners are organized that cannot be disregarded. Of course the quality of learning is markedly influenced by environmental and organizational factors. Effective techniques and devices also have their place. In *Alice in Wonderland* the King said: "The horror of that moment I shall never, *never* forget!" "You will, though," said the Queen, "if you don't make a memorandum of it."

In this chapter we will review factors that are often looked upon as discrete, but can be seen to fit together as part of the total living environment. This environment is emotional as well as physical. It used to be considered that all students were members of a class, or group; now we see that many kinds of learning are experienced as an individual. This means that the environment for individualized learning is important, but so is group organization and so are facilities and devices. We have not attempted to be comprehensive; as examples, we have chosen those forms and devices which seem to be best suited to illustrate the principles which have been discussed in previous chapters. The reader is asked to keep these principles in mind and consider how they may be planned for. He is also requested to remember throughout Emerson's observation: "Ends pre-exist in the means."

It should not be assumed, as noted, that learning must always take place in a group of some kind. But this is often the case. Sir Richard Livingstone, who can scarcely be considered to bear the stigma of "groupism," once said:

> Even in education man remains a social animal. Consider how often education has burned most brightly at a common hearth, where men gath-

234

ered together in company to warm their hands at its flame; in antiquity, Socrates in the marketplace and the gymnasiums, the great classical schools of the Academy, the Lyceum, the Stoa, the Museum of Alexandria: in the Middle Ages, the universities, culminating in the residential university, recognized, at least in the Anglo-Saxon world, as their ideal form. These examples may teach us something. No doubt the lamp of wisdom can burn in solitary shrines and even in dismal lecture halls, but for the many it will not burn brightly, if at all, unless fanned by that social corporate life which both educates and makes education attractive.[1]

This chapter will concern itself with social and with solitary forms of learning, both of which are rewarding and complementary experiences for most learners.

Emotional Climate

In Chapter 4 we noted the importance of emotions in the education of adults. An environment that is perceived by the learner as hostile, or fiercely competitive, while it may be intellectually stimulating, is not the best place for most adults to begin. There have been cases of part-time and older students being admitted to college or university only to find that the younger students and the younger professors made the atmosphere tense by immediately demanding high standards of performance before the older student had time to adjust or settle in. Too often the result would be an early drop-out, whereas, if some of these able students had been welcomed, encouraged, perhaps given assistance with study skills, their performance a few months later might have equaled the best.

People who have never been in institutions such as a library are sometimes repelled by certain environments. Those who have failed at school do not return with enthusiasm as adults to night school. Some adults with rural backgrounds or backgrounds of factory work are intimidated by the forbidding appearance of some universities, colleges, museums and galleries. They do not perceive these institutions to be for them and are doubtful of their ability to cope. If such places are manned by clerks or receptionists who are officious or not helpful, or if there is an inflexible registration process, the learning process may be over before it has begun.

It should not be difficult to provide an emotional environment for older students that at least is welcoming and supportive, with rules that are made and administered for the welfare of the learner and not the ease and comfort of the personnel in the educational institution. These matters seem so simple, but when older students are interviewed about difficulties in their educational courses, again and again they report:

- Rigidity, lack of communication, coldness and impersonality of the registration procedure.
- Coldness, hostility, indifference of faculty and other students.
- Lack of facilities designed for needs of older or part-time students.
- Lack of assistance in mastering the complexities of the institutional environment.
- Lack of assistance in mastering the first tests or assignments.

In plans for learning, wherever it is to occur, thought is needed to devise an emotional and physical environment that stimulates and supports learning.

The Individual Learner

The physical factors favoring, supporting, and reinforcing the individual learner are no different from those in social situations; namely, such things as good illumination, absence of distracting sound and glare, appropriate temperatures, and fresh air. It is important to recognize that the focus of much or most learning is the home, the place of work, the motel, the automobile, the bus, train, airplane, and other means of transport, as well as the library. With the possible exception of the library, none of these environments are planned for learning. Few libraries are well designed for learning; they may have reading rooms, with prominent signs demanding SILENCE (or as in a library in India: "Let thy voice be low"), but the reading stations, study carrels, and places for sound reception or perception of visual materials, are still comparatively few. No builder or interior decorator, so far as one knows, has designed the home as the main theater for learning. Now that there are increasing numbers of programs, like the "Open University," and the "University Without Walls," as well as programs of learning while traveling, more attention will be given to the learning needs of people at home and on the road. There are a few commuter trains, in Sweden for example, where daily travelers can study languages with the benefit of appropriate illumination, study tables, electrical outlets for tape recorders, projection screens, etc. Motels and hotels now accommodate seminars as well as conferences. A few are adequately planned and equipped for such purposes, though most are not, and even fewer consider their guests as learners and plan facilities accordingly. No factory or store we have ever visited provides for the individual learner, although many have plans for group instruction, and some factories in Russia and a few other countries have libraries. Until such environments are planned for these needs, individual learners will be obliged to arrange for appropriate "learning spaces" in their own homes and work places and organize their own equipment, travel, luggage, transport accessories for this purpose. The problem is to recognize the need. Once that is done, solutions can be found.

Social Learning

Much learning still takes place in classrooms and other social settings, but the need for well-planned facilities is not always recognized. For example, most large hotels and airport motels now cater to conferences and seminars, often in Canada and Europe for persons using different languages, yet few such facilities are wired and equipped for instantaneous translation. Even in most of the libraries, universities, colleges, and night schools that we have visited, the learning environments, for group or individual study are rarely as well planned as the heating system or the cafeteria.

The facilities in which learning is carried on can vary tremendously in size, in character, and in relative comfort offered. Those who associate quality of learning with puritan virtues used always to recommend Spartan simplicity and even some physical hardship. But it is quite clear that learning is not aided by "mortifying the flesh." Luxury is not required, but comfort, excellent illumination without glare, absence of disturbing sounds or movements, provide a setting in which the chances for effective learning are increased. The atmosphere, whether fresh or stifling, may determine whether the person is an attentive participant, a slumberer, or a man whose energies are bent just to keep himself awake. Many of these factors that facilitate good sight and hearing were reviewed in Chapter 3.

The very size and shape of the facilities may have some impact. One of Winston Churchill's most eloquent speeches took place at the end of the war when the damaged House of Commons was to be redesigned. Churchill maintained that the physical form of the house would substantially modify decisions taken there for generations to come. Parkinson, in his book *Parkinson's Law* has some amusement with the same idea, but the laughter does not obscure the author's serious intentions!

. . . The House of Commons is so arranged that the individual Member is practically compelled to take one side or the other before he knows what the arguments are, or even (in some cases) before he knows the subject of the dispute. His training from birth has been to play for his side, and this saves him from any undue mental effort. Sliding into a seat toward the end of a speech, he knows exactly how to take up the argument from the point it has reached. If the speaker is on his own side of the House, he will say "Hear, hear!" If he is on the opposite side, he can safely say "Shame!" or merely "Oh!" At some later stage he may have time to ask his neighbour what the debate is supposed to be about. Strictly speaking, however, there is no need for him to do this. He knows enough in any case not to kick into his own goal. The men who sit opposite are entirely wrong and all their arguments are so much drivel. The men on his own side are statesmanlike, by contrast, and their speeches a singular blend of wisdom, eloquence, and moderation. Nor does it make the slightest difference whether he learned his politics at Harrow or in following the fortunes of Aston Villa. In either school he will have learned when to cheer and when to groan. But the British system depends entirely on its seating plan. If the benches did not face each other, no one could tell truth from falsehood, wisdom from folly, unless indeed by listening to it all. But to listen to it all would be ridiculous, for half the speeches must of necessity be nonsense.

In France the initial mistake was made of seating the representatives in a semicircle, all facing the chair. The resulting confusion could hardly be imagined if it were not notorious. No real opposing teams could be formed and no one could tell (without listening) which argument was the more cogent. There was the further handicap of all the proceedings being in French—an example the United States wisely refused to follow. But the French system is bad enough even when the linguistic difficulty does not arise. Instead of having two sides, one in the right and the other in the wrong—so that the issue is clear from the outset—the French form a multitude of teams facing in all directions. With the field in such confusion, the game cannot even begin. Basically their representatives are of the Right or of the Left, according to where they sit. This is a perfectly sound scheme. The French have not gone to the extreme of seating people in alphabetical order. But the semicircular chamber allows of subtle distinctions between the various degrees of rightness and leftness. There is none of the clear-cut British distinction between rightness and wrongness. One deputy is described, politically, as to the left of Monsieur Untel but well to the right of Monsieur Quelquechose. What is anyone to make of that? What should we make of it even in English? What do they make of it themselves? The answer is, "Nothing."

All this is generally known. What is less generally recognized is that the paramount importance of the seating plan applies to other assemblies and meetings, international, national, and local. It applies, moreover, to meetings round a table such as occur at a Round Table Conference. A moment's thought will convince us that a Square Table Conference would be something totally different and a Long Table Conference would be different again.[2]

This is a subject for more than humor. Much is already known about the advantages of face-to-face communication that is possible in a circle or U-shape arrangement of chairs. Much is also known about the inhibiting effect of the traditional screwed-down rows of seats or desks in a classroom or auditorium. Now that attempts are being made to design and plan *facilities specially for the learning of adults* [3] instead of having adults take over something planned for someone else, there may be considerable improvements in the environment provided for adult learning. Indeed, the improvements in design of many of the community colleges, and a few of the newer universities indicate how much can be done with little or no increase in cost if they are planned for at the time of construction.

IN THE CLASSROOM

The one form of institution planned particularly for adult education has been the residential school and conference center. Such residential centers are found in many countries, naturally displaying many differences in size, location, quality of facilities, and variety of activities, and sponsoring agencies. Some of the facilities have been planned for the purpose; many others are buildings designed as a "great house" or villa or hotel, and now adapted for this new activity. However, despite these differences, there are underlying similarities of purpose, which can be stated as an attempt to provide a physical and social environment which will maximize the possibility for learning of excellence.

Some of the most important names in adult education have written about residential education—Sir Richard Livingstone and Frank Jessup in England, Margaret Mead and C. O. Houle in the United States. Many of the principles of planning the environment and operating a residential center have been described by Harold J. Alford in the book, *Continuing Education in Action*.[4] Professor Houle had compared differences in purpose, environment, auspices, and program of centers in Europe as well as in North America. In his booklet, *Residential Continuing Education*,[5] he offers two passages about the environment which sum up both the problem and the notable opportunity. From Margaret Mead, in a negative vein:

The conference room that is not cleaned in the morning, in which smoke of last night lingers over the table, the dreary meal in a dreary restaurant that precedes so many scientific meetings, the bad coffee or the lukewarm cocoa that a meager and grudging budget provides, the equipment that is inadequate, that breaks down and is neither repaired nor replaced—these are the things that dampen not only the spirit but the imagination.

Cardinal Newman, after an exhilarating conference:

The general principles of any study you may learn by books at home; but the detail, the color, the tone, the air, the life which makes it live in us, you must catch all these from those in whom it lives already. . . . Not even scientific thought can dispense with the suggestions, the instruction, the stimulus, the sympathy, the intercourse with mankind on a large scale, which such meetings secure. A fine time of year is chosen, when days are long, skies are bright, the earth smiles, and all nature rejoices; a city or town is taken by turns, of ancient name or modern opulence, where buildings are spacious and hospitality hearty. The novelty of the place and circumstance, the excitement of strange, or the refreshment of well-known faces, the majesty of rank or of genius, the amiable charities of men pleased both with themselves and with each other; the elevated spirits, the circulation of thought, the curiosity; the morning sessions, the outdoor exercise, the well-furnished, well-earned board, the not ungraceful hilarity; . . . the brilliant lecture, the discussions or collisions or guesses of great men one with another, the narratives of scientific processes, of hopes, disappointments, conflicts, and successes, the splendid eulogistic orations; these and the like constituents of the annual celebration, are considered to be something real and substantial for the advancement of knowledge which can be done in no other way. . . . They issue in the promotion of a certain living, and as it were, bodily communication of knowledge from one to another, of a general interchange of ideas, a comparison and adjustment of science with science, of an enlargement of mind, intellectual and social, of an ardent love of the particular study, which may be chosen by each individual, and a noble devotion to its interests.[6]

Newman is describing a special kind of meeting in residence, and the picture is idealized. But it does contain many of the attributes of good learning anywhere, established in an environment that nourishes and stimulates excellent response.

Because many of them display imagination in designing environments for the study of adults, the residential centers may become, indeed have become, the laboratory for observing most environmental principles for learning.

OUTSIDE THE CLASSROOM

We have noted that many of the most important kinds of learning take place outside of educational institutions. It may happen in museums or art galleries, or in theater, cinema or concert hall. But also it may be in a political party or in social action.

In the 1960's many residential centers for adult education were built, often in places where men and women could get away temporarily from conditions of conflict and stress. However, even more frequent and just as notable were the cases of education planned to take place in the midst of the deepest social problems, with learning derived from the attempts to study and act in solving those problems. More and more young professional people obtained their practice as lawyers or doctors in downtown clinics and centers, and other adults learned about themselves and about human problems by participating in the attempts to bring about needed social change.

Many writers have spoken with enthusiasm about the value for learning of the environments provided by travel, by field trips, by sports, by involvement in social action. Respecting the latter, it is often observed that social processes need to be diffused with educational processes so that the actor or participant is learning and so that the learner who has profited from education will take some part as a citizen in affecting social change.

However, we have all known examples where little was learned in these environments. To take a simple example, the visit to the factory or the political committee room on election night brought little understanding of what was happening because of the noise and the confusion.

Educators sometimes assume that since the stimulus in an environment outside the classroom is strong, that interest or excitement or tension are conditions to insure good learning. What should be remembered is that where there are fewer opportunities for controlling the environment, greater, not less attention to environmental factors needs to be paid. This can be done by providing places and planned opportunities where the learners can pause, reflect, obtain feed-back, seek further clarifying information or experiences, begin to sort out and assess what has been happening to them. It is partly for those reasons that a good film about social action may provide a different and complementary learning experience to that of being a participant. In the film there has been some control of the stimuli and also of the environment. Or to take another simple example, if people are to learn from their participation in sport, the opportunity for learning must be ensured. The environment of a windswept outdoor hockey rink in zero weather provides for some learning experiences, but not for others. Nor is the dressing room usually the best environment for obtaining objective feedback and reflection. In one YMCA, a room was arranged, next to the dressing room, where players, coaches, referees, parents, could meet in small groups or all together to consider what had happened and how to improve the experience, including the need for changes in training diet, scheduling, officiating, managing, coaching, attitudes, behavior, etc.

Most learning projects, including field trips and "educational travel," require a very clear understanding of what are essential features of the environment if effective and positive learning is to happen. Any political party, any community clinic, any social action undertaking, any sport, any travel should be seen to have a learning component, and an appropriate environment should be considered and provided: conditions making it possible to study, talk it out, obtain feed-back, test out solutions, and evaluate.

Forms and Devices

The environment for learning consists of more than an emotional climate and furnishings. In one sense, at least, it includes organizational forms, methods and techniques, and devices. We will review some of these, not to describe step-by-step how they are used in a learning process, but to understand their choice and their place as part of a total milieu for learning. It has been to the advantage of adult education that such a variety of forms and devices for learning have been utilized. The schools and universities have much more severely standardized the ways in which learning is carried on. The most obvious example of this is in the building of classrooms. A visitor to the schools of North America might soon form the opinion that the Almighty has decreed, or a law has been passed, ordering that education must be carried out in a rectangular room and that learning only happens where there are forty students and one teacher. Of course we know that learning can happen in a variety of settings. We know, equally, that with well-planned use of audiovisual materials certain kinds of facts and information can be taught to 1,000 or 2,000 as readily as to 40, but that for the quick mastery of the "sound" of a new language, a class of five or six may be the maximum for best results.

It is interesting to note that the preferences or prejudices in favor of one practice or another rarely have much to do with the relative effectiveness for learning of each form. There are teachers of adults who feel that it isn't learning unless it is by lecture; there are others who feel that no souls are saved except in group discussion. In one demonstration a group of adult students lampooned the idea that all learning must take place in a discussion group by producing a play in which new and inexperienced sailors are taking out a sailboat for the first time. Their procedure is to take turns reading aloud the manual of sailing instructions before agreeing to change course or "go-about." As a result of following a course of action that is excellent in another context, they were soon high and dry on a reef!

We have noted that traditional values still influence every decision about schools, despite the emergence of "open classrooms" and other recent innovations. Views and prejudices about the way learning occurs can still be held tenaciously in adult education.

One can also note that there are fads and styles in adult education practice and even in the descriptive terms employed. In many organizations the panel is used on almost every conceivable occasion. The term *workshop* was widely used for a number of years and applied to almost any activity, "where two or more people were gathered together." Some of the more common aspects of such workshops were described in an article entitled "The Folklore of Workshops." [7] The authors of the article had a number of amusing things to say; they also pointed out how harmful, how foolish, are some of the practices followed. Terms have been applied very loosely. It was amusing to note, not so long ago, that when the word went round that a certain foundation was dissatisfied with the results of "seminars" for which it had provided grants, all the new applications were for "institutes" and "conferences." We are all familiar with the fact that certain terms cannot be used in certain places. In a branch of the armed forces of Canada one could include any topic or interest having to do with learning, from shooting a rifle to Shakespeare, under the head of "training" but never, *never* employ the word "education."

But if learning of quality is to happen, the choice of form and technique is a matter of some consequence. Where the aim is excellence there is a need of careful selection. And the selection ought to be made with a full knowledge of possible opportunities and consequences. It ought not to be arbitrary, like that of one personnel manager years ago who used to hire dark-haired men on Monday and Tuesday, light-haired men on other days, and red-headed men on the 29th of February.

Nathaniel Cantor was once illustrating the error of misusing what can be an effective educational method:

> The celebrated Mr. Dooley was visiting a progressive school in the days when the bonds of formalism were first beginning to be loosened from the classroom. Accompanied by a member of the school staff, he came upon a group of boys talking excitedly together. Voices rose, accusations resounded; there was a quick left to the jaw and one boy was down.
>
> "And what," asked Mr. Dooley, "are these boys learning?"
>
> His guide, abashed, was silent for a moment and then replied, "They are learning, I think, the futility of human endeavor."
>
> More accurately, they were learning the fultility of trying to hold a discussion group when they did not know the conditions necessary for making a discussion group a profitable learning experience.[8]

We need some assessment of the possibilities of each form for learning and to be better informed about the ways in which learning does happen with respect to each form.

One of the most useful kinds of investigation carried on at the Center for the Study of Liberal Education for Adults, and in several other places, has been a comparative study of teaching styles.

In his paper, "Guide to Styles, Groups, Methods" Hugh Gyllenhaal [9] provides both a summary and also a guide to the selection of forms and devices. The steps he lists are familiar:

- What do we want to accomplish?
- What sort of affair is called for?

- What subgroupings should we have?
- What presentation methods should we use?
- How to get the audience more involved?

The material is organized according to type of meeting, kinds of groupings, and presentation methods.

EXAMPLES FROM "TYPE OF MEETING"

Purpose	Type	Features
To plan, get facts, solve organization and member problems.	Work conference.	• General sessions and face-to-face groups (15 or less). • Usually high participation. • Provides more flexible means for doing organization's work.
To share experience among "experts."	Seminar.	• Usually one face-to-face group. • Discussion leader also provides expert information.

EXAMPLES FROM "KINDS OF GROUPING"

Purpose	Type	Features
To take official action.	Plenary session.	• Includes voting members and takes care of only official business.
To work on specific problem.	Work groups.	• Mixed membership from total group. • May meet once or several times. • Report usually expected.

EXAMPLES FROM "PRESENTATION METHODS"

Purpose	Type	Features
To present information for several points of view.	Symposium.	• Two or more speakers. • Speakers help audience get understanding of specific subject. • Chairman summarizes and directs questions. • Audience usually does not participate verbally.
To help audience analyze individual or group action in "natural" setting.	Situation presentation.	• Members of group present role play, vignette or case study. • Commentator may call attention to specific points as situation progresses. • Audience gains a common experience for discussion afterwards.

Some such schematic form in which the leading objectives are clearly stated and where organization and methods are specified with respect to objectives can be very useful.

We may also need to remember, however, that an activity may be chosen for reasons other than the possibilities of learning in it.

It has often been argued, for example, that the discussion group is a suitable form of adult education because it is inexpensive to provide. Such a claim needs to be examined critically; good education, like good anything else, rarely comes at a bargain counter. Similarly it has been argued that the discussion group, in addition to any learning that results, has a highly valued by-product, because the participants experience and practice some of the skills of democratic living. The discussion group and other forms have also been favored for other reasons, such as therapy. While there may be several purposes or achievements for a single activity, it is important to be clear about the primary goal. Not so long ago in one organization a dispute arose in connection with a film discussion project. Two different techniques were advocated. Staff members took sides, and the strife was such that it resulted in temporary paralysis in the organization. Then cooler heads prevailed, whereupon it was discovered that the two approaches were based on two different assumptions about what the project was to accomplish, one concerned primarily with decisions about social action and the other with therapy. Different goals in a single project may be maintained providing there is some precision and clarity about both goals and methods.

Another source of confusion, pointed out by Coolie Verner, is in the use of terms, particularly between *methods* and *techniques*. Discussion is used to designate the method as in "discussion method" and to indicate the technique as in "group discussion." In addition, there are many instances in which the properties of a method or technique are ascribed to materials or devices that are actually adjuncts of a method or technique. Audio-visual aids, bulletins, and such are frequently referred to as methods when in reality they are devices. Verner himself defines both methods and techniques, and urges that the terms be used with more care and discrimination:

> Method, then, may be described as the relationship which exists between the learner, the knowledge, and the institution which has knowledge to diffuse in order to bring about changes in attitudes and behavior. . . . Once the method has been determined, a second stage in the diffusion process comes into play. . . . The agent may employ a wide variety of established procedures or invent new ones that, in one circumstance or another, prove useful in furthering learning. These processes are the *techniques* of adult education.

Not all techniques can be used appropriately with all methods but some are useful with many methods. Thus a university conducting a program of correspondence study (the method) would not use role playing (a technique). However, an agency using discussion (a method) would use group discussion (the technique) or role playing and "buzz groups." Within the framework of the assembly or convention method, for example, the adult educator might utilize lecture, panel, forum or group discussion techniques.[10]

Some observers, who are concerned about the large number of adults that take no part in any educational activity, have noted that some forms of organization not only do not attract, but actually seem to intimidate adults who have had little academic experience. We have noted this point before. Recent research evidence indicates all too clearly that many groups and individuals do not feel that certain facilities are for them. The university, even the public library, may seem for some to belong to another social class. A Great Books program may appear remote and unprofitable. Further research and experimentation is needed concerning the forms and devices which people with little formal schooling will find attractive and in which they may undertake study that is satisfying to them. Experience with rural groups, workers, community development, and social action projects may all be useful toward this end.

SELECTION OF PARTICIPANTS

The choice of the participants in any learning activity may have a major influence on the outcome. We noted earlier that there are three significant relationships in a learning situation: learner-teacher, learner-with-fellow-learners, and learner-subject-matter. Though all these are important, it is quite apparent that, in some cases at least, the second of these relationships affects all the others.

Size of Group. We have already referred to the most elementary part of this; namely the size of the group. If the main purpose of activity is to have free and full interaction between the participants, such as is the goal of group discussion, then the limit in group size is the number of people one can easily relate to. In practice this is about five to ten, depending upon circumstances. But if the purpose is to produce an effect of solidarity behind a single idea, or sentiment, the great mass rallies of totalitarian nations, such as Hitler's demonstrations at Nuremberg, may be the chosen form.

Group size is related not only to the extent and quality of group relatedness but also to the means of communicating chosen by the teacher or the leader. We shall note later that ways have been devised in large groups for gaining some of the same quality of attention and participation that characterizes small groups.

Who Chooses Whom? But, size apart, who chooses the actual participants? What relationship does this act of choice bear to the way that the participants relate and interact?

There has been a growing interest in *sociometry*, in the improvement of response or performance in certain situations because the participants have chosen themselves and each other. Sociometry is a scientific variation of the old parlor game "Whom would you like to have for a companion if you were marooned on a desert island?" It has been found in some situations, for example, that when boys and girls choose their own tent or cabin mates at camp, there is more satisfactory participation by the campers in many phases of camplife than if the choice is by chance, or made by the director or even the counselor. The same principle has been applied, during the war, to many dangerous combat missions, so that men whose lives were dependent upon each other's effort and responsibility were given the opportunity to select their own mates. In certain work situations the self-selected group has attained records of high productivity, always providing that other factors leading to good productivity were also present. The same has been found true, experimentally, of learning, particularly in seminars and workshops where member participation is of maximum importance. If the participants in a learning activity have a part in the choice of their fellows, at least one of the factors in good learning has been provided for.

But such results should never be applied without discrimination to every conceivable situation. There is a large place for individual effort, and a primary object of all education is the unfolding, the expansion of an individual, not his contraction or smothering in any kind of group or mass. "Each individual," said Whitehead, "is a more complex structure than any social system to which he belongs. . . . If a man is wholly subordinated to the common life, he is dwarfed."

Earlier we quoted such diverse scholars as Murphy and Livingstone, who both pointed out that the life in a group may be an excellent place for the individual personality to flourish. But the group also has within it the possibility of the stunting and the shrinking of human personality, and we need to be clear-eyed about this.

Moreover, as we have noted, learning and all kinds of growth arise in part through the excitement and stimulation of difference and tension, not just from a condition of well-being. For some purposes, for example, a workteam studying the effects of radiation, the participants would all need to be possessed of experience and skill to a high degree. Here a measure of homogeneity in interest, capacity, and experience is essential. For other purposes learning is most likely to happen if there is considerable divergence in background and experience. Here, heterogeneity is desirable. A discussion group in which every member knows every other member so well that he can predict the views and position that every other member will take on any new question may provide little zest, and a large part of the possibility for learning is also lost.

There are two other factors which may appear in classes or groups of adults. First, some members of the class may feel that they are "different," or a minority, even not wanted by the majority. They might be a handful of older students in a college class, or five or six younger people, or a particular ethnic language group. Sometimes, perhaps most times, these differences may be accommodated in the same group, but there may also be the occasion for special grouping, at least as a temporary measure. Secondly, class members may come to the course with very different experiences or levels of performance in the subject or the skill that is being learned, or with different rates of learning. These factors may also be important enough to form the basis of decisions about class grouping. Again, however, if class size is not too large, considerable differences can be accommodated in the same class with advantage to all.

LECTURE-TYPE ACTIVITIES

Despite the present popularity of the discussion group more use is still made of the talk, lecture, speech, address, and similar forms than of anything else. By similar forms we refer to the symposium, the forum, the panel and, to some extent, the debate. We also would include most classes and most large meetings although both of these are mixed forms.

These forms can be listed in order of increasing participation. (We should say *apparent* participation for, as we shall see later, it is not easy to be completely sure about the amount or quality of participation.)

- *The lecture*—one voice speaking to an audience.
- *The symposium*—two or more speakers giving prepared statements which are on the same or related subjects. (Many so-called "panels" are really symposia.)
- *The forum*—one or more speakers, sometimes with some interaction between forum participants and almost certainly some interaction with members of the audience, usually by questions, but sometimes with observations and comments from the floor.
- *The panel*—in its original usage the term panel was applied to a small intimate, face-to-face group that conducted a "conversation" about a subject with the audience eavesdropping or listening in.

The advantages of these forms, particularly the first three, are that people with special knowledge or competence are able to organize facts and ideas and present them in an orderly way with a minimum of time and effort.

If the primary purpose is simply the learning of facts, it matters not at all that only one or at the most a few persons are being heard, providing that the facts are accurate. But, if opinions or values are being considered, the number of speakers, the points of view that they hold, and whether or not there is provision for rejoinder are important. If the topic is the number of pupils in elementary schools in the United States and their average gain in height and weight each year, no one will care particularly who presents the data. But if the subject is the integration of elementary schools in the Southern states the hearers will take a different attitude both to the number and the credentials of the speakers. However, our main interest here is *how much is learned how well.*

We have noted in several places that a lecturer directly, or by radio, or on film, can present material so that learning takes place, particularly if the substance is factual. We have also seen that it is rare for attitudes to be substantially altered in this way, and that most skills or processes can better be learned by demonstration and practice than by having someone talk about them. It is possible to teach a woman how to bake a cherry pie, or a man to build a canoe, simply by talk, but there are easier and more effective ways to accomplish this objective. The talk or lecture is primarily for the presentation of information or ideas where their order and relationship are important.

But if learning from the lecture is to be effective, several factors are of primary importance, such as motivation of the learner, relevance to the learner, attainment of satisfaction by the learner and the extent to which the activity is a two-way process.

We have already asserted many times that without motivation the likelihood for learning is minimal. This is especially true where we depend upon a talk as the main stimulus for learning. Most adults have been exposed countless times to talk; sometimes they have been uplifted; but too often they have been bored. They have become adept at *tuning out* any speaker. Accordingly, it is imperative if any learning is to happen that their attention be engaged. There are many ways to do this. One of the most common is the introduction of the speaker. Most *intruders* seem to be oblivious of their particular role in the learning process. Frequently they seem to feel their task is to weave pleasant platitudes around some real or assumed virtues of the speaker, or proceed to demonstrate that at least, they have read his *curriculum vitae.* However, their real purpose is easily understood, and can be readily stated:

- To win attention for the speaker.
- To show briefly how what he brings is related to, and consonant with, the goals of the members of the audience.

This raises immediately the subject of relevance. Children may attend to and learn many things that they are asked to; adults need to believe that the new is relevant. This is true about learning where no deep feelings are present, but even more so when emotion is strong. Some people believe that little or no learning happens as a result of speeches at a service club, because the subjects are so varied, and attention is desultory. But in a recent study in selected communities about the growth in understanding of international affairs, the surveyors found that considerable learning had taken place as a result of service club meetings. The writers had assumed that local business men would not consider that foreign affairs would mean much to them. Yet some business men are beginning to think about the implication of what Clarence Randall, a well-known industrialist stated: "The business man must now bring to the consideration of world problems the same hard sense of social responsibility which he is beginning to learn and to practice in his own community." [11] In any event club members had been persuaded that the study of world affairs was really a responsibility of their club and of themselves. When this was done, the result in learning and changed behavior was substantial.

But what about satisfaction? How can this result from a speech? Perhaps through achieving an increased ability to grasp, and talk about, the subject, perhaps through the efforts to see a new relationship, perhaps even by understanding that the subject is more difficult, and therefore more challenging, than had been considered. However, there is little satisfaction if the speech increases confusion, or brings a sense of defeat, or if the task seems too easy to be worth any effort.

Is the talk or lecture an example of one-way or two-way communication? Are the conditions of a *learning dialogue* established, where the mind of the learner is engaged with the words and ideas of the lecturer? This sometimes happens without any outward sign although such participation may be exhibited by gestures and facial expressions. It is much more likely to be present if opportunities are provided for the learners to respond, to ask questions for clarification, to react to the speaker's point of view, to express disagreement. Only in this way is there much surety that learning is actually happening. Moreover, only in this way can there be release of feeling which might inhibit learning, feelings which may have resulted from a misunderstanding of what the speaker meant. Without such an opportunity the lecturer cannot know he is making effective contact.

Much has been made of the necessity for winning attention. This is seen to be a more important consideration than ever before because there are so many competing claims to attention. The approaches used are many: humor, flattery, cajolery, even threat and shock. A minister one hot Sabbath morning sensed that his congregation was dozing. Raising his voice, he shouted, "Well, I'll be Goddamned!" There was a moment's stunned silence, but all eyes were now upon him. "That's what I heard a man say yesterday," said the minister, and proceeded to give a talk about the evils of profanity. But shock is seldom a useful tactic, and must be used with care if the result is to be as intended.

A number of facilities have been developed and continue to be devised for increasing the level of attention, particularly in large meetings. One well-established mode is known, at least in some places, as 66. It is extremely simple. After a speech the audience is quickly numbered in groups of six, by having three persons sitting in each alternate row turn around and face the three people behind, thus forming a face-to-face unit of six. The six people then introduce themselves to each other. Already a subtle change has occurred. Individual members of the audience who had no previous relationship (and therefore no obligations other than to themselves) are now "members" of a loose-knit group. They are now given a task, usually that of selecting a question to be put to the speaker. (Notice that the task given must be one that can be managed in a short time and by a group that has very little cohesion. A complicated task, such as summarizing what the speaker has said, would almost certainly lead to failure and to dissatisfaction.) The six people in choosing a question tend to act in a responsible way, tend to weed out questions that seem irrelevant or of limited significance, or are poorly phrased, or those which are asked simply to exhibit one individual's "hobby" or prejudice. Through this sifting process there has been an improvement in the quality of many of the questions. Moreover, each group of six, armed with their question, are better prepared to take part in the question period. Most significant of all, the individuals are much more attentive. They are interested to find out if other groups are asking the same question, if the questions of other groups are as pointed, as significant, as subtle as theirs. They tend to listen to each other and to the speaker's replies in a fresh way.

This procedure is useful after the speech and just preceding the question period. It can also be used effectively, just as the meeting starts, in order to inform the speaker about the kinds of issues with which his audience want him to come to grips. "Buzz groups" (small informal groups meeting for a limited time and with a carefully defined task) can be employed in the same fashion.

Another device for enriching the quality of attention is to assign a task of attention to members of the audience. The traditional auditorium has three sections of seats, left, center and right. The chairman can invite the audience to form three "listening teams." Those in the left section may be asked to pay particular attention to the points or arguments in the speech where further amplification, or clarification, or illustration is needed. Those in the center section may be asked to attend to the key arguments or observations of the speaker which need emphasis. People on the right may be asked to note the points where they disagree with the speaker. When a listener has assumed some obligation in connection with a talk, his attention has been won.

Notice, that from one point of view we have been talking about the methods and techniques used by a teacher or organization. But seen from another perspective, these decisions about organization, method, technique, and device have been attempts to ensure that the learner's environment is supporting, stimulating, reinforcing. The task of the teacher, as will be discussed in Chapter 11, is very much one of planning and enriching the learning environment.

GROUP DISCUSSION

We have selected "small group discussion" as a special example for consideration of environmental factors because the form is used for so many purposes and in so many ways. We shall consider only the application of certain learning principles and not attempt detailed description or analysis.

A great deal has been written about group discussion. Some of it is singularly misleading because little or no attempt has been made to distinguish between the purposes intended, which in turn determine what environment is required and the special technique or practice to be followed.

Earlier we stated an obvious but sometimes neglected point, that "small group discussion" is not a form that is satisfactory for every kind of learning. However, the range of use is very wide. Consider some examples:

- Business men studying industrial administration through the discussion of a typical case.
- Mothers meeting together because of their concern about safe play areas for their children.
- Union members trying to work out a plan of seniority that is as fair as possible for all concerned.
- Neighbors gathered in a local hall or club to talk about community issues.
- Farmers dealing with problems affecting all of them such as marketing and soil conservation.
- People with marital difficulties seeking help in a "marriage clinic."

What goes on in these discussion groups can hardly be classified under the same category, yet many discussion manuals talk about the activity, and many discussions groups are organized, as if one set of rules or practices must always be followed. The first danger to be avoided, therefore, is the "bed of Procrustes" approach. It is not a law of God or man that all discussion groups must be held in a library or be of an identical size and follow the same pattern. A related danger, to which reference has also been made, is that people who have found a particular practice suitable for achieving their particular goal will try to have that practice adopted by everyone else.

One could plot most of the uses of the discussion group along a continuum. At one end would be the activities which are largely intellectual or task oriented in purpose and at the other end activities which are largely for the purpose of releasing and understanding feelings. At the one end, the group would attempt rational exploration of facts, opinions, and experiences, hoping for the achievement of knowledge, the understanding of a particular subject matter, the improvement of a skill or process, perhaps the making of decisions. At the other end there would be a free expression of feelings leading toward self-understanding, although subject matter might also be involved. In one case the members of a discussion group might agree to be rigorous in limiting what was said to the particular issue chosen for discussion, applying self-discipline, or asking the chairman to rule out anything that seemed irrelevant. Here a more formal setting may be appropriate. In the other case, it might be essential to have every member feel that any ideas, opinions, or feelings that he may bring to the group will be welcomed and respected. At this end of the continuum there would be no real dividing line between a discussion group and a "sensitivity" group experience, and the place where the activity occurs should provide for intimate, face-to-face conversation with privacy respected.

Nevertheless, while considerable flexibility in practice is required, depending upon the objective of the discussion, there are also many common elements.

The "subject matter" of a discussion group is brought in through the members' sharing of their experiences, ideas, and feelings, or provided for in some planned way. A discussion group cannot be carried on effectively without any subject matter; it is not "pooled ignorance." If facts are essential, and they are lacking, they must be provided in some way. If the task is mainly an intellectual one, and if most of the facts or theories for vigorous discussion are not within the experience of the group, some other form of learning will usually be more successful.

The usual focus of any discussion group is on an issue, something about which people have different opinions or feelings or values. An *issue* is not a *fact*. One can argue about a fact but one cannot really discuss it. A fact is *so*, or it *isn't*; and this can be verified. For example, you may argue heatedly about whether there are more Republicans than Democrats in the state of New York, but this is waste talk; you would be better employed finding out how many voted for these two parties in the last several elections. Such a matter is barren ground for group discussion. However, if one asks, "Should everyone in New York state be obliged to vote by law?" (as the Australians do) one has an issue which can be discussed with considerable profit and around which one may learn a great deal about theory and practice in a democratic country. About such an issue people do have different feelings and opinions and they realize it is a matter of some importance. At this point the facts about how many people actually vote, take on some significance. The participants will also need to know or learn many other facts if the discussion is to move very far and be productive.

Some topics are far more productive of discussion and learning than are others. A rough test for choosing a topic is this:

- Can you state it as a question?
- Do people differ in their attitudes in response to the question?
- Are people likely to feel that the questions are worth some effort to answer?

Naturally enough, a question that leads to a Yes or No answer does not get us very far.

Some questions are what might be called neutral in their tone, others are highly charged with emotion. Among certain groups a discussion of integration in the schools can be conducted rationally and objectively; in others it might be difficult to maintain any kind of control. Discussion of neutral or controversial questions may be equally productive, but if there is to be any learning in a situation of excessive emotion, special attention would have to be given to ways of lessening the tension. As we have seen before, people are not likely to change their attitudes under conditions of threat or fear, real or imagined.

If the objective of the discussion group is learning a particular subject matter, if a decision is to be taken or a problem is to be solved, it may be necessary to follow a plan or pattern which may go somewhat like the following:

Stage 1. Ensuring that the problem is recognized.
Stage 2. Having the problem defined in terms that have the same or a similar meaning for each member of the group.
Stage 3. Discovering the nature and causes of the problem and agreeing on a standard by which possible solutions can be judged.
Stage 4. Surveying possible solutions.
Stage 5. Choosing what seems to be the "best" solution.
Stage 6. Checking the solution against the problem as originally defined.

Many of the principles involved in good learning are present in such a plan, assuming that efforts have also been applied in motivating the members and securing attention. However, a good many discussions are carried on with considerably less form than this. And as noted earlier, the process followed when the object is more "therapeutic" than intellectual, will follow a different model.

Satisfaction and reward in discussion always depend upon the purpose. A man and a wife may come to a group in a marriage clinic, each of them distressed at the lack of harmony in their home and additionally anxious because of feelings of guilt. Without stating it, they may feel there is something different, perhaps something a little strange, about themselves. At first in the discussion very little may happen except some faltering exchange of experience. But eventually there may appear the dawning realization on the part of each individual that other people have difficulties too, and that one need not accept defeat or the feeling that one is different or queer. At this stage it may be that some changes or improvements are possible.

Satisfaction, and what is learned from such a discussion, of course, is somewhat different from that obtained by a group of business executives who have talked together about an industrial case, how they might have handled it, and how they might face similar problems. In the latter, the satisfaction gained might be through achieving a fuller understanding of some problems, seeing new relationships, facing new ideas or approaches to a problem, seeing fellow participants in a new light, or even coming to some decisions about a problem.

There is usually room for controversy in discussion. But mere displays of pugnacity result in very little learning. The primary purpose of the discussion group is the sharing of experience and the search for truth, not defeating opponents, rooting out heretics, or converting the heathen. These may be worthy objectives on other occasions, but there is no place for them in discussion groups.

In few reported studies of the use of group discussion, except in residential schools for adults, have there been investigations of the environment in total, or even of all or most of the variables in the environment. Studies have, of course, been made of methods, techniques, devices, and leadership. Many observers have reported that group discussion is successful to the degree that the leadership is effective. Some organizations insist on the employment of specially trained leaders: others do not. J. E. Anderson [12] studied the use of discussion in eight agencies in Wisconsin. He reports that although five of the agencies used discussion as their main technique, leaders were sometimes selected for their local prestige rather than for competence in discussion leadership. Some leaders tended to use their position as a means of disseminating information or opinions rather than providing a free exploration of issues. Often the less well-trained leader did not allow sufficient time for issues that arose to be explored or, where desired, for agreement to be reached.

In another study, Abbott Kaplan [13] was interested in the response of group members to the behavior of the leader. Many of those with less than average education seemed to want strong directive leadership in their group. But the better-educated resented a leader who dominated the group.

SKILL AND PROCESS LEARNING

Are there any practices to be followed in the learning of such different skills or processes as first aid, figure skating, a game like tennis, using a micrometer, or how to drive a car?

It is clear that there are. It is also clear that the environment must be carefully planned for skill learning, with all the elements for practice and reinforcement close at hand.

First of all, it is well established that any skill can be learned with greater facility if the learner is given some understanding of the reasons that it is being learned. He needs to know the place or importance of that skill in his life, and also what he may expect to happen as he proceeds to learn. If there is to be difficulty or danger this information may actually lessen his anxiety. Most important, he has some framework upon which to build as he makes his first few efforts. This is akin to the principle of relevancy. The explanation, which need only deal with the essentials, can precede practice, or may come soon after the beginning of practice.

Second, in connection with most skills, there is also a body of information to be mastered and this of course must be clearly presented, preferably in a sequence related to his mastery of the skill. In *first aid* one ought to be learning the facts about how bones "set" at the same time as one is practicing how to care for fractures, not when one is practicing artificial respiration.

Third, it has been well-established that learning a skill happens with greatest effect if the practice of that skill is carried out under *actual* conditions and in the *actual* setting. The place to practice the use of the micrometer is in a machine shop; the place to practice the forehand drive is on a tennis court.

For speedy mastery of the skill or process an overview of that skill or process should be provided. An overview of a sport such as tennis should provide an introduction to the entire game, its strategy, its ebb and flow, and the relationship of the new skills to those which the learner may have acquired previously. Once the learner has some grasp of the *whole* problem, the strength of his motivation has been reinforced. It is now time to demonstrate, analyze, and practice particular aspects of strokes of the game. Errors in performance should be corrected, followed by further demonstration and practice. Only when there has been some mastery of one particular skill should one go on to the next. The procedure is always similar; identify the skill, demonstrate the technique, follow by practice by the learner.

As we have seen earlier, good practice in the case of very complicated physical skills, like a "full twisting" dive, may require that the body is put through the required action, under conditions of comparative safety, until the pattern of response has been traced out and "learned" by the nerves and muscles.

DEMONSTRATION

Many skills and processes are taught by demonstration. This has long been the favored practice followed by agricultural extension workers, home economists, trainers in industry, and in the armed services.

The demonstration may be perceived through several senses and, if well planned, gives the individual learner a chance to practice each of the successive steps.

As one would anticipate, learning happens most readily when both the purpose and the practice are clearly understood. Again, this is provided in advance, as well as at each step in the demonstration, relating the separate factors to the whole. The demonstrator needs to organize his material in a step-by-step form, and needs himself to be adept at the skills so that he can demonstrate them clearly, with an air of confidence, in an orderly sequence. A gingerly, apprehensive approach to the demonstration creates added difficulty for the learner.

It is very important in the demonstration to plan time for questions, so that all points of difficulty are cleared up, along with ample time for practice by the learner. This requires an environment offering good conditions for such a function.

Simulating the Real

Some psychologists studying learning have done so in the classroom or under contrived conditions in the laboratory. Others have drawn inferences from learning behavior wherever they have been able to observe it. But all agree that learning is most effective if carried on under conditions similar to where the knowledge, skill, or attitude will be practiced. By *effective* we simply mean the likelihood that what is learned will be utilized and applied.

Our literature is filled with such aphorisms as that life itself, or experience, is the best teacher. This is true, but only up to a point. Learning from life, or from nature, requires at least two conditions. The learner needs some conceptual frame by which to understand and relate what he learns. Lacking this, the evidence of the senses may lead to error. Without a theory of roundness men perceived the earth incorrectly for thousands of years. Or life can be too massive, too complex, or too tiny, for us to comprehend unless there is some selecting, simplifying, unifying principle. You cannot "take in" a city; it is much too complicated and baffling. You must see a map, know about its economic organization, its power structure, the kind of people in it, where they live, and what they do, before you can begin to understand or make any sense out of a city. Real experience is the best teacher only if it has been given some organization.

In earlier societies many of the most important principles and practices of living were embodied in dances, rituals, drama, and taught in this form. Many societies today also exhibit this tendency, but it is most readily observed in a relatively uncomplicated society. Thus in Jamaica, farm and village people still play singing games in which many of the skills and attitudes of living are displayed and practiced, and young people growing up learn actual skills along with a body of beliefs and attitudes common to those communities. In the "new education" going on at present in China, plays and dramatic sketches are the chief means of teaching.

Our own learning methods are beginning to follow similar practices. Increasingly, we are devising means of learning in which the conditions of real life are simulated. Examples of this are various kinds of simulated role playing, use of audiovisual materials, and "mock-ups" of actual machines in training. An example at a more abstract level is the "case study."

ROLE PLAYING

The use of various forms of drama in learning is as old as man, but the body of practices which go under the name "role playing" has been developed in more recent years, dating from the publication of the books and the demonstration by J. L. Moreno. Moreno's book *Who Shall Survive?* was published first in 1933.[14]

Moreno used the psychodrama for both study and therapy in regard to certain kinds of personality disorder. Before long, other applications began to be made, particularly in training.

In role playing, members of the group act out a problem situation, usually without a script. The scene is customarily followed by discussion and may be replayed with variations of personnel or circumstances. The purpose is to provide an experience close to reality for personal understanding and insight. It is assumed that to the extent that the student is able to identify and involve himself with what is being enacted, he may be able to appraise his own actions or understand the relationship in which he is involved.

In discussing the merits of role playing for learning, Alan Klein writes:

It introduces the actors as well as the observers to the situation with dramatic impact. It draws the group from a purely intellectual exercise into an emotional experience. The entire meeting is pulled into the stream of events which the members can feel as well as hear about. . . . When the meeting is focused on a problem or incident to this extent, discussion follows easily and can have depth. We do not need then to be concerned with how to cope with apathetic members and uninteresting meetings.

Such an exercise is a practice in human relations. One might liken this to scrimmage practice of the football team in its training session. The team play is perfected, mistakes are observed and corrected and the players learn how to cope with the problems of the game. Role playing is useful to learn how to work with other people, how to handle ourselves, and to observe and correct our human relations mistakes as we practice coping with the problems of group life.[15]

Klein then goes on to say that the main uses of role playing are (1) training in leadership and human relation skills, (2) training in sensitivity to people and situations, (3) the stimulation of discussion, (4) training in more effective problem solving by the group. Role playing is frequently used to practice such skills as negotiating a contract, or meeting in a committee to deal with a social problem like juvenile delinquency. It provides an excellent opportunity for people to learn what it may feel like to face a situation in which deep hostility may be expected. One can thus study the issue, without some of the threats that one finds in a genuine conflict.

Mistakes can be made in such practice which might be crippling in a real situation. The assumption is that one will be able to deal more calmly, more objectively and more understandingly with real conflicts through practice in simulated conflict situations where real feelings are released. In discussing a problem involving a minority group, members of the majority group can be asked to take the reverse role. Or if there are two or more sides to a dispute, representatives may be asked to take opposing sides and state that point of view to their opponent's satisfaction. Members of an "action-minded" local committee, impatient with delay, may be asked to act out a meeting of city council faced with all the conflicts involved in providing better transportation or better recreation.

In the 1960's utilization of these methods increased. The frequent attempts to learn about society by being involved and participation in community development and social action have been noted. There have been new forms of "internship" and apprenticeship offered in various fields of education. An array of simulation projects from elementary "in-basket" projects to elaborate and complex exercises involving entire industries or whole community agencies have been tried out. Simulation and games have become favored methods for teaching certain subjects such as political science. Computers have been utilized in the games and simulation and so have television and videotape recordings.

One of the by-products of use of simulation and other such practices is that the teacher is forced to consider the total environment, in order to simulate it, or even to use effective simulation for learning. Even such a simple device as an "in-basket," in which one comprehends most of the learning problems that a man may encounter on his job, requires not only clarity about goals but orderly attention to all the factors that influence learning.

CASE METHOD

There is nothing particularly new about learning through the study of an event, but the careful refinement of using selected examples of experience for teaching has come about rather recently. Case studies have been a feature of legal education for more than two thousand years, at least since Solon prepared such cases for instruction in Greece. Confucius also used case studies. Today the "case method" is usually identified with the Harvard Graduate School of Business Administration, and it has often, though not always, been applied to learning which has to do with business. One definition of a case is this:

> A record of a business issue which actually has been faced by business executives, together with surrounding facts, opinions and prejudices upon which executive decisions had to depend. These real and particularized cases are presented to students for considered analysis, open discussion and final decision as to the type of action which should be taken.[16]

What makes a particular case useful is its reality, its relevance to problems faced by others, the completeness of available data, and the significance of the issues or values at stake. In other words, it is effective only when all of environmental factors have been accounted for.

It has sometimes been alleged that the "case method" is used only to teach the application of certain practices, that its main purpose is propagandistic. There is no such inherent weakness. The main purpose of the study of a case is analysis, identifying fact and opinion, weighing and testing alternatives, considering values. It is an approach of equal merit for studying ethics or philosophy, as in examining the soundness of certain market practices.

The explicit purpose of the case method is application in the actual world. It is not just the memorization, or even the understanding of principles, but the deliberate effort to interpret these principles in a real situation. The problem of such learning has been illustrated in a limerick:

A student of business with tact
Absorbed many answers he lacked.
But acquiring a job,
He said with a sob,
How does one fit answer to fact?

The case method has application particularly to fields where there are few or no final answers, and where judgment is the essential quality. Many of the characteristics of a small discussion group must be present if there is to be genuine learning. Its reality, and the effort to state principles in terms of good practice, even to test out these principles in reality situations, makes it an approach of particular value to many adult groups.

T-GROUP

As we have seen, the T (for training) group was devised for training in human relations at the National Training Laboratory.

There are three essentials in the process of a T-group:

- Developing a group, rather than a collection of individuals, in which there may be found group cohesion, group standards, and growth in group maturity and productivity.
- Developing an atmosphere of support and objectivity in which there are encouragement and support for individual growth and awareness about oneself.
- Developing effective use by the group of methods of analysis and experimentation.[17]

The most significant fact, of course, is that learning in the T-group is learning through experience, through participation in a group activity and the examination of one's own behaviors and one's own feelings in this activity. The T-group has a number of objectives:

- Developing a mental attitude of observation about oneself and about others, developing sensitivity in regard to oneself and others.
- Learning about control, and how it may be exercised under different conditions, particularly about how the group can learn to manage itself.
- Becoming aware that communication can go on at different levels.
- Gaining competence in problem solving in the group.

This is learning of different kinds, as well as degrees, and no single set of principles can be used to assess all the results. The method is one deserving careful study for possible implications for other kinds of training.

LIMITATIONS

In all these forms in which the real is simulated, one can anticipate an interest and keenness that may not be present in other forms of learning. It is no exaggeration to say that many of the most interesting advances in learning theory and practice in recent years have been of this kind. But there are a number of limitations.

These forms and devices require considerable time to prepare and to use. An excellent plan is required, and considerable time must always be allotted for discussion and for identifying principles and practices. Learning in this fashion may have little consequence, even if the case, or play, or exercise is well presented, unless the essential task of analysis, understanding, and application is carried on systematically. Requirements of planning and handling the environment are usually greater, not less, than in a traditional classroom setting.

There is another obvious difficulty. There is considerable evidence to show that learning is increased if there is some variety in methods. But no one meeting should be crowded with too much content or too many shifts in method. Adults in particular need some time to adjust themselves to shifts in attention and pace.

Role playing, in particular, requires very careful planning and execution. If used in clumsy fashion people can feel threatened or embarrassed in the process, especially if they are asked to play themselves or if the particular situation allows any participant to "be put on the spot."

Recently a professor was asked to give a lecture to a minority group on the subject of racial prejudice. Without letting anyone know, he arranged for two of his students to enact a situation, just before he began to speak, in which prejudice was exhibited in a very direct form. The result was the galvanization of such hatred in the group that for the first hour of the meeting he was able to do little more than allow the group members to release their hostility. At that point he was able to interpret what had happened and have the group think together about hostility and prejudice in a constructive way. But had he not had enough skill to deal with the situation and the near-violence (which he had not anticipated), the result would have been negative learning of the least desirable kind. Role playing for *therapeutic* purposes is a matter only for people with special training. For other purposes it is a useful device, but to be approached with the same thought and care that one would give to any important meeting.

Motion Pictures

Thomas A. Edison and the Lumière brothers, who had most to do with early development of motion pictures, believed that their inventions would find chief application in education. However, motion pictures were early associated with *entertainment,* and the use of this medium for learning, with some notable exceptions, did not make much headway until after 1930. This was the time when 16-mm. sound motion pictures began to be distributed. This was also the beginning of the documentary film, in which all the arts and skills of motion picture production were first employed in connection with subjects concerning man and how he lives. But if films were to be used for education, not entertainment, more than changes in film content and technology were required. It required changes in the environment in which they were to be perceived, a fact that took much longer to register.

Radio has been utilized for learning for thirty years and more. Wire and tape recorders, although the main principle had been known since 1905, did not come into common use until near the end of Word War II. Aural cassettes and videotape recorders were developed in the 1960's and video cassettes in the 1970's. All of these are now used for a wide variety of purposes:

- Providing information, facts or theories
- Showing the proper execution of skills and processes
- Raising questions and providing a background of experience for group discussion
- Motivating study and action
- Stimulating appreciation of the arts
- Research in learning theory and practice

All these media have particular as well as general uses. We shall illustrate by reference to the sound motion picture, although the greatest impact of media may be in their combined, and not their singular, use. Motion pictures have a number of special properties that are of advantage to learning. People like to see them, and rarely need encouragement or special motivation. This seems to be equally true of men and women all over the world. Films are concrete and real; often closer to the experience of men and women than are more abstract printed materials.

Films may combine all the arts—drama, music, photography, graphic arts, dancing—in interesting and unusual combinations. They are thus able, not only to attract an audience, but to hold attention. For the same reasons they appeal to, and influence, the feelings. There is an emotional as well as intellectual response to films. It is not always known clearly why this is so or how to control it, but the fact that it exists is a matter of importance.

The motion picture is in some respects better suited to learning than is nature or actual experience. Telescopic photography can bring distant objects close up for study; microscopic photography can allow direct observation of objects otherwise too small; time-lapse and slow-motion photography make possible the study of growth or motion which one otherwise could speculate about but never observe. Artistry in film-making can provide insights just as does any other art—insights not possible through rational processes.

The use of motion pictures in learning requires good planning and effective presentation. We have noted that attention to the environmental factors for good learning did not appear as early as changes in technology. A number of books are now available which give detailed suggestions of use. One essential fact about motion pictures is that although people will view a film with some eagerness, they may also approach it with some of the same attitudes they bring to any other entertainment. That is, they expect to be interested, distracted, or amused, and may take no responsibility to put themselves out, to understand, or to do anything about the new experience. Respecting educational purposes, the setting is extremely important. A large theater reinforces expectations of entertainment, little involvement, no commitment, and disengagement at the conclusion of the experience. A different environment is needed if the observer is to attend carefully, and then take part in examination of the film and its consequences for his behavior and follow-up action.

In using films in place of a talk or lecture, one needs to remember that there are certain requirements. Of course, illumination, size of image, sound quality, and freedom from visual or audio distraction should be provided. Just as it is important that a speaker be introduced, so it is imperative that any medium should be. There is evidence to show that an effective introduction, motivating the learner and securing his full attention, will double the amount that is learned from a film, and that what is learned will be retained longer. It is just as essential with a film as with a speaker to find out if the points of the film are established. If this did not happen, it is often useful to screen the film again. In using film or filmstrips for teaching a skill like tennis or learning a language, the particular sequence may need to be repeated several times. For this purpose, the film loops, which allow a single portion of the film to be repeated and repeated, are most useful.

Most films are not designed for group discussion—that is, their purpose is not to raise questions, but to assert, inform, instruct, preach, indoctrinate. If, however, there are significant questions implied in the film, discussion can develop. The film presentation does provide a background of common experience out of which consideration of the topic develops. But in the presentation of the film attention needs to be focused on the issues. Of course opportunities for discussion and additional reading, study, and testing should be planned for and accessible.

One of the most valuable uses of film is much like that of role playing. Some films present a social problem in dramatic form with which the participants can identify. The members can then consider together the implications or some related issues that may have been suggested by the film. This may provide a satisfying release of one's feelings, as well as a means of becoming more objective about one's own experience. In one such discussion a woman said: "I have known this [a particular practice in child care] all my life. If I had been given a written examination about it, I could have passed it any time. But I never fully understood it till tonight *when I heard myself saying it.*"

Application

This has been a chapter of *application.* No new principles have been advanced, but most of the major factors in learning have been reviewed, this time in a different context, and in the kind of setting in which a practitioner is most likely to confront them.

There is no hierarchy of values in learning; every factor can be of critical importance—on occasion fresh air may be as important as fresh ideas. Environment, the place, shape, and character of the facilities, all affect the amount and quality of learning.

An astonishing variety of forms, methods, techniques, and devices are available to the agent in adult learning. But ability in selection is required, and this is one of the chief skills of the teacher of adults. For example, it is possible to convey facts to very large groups of adults, but the sound patterns of languages are best learned in groups no larger than six. Where skills are being taught, ample opportunity and facilities must be provided for practice.

In every activity arrangements must be made for the expression of a number of factors—for example, anticipating and dealing with apprehension or resistance to learning, gaining and holding attention, providing for clear exposition, allowing for a two-way flow of communication, ensuring that there is testing, application and appraisal of the knowledge, skill or attitude.

The experienced practitioner may feel that our references, again and again, to the total learning environment as well as to the variables within it have been repetitious and redundant. Perhaps so, but it is our observation that, along with the failure to discern and articulate learning objectives, failure to provide an environment that supports these objectives is much too common. Millions of dollars have been invested in facilities and devices, but too often the learning environment, though improved, is still lacking in fundamentals. The situations for studying and examining environmental factors are all around us. It is an absorbing experience, for example, to observe or take part in four kinds of experience:

- An activity in a center planned for adult education
- An event associated with attempts by a university or college to participate in the improvement of social conditions
- A discussion group
- The use of a film or television in a group learning project

In each case the environmental features present or absent should be noted.

The key to learning is engagement—a relationship between the learner, the task or subject matter, the environment, and the teacher. Some of the factors within this relationship are already established by the nature and experience of the learner, but many of the factors are not fixed in any way; they can be modified and improved with planning and practice.

With this chapter we complete the cycle of theory, practice, and application. We shall next review the entire teaching-learning transaction.

REFERENCES

1. Richard Livingstone, *On Education* (New York: The Macmillan Company, 1942).
2. C. N. Parkinson, *Parkinson's Law* (Boston: Houghton Mifflin Company, 1957). By permission of the publisher.
3. Commission on Architecture, *Architecture for Adult Education* (Chicago: Adult Education Association, 1956).
4. Harold J. Alford, *Continuing Education in Action* (New York: John Wiley and Sons, 1968).
5. C. O. Houle, *Residential Continuing Education* (Syracuse: Syracuse University Notes and Essays on Education for Adults, 70, 1971).
6. John Henry Newman, *University Sketches* (Dublin: Browne and Nolan, Ltd., text of 1856).
7. Dennis Trueblood and Franklin Roberts, "The Folklore of Workshops," *Adult Leadership* (Chicago: AEA), Vol. 7, No. 7.
8. Nathaniel Cantor, *Adult Leadership* (Chicago: AEA), Vol. 1, No. 10.
9. Hugh Gyllenhaal, "Guide to Styles, Groups, Methods," *Sales Meetings*, Jan. 4, 1957.
10. Coolie Verner, "Methods and Techniques," *An Overview of Adult Education Research* (Chicago: AEA, 1959).
11. Clarence Randall, *Toward the Liberally Educated Executive* (White Plains, N.Y.: Fund for Adult Education, 1957).
12. J. E. Anderson, "Teaching and Learning," *Education for Maturity* (New York: William Morrow & Company, Inc., 1955).
13. Abbott Kaplan, *A Study of Liberal Arts Discussion Programs for Adults in the Metropolitan Los Angeles Area* (White Plains, N.Y.: Fund for Adult Education, 1958).

14. J. L. Moreno, *Who Shall Survive?* (Boston: Beacon Press, Inc., rev. ed., 1953).
15. Alan Klein, *Role Playing* (New York: Association Press, 1956).
16. Kenneth D. Andrews, *The Case Method of Teaching Human Relations and Administration* (Cambridge: Harvard University Press, 1958).
17. National Training Laboratory, *Explorations in Human Relations Training* (Washington, D.C.: National Education Association, 1953).

SUGGESTED READING

Blakely, Robert. *The New Environment: Questions for Adult Educators.* Occasional Paper, No. 23. Syracuse: Syracuse University Publications in Continuing Education, 1971.

Burns, Hobert W., *Sociological Backgrounds of Adult Education.* Syracuse: Syracuse University Publications in Continuing Education, 1964.

Castaldi, Basil. *Creative Planning of Educational Facilities.* Chicago: Rand McNally, 1969.

Drucker, Peter. *The Age of Discontinuity: Guidelines to Our Changing Society.* London: Heinemann, 1969.

Etzioni, Amitar. *Studies in Social Change.* New York: Holt, Rinehart and Winston, 1966.

Hunsaker, Herbert C., and Pierce, Richard. *Creating a Climate for Adult Learning.* Syracuse: Syracuse University Publications in Continuing Education, 1959.

Hutchins, Robert M. *The Learning Society.* New York: Frederick A. Praeger, 1968.

Johnson, Eugene I. *Metroplex Assembly: An Experiment on Community Education.* Reports, No. 213. Syracuse: Syracuse University Publications in Continuing Education, 1965.

Ruddock, Ralph. *Sociological Perspectives on Adult Education.* Manchester: University of Manchester, 1972.

Shaw, N. C., ed. *Administration of Continuing Education.* Washington: National Education Association, 1969.

Sherif, Muzater. *Social Interaction: Process and Products.* Chicago: Aldine-Atherton Publishers, 1971.

Toffler, Alvin. *Future Shock.* New York: Random House, 1970.

10

The Learning Transaction

So far in our inquiry we have set out certain hypotheses about the self and about learning, examined many sources of information about the learner, considered how these factors have been woven into theoretical formulations, observed how they work out in certain fields of practice, and examined the environmental and organizational circumstances affecting learning. Hypothesis, study, formulation, testing of theory, observation, all have gone on. Now we shall attempt some application of what we have found out, first setting out some of the main considerations in regard to the whole process of learning and then concentrating upon the *teacher* or *leader* or *practitioner* in the process.

John Dewey often wrote about learning as a transaction. He said that active perception, interpretation, or understanding comes as a result of a transaction in which are linked the interpreter and the interpreted, or between the observer and the observed. In the marketplace, unless both the buyer and the seller bring something of value, there is no transaction. So it is with learning. Many students of learning over many centuries have also used this term because they have been acutely aware of both process and *continuity*—continuity between the learner and his past, the learner and his environment, the learner and the content, the learner and his teacher.

We have already seen that learning involves change and growth in the individual and in his behavior. "You don't change," said Eduard Lindeman, "until you do something. You don't change by listening. You don't change by talking. You actually change when something happens to your muscles. When you step or move in a new way, then the change becomes really significant." [1] What may be involved is cognitive learning or motor learning, or affective learning—or all in the same process—but always there is change and growth.

We have also had a glimpse of the nature of the *self* and have seen how the self must become committed or involved if effective learning is to happen.

We have established that adults have the physiological equipment and the capacity for learning, and even where there has been some physical or sensory impairment, there are also means of overcoming most of the disabilities. Sometimes learning is an individual act, sometimes it happens in a group or social situation where the transaction has at least five elements:

- the learner
- the teacher
- the group (usually)

- the setting or situation
- the subject matter

But the main protagonists in the transaction are still the learner and the teacher. This is often true even in self-directed learning because, as Allen Tough reports in *The Adult's Learning Projects*, self-directed learners frequently seek helpers or teachers for particular goals.

At the risk of boredom induced by repetition, let us once more ask ourselves what the learner brings to the transaction. What are his perceptions about the need for change? How deep is his uneasiness, his dissatisfaction with the present or his desire for the new? What are the inhibitions to learning that he brings, his ambivalence, his resistance to change, his refuge in the present? What does he know about his own capacity for learning? Does he perceive the content as abstract and irrelevant? Does he expect understanding and helpfulness from the teacher or some kind of threatening behavior? Does he feel a part of, or rejected by, the group?

Learning may be an adventure, but for the learner it may also pose unknown difficulties or raise images of past failures. Does the learner perceive the situation as it is or are his perceptions distorted? Is he likely to protect himself by verbalizing about the subject matter without internalizing or reorganizing it within himself. Whitehead has warned that passive learning of "inert ideas" may be not only wasteful but actually harmful, since the result is a decrease in satisfaction gained from learning and probably an increase in resistance to further learning.

What does the teacher bring? Like the learner, the teacher also brings a great deal to the transaction, much more than his mastery of a skill or his knowledge of subject matter. Does he have awareness of the continuity or the interaction that is involved? Does he look on it as an encounter with another self, or perceive himself simply as a transmission system for presenting certain material? Nothing is more deeply belittling than the self-image that some teachers have of themselves as being but a repository of facts or ideas, ready to display them before others, but themselves taking little part except as transmitters. In such cases a tape recorder might do as well; a computer could do even better; at least it would react to the questions asked.

How well is the teacher aware of the delicacy of his role, of the need that the learner has to be both dependent upon, and independent of, him? How well does he understand his own needs, his need to control people, or his need for affection, or his fear of hostility from the learner? How well is he able to accept the learner, not just as pupil but as a person?

Within the group, its experience, its skill in supporting the learner, its encouragement to him to stretch out, its capacity for obtaining assistance from the teacher, and so on, are factors of considerable consequence. As we have seen, this is equally true of what might be called the environmental factors and the subject matter.

For the purposes of summary and application we shall now look at the learning transaction according to a somewhat different plan. To a considerable extent we shall be reviewing and recapitulating—but with illustrative examples and with some expansion of principles. We shall also follow a three-step time sequence that is usually present in any learning transaction— that is, planning the curriculum, establishing the learning situation, and evaluating. The same dominant notes and chords will be struck as in earlier chapters, but we shall now experience them in the kind of frame or setting most applicable to educational or training institutions.

We cannot escape some dangers here. No one statement can do justice to differing points of view that still exist concerning philosophy or method. Nor can it apply equally well to learning situations as different, for example, as teaching the use of the slide rule in a factory and the study of comparative religion; or the relatively free exploration of poetic forms and the teaching of a catechism or the preparation of a night-school class for an examination in mathematics. These situations are far from identical and any statement of practice, no matter how flexible, can be applied only with the exercise of considerable ingenuity. We believe, however, that what is suggested here does have application to most learning situations for adults.

The study of curriculum for elementary and secondary schools, colleges, and universities has been going on for a very long time. Less systematic attention has been given to program planning or designing curricula for adults, although that situation is changing for the better. While many adult curricula have the virtue of flexibility, far too often there are serious weaknesses.

However, as George Aker reports in *Materials and Methods in Adult Education*,[2] considerable sound systematic development work is now proceeding under such labels as curriculum, course, or project development.

One of the essential differences between adult education and the curricula often planned for children is that the adult learner, far more than the child, may expect to take a more active part in the consideration and selection of what he is to study. With children the amount of choice, and the degree of participation in the choice of learning materials and experiences will usually be limited. But with adults there can be a very wide range from dependence upon the teacher to the stage where the choice of learning objectives and the curriculum are made by the learners. Where examinations are set by some authority, or where the readings are already established (as in the case of a Great Books program), choice may be considerably restricted, but even in these cases there may be considerable opportunity for variety of illustrations or applications of principles. Whatever the limits, it is clear that where the learner does take part in the development of the curriculum, this act leads to a learning experience that is markedly different in quality. However, as we shall see in the next section, the learner may not have had any previous practice in choosing what to study. This may at first be a strange and perhaps even forbidding task for him, and he may need guidance in trying it.

A number of scholars have contributed considerably to our understanding of curricula; among them Malcolm Knowles, C. O. Houle, Virginia Griffin, and Robert Mager, to name only four.

For our purpose we will begin with a short analysis derived mainly from *Basic Principles of Curriculum and Instruction* [3] by Ralph W. Tyler; who identifies three general sources for learning objectives:

- The learner himself
- Contemporary life and the society in which the learner lives
- The subject matter fields such as history and literature

Since we are concerned with cognitive, systematic, and effective learning, and since in some cases the main decisions about curriculum are made by the learner himself, in others by the students sharing in curriculum planning, and in still others by the teacher, there will be many variations in practice, but the same general procedure can usually be employed.

Needs of the Learner

We have dealt with the learner at some length. In Chapter 5 we identified two kinds of needs, both of which have some application in curriculum building:

- A need in the sense that the learner lacks some information or skill that it is assumed he should have, or that is enjoyed by most members in society.

- A need in the sense of a tension or disequilibrium—for example, if the body lacks food, or if the person lacks affection, or lacks a philosophy of life.

A study of the needs and wants of the adult learner is one means of beginning the development of a curriculum. Needs are so many and so varied that one must have some way of bringing them into order. One rough classification is (1) health (2) family and friendship relations (3) sociocivic relations (4) consumer aspects of life (5) occupation (6) recreation (7) religion and philosophy.

Many ingenious ways have been used to identify both needs and interests, employing questionnaires, interviews, and similar devices.

Objections have sometimes been raised to the employment of such information in developing a curriculum. It is claimed, for example, that information about interests may give the *range* of interest but not the intensity. It is also possible that adult students may come with mixed, or twisted, or unworthy interests and goals.

A further objection is that placing too great a reliance on individual "interests" may result in the slighting of information gained from community surveys and the analysis of social patterns and social groupings which, in practice, have been the source of many useful ideas for educational activities for adults.

The most frequent criticism is that an interest-based curriculum will result in reinforcing what may be a degraded level of taste. It is clear that some producers of the mass media in "giving the people what they want" are not only underestimating what people really want, but are themselves modifying wants and interests.

The errors here are threefold. The first is to assume that people have had enough experience to know all that will interest them. One way to help people discover an interest is to expose them to a range of experiences. As William E. Hocking once said, "There is many a horse which does not know it is thirsty and which, when led to water, finds that it wants to drink." This is often true of the adult student whose horizons of experience have been restricted. How can he know how fascinating some of the "unknown countries" may be? The only way he can discover this is by exploration which sometimes may be difficult and unrewarding, but may also prove a great adventure.

A second error is putting undue reliance upon superficial interest-finders of the questionnaire type, using inadequate sampling procedures. Results of such measures usually are very limited. On the other hand, well-conducted interviews, or thorough investigations, have revealed a surprising range and depth of interest among adults. One study of radio listeners in

England by Joseph Trenaman [4] reports that there are desires for learning among "ordinary people" of a kind that are seldom supplied in the daily run of broadcasting. The large numbers of people that have not enrolled but "listen in" to the Open University is another example. It seems probable that such results can be obtained in most countries.

A third error can arise in the decision about a course of action based on what has been found out about the interests of learners. Supposing one discovers that men in a certain work gang read nothing but comic books. One then has the choice between supplying them with even more comic books or continuing the search for an interest or need around which other forms of reading or study may take place. Of course it is possible always to capitulate and accede to any want that is expressed. A well-known American comic once claimed, "My audience is made up of high school kids. High school kids like to see me spit on people. So I spit on people." But it is also possible to use information about interests and needs in a responsible way. A study of comic books carried out for an institution, Frontier College, working in the bush camps of Canada, revealed a number of interests that became the basis for several courses of study.

The main reason, of course, for the concentration on interests as a source for educational objectives is the close relationship that this seems to bear with gaining the attention of people and having them participate in educational endeavors. Considerable study has been given to those adults in society who are infrequently or never found in educational activities. Despite recent growth in enrollment in adult education, the number of men and women who never take part in formal or informal activities must still be very large; particularly, it has been found, amongst those who have less than an eighth-grade education, are over fifty-five years of age, are laborers or service workers, and are close to a subsistence level of living. Many who have studied nonparticipation believe that if more adults are to be brought into educational activities, not only must the curriculum be modified to accommodate other interests but also many of the traditional forms of organization may have to be revised.

Curriculum

Those devising a curriculum may search contemporary life for clues to the selection of learning experiences. Here, just as much as in analyzing interests, the amount of material is so vast and complicated that some categories or other organizing devices are required.

Sources for this purpose are many. They include different kinds of data as supplied from the census, or from studies of society by social scientists, or from novels and plays.

Subjects may be suggested that have occupied the attention of men in all ages; or they may be about contemporary phenomena such as the impact upon people of industrialization and urbanization, particularly of the "great city" where many millions of men and women are now linked together in a gigantic aggregation of living and working.

Objections can be and are raised against a narrow restricted use of contemporary material. For example, if a study is undertaken of a single institution, or activity, or social problem, without seeing it in its wider setting, or without any principles for wider application, the study may not be very rewarding. But the reverse of this would be equally barren. Few people believe any longer what used to be a common assumption, that a few basic principles are all that are needed; that these can be readily learned, and that when learned they can be applied to any new situation. It is now well established that learning happens with greatest efficiency where there is some similarity between the learning situation and the life situation. It is a caricature, of course, but still there is some force in the complaint of the young man who claimed: "I have an education that has equipped me in every respect to be a Roman emperor, but, alas, I am going to become a father!"

THE FIELDS OF STUDY OR SUBJECT MATTERS

An excellent source of learning objectives is in the established fields of study, such as mathematics and history. This has long been recognized in adult education, and not much comment is necessary. But there have been curious gaps. For example, although we live in an age that is often described as the "scientific era," the time allotted to science in the curriculum for adult education has been only a tiny fraction of the whole. Moreover, the use of subject matter has been for learning objectives that have been surprisingly narrow. Often it has included little more than the acquiring of information. To take the example of science again, it is claimed that there are at least four main educational objectives for any *ordinary citizen* studying science:

- To contribute to the health (both physical and emotional) of the learner through his changed behavior.
- To contribute to the conservation of natural and other resources as well as the improvement of his occupational capacity.
- To give the learner a more accurate, more satisfying picture of the world and his place in it, including the release of some of his fears through a better understanding of what may now appear strange.
- To help him adopt more effective methods for studying and for solving problems.

By seeking the aid of the subject matter specialist in developing a curriculum, not only can important fields be covered, but they can be opened up in the depth and breadth that they deserve.

In these three ways far more educational objectives will be identified than can possibly be followed up by any single educational agency. How can selection be made of those of greatest worth? Tyler proposes two main "screens" for selection—one's educational philosophy and the understanding that one has of what learning is or can do.

Educational Philosophy. We have already listed a number of questions in educational philosophy. These need to be asked with respect to any educational objectives proposed. There are additional questions, for example, "Should the same kind of learning experience be provided for a man in a labor union as in a chamber of commerce?" The rigorous application of these questions to a proposed curriculum may make it possible to develop some priorities; those educational objectives in harmony with one's philosophy will be identified. However, in order to do this, it is essential that one's educational philosophy be stated lucidly and the main implications for educational objectives may have to be spelled out.

Understanding About Learning. The second screen to be applied is made up of what we know about the educational process. There are some learning objectives that are potential only, there are some that are possible only with years of application, there are others that can be accomplished in a single course, or a single presentation. We know, for example, that it is possible in therapy for a considerable reorganization of the personality structure of an individual to be effected. But this is most likely to happen only over periods of time. One ought not to expect revolutionary outcomes from a week-end course labeled "Personality 101."

From our knowledge of learning we can more readily organize material in time sequences. Some content may come first because it can be mastered more easily or because it provides necessary background, or a system for understanding what is to follow. It may seem an odd remark to make but another useful guide is our knowledge about "forgetting." A college student, for example, may forget as much as 50 per cent of what he learns in one year, or as much as 80 per cent in two years. But if he practices or uses the new he is not so inclined to lose it. It is desirable therefore, to choose learning sequences which the adult student is in a position to practice and apply. Moreover, things that are learned that are consistent with each other tend to reinforce and those that are inconsistent tend to interfere. This understanding can also guide us in selection of subject matter. We have seen that material which is inconsistent with the learner's view of the self is likely to be rejected or distorted. Where such material is a necessary part of the curriculum it ought to be introduced with some care and in ways by which the learner may be aided to face up to the implications squarely.

Some decisions may need to be made about the objectives that are "educational" and those that require some other form of behavior. For example, some of the problems faced by an unemployed laborer with five children may be dealt with through education; others may require action through welfare, therapy, or politics.

Two final actions are required in the development of the curriculum; a careful statement of objectives and selection of the actual learning experiences.

STATEMENT OF OBJECTIVES

In the ways already outlined a group of major educational objectives can be listed. If they are to be developed into actual learning experiences they must now be stated precisely.

On several occasions it has been noted that the important thing about learning has to do with changes in the learner; it is not behavior by the teacher, or kinds of subject matter. Accordingly educational objectives ought to be stated in a form which identifies the expected changes in the student. It is not enough to state that a learning objective is history or shopwork, or even in some generalized form such as "History develops an historical point-of-view." Two elements should be included in the statement —the kind of behavior change expected and the subject matter to be employed. Examples:

- To prepare a clear and well-organized newspaper article about the reorganization of city government.
- To develop an appreciation of modern architecture.
- To achieve familiarity with dependable sources of information about the teaching of mathematics.

In this way there is clarity about the selection of specific learning experiences. Moreover the objectives are stated in a form that is required if there is to be any satisfactory form of evaluation.

SELECTION OF LEARNING EXPERIENCES

The final step is the selection of the actual learning experiences. How this is done has already been suggested by what was said earlier about learning practice. If the objective has to do with a skill like reading or discussing, or using a tool, the experience must provide both the necessary content and the opportunity to practice that skill. The learning experience must be one in which the learner gains the kind of satisfaction set out in the objectives. We have all suffered occasions where this has not happened. If, in a course in musical appreciation, in the way that musical examples and musical form are analyzed the learner comes to hate music, there has been a disastrous error both in selection of the learning experience and probably in the methods employed. The learning objective needs to be gauged as being within the possible range of accomplishment by the learner at his present level of experience. Discomfort will be produced if it is too elementary just as it will if there is too great difficulty.

While Tyler's principles can be applied to most situations in adult education, and have been widely utilized, many adult educators have developed valuable constructs. The model by Houle [5] is especially useful in action-oriented programs, although it, too, has wider applications:

1. Identify the *problem* and the contextual *situation*.
2. Make a judgment about the appropriateness of possible educational projects. Are there "educational solutions" to this problem or are other measures, such as law, required?
3. Develop and refine a statement of objectives, including specific outcomes in changes of behavior.
4. Design a suitable program:
   a. Format—content and style of presentation.
   b. Leadership—who and by what criteria are leaders selected?
   c. Methods.
   d. Materials.
   e. Group health and morale, common purpose, and reinforcement.
   f. Individualization—individual needs as well as group.
   g. Awareness by all concerned—of goals and procedures.
   h. Evaluation—what objective, measured in what ways, using what data.
5. Provide administrative supports:
   a. Guidance—to program leaders and to individual participants.
   b. Finance.
   c. Interpretation and "public relations."
6. Carry out learning activities, utilizing appropriate feedback at all stages.
7. Measure the progress achieved, at varying stages.
8. Make an appraisal of the whole project, including some sharing and diffusion of what has been learned.

The work of Robert F. Mager,[6] reported in two books, *Preparing Instructional Objectives* and *Analyzing Performance Objectives*, has been influential in vocational education and adult education generally. Mager is a model of lucidity in stating objectives and putting them in a form where it is possible to measure changes in behavior and performance. The care in delineating objectives, paralleled at many points in managerial training (note "Management by Objectives,") has proceeded simultaneously with efforts to organize the instructional materials into smaller, more manageable units or modules.

To summarize: choosing a curriculum for adults means several things. It means understanding the needs and interests of the learner, understanding the situation in which he lives, and the kinds of content that may serve his needs. It means a careful statement of objectives in a form that sets out the desired changes as well as the subject matter. It means selection of the precise learning experiences that may best accomplish these objectives. It assumes the fullest possible participation by the learner in curriculum building.

Moreover, it is now clear that devising suitable curricula for adults, though a fascinating enterprise, is somewhat complicated. If the learner is himself to play a large part in this, it is essential that more assistance be provided to him. Houle, in his survey of adult education in the armed forces, and in his books since has reiterated that counseling, both in the development of curriculum and in the selection of studies, ought to be provided in every educational situation for adults. He and others have maintained that since in adult education the possibilities of choice are usually greater than in most schools or colleges, it is even more essential for the adult student to be able to secure counsel in making an effective choice.

The Learning Situation

With the curriculum chosen we can look at the second phase or aspect of what is really a continuous process.

Whether the learning occurs through individual effort or in some kind of educational or training institution, the key concept is the same. As we have noted it is best expressed in the word *engage* (particularly in the French *engager* from *gage*, or pledge) meaning "to bind oneself, to pledge oneself, to become engrossed, to become involved." Learning happens as the result of engagement, and the task of those guiding learning is to bring about engagement.

Naturally this does not happen by chance or by luck. It must be carefully planned. We say naturally, but it is not always deemed so. Since there is often considerable stress put upon informality in the learning of adults, and the term "informal education" is sometimes used as a synonym for adult education, it has been assumed by some that the learning transaction can proceed as an improvisation. But improvisation is possible, just as in music, only where there is a *mastery* of all the principles that must be brought into some harmonious arrangement. It requires planning and practice, even if it might appear artless.

There are a number of related aspects to this plan and practice:

- Exploring needs for, and resistance to, the learning objectives.
- Making decisions and taking action about the learning environment, i.e., physical arrangements, selection of forms, and devices.
- Achieving helping characteristics within the group if it is a social and not an individual project.
- Exploring the content.
- Testing and applying.

These aspects have some parallels with the phases that Lippitt has identified as occurring in any example of planned change (we substitute the word *learner* for *client*, and *teacher* for *change-agent*):

Phase 1: The learner discovers the need for help, sometimes with stimulation by the teacher.

Phase 2: The helping relationship is established and defined.

Phase 3: The change problem is identified and clarified.

Phase 4: Alternative possibilities for change are examined: change goals or intentions are established.

Phase 5: Change efforts in the "reality situation" are attempted.

Phase 6: Change is generalized and stabilized.

Phase 7: The helping relationship ends, or a different type of continuing relationship is defined.[7]

Lippitt's phases and his more generalized concepts represent a careful extension of the traditional three-stage model—presentation, analysis, testing and application, which has been followed by many teachers for centuries. The three stages have never been more clearly stated than by the rural minister who was asked how he went about preparing his sermon, and replied: "First, I tells 'em what I'm going to tell 'em; then I tells 'em; finally, I tells 'em what I tole 'em."

EXPLORATION OF NEEDS

If he is to become deeply engaged, the learner must perceive his needs and the relationship that the subject matter has to them. It may be useful for him to have some verbal discussion of this. Some teachers make the exploration of needs, as seen by the learners, the central core of the opening session of a course. It may also be useful to have some open discussion of blocks and limitations to learning that may be expected. Sometimes it is useful to have some expression of anxieties, that one is too old, or "rusty," or has been unsuccessful in such kinds of situations before. Sometimes it may help if the teacher warns the members what to expect. For example, they may be told that the subject matter may be difficult until a certain stage is achieved, and that perseverance will be required.

It ought not to be expected that this exploration will take place without incident or some difficulty. People who have been used to governing their own learning will take part in such a preliminary as a matter of course. But what of the adult student whose previous experience has been of a very different kind? Perhaps in any previous educational situation he was *told* how and what to study. Now you are expecting him to assume some responsibility for his own learning. He may feel somewhat puzzled, or frustrated, or even threatened by a situation unlike anything experienced before.

When we ask an athlete to try out a forward somersault dive his muscular contortions may at first be violent.

When we ask a woman to try out a delicate embroidery operation the initial result may be clumsy.

When we ask any human being to behave in a way that is outside or runs counter to all his previous experience the immediate response will be uncertainty, at the very least.

In all cases the individual may need encouragement. This is not mollycoddling, or sugar-coating, or soft pedagogy. This is simply understanding and cooperating with the dynamic way in which a human being grows and changes.

The principle is simple enough to understand and even to state as a generalization, but it is endlessly variable and fascinating in practice.

If the learner has never had the experience of sharing in the planning of his own study, if he has always been in a class or squad or gang where he was expected to listen, repeat certain kinds of instructions when ordered, or reproduce the thinking of his teacher, then the first occasion when he is confronted with the opportunity for greater participation is likely to be difficult. There may be the emergence of negative feelings, perhaps very strong ones. These may be slow to appear, because the tradition is that "the teacher is always right," but it may not be long before someone will blurt out that "time is being wasted," or that he "didn't come there to listen to some other students," or that "the teacher ought to take charge and get on with the teaching."

Naturally, unless these negative feelings can be expressed, there is little chance of the development of much understanding of what has produced them, or acceptance by the learner of a greater degree of responsibility. But if the learner finds that he can express feelings without being condemned, if he can take action or try out ideas that will not lead to his rejection by the teacher or by the class members, he has little need for a brittle defensiveness. If no one is attacking, blaming, or condemning him, he is freed to face his own ambivalent feelings. Not having to face hostility all about him, he can decide to face or not to face himself in regard to the particular learning goals. It is not enough for the teacher to be patient with the learner. He must himself be prepared for the puzzlement, frustration, even the hostility that may be expressed. If such feelings catch him "off guard," his own protective responses such as returning hostility, ridicule, or censure, will serve to increase the tension and thus the learning difficulties.

One more point: the student not only needs to be prepared to handle his own difficulties but he may need the incentive of some forward view of the results. The superintendent of a park in the Rocky Mountains once reported: "We found that as soon as people could see the peak from every point on the road, many more completed the climb to the top."

SELECTION OF SPECIFIC FORMS AND DEVICES

In any field where there is richness of opportunity the process of *selection* becomes more important and correspondingly more difficult. In the old one-room school, with no aids to learning but a slate and a tattered arithmetic book, the teacher had few problems of selection. But a teacher or leader of adults today best demonstrates his competence by his understanding and skill in the selection and use of an astonishing range of alternative resources and forms. Of course, selection must be based on what is required for the learning objectives. This was discussed in Chapter 9 in connection with the outline of Hugh Gyllenhaal.

It is essential to make sure that all arrangements are in accord with what we know about learning. This will include at least the following:

- Planning the environment in line with the program objectives.
- Having all equipment in excellent condition, set up for immediate use, or available for practice at the time when needed.
- Applying the suggestions devised to help overcome some of the sight and hearing limitations of older people.
- Arranging the learning sequences in time units that challenge but do not fatigue or dull the interest of the adult learner.
- Taking care that the pace of presentation is not too rapid, particularly for the older adult.

CHARACTERISTICS OF THE GROUP WHICH SUPPORTS LEARNING

We shall not attempt to repeat here the material about groups and learning that was presented in Chapters 8 and 9. Instead we shall simply note at least three characteristics that need to be present in the group if effective learning is to take place:

- *A realization by the members of the group* that genuine growth stems from the creative power within the individual, and that learning, finally, is an individual matter.
- The acceptance as a *group standard* that each member has the right to be different and to disagree.
- Establishment of a group atmosphere that is free from narrow judgments on the part of the teacher or group members.

EXPLORATION OF THE SUBJECT MATTER

We have seen that the presentation of the subject matter can take many forms, such as reading, lectures, observation and experiment, or practice of reality situations. If the attention of the learner is fully engaged he will want, in increasing measure, to experience the subject matter in all its fascination, or its difficulty, even its bewilderment. He may want or need the information or opinion of an "expert." Or he may be prepared for frank exchange of views. Some differences of opinion are healthy: the I-think-this-for-this-reason kind; rather than you-are-wrong kind which we usually call an argument, and which usually is quite sterile as far as learning is concerned.

This exploration can and should go on, in depth. But there are also endless possibilities for breadth. With so much experience among the group members to start from, the possibilities of generalizing and of perceiving new relationships are many. This potential richness of generalizing is, for writers like Peter Siegle,[8] one of the chief marks of and the most absorbing aspects of adult education. Possibilities for the curriculum associated with travel and field trips, as well as education as part of community development and social action, open the field wider still but make all the more necessary a firm grasp on what are the learning objectives.

In the case of a skill, or motor learning (like learning to play tennis), little result can be anticipated without opportunity for practice. Actually this principle is valid not only for motor learning, but it is not so well recognized in other fields. Along with the presentation, exploration, and relating of subject matter must go the practice of ideas and skills, the try-out and testing of assumptions and hypotheses, checking them against alternatives, and counterclaims, estimating their validity with respect to inner logic or in application in real life.

If the learning has to do with the acquiring of new skills and attitudes, an essential part of the learning process will be imaginative applications in the home setting. The learner may want and need help in diagnosing the forces that may be resistant to change, in measuring his own strengths and weaknesses, and in seeking to re-establish himself back in his own situation.

The learner may also need help in developing a "continuing system" of learning. If he has attained satisfaction in learning, already he has a "bent" for more. What he may also need is to improve his skill in learning, to use more scientific methods of observation and analysis, to become more sensitive and understanding of his own inhibitions to learning (and through understanding reduce these resistances), to become more self-accepting, and, through gaining more security and becoming less defensive, freer to perceive without distortion.

This entire learning transaction proceeds most effectively if it is guided by "feed-back" and evaluation.

Evaluation

We shall now turn to the third phase of the transaction—*evaluation*. In recent years so much attention has been directed to this subject that the word itself has become invested with feelings and is something of a semantic battle ground. Unfortunately, as in the case of the weather, there is still much more talk than constructive action.

The function of evaluation was stated succinctly by a national committee of the Adult Education Association:

- The purposes of education are growth and change—change in behavior of individuals and groups. People behave differently as a result of education.
- The primary purpose of evaluation in education is to find out how much change and growth have taken place as a result of educational experiences. One evaluates a total program or major parts of it to find out how much progress has been made toward program objectives.[9]

In some cases, measurement of results is relatively simple. An agricultural extension worker does not have to guess about outcomes: he either can or cannot find actual changes in practice. So can a political organizer. The test of some educational programs in social action is how many improved conditions were brought about. The American Library Association once stated what were termed as "four basic steps" respecting evaluation:

Those taken before the activity
    1. setting of goals—what specific outcome is expected?

2. establishing a base-line—what is true of this situation now?
Those taken after the activity
3. noting and recording change—what happened?
4. considering the change in the light of circumstances—what does it mean and what should be done about it? [10]

This model may not suit all forms of education but it can be adapted to most.

Earlier we also asserted that evaluation should be carried out with respect to specific learning objectives. Indeed, one of the principal reasons for being sharp and clear in the statement of one's objectives is so that appraisal can be conducted in a meaningful way. If, to take an earlier example, the learning objective is "to develop familiarity with dependable sources of information about the teaching of mathematics" it is not too difficult to devise an interview or questionnaire, or task, by which that objective can be appraised.

We have also claimed that evaluation should be carried on as a *regular, ongoing* part of the total learning process.

Now if the objective of the learning program were merely the reproducing of information supplied by the teacher, or giving back the opinions of the teacher, evaluation might be expressed as some measure of facts or opinions committed to memory.

Usually, however, the objectives have to do with *changes* in observing, identifying, analyzing, understanding, organizing, applying, and testing information as well as the development of certain work habits, skills, and attitudes. Some way must therefore be found for measuring the changes, directly or by inference.

It is well to stress a variety of measures because it has often been assumed that evaluation means the use of pencil-and-paper tests. Obviously written tests have a part in evaluation. So do tests of performance in certain skills (for example, typing, gymnastics, welding, dissecting, leading discussion). So also does appraisal of samples of performance, such as selections from a student's writing. So do oral examinations of many kinds.

Not only does evaluation mean the measurement of changes in behavior but it usually signifies more than one test, more than a final examination. If evaluation is to mean much there must also be pre-examination, so that there is a base from which growth can be measured. There is also systematic ongoing evaluation which we shall discuss in a moment under the term "feed-back." There is testing at the conclusion of the program. And there is further assessment at some point in time afterwards, to note any application of the learning. In reporting on the research concerning the teaching of the facts of nutrition we have seen that at the end of the formal program of instruction the women all seemed to have acquired about the same amount of information about nutrition, but six months later, when tested concerning what they had done about the facts that they had learned, some of them showed considerably more gains than the others.

In his book, *Informal Adult Education*,[11] Malcolm Knowles reports that "to most adults the words 'test,' 'quiz' and 'examination' call forth such unpleasant memories that it is often difficult to use them in voluntary adult groups." This seems to be true, and thus far there have not been devised many satisfactory substitute methods. One difficulty we have dealt with already. If the learning objective is not defined in a precise way it is difficult or impossible to make any assessment of progress. However, various kinds of written "objective" tests have been adapted from schools and universities. These are of the sort in which the learner indicates whether he thinks the statement is true or false, or in which he makes a choice among several statements.

But little attention has yet been directed toward developing these for adult purposes. In adult education in England, particularly in the classes of the Workers' Education Association, it is expected that every student will write a number of essays and much of the effort of the tutor in guiding the adult students comes in connection with this written work. Essays and projects are not unknown but are much less common in North America.

Some attempts have been made to use projective tests (notably the Rorschach "ink blot" test) in which the learner constructs an imaginary story or describes how he feels or what he sees when certain unstructured shapes are presented to him. Analysis by a trained psychologist of his responses can give a good deal of information about his attitudes, social adjustment, and personality structure. But such use is rarely possible except in psychological clinics and institutions; it is not at all for general purposes unless highly trained professional staff are available.

Some teachers have made use of studies of attendance, and of "dropouts," in evaluating their program. However, such statistics by themselves do not reveal very much unless it is possible to follow them up with interviews with a selected number of individuals. Studies of participation are becoming more common, as we have noted in another connection.

Each teacher can and does make some subjective assessment of the performance and growth of the learners. But that is rarely satisfactory in furnishing data for any kind of comparisons.

Kropp and Verner [12] have developed an attitude-scale technique for evaluating the changes that occur in a single meeting or conference, which they feel will provide results that can be compared. The scale is based on the feelings and judgments that the learner has about the experience in which he has just participated.

The *agent* of evaluation may be very important. If the learning objective is simply reproducing what the teacher has taught, the result may just as well be measured by the teacher. But if a primary learning objective is for the learner to become increasingly autonomous, to begin to take over direction of his own learning, then it is highly important that he take a large share, if not the complete control, of the evaluation. Now that it is better understood how much self-directed learning goes on, a major task of education will be to equip individuals with the attitudes and the skills required for curriculum planning and evaluation of their own programs of study.

In many learning situations, the participation by the learner in the evaluation is difficult to manage. Where there is a standard program of teaching skills, such as lifesaving, there is usually a fixed examination system. A factory, a school or university may also have an established examination procedure which is required by law for licensing, or to receive the payments of grants, or because it is backed by some other sanction. What can be done in the face of such rigidities?

First of all, it should be repeated that the measuring of performance against certain objective standards is an excellent way to obtain knowledge about oneself if the learner is himself making these comparisons, and if the process is carried out without some form of punishment for poor performance. Films or tape recordings by which he can observe good work, and appraise his own performance against what is excellent, provides one means of doing this. It is also important for him to measure his performance against his own previous performance and against his learning objectives. Again, the use of tape recordings, particularly videotape recordings, makes this possible in many fields. Motion picture film is regularly used for appraisal in sports like football.

In the classroom many teachers, obliged by the institution to give some test, have experimented with various means of testing that are also conducive to the development of self-appraisal. One practice is to have the class members themselves prepare the test form. Contrary to what might be anticipated, the resulting test is often more rigorous than that which would have been devised by the instructor. Another variation is where the students are asked to state a dozen or so major propositions in regard to their subject, bring them to class, and then be examined critically on their understanding and application of a selection of these propositions.

But where academic credit is not an issue, the number and variety of "examinations" used is surprising. Often the test is some form of application of the subject matter and principles learned. For example, in one school for trade unionists where they had been studying collective bargaining, the class members were asked to nominate five of their number to take part in a full-day "case," along with an equal number of business men, and guided by three industrial conciliators. During the proceedings a special "chair" was left open so that any class member who sat there would be recognized by the chairman and allowed to make an observation or ask a question. Two- or three-day exercises which feature the direct applications of principles have been devised in projects of in-service training for the staffs of national organizations. Participation in a political party or in social action respecting urban renewal have been the forms of evaluation and application of some political science courses. In a one-week-long intensive seminar on Shakespeare, the participants read, hear lectures, and attend performances of the plays. For their examination, the entire seminar group utilize the knowledge they have gained about the stage, the actors, design, costumes, and Elizabethan music and apply it in the design of a production of a different Shakespearian play. In this case, the seminar participants themselves decided upon the form of examination. They also identified the criteria to be used and methods to be followed in appraising their own performance.

The important factor of course, is not just interest in the activity, but how much engagement of the person can be attained in the process of measuring and understanding his own progress. Evaluation of the learner in more traditional ways has sometimes been criticized as resulting in a restricted curriculum. The complaint is made that the teacher prepares students "for the examination" rather than pursuing the subject. It is sometimes claimed that the "examination system" does violence to the learning transaction itself. Carl Rogers, from his experience has come to the conclusion that *anything but* self-appraisal may have harmful results:

> As we have struggled with this problem of grades and academic bookkeeping, and have contrasted it with those experiences in which students are free to evaluate themselves, we have reached a conclusion which to some will seem radical indeed. It is that personal growth is hindered and hampered, rather than enhanced, by external evaluation. Whether the evaluation is favorable or unfavorable, it does not seem to make the development of a more mature, responsible, or socialized self, but indeed tends to work in an opposite direction.[13]

And Donald Snygg has had similar comments to make about traditional measuring devices:

> It is very questionable if our traditional marking system is able to give the student the feeling that he is making progress. The marking standard is based on the class mean. The student who progresses at the same rate as the class does not improve his mark and the student who progresses more slowly sees his mark drop even though he is making progress. . . .
> Another defect is the fact that since the mark is one official symbol of

success, the mark itself, rather than growth and progress, becomes the student's goal. . . . If students can get a mark without changing their opinions they will do so.

We shall have to find better ways than marks to help students perceive and evaluate their progress. More appreciative comment on student papers, more attention and respect for student ideas will help, and I should like to say that that implies serious discussion and constructive criticism. Perfunctory acceptance of all a student's ideas does not mean respect. It means indifference and sooner or later the student finds it out. But the best promise seems to lie in giving the student more opportunities to work on real problems which he recognizes as important and on which he can evaluate his progress by objective results.[14]

Whether one accepts these views or not, it is not difficult to note the different behavior of students when they are working toward and appraising learning objectives which are their own. Recently a group of school superintendents took part in a month-long workshop. At the beginning it was not known if formal credit for achievement in the workshop would be allowed or not. For the first two weeks the men worked assiduously, both individually and collectively, in the study and consideration of subjects and problems which they selected themselves. But at this stage the department of education announced that credit would be given for the work. Now class members who had worked with some help from the staff but with a certain assurance on matters *they knew* were of importance and concern began to ask what the *instructor thought* was important, and what the instructor said should be studied.

The professor directing the workshop claims that tensions increased and that satisfaction and deep application diminished in the second period.

We have seen in the reports on studies of communication that when a message is being communicated from one person to another, if there is an opportunity for the recipient to report back what he is receiving, a great deal of error is eliminated.

Feed-back is the process by which, in any communication, or any learning process, the recipient or learner is able to state what is his perception of the situation at any given time.

Examples of this are many. The members of a class, at the end of a lecture, may state what they understood from the lecture. Feelings they have about what has transpired may be identified as well as facts. Much of the value of the feed-back is to discover with what feelings the activity or content is being received, and this can be used to guide both teacher and learner. At the conclusion of the first day of a conference the members may indicate to what degree the sessions are meeting the objectives that had been established for the conference, as well as some of the personal objectives that each of them had. They may also state what is lacking; what issues or emphasis ought to be included, or what has been unclear. The use of such material in planning subsequent lectures or sessions is obvious.

There are other by-products. The practice of regular assessment of what is occurring leads to improved performance in self-appraisal. Moreover, being able to measure his own success is perhaps the strongest motivating force for an adult to continue or to put fresh energy into the chosen study.

Devices for obtaining "feed-back" sometimes used are simple meeting reaction forms filled out quickly by every participant, or detailed questionnaires, or interviews, brief or sometimes in depth.

EFFECT OF EVALUATION

It seems to be clear from all the evidence that adults, even more than children, are interested in the application of what they learn. Adults seem to be more interested in the directions in which their learning is taking them. The motivation of adults, since they engage in most activities from free choice and not by law, is dependent upon their being convinced that progress is being made toward some goal. For all these objects evaluation is essential.

Adults want to know in what ways they have been changed. Several years ago the late Eduard Lindeman reported that a class of trade union members, studying international affairs with him, wanted to know if their study had changed them in any of the following respects:

- Has it increased my usable fund of reliable information? (The principal feature of their concern appeared to be (a) the relationship between different bodies of facts and (b) ways of distinguishing the various grades of reliability of information.)
- Have I changed my vocabulary? Have I, in other words, learned how to make use of some *new concepts?*
- Have I acquired any new skills? (e.g. learning how to interpret statistical tables and graphs.)
- Have I learned how to make reliable generalizations?
- Have I learned how to sort out the moral ingredients in the various situations considered by this study group? Have I learned to think in terms of values?
- Have I altered any attitudes? [15]

It is quite clear from this list of questions that Dr. Lindeman was assisting his class to learn how to evaluate, as well as how to read and study. It is not enough to recognize the importance of self-appraisal for the adult learner: he will need guidance in how to go about it, starting, as we have seen, with the statement of learning objectives.

Recently some effort has been made to measure progress in the reading of adult students, not in terms of simple speed, recall, or comprehension tests, but in terms of the *mature reader* concept that was discussed in Chapter 2. As more and more becomes known about the mature adult learner, and the self-motivated learner, these concepts will add useful tools for evaluation. It is possible that an institution may one day be evaluated on some such basis as the number of self-directed learners that have been enrolled.

One final word: we have seen that most adult learners have both educational and what might be called noneducational motives. For example, belonging to cohesive social groups may, as was reported earlier, affect the amount of growth or educational change. But many of the instruments presently used for evaluation take no account of factors such as this. Evaluation in its full sense is a more subtle complex process than is yet represented in the techniques that are usually employed. Accordingly, any results of these devices should be interpreted with some care.

REFERENCES

1. Eduard C. Lindeman, *The Meaning of Adult Education* (Montreal: Harvest House Ltd., 1962).
2. George Aker, "Curriculum Development" in *Materials and Methods in Adult Education* (Los Angeles: Klerens Publications, 1972).
3. Ralph W. Tyler, *Basic Principles of Curriculum and Instruction* (Chicago: University of Chicago Press, 1950).
4. Joseph Trenaman, *Education in the Adult Population* (Oxford: Oxford University Press, 1959).
5. Cyril O. Houle and Others, *The Armed Services and Adult Education* (Washington, D.C.: American Council on Education, 1947).
6. Robert F. Mager, *Preparing Instructional Objectives* (San Francisco: Fearon Publishers, 1962).
7. Ronald Lippitt, Jeanne Watson, and Bruce Westley, *The Dynamics of Planned Change* (New York: Harcourt, Brace and Company, 1958).
8. Peter E. Siegle, "Mountains, Plateaus and Valleys in Adult Learning," *Adult Education* (Chicago: AEA), Vol. IV, No. 4.
9. Adult Education Association, *Program Evaluation in Adult Education* (Chicago: AEA, 1952).
10. American Library Association, *Guide to Activities* (Chicago: ALA, 1957).
11. Malcolm Knowles, *Informal Adult Education* (New York: Association Press, 1954).
12. Russell P. Kropp and Coolie Verner, "An Attitude Scale Technique for Evaluating Meetings," *Adult Education*, (Chicago: AEA), Vol. 7, No. 4.
13. Carl R. Rogers, *Client-Centered Therapy* (Boston: Houghton Mifflin Company, 1951).
14. Donald Snygg, *Some Motivational Aspects of College Training* (Syracuse: University College of Syracuse University, 1956).

15. Eduard C. Lindeman, "Adults Evaluate Themselves," *How to Teach Adults* (Chicago: AEA, 1956).

SUGGESTED READING

Axford, Roger W. *Adult Education: The Open Door*. Scranton, Pennsylvania: International Textbook Company, 1969.

Bugelski, B. R. *The Psychology of Learning Applied to Teaching*. New York: Bobbs-Merrill, 1964.

Charters, Alexander N. *Toward the Educative Society*. Notes and Essays on Education for Adults, No. 67. Syracuse: Syracuse University Publications in Continuing Education, 1971.

Crow, Lester D., and Crow, Alice L., eds. *Readings in Human Learning*. New York: David McKay Co., 1963.

DeCecco, J. P. *Human Learning in the School: Readings in Educational Psychology*. New York: Holt, Rinehart and Winston, 1963.

ERIC Clearinghouse on Adult Education. *Abstracts of Papers Presented to the National Seminar on Adult Basic Education Research*. Syracuse: The Clearinghouse, 1968, 1969, 1970, 1971, 1972, 1973.

Jensen, Gale, Liverright, A. A., and Hallenbeck, Wilbur. *Adult Education: Outlines of an Emerging Field of University Study*. Washington, D.C.: Adult Education Association of the U.S.A., 1962.

Krumboltz, John D., ed. *Revolution in Counselling*. Boston: Houghton Mifflin Co., 1966.

Powell, J. R. *Learning Comes of Age*. New York: Association Press, 1956.

Smith, C. K., ed. *New Teaching New Learning, Current Issues in Higher Education*. San Francisco: Jossey-Bass Inc., Publishers, 1971.

11

The Teacher in the Learning Transaction

In Chapter 1 we stated that this book was planned primarily for practitioners who have some part in adult learning—teachers, librarians, training directors, coaches, foremen, perhaps educational administrators.

It is interesting to note that in English we do not have any term that describes quite what is needed here. We use the word *teacher* for want of something else. What is needed is a noun that means "he-who-assists-learning-to-happen," or the "manager of learning," as some writers put it. In the book *The Dynamics of Planned Change* [1] the authors use the term "change agent" to express this idea and it might serve if it were not so clumsy, and if it had no misleading connotations. The French term *animateur* has many of the same meanings.

Nearly everything that has been written about learning refers to what happens to someone else. It is usually about *them*, the students. But this chapter is about *us*, those of us who take some part in bringing about learning. Our inquiry started with us, it has now gone full circle. What do we do? What are we like? What do we need to remember? What growth should we try to bring about in ourselves?

The research about self-directed learning indicates that all of us, at some time or other, are both teacher and learner. In this chapter our attention is upon the role of the agent who animates learning. We will usually employ the single name *teacher* to include the various tasks and responsibilities that are involved in the learning transaction.

Different Roles of the Teacher

By now it must be sufficiently clear that in stimulating and guiding learning there are many different roles. The traditional, somewhat romanticized picture of a teacher, a Mr. Chips who inspires, cajoles, exhorts, stimulates his students to vigorous intellectual effort, covers only one part of this. Commonly we think of a person who is lecturing or giving a talk as being the chief actor in the drama of learning. Yet, from our own experience, we may remember that the one whose contribution was critical in achieving learning was the janitor who saw to it that there was enough fresh air so that nobody became inattentive or fell asleep. Or the members of the committee who welcomed the newcomers at the door and somehow were able to convey that the occasion was one of significance, requiring unusual effort. It could have been an anonymous photographer or film editor who supplied the main content for the evening, or it may have been Plato with whose ideas the members grappled so that their understanding enlarged.

In attempting to gain some appreciation of the significance of roles in teaching, there is much that is relevant in what has been written about leadership. As we have seen in Chapter 7, some writers have described leadership as consisting of a number of actions which one designated person, the leader, or several of the participants, may carry out. Similarly there are many possible actions in regard to teaching, such as the following:

- Animating or inspiring attention and commitment
- Presenting information or demonstrating processes
- Raising relevant questions, developing habits of self-questioning
- Clarifying difficulties or obscurities
- Drawing parallels or finding relationships
- Reflecting feelings
- Expressing agreement and support
- Evaluating, or developing the learner's capacity for self-evaluation

One needs to understand these distant roles and also how they might be "orchestrated" in a complete teaching process.

But just as one needs to remember that any task that leads to an educational result is worthy of respect, it is equally important to remember that there is no learning situation so minute, so self-contained, or so well-defined that other learnings are not implicated. No teacher can claim, for example, that because his task is elementary or modest, because what he teaches is limited to a routine skill, such as instructing in the operation of a simple machine, he doesn't need to know or to care much about other kinds of learning. On the contrary, whenever a human being is the learner, no matter how rudimentary may be the specific subject of instruction, a whole complex personality is engaged. It should not be necessary here to repeat any clichés such as that "the whole person is involved in any learning transaction." Still, this truism, like most, represents an idea of great importance.

We have talked about the teacher as if he were a "tutor" of an individual or an instructor of a class. But many educationists may act as consultants and may have as their "client" an association or an institution. They may be responsible for *public* education, or at least the education of selected publics, such as "the nursing profession" or a trade union. In Chapter 2 we quoted Alan Thomas's analysis of the importance for learning of *membership* rather than *studentship*. In an organization having many members, one or more persons, such as program organizers, may have a major influence on what is learned and how well, yet we would rarely address them as teachers.

Naturally, the role of an educational guide to a client system, such as a consultant to a minority group seeking better education and equal rights, is not identical with that of a teacher of automobile mechanics, but there are many underlying similarities.

All the roles and acts respecting teaching have their place and importance: all may be utilized at one time or another. Most of them are based upon or require a particular kind of skill or understanding. The successful practitioner not only values any role that does contribute to effective learning but attempts to become competent, at least, in many or all of the required skills.

No Blueprints for Teachers

Several hundred volumes of how-to-do-it books about teaching have been published with a sale of millions of copies. So far there is none that describes adequately how to be a teacher. Of course, one might quail if such a book were offered. Still, it is somewhat surprising how few books there are about the teacher, and how few apt descriptions or analyses of him. If you talk with teachers themselves, the only book to which many will refer is *The Art of Teaching* [2] by Gilbert Highet. In English adult education, the tutor has a recognized kind of role and responsibility, and there are a number of books dealing with the training and responsibilities of tutors.[3]

Some of the most useful, and readable, pages in Highet's book contain his remarks about teaching style. He tells us, for example, that in Scottish universities there is a direct form of two-way communication between audience and lecturer:

> When they admire a phrase or an idea, the students applaud by stamping, none too gently; and when they miss something they shuffle their feet until the sentence is repeated. It may sound odd, but it is extremely helpful to the lecturer, and also ensures that the Scots get full value of their fees.

Highet also, by quoting Conan Doyle, tells of the kind of speaker that is still to be found in our midst, even when public address systems are in general use, and in more countries than England:

> Professor Brown will, I am sure, excuse me if I say that he has the common fault of most Englishmen of being inaudible. Why on earth people who have something to say which is worth hearing should not take the slight trouble to learn how to make it heard is one of the strange mysteries of modern life. Their methods are as reasonable as to try to pour some precious stuff from the spring to the reservoir through a nonconducting pipe, which could by the least effort be opened. Professor Brown made several profound remarks to his white-tie and to the carafe upon the table, with a humorous, twinkling aside to the silver candlestick upon his right.

In recent years there have begun to appear writings by able teachers of adults, dealing directly with the art of teaching, or reflecting their experience. Richard Hoggert, in England, has written lucidly about teaching subjects such as literature to adults. *Teaching and Learning in Adult Education* [4] reflects the wide experience of H. L. Miller, and so do the more general books of C. O. Houle and Malcolm Knowles.

There have been more frequent examples of the various functions of a teacher coming under research scrutiny by psychologists such as Robert Gagne, much of it reported in the *Handbook of Research and Teaching*, edited by N. L. Gage. [5] Stanley Grabowski has edited an excellent collection of research reports, *Adult Learning and Instruction*. [6]

Specifically in adult education there has been some investigation of the differences in "teaching styles." Teaching styles are often expressed as opposite tendencies or as positions along a continuum. Examples:

- Permissiveness versus control
- Aggressiveness versus protectiveness
- Emphasis on content versus emphasis on participation

A number of such styles have been identified and the requirements, effectiveness, and limitations of each are being studied. Just as there are many acts and roles, there may be several kinds of teaching styles, each of which may have particular advantages for certain learning situations. There are many analyses, as well, to management styles.

Successful teachers have always developed their own styles, based on their own experience and to some extent through the observation of others. For most of us, the opportunity for observing good teachers has not been too frequent, but, potentially at least, we now have sizable stocks of materials for studying effective teaching. Many hundred aural and video tapes and films now exist in which teachers are recorded on hundreds of subjects, following varied teaching styles, in scores of different learning situations. With a little bit of ingenuity and organization these tapes and films can provide excellent material for observing and analyzing at least some of the qualities needed in the learning process. By utilizing VTR teachers can "observe" themselves and their own teaching behavior in order to make improvements.

There are excellent precedents for this. Years ago, through the work of Thomas Fansler [7] and others, many adult leaders improved their skill in group discussion by studying transcripts of discussion. Students in social work listen to tapes and study records of interviews and group meetings. Excellent results of a similar kind have been achieved in the study of non-directive counseling under Carl Rogers.[8] It should be noted, however, that most of these recordings are concerned with one or two of the roles of the "teacher," not with his whole repertoire.

No text or blueprint exists which sets out in any definite way all the arts or skills needed by the teacher, but many of the tools for his practice and study are available, if he will organize and use them.

The Teacher as Learner

When asked what was the most important attribute of the teacher, Harry Overstreet once replied, "He must be a learner himself. If he has lost his capacity for learning he is not good enough to be in the company of those who have preserved theirs." Dr. M. M. Coady, former director of the Antigonish Movement, once put it even more bluntly. "The man who has ceased to learn," he said, "ought not to be allowed to wander around loose in these dangerous days."

From our examination of attributes and motivation it is quite apparent why a teacher must be a learner, must himself possess strong motives and a positive attitude toward learning. For, as we have seen, it is this attitude which itself communicates most forcibly, not his words. Nothing is as transparent as the attitude of another to learning. And no one sets up such a block for others as he for whom learning seems so unimportant that he is not bothering with it himself, even though he claims it might be useful for others.

Unfortunately, most of us know parents who frequently admonish their children and urge them to learn, but never provide an example of themselves learning. Teachers sometimes exhibit a model of successful teaching, but not of successful learning, which might be a more useful example for the students. We know of extension directors, and professors of education, who are prepared to help any corporation, government, or profession establish programs in continuing education, but have done nothing about the continuing education of themselves.

We must have long since concluded that learning is such a complicated affair that one never fully masters it; one needs to be constantly alert for new manifestations. Keeping up to date in regard to learning is only comparable with keeping up to date in regard to medical practice. Every good doctor assumes such a responsibility as part of his job; any good practitioner in education has a similar obligation.

An important part of the continuing education of the teacher is the development of skills. We have already noted that each role or each style may require a special kind of skill, and few of these are easily acquired. Skills such as presentation, developing curricula, evaluation, and administration can be practiced and learned but this happens most readily when one has most need of them. These are not skills to be mastered early at college and always kept burnished and complete: they must be worked over and maintained by use.

As is true of some other fields, the agent in learning is not only an artist, but a craftsman as well and needs to take over some of the attitudes, such as the concern about skill, the devotion to self-improvement, the slow maturation of skill that is the hallmark of the genuine craftsman.

Most schoolteachers have become aware of the need to learn more about the differences in background of their students. This is even more important for adults, since the differences are usually much greater.

What may be more important is for the teacher to learn about himself. Robert Luke has suggested some practical means of self-investigation in Chester Klevins's book, *Materials and Methods in Adult Education.*[9] Leland Bradford has also written about this need.

> In learning about ourselves, we need to understand, as well as we can, our own motivations. Obviously none of us can understand all his motivations, but the clearer we are about why we are doing what we are doing, the more capable we are of directing our behavior and understanding ourselves and others.
>
> We need, second, to recognize the consequences of our behavior on others;
>
> We need, third, to understand the consequences of others' behavior on us. Frequently we don't have adequate insight into how other people really affect us or how we react in human situations;
>
> Fourth, most of us have not developed the ability to listen. We think we listen but we only hear a small portion of what's trying to be said. We hear on only a surface level, and we don't really understand the other;
>
> Finally, we have many resistances to accepting suggestions and reactions. We resist cues telling us something about our behavior and how we are

relating to others. We thus lack the basic ability to continue learning through experience.[10]

It will be noted that there is a very close similarity between what is here advocated, that a teacher should learn about himself, and "sensitivity training" for industrial managers described by Tannenbaum in Chapter 8.

Dr. Overstreet has stressed the importance of a different kind of learning competence by the teacher: "The adult educator cannot be simply a person of good will and generous impulses—and large ignorance. He must know something well." [11]

If the teacher is himself a learner this will mean periodic change in his beliefs, theories, and practices. Ordway Tead once remarked that the good teacher should "recognize the priceless asset of intellectual integrity and rational candor; let him eschew also the constant driving for agreement with his own doctrine."

Developing a particular field is one defense against an affliction which may attack anyone in adult education. As we shall note later, most practitioners are generalists and part of their usefulness grows out of that fact. But they live "in an age of specialists" when most people have a function in life which is well defined and at least partially understood. If a man is asked what he does, and he is able to reply that he is a lawyer or salesman or carpenter, the inquirer may not know precisely what he does but he is satisfied that this is a proper function in life. If his answer is *adult educationist*, or something like that, the next question can easily be predicted—"What's that?" People who are generalists, or are performing a kind of service which most people don't yet understand, sometimes feel ill at ease or become defensive about this. The generalist may fear he is nothing more than "a jack of all trades." The development of some competency, even if it may not always be understood or appreciated, assists in bringing and maintaining the self-respect and self-assurance upon which good performance depends.

This is particularly true for the many whose main tasks in regard to learning are in organization and administration. It is scarcely a revelation to say that sound learning principles must permeate all parts of the organization responsible for the learning situation. Administrative practices must be consonant with the best thinking about learning.

Some administrators and organizers are assailed occasionally by feelings that their role is insignificant or, even if very important, that it has little to do with the central objective, namely, learning. But there need not be any chasm between the learning situation and administration if the same general principles govern both. Administration, of course, can be an intensely creative job.

There is a corollary to all this. The administrator who has the taste and skill for it, and who manages to find the time for teaching in at least one activity, has a much better opportunity for keeping in touch with the whole learning enterprise and also keeping alive intellectually.

Overstreet believes that a teacher or administrator needs at least four qualities:

> He must himself want to go on learning; he must have some expertness that gives, as it were, a vertebrate character to what he says and does; he must have a sense of relationships broad enough to redeem him from narrow specialization; and he must have a sense of community—a power to think and act in terms of the real problems and resources of real places where real people live.

A great deal is said and written about the necessity for teaching and research to go hand in hand. What is meant by research is not always clear —is it simple fact-finding, is it analysis, is it model building, is it some new contribution to knowledge? Few other than university teachers have the time or facilities for rigorous and long-term research efforts. A few practitioners do carry out significant and basic research because they are curious and impelled to do so—but most do not and it would be ridiculous to expect that they would.

But there are some favoring circumstances. Not the least is that there is so much that has not been done. The law of diminishing returns does not yet apply to adult learning. As we have seen, systematic research in connection with adult learning has been infrequent and incomplete. One need not fear the fate of many workers in other fields, where study is not so much *to learn* but for the sake of learning a method, because the important questions have already been studied or are being studied with much more ample resources. In almost any field of adult learning, careful observation, careful recording, analytical thinking will by itself make a contribution, will add something to what is already known.

We noted in Chapter 7 that many of the additions to learning theory have come from practical fields of work where the experience was organized and gathered by a teacher or trainer. Any teacher of adults is on the "learning frontier."

Second, adult students can be enlisted in many inquiries. They may be just as able and just as resourceful in pursuing the inquiry as the teacher. There are actually many examples where the members of adult classes have participated in such an inquiry with considerable benefit in terms of what they themselves learn as well as adding somewhat to the store of knowledge about a particular subject. Much of what has been recorded about the folk arts in Trinidad, for example, has been observed, classified, identified, and discussed by "students" in university extension classes in that island. In this process of fact finding they have also seriously studied how people brought up under one culture are quickly taking over many of the attributes of a different culture, which is one of the most important practical problems in learning theory.

Enough has been said earlier to underline the probable effectiveness of an activity in which the participants are sharing fully in a project of research, when they are having a part in the plan and conduct of the project.

There may be a further by-product when a teacher and students engage in some form of research. Most of us have developed the ability to find praiseworthy reasons for *not* tackling some difficult problems. One of the preferred explanations for refusal to face hard facts, or hard actions, is to say "we don't know enough," "we must wait until there is more research." This device loses much of its efficacy with men and women who are themselves engaged in some form of organized research. In such a procedure they come better to understand ways of obtaining information necessary for sound action, and at the same time become more aware of the limitations of research.

It is true, unfortunately, that a number of studies that have been called research in adult education have not been very profitable for anyone. When the process becomes one of counting noses, in the absence of any useful hypothesis, or any rigorous analysis of the data collected, the effort may be more frustrating than rewarding. There are many problems of adult learning in which the greatest hope for solution must come from hard thinking more than from any other activity. It may not have the vogue enjoyed by certain techniques devised by the social scientists, such as multivariate analysis using computers, but there is, of course, nothing at all unscientific about persistent, vigorous, and critical thought.

A number of conceptions have been reported in Chapter 2 that seem worthy to guide, and be tested by, speculation. Observations of study in which there has been some shift in the methods of teaching, may also throw considerable light on learning. Examples of long-established fields in which the teaching-learning methods are being substantially revised are mathematics and languages.

But the chief part in research which most practitioners will play is to share in the research undertaken by colleagues in the social sciences. Otto Klineberg has pointed out that when attempts are made to appraise social action projects, the adult educationist is in the best position to supply statements about the goals of social change that are to be measured. But if he is to be an effective collaborator, Klineberg argues, he must develop the capacity for stating such goals with much greater clarity:

If it is a project in fundamental education, for example, it is usually beyond the competence of the social science consultant to formulate the goals; without such formulation however, his aid may be greatly restricted, and may be worthless. Something can of course occasionally be done to study the effects of a program without too much concern with goals. If one has asked merely what has happened as a consequence of establishing a new school, or a change in diet, it may be possible to give a partial answer. We might refer to this as the natural history approach to evaluation. More frequently, however, the techniques of evaluation must be adapted to the goals. That means that practitioners must be prepared to supply to their social science consultants, in the clearest and most direct form, a statement of the general principles under which they are operating, as well as the specific purposes for which the project has been launched in the particular case. Such a clear formulation has not always been forthcoming.[12]

Practitioners, then, can identify problems for research, collect data, involve their students in data collection and analysis, test out theory and organize pilot demonstrations. All of this is beneficial to the research enterprise and will enlarge and advance the quality of their own instruction. The practitioner who has the taste for more vigorous research should also be encouraged and aided to find the time and resources for it.

Other Traits or Skills

One hesitates to begin to list desirable traits for the agent in adult learning. There is considerable doubt about the practical value of any list of traits, either about reaching agreement on the items in the list, or learning from it. Such a list may reveal more about the list-maker than about the subject. However, certain traits have been selected for special attention in nearly all speeches and writings about adult education. These can be identified and quickly summarized.

It goes without saying that the teacher must be clear in spech and writing. Or can we assume this? These qualities are not common, one is not born with them; they come only with hard work. It used to be believed by some that certain kinds of obscurity were not only to be tolerated, but to be cultivated. Dickens's picture of schoolmaster Squeers is not a bit overdrawn:

Philosophy's the chap for me. If a parent asks a question in the classical, commercial or mathematical line, says I gravely, "Why, Sir, in the first place, are you a philosopher?" "No, Mr. Squeers," he says, "I ain't." "Then, Sir," says I, "I am sorry for you, for I shan't be able to explain it." Naturally the parent goes away and wishes he was a philosopher, and equally naturally, thinks I'm one.

Everyone is in agreement that for a field of work that is relatively new, and where there are more unresolved problems than certainties, enthusiasm and a sense of humor are indispensable. Whitehead used to argue for the necessity of irreverence in education: "Laughter is our reminder that our theories are an attempt to make existence intelligible but necessarily only an attempt, and does not the irrational, the instinctive, burst in to keep the balance true by laughter?"

Most writers are equally in agreement that one engaged in adult learning must himself have a rich experience of living. Some individuals who throughout history have markedly affected the art or thought of the ages were men who held themselves somewhat aloof from their fellows. But most great teachers seem to have been men who have had more, not less, experience of living than anyone around them. The good teacher seems to be the one who is at home with people, and they with him, because he has walked and talked with all kinds. In saying this, one does not deny for a moment the value of developing graduate courses in adult education. But it is to be hoped that those who will guide adult learning will, in addition, have spent some time in kitchens and workgangs as well as in colleges; on shipboard or even in taverns as well as in churches, libraries, or lecture halls.

Perhaps the most important trait is imagination. Or so Whitehead believed:

> . . . so far as the mere imparting of information is concerned, no university has had any justification for existence since the popularization of printing in the fifteenth century. Yet the chief impetus to the foundations of universities came after that date, and in more recent times has been increased.
>
> The justification for a university is that it preserves the connection between knowledge and the zest of life, by uniting the young and old in the imaginative consideration of learning. The university imparts information but it imparts it imaginatively. At least this is the function which it should perform for society. A university which fails in this respect has no reason for existence. This atmosphere of excitement, arising from imaginative consideration, transforms knowledge. A fact is no longer a bare fact; it is invested with all its possibilities. It is no longer a burden on the memory; it is as energizing as the poet of our dreams, and as the architect of our purposes.[13]

Another trait that is on everyone's list is balance. Perhaps no two observers mean the same thing by balance. But one can guess what they intend. It usually has something to do with the old Greek virtue of moderation. It may mean the ability to benefit from different points of view without being lost in partisanship. We have noted, for example, that several of the "schools" of psychology and philosophy have provided insight and understanding useful in adult learning even though, temporarily, there seemed to be much conflict between them. A vigorous, questioning spirit directed at any proposal or theory is not out of place in a teacher who is also patient enough to wait until he thoroughly understands a proposition before endorsing it or assailing it.

One more trait, and we shall conclude. It is that those who are engaged in adult education need to learn how to deal effectively with controversy. A famous report on adult education has had a good deal to say about such matters:

> The remedy for one-sidedness in education is, in short, more education. . . . We do not think that the controversial character of many of the subjects most commonly studied by adult men and women prevents them from possessing a high educational value. If it makes it especially necessary to guard against onesidedness of presentation, it also gives them the advantage of appealing to interests which are vivid and strongly felt. It seems to us a positive gain, indeed, that topics which are discussed with partisan heat on the platform or in the press should be sifted at leisure by groups of students with the aid of books and in an atmosphere of mutual criticism. The course of wisdom, we suggest, is not to attempt the impossible task of restricting education to subjects which are not contentious but to ensure that whatever the subject, those who desire to form a reasonable judgment may be aided to do so by seeing that facilities for study with regard to it are available. Provided that discussion is free, and that the teacher takes pains to call attention to aspects of the truth that are in danger of being overlooked, one point of view tends to supplement and correct another.[14]

All teachers face this directly. Members of the class will be curious to know what the teacher himself thinks about questions of public interest. In some programs, such as Great Books, where many and differing opinions are provided in the readings, the method is to try to understand, and to be able to state clearly, the differing points of view. In such a case, a vigorous airing of conflicting opinions is already provided for, and the leader is bound by the arrangement already understood. But in other cases he may properly be asked for his opinion, an opinion to be supported with what evidence is available and to be subjected to the same kind of questioning that would be directed to any other material or point of view dealt with in the course.

The teacher or agent cannot expect that he will always have an easy time of it. President Neilson of Smith College once wrote:

> There are many teachers who through principle, or indolence, or lack of imagination, failed to connect their subjects with the living issues of the day; not only failed themselves, but bitterly attacked colleagues who labored in season and out to arouse their students to the dangers which everyone recognized at last.

Courage in dealing with controversy is required; it doesn't always lead to popularity either with one's colleagues or the public. How to deal effectively with controversy is a subject of considerable importance on which there has been much thought. One issue of *Adult Leadership* publishes a series of papers on handling controversial issues, dealing with such matters as gaining perspective, timing, studying consequences, and the art of constructive compromise.[15]

In most fields of controversy and social action there is a need for rationality precisely because so much that happens is irrational, emotional, and unreasonable. However, the practitioner need not feel that he should operate as a philosopher or an umpire on the sideline; he will find it difficult not to become a participant, perhaps a partisan. What he needs most may be emotional balance to live with tension and the faculty of scrutinizing his own motives, aims, methods, and feelings.

Before S. I. Hayakawa became a central figure in one nationally publicized university struggle, he had described how tensions between two individuals may be lessened where the conditions of listening and communication are maintained:

Mr. A. has listened to Mr. B. and instead of trying to shove things down his throat he is permitting the messages to come through. Nothing is so relaxing as being listened to, and Mr. B. begins to moderate the rigidity of his defenses. When this happens there is a direct linguistic reflection of this in the fact that Mr. B.'s statements from here on out become less dogmatic, less absolutistic, not only in tone of voice, but in their actual verbal content. . . .

All linguistic processes being processes of social interaction, the relaxation of B. means the relaxation of A., and the relaxation of A. becomes the relaxation of B. As you become less afraid of Mr. B. and less horrified by his position this reveals itself in your facial expression and the very posture of your body as you sit there listening to him. And this change in postural stance is subliminally sub-verbally picked up by the other fellow and in turn relaxes him and ultimately both of you may be making sense.

But there is a point at which (and this I think is the most important point) when, after receiving Mr. B.'s communications, Mr. A. is finally able to say, "I still don't agree with you, Mr. B., but I can see why you believe as you do. I can see why you feel as you do." I think this is the real turning point in communications and therefore in all human relations. "I don't agree with you, but I can see how you get to your present position." When you say this, you are, in a sense, admitting the other individual into the human race. Isn't that right? That is, you are admitting that this other person has rational processes, starting on different assumptions from mine, and therefore coming to different conclusions from mine, but nevertheless, traceable rational processes. And once this admission that you too have rational processes as well as me is made, then communication is possible.[16]

Responsibility of Teacher

Anyone who is engaged deliberately in producing change—and as we have seen, all learning involves change—must sometime be confronted by uneasiness. In what ways and by what right is he helping to bring about changes in the thinking, behavior and attitudes of another human being? Is he manipulating another self?

This is not the place for any exhaustive discussion of the moral and ethical problems confronting anyone engaged in adult learning. But it is necessary to identify at least one or two aspects of it.

It has been the assumption throughout, both implicit and explicit, that the teacher or leader, in dealing with adults, will present the truth, as far as he knows the truth, and will subject all truth to the same kind of inquiry. He will also, as far as his self-knowledge goes, make known his own biases, so that they can be allowed for. He will not delude his class or group. But neither should he delude himself. Particularly should he not deceive himself that he can ever, in a class or in some form of community action, behave *simply as a catalyst*, unchanging. All actions, his own not excluded, have consequences. He can, of course, withdraw from any contact with others, in which case he will still have influence of a negative kind. He needs to understand *and accept* the fact that he has considerable influence.

The stresses faced by any agent of learning have been well described in *The Dynamics of Planned Change*:

> Sometimes the change agent himself will experience uneasiness about the justification for what he is trying to do. The causes of his uneasiness may be rational or irrational, and the uneasiness itself may assume any one of a number of forms. The change agent whose clients refuse his help may wonder, for instance, if he really has much to offer them. Or he may wonder about his own emotional involvement in his client's problems; perhaps he cares too much or too little, or perhaps he is merely attributing to the client certain problems which are really his own. . . .
>
> Often the uneasiness of the change agent may arise from his unconscious tensions and anxieties. Unresolved personal problems may inhibit his ability to respond to others in an appropriate and helpful way. . . . By no means, however, can all of the emotional stress experienced by change agents be attributed to unconscious personal difficulties. The task itself—trying to help other people—often creates special strains.[17]

The authors go on to point out that such uneasiness, where it exists, is readily communicated to the learner and may interfere with the learning objective. What the teacher requires to do, as Luke and Bradford have also stated, is to make a thorough self-examination.

> He needs to think through for himself the reason why he wants to help others. Included in this question is the matter of what rewards he wants for himself—money, prestige, professional advancement, research data, emotional support, or simply satisfaction in seeing an important job done well.

These personal needs of the teacher, the authors say, must then be examined in terms of what the learner needs and is able to give. If it seems that the learner's needs can be fulfilled, "the work at hand can proceed." The teacher who accepts himself, with some understanding of his will to dominate, may continue with his task free from some of the internal stress that might otherwise be his lot, less likely to manipulate the learners "for their own good" or become the victim of the delusion that he has no responsibility for what is transpiring.

What is the teacher's responsibility and how can one identify good teaching? Malcolm Knowles [18] asked that question, and suggested there were at least several parts to the answer including:

1. His ability to understand the goals of the course, and whenever possible, to see that the student shares in shaping the goals.
2. His attitude, acceptance and respect for personality.
3. His planning of the environment.
4. His facility in encouraging full participation by all learners.
5. His versatility in choosing methods and media.
6. His awareness that learning should be satisfying and free of compulsion.

No answer can ever be complete. My own answer is not complete, either; it is in the form of a decalogue.

TEN COMMANDMENTS FOR EDUCATORS

1. Thou shalt never try to make another human being exactly like thyself; one is enough.
2. Thou shalt never judge a person's need, or refuse your consideration, solely because of the trouble he causes.
3. Thou shalt not blame heredity nor the environment in general; people can surmount their environments.
4. Thou shalt never give a person up as hopeless or cast him out.
5. Thou shalt try to help everyone become, on the one hand, sensitive and compassionate, and also tough-minded.
6. Thou shalt not steal from any person his rightful responsibilities for determining his own conduct and the consequences thereof.

7. Thou shalt honour anyone engaged in the pursuit of learning and serve well and extend the discipline of knowledge and skill about learning which is our common heritage.
8. Thou shalt have no universal remedies or expect miracles.
9. Thou shalt cherish a sense of humor which may save you from becoming shocked, depressed, or complacent.
10. Thou shalt remember the sacredness and dignity of thy calling, and, at the same time, "thou shalt not take thyself too damned seriously."

Most great teachers have associated learning with *light*. Illumination, opening up the dark patches, these were the constant themes for Bishop Gruntvig, founder of the Danish folk high schools. "I can always tell a good teacher," Dr. M. M. Coady once said. "All I have to do is to speak to him of some transforming idea and then watch him light up just as an electric bulb does when the current is connected."

But perhaps the most profound thing that can be said of the teacher is that he can't help it! Searching for and revealing truth, assisting in the way that others grow—these are the means by which he comes to grips with and expresses the life that is in him. Four centuries ago Francis Bacon said: "I would address one general admonition to all: that they consider what are the true ends of knowledge, and that they seek it not either for the pleasure of the mind, or for contention, or for superiority to others, or for profit, or fame, or power, or any of these inferior things; but for the benefit and use of life." [19] For the teacher the "use of life" is learning—for himself and for others.

REFERENCES

1. Ronald Lippitt, Jeanne Watson, and Bruce Westley, *The Dynamics of Planned Change* (New York: Harcourt, Brace and Company, 1958).
2. Gilbert Highet, *The Art of Teaching* (New York: Alfred A. Knopf, Incorporated, 1951, and Toronto: McClelland and Stewart, Ltd.).
3. British Institute of Adult Education, *The Tutor in Adult Education* (Carnegie: United Kingdom Trustees, 1928).
4. H. L. Miller, *Teaching and Learning in Adult Education* (New York: The Macmillan Company, 1964).
5. N. L. Gage, *Handbook of Research and Teaching* (Chicago: Rand McNally, 1963).
6. Stanley M. Grabowski, ed., *Adult Learning and Instruction* (Washington: Adult Education Association of the U.S.A., 1970).
7. Thomas Fansler, *Creative Power Through Discussion* (New York: Harper and Bros., 1950).

8. Carl R. Rogers, *Counselling and Psychotherapy* (Boston: Houghton Mifflin Company, 1948).

9. Chester Klevins, *Materials and Methods in Adult Education* (Los Angeles: Klevins Publications, 1972).

10. Leland P. Bradford, "A look at Management Growth and Development," *Journal of the American Society of Training Directors,* Vol. 12, No. 7.

11. Harry Overstreet, *Leaders for Adult Education* (New York: American Association for Adult Education, 1941).

12. Otto Klineberg, "Introduction—the Problem of Evaluation," *International Social Science Journal,* Vol. 7, No. 3. By permission of UNESCO.

13. A. N. Whitehead, *The Aims of Education* (New York: Mentor Books, 1949). By permission of the Macmillan Company, copyright owners.

14. *A Design for Democracy,* an abridgment of "The 1919 Report" by the Adult Education Committee of the British Ministry of Reconstruction (New York: Association Press, 1956).

15. Adult Education Association, "Workshop—Handling Controversial Issues," *Adult Leadership* (Chicago: AEA), Vol. 2, No. 6.

16. S. I. Hayakawa, "Success and Failure in Communication," *Journal of the American Society of Training Directors,* Vol. 12, No. 7.

17. Ronald Lippitt and others, *op. cit.*

18. Malcolm Knowles, *The Modern Practice of Adult Education* (New York: Association Press, 1970).

19. Francis Bacon, *The Great Instauration* (London: Spedding, Ellis and Heath, 1904).

SUGGESTED READING

Amidon, E. J. and Flanders, N. A. *The Role of the Teacher in the Classroom.* Minneapolis, Minnesota: Paul S. Amidon & Associates, Inc., 1963.

Corey, Stephen M. *Helping Other People Change.* Columbus, Ohio: Ohio State University Press, 1963.

Dees, Norman. *Approaches to Adult Teaching.* Oxford: Pergamon Press, 1965.

Freire, P., *Pedagogy of the Oppressed.* New York: Herder and Herder, 1970.

Grabowski, Stanley M., ed. *Adult Learning and Instruction.* Syracuse: ERIC Clearinghouse on Adult Education and Adult Education Association of the U.S.A., 1971.

Hely, A. S. M. *School-Teachers and the Education of Adults.* Paris: UNESCO, 1966.

Houle, C. O. *The Design of Education.* San Francisco: Jossey-Bass, Inc., 1972.

Jensen, Gale E., ed. *The Dynamics of Instructional Groups.* Chicago: University of Chicago Press, 1971.

Kreitlow, Burton W. *Educating the Adult Educator, Part I—Concepts for the Curriculum.* Washington, D.C.: United States Department of Agriculture and United States Department of Education, 1965.

Mager, Robert F. *Preparing Instructional Objectives.* San Francisco: Fearon Publishers, 1962.

Mayer, Frederick. *The Great Teachers.* New York: Citadel Press, 1967.

Miller, Harry L. *Teaching and Learning in Adult Education.* New York: The Macmillan Company, 1964.

Miller, Marilyn V., ed. *On Teaching Adults: An Anthology.* Syracuse: Syracuse University Publications in Continuing Education, 1960.

Nadler, Leonard. *Developing Human Resources.* Houston: Gulf Publishing Company, 1970.

Peterson, A. D. C., ed. *Techniques of Teaching: Tertiary Education.* London: Pergamon, 1965.

Rogers, Jennifer. *Adults Learning.* London: Penguin, 1971.

Stephens, M. D., and Roderick, G. W. *Teaching Techniques in Adult Education.* London: David Charles, 1971.

Index

achievement, 110
Adler, Mortimer, 26, 151f.
Adult Basic Education, 197
Adult Education Association (AEA), 283
Adult Leadership, 304
Adult Learning, 21
Adult Learning and Instruction, 295
American Library Association (ALA), 283
Adult Psychology, 10
adult students, 207, 290, 299
  abilities of, 33
  continuing education for, 208f.
  as nonlearner, 132
  see also learners
Adult's Learning Projects, The, 269
aging, 49, 54ff.
  changes in interests, 113f.
  and conservatism, 116
  and death, 143ff.
  and disengagement, 141
  limiting factors associated with, 67f.
Aker, George, 270
Alford, Harold J., 239
Alinsky, Saul, 227
Allport, Gordon, 115, 125
  and concept of becoming, 138f.

Analyzing Performance Objectives, 277
Anderson, J. E., 255
andragogy, 36
anger, 98f.
Angry Book, The, 97
Angyal, A., 43
Animal Intelligence, 162
animateur, 197, 223, 292
Art of Teaching, The, 294
As You Like It, 53
Asch, S. E., 214
association, 162f.
attitudes, 115ff.
Audio-Visual Methods in Teaching, 219
Augenstein, Dr. Leroy G., 73f.
Ausubel, David, 25, 181f.
autohypnosis, 186
aversion, 168
aversive conditioning, 111
awareness, 62

Basic Principles of Curriculum and Instruction, 271
Bayley, N., 86, 87
behavior modification, 111, 212
behavior therapy, 111

behaviorists, 24, 160
  see also conditioning
Benne, Kenneth, 24
Berlyne, D. E., 39, 109
Bernard, Luther, 107
Berne, Eric, 139
bio-feedback, 186
Bion, W. R., 178
Birren, J. E., 8, 54, 141
Bischof, Ledford, 10
Blake, Robert, 110
Blakely, Robert, 43
body, instability of, 56f.
Bradford, Leland, 297
brain research, 72f.
brain rhythms, 186
Brenner, M., 214
Broadcasting for Adult Education,
  219
Browne, Sir Thomas, 11
Browning, Robert, 54
Brubacher, John S., 150
Bruner, Jerome J., 25, 180, 181
Buhler, C., 138
Busch, Henry, 210
buzz groups, 251

Cannon, Walter B., 56
Cantor, Nathaniel, 243
case method, 260f.
Center for the Study of Liberal Education for Adults, 243
change, 117f., 199f.
Classrooms in the Factories, 32
closed-mindedness, 182
Coady, M. M., 151, 296, 307
cognitive desensitization, 73, 111
cognitive learning, 24, 25
communications media, 216f., 224ff.,
  262ff.
  readability, 220f.
  two-way, 222f.

community psychiatry, 185
concepts, 182ff., 220
Conceptual Systems Theory, 184
conditioning, 166ff.
Conflict, Arousal and Curiosity, 109
connectionism, 162ff.
Conrad, Herbert S., 77
conscientization, 158
consciousness, altered states of, 185
continuing education, 208f.
Continuing Education in Action,
  239
Corey, S. M., 26
counseling, 228
crisis of identity, 126, 140f.
cultural exchange, 230f.
curiosity, sense of, 39, 108f.
curriculum, 273ff.
  choosing, 277f.
Currie, Sir Arthur, 47
cybernetics, 188

Dale, Edgar, 219
Davidson, Lionel, 126
Day, H. I., 39, 109
death, 143
  seminars on, 144f.
Deutsch, Karl, 217
Dewey, John, 112, 268
  on theory and practice of education, 152f.
Diffusion Process, The, 199
discovery learning, 180
discussion group, 245
Dollard, John, 15
Drever, J., 94
drives, 102
Duncan, James, 135, 200
Dyer, John, 34
Dynamic Administration, 210
Dynamics of Planned Change, The,
  292, 305

Ebbinghaus, Hermann, 187
education
    distinguished from learning, 15
    purposes of, 283
    task of, 47
educational objectives, 276
educational philosophy, 275
Emotional Dynamics and Group Culture, 178
emotions, 93ff.
    constellations of, 97
empathy, 215
engagement, key to learning, 266, 278
Erikson, Erik, 132, 137, 141
Essay on the Human Understanding, 162
esteem needs, 108
Estes, W. K., 188
evaluation, 283ff.
    agent of, 286f.
    effect of, 289
existentialism, 155f.

Fansler, Thomas, 296
fear, 99ff.
feedback, 108, 188, 241, 283, 288f.
feelings, *see* emotions
Ferguson, G. A., 182
field theory, 150 ff.
fields of study, 274f.
Flaherty, Josephine, 188f.
Flesch, Rudolph, 221
Follett, Mary, 210
Frank, L. K., 94
Freire Paulo, 157f., 221
Freud, Sigmund, 177f.
Future Shock, 8

Gage, N. L., 295
Gagne, R. M., 182, 295
Galton, Sir Francis, 58

Gestalt psychology, 170ff.
Gestalt therapy, 173
    criticisms of, 174
Gibbs, Dr. Fredric, 72f.
Gilson, Etienne, 150
Ginsberg, Morris, 134
Goldstein, Kurt, 173
Grabowski, Stanley M., 32, 295
Granick, S., 87
Gray, William S., 44
Great Books program, 246, 271, 303
Griffin, Virginia, 271
group discussion, 252ff.
    schema for, 254
group dynamics, 210ff., 282
group therapy, 178, 228
groups, 212ff., 226f., 246ff.
Guilford, J. P., 74, 75
Guthrie, E. R., 167, 168f.
Gyllenhaal, Hugh, 243, 281

habits, 117f.
Hallenbeck, W. C., 34
Handbook of Research and Teaching, 295
Harlow, H. F., 181
Harris, Thomas A., 140
Havighurst, Robert J., 17, 138
Hawthorne experiments, 201f.
hearing, 64f.
    overcoming limitations in, 68
Hebb, D. O., 89
Heidbreder, Edna, 147
Hendry, Charles E., 204
Hershberg, Frederick, 203
Herzberg, Frederick, 110
Highet, Gilbert, 294
Hilgard, E. R., 188
Hocking, William E., 272
Hoggert, Richard, 295
Horney, Karen, 44, 178

Houle, C. O., 27, 47, 206f., 239, 271, 277, 295
Hull, C. L., 150, 187
humanists, 24
Hunt, David, 25, 184
Hunt, J. McV., 108
Hutchins, Robert, 27
hypnosis, 185

Illich, Ivan, 9, 157
illiteracy, 9
I'm O.K.—You're O.K., 140
individual learners, 236
Informal Adult Education, 285
information retrieval, 89f.
Innis, Harold, 217
institutional change, 9
intelligence
    cross-sectional studies, 76ff.
    kinds of, 75, 189
    longitudinal studies of, 86f.
    and vocabulary, 85
intelligence tests, 20, 75
    Conrad and Jones Study, 77f.
    cross-sectional studies, 76
    Thorndike Studies, 78f.
    time as a factor, 82f.
interests, 112ff.
intervention therapy, 185
Intrinsic Motivation, 108
Introduction to Group Dynamics, 213
I.Q. (intelligence quotient), 21, 75, 76, 81, 87
Is Anybody Listening?, 225
issue, 253f.

James, Bernard, 32
Jessup, Frank, 239
job enrichment, 203
Johnstone, John W. S., 31

Jones, Harold E., 77
judgment, 75, 91

Kaplan, Abbott, 256
Katz, Elihu, 225
Kelly, Walt, 13
Kilpatrick, William, 153f.
Klein, Alan, 258
Klevins, Chester, 297
Klineberg, Otto, 300
Knowles, Hulda, 213
Knowles, Malcolm, 27, 36, 41, 213, 271, 285, 295, 306
Koffka, Kurt, 170
Kohler, Wolfgang, 170ff.
Kreitlow, Burton, 135, 200
Kropp, Russell P., 285
Kuhlen, Raymond G., 40, 132
Kuhn, Thomas S., 182

language, 88, 228f.
Lazarsfeld, Paul, 225, 227
leadership, 204, 212, 214f., 255f., 293
    kinds of, 177
learners
    description of, 15
    individual, 236
    needs of, 271ff.
    number of, 31
    motives of, 32
    and relationships with emerging self, 129ff.
    and teacher, 269f.
    see also adult students
learning
    age as factor in, 21f., 80
    barriers to, 35, 221
    capacity of adults for, 7, 18, 79, 80
    concepts in, 182ff.

learning (*cont.*)
  conditions for, 13ff., 119ff., 129ff., 180
  continuity in, 268
  contributions from other disciplines, 158f., 205, 213
  by demonstration, 257
  dictionary definitions of, 14
  distinguished from education, 15
  emotions and, 93ff., 161, 178, 235f.
  facilities for, 237f.
  forms and techniques of, 242ff., 281f.
  general theory of, 188f.
  groups of six (66), 251
  in the classroom, 239, 242
  and language, 88
  lecture-type activities, 248ff.
  limits to, 17ff., 80
  main uses of, 24
  motivation and, 91, 100ff.
  outside the classroom, 240f.
  philosophy of, 26f., 150ff., 275
  practice charts, 169f.
  psychology and, 159ff., 177ff.
  purpose as factor in, 165f., 178
  rate of, 61
  selection of participants, 246ff.
  social, 237ff.
  special factors in, 133ff.
  theories of, 150ff.
  as a transaction, 268ff.
  two conceptions of, 128
  use of communication media in, 218f.
learning dialogue, 250
learning experiences, 276f.
learning group
  leadership as factor, 177
  other factors, 248f.
  relationships in, 136f.

Learning to Be, 124
lecture-type activities, 248ff.
Leighton, Alexander, 207
level of aspiration, 133
Lewin, Kurt, 117, 175ff., 188, 210, 227
library, 236
Life: A Psychological Survey, 40
life space, 175, 176
Lindeman, Eduard, 154, 289
Lippitt, Ronald, 279
Livingstone, Sir Richard, 26, 155, 234, 239, 247
Locke, John, 162
Lonely Crowd, The, 44, 103
longitudinal studies, 76, 86f.
Lorge, Irving, 80, 81, 82, 83, 85, 96, 214, 221
Love, Robert, 32
love needs, 108
Luke, Robert, 297
Lynd, Robert S. and Helen M., 104, 134

McClellan, David, 102, 110
McClusky, Howard, 33, 36, 48, 132
McGregor, Douglas, 110
McLuhan, Marshall, 11, 175, 217, 218, 219
Mager, Robert, 27, 271, 277
Managerial Grid, 110, 204
Manual on the Collection and Analysis of Adult Education Statistics, 31
Maritain, Jacques, 150
Maslow, Abraham, 25, 107, 127, 128, 142, 143
Materials and Methods in Adult Education, 270, 297
mathematical models, 187f.
Mathetics, definition of, 23, 156

maturity, 43ff.
   physiological, 59
   as developing state, 137f.
Maturity in Reading, 44
May, Rollo, 186
Mead, Margaret, 239
meetings, schema for, 244
member, role of, 42, 185
memory, 89f., 180
Mentality of Apes, The, 171
method vs. technique, 245f.
Middletown, 104, 134
Miles, Walter R., 62, 79, 91
milieu therapy, 185
Miller, H. L., 295
Modern Philosophies and Education,
   150
Montagu, Ashley, 98
Moreno, J. L., 173, 258
Moses, Stanley, 183
motion pictures, 262ff.
motivation, 91, 93, 172, 290, 297
   attitudes, 115ff.
   definition, 101, 102
   educational, 106ff.
   interests, 112ff.
   intrinsic and extrinsic, 103, 108f.,
      182
   maintenance vs., 110f.
   Theory X and Theory Y, 110
Motivation and Personality, 143
motives, 102
   primary and secondary, 104
   social, 106
Murphy, Gardner, 49, 95, 104, 247
Murrow, Edward, 194

National Training Laboratory,
   211ff., 261
*Nationalism and Social Communi-
   cation,* 217
needs, 107, 129

New Understandings of Leadership,
   204
Newman, J. H., 155, 239
Noyes, Alfred, 208
Nyerere, Julius K., 157

Oden, M. H., 86
operant conditioning, 167
Oppenheimer, Robert, 194
organism and self, 127
Otis Mental Ability Test, 87
Overstreet, Harry, 44, 296
*Overview of Research in Adult Edu-
   cation,* 10
Owens, W. A., 86, 87

Parkinson, C. N., 237
Parkinson's Law, 237
part-time students, 34
patterning, 161
Patterson, R. D., 87
Pavlov, I. P., 166
peak-experience, 142f.
Peers, Robert, 21, 83f.
Penfield, Wilder, 73, 228
Perls, Fritz, 11, 25, 173, 174
Personal Influence, 225
personality, 141
   characteristics of noted people,
      127f.
physical work, 60
Piaget, Jean, 179
planned change, 279
population, 8, 22
practice charts, 169f.
Preparing Instructional Objectives,
   277
Pressey, Sidney L., 40
problem solving, 90
Problems of Aging, 40
psychoanalysis, 177f.
psychodrama, *see* role playing

phycholinguistics, 88
*Psychological Development Through
   the Life Span*, 40
*Psychological Studies of Human De-
   velopment*, 40
psychologists, categories of, 24f.
psychology, 159ff.
Psychology of Aging, The, 8
*Psychology of Wants, Interests and
   Attitudes, The*, 103
*Purposive Behavior in Animals and
   Men*, 165

radio, 263
Randall, Clarence, 250
Rank, Otto, 178
readability, 220f.
reasoning ability, 91
Residential Continuing Education,
   239
Reveille for Radicals, 227
Review of Education Research, 33
Riesman, David, 43, 103
Rivera, Ramon, 31
Rogers, Bernice, 44
Rogers, Carl, 25, 44, 100, 127, 128,
   209, 287, 296
role, 40, 41
   horizontal, 132
   vertical, 131
role playing, 258ff.
   limitations of, 262
   see also simulating the real
Roper, Elmo, 225, 226
Ross, Murray G., 204
rote learning, 89
   vs. meaningful learning, 181
Rubin, Theodore, 97

safety needs, 107f.
Schneidman, Edwin, 144
science, study of, 274

Sechenov, Ivan M., 88
*Seeking Common Ground in Adult
   Education*, 156
selfhood, 128ff., 178, 268
Selye, Hans, 175
seminar, 243
sensitivity training, 204, 211, 298
Seven Psychologies, 147
Shape of Things to Come, The, 7
Sherif, M., 214
Shorey, Leonard, 183
Siegle, Peter, 282
simulating the real, 257f.
   see also role playing
skill learning, 256f.
Skinner, B. F., 25, 166
Smith's Gazelle, 126
Snygg, Donald, 43, 287
social change, 8
social class:
   definition of, 134
   as influence in learning, 135
social learning, 237ff.
sociometry, 247
Sorenson, Herbert, 33
span of attention, 105
sports, 66
S-R (Stimulus-Response) formula,
   132f., 162, 164
Stock, Dorothy, 178
stress theory, 175
Strong, Edward K., 113, 114
*Structure of Scientific Revolutions,
   The*, 182
student, role of, 42
Suchman, J. R., 108f.
surgency, 215
systems analysis, 209

tabula rasa, 120
Tannenbaum, Robert, 204

Taxonomy of Educational Objectives, 93
teacher:
　definition of, 292
　development of skills, 297
　qualities necessary, 299, 301ff.
　responsibilities of, 305ff.
　roles of, 293
Teaching and Learning in Adult Education, 295
teaching styles, 295f.
Tead, Ordway, 39, 298
Terman, L. M., 57, 77
T-group, 261
Thelen, Herbert, 178
theories of learning, 150ff.
Thomas, Alan M., 41, 42f., 185
Thompson, G. G., 40
Thorndike, E. L., 21f., 78, 103, 118, 162ff.
　and three laws of learning, 164
Tilton, John W., 81
Tolman, E. C., 149, 162, 165f.
Tough, Allen, 48, 50, 269
Toynbee, Arnold, 144
training programs, 195ff.
　agricultural extension, 198ff.
　in the armed forces, 205f.
　functional literacy, 197
　industrial, 200ff.
transactional analysis, 139f.
translations, 8

Trenaman, Joseph, 273
Tuckman, Jacob, 96
Tuddenham, Read D., 81
Tyler, Ralph W., 271

United States, 8, 22

valence, 176f.
Verner, Coolie, 35, 245, 285
vision, 62f.
　overcoming limitations in, 67
vocabulary, 84f.
Volunteers for Learning, 31

Walden II, 166
Walkup, L. E., 187
Waniewicz, Ignacy, 219
Warner, Lloyd, 134
Watson, John B., 88, 168
Wechsler, David, 80
Wechsler Adult Intelligence Scale (WAIS), 80
Welford, A. T., 83
Wells, H. G., 7
Wertheimer, Max, 170
Whitehead, Alfred North, 101, 247
Who Shall Survive?, 258
Wiener, Norbert, 188
Woodworth, R. S., 164
workshop, 242f.
World Conference on Adult Education (1972), 31

Southern Methodist Univ.   br
LC 5219.K5 1973a
How adults learn /

3 2177   00969   1583